EXAMKRACKERS MCAT®

PSYCHOLOGY & SOCIOLOGY

10TH EDITION

OSOTE

PUBLISHING

Major Contributors:

Kaitlyn Barkley

Jennifer Birk-Goldschmidt, M.S.

Stephanie Blatch, M.A.

Erin Glennon

Lauren Nadler

Laura Neubauer

Contributors:

Mark Alshak

Emily Barrios

Kristin Bater

Max Blodgett

Jacob M. Burton

David Collins

Erik Davies, M.Ed.

Claudia Goodsett

Xintong Li, M.D.

Erica L. Smearman, Ph.D.

Christina Snider

Richmond Woodward

Art Director:

Erin Daniel

Designers:

Dana Kelley

Charles Yuen

Illustrator:

Poy Yee

ISBN 10: 1-893858-86-3 (Volume 5)

ISBN 13: 978-1-893858-86-2 (6 Volume Set)

10th Edition

To purchase additional copies of this book or the rest of the 6 volume set, call 1-888-572-2536 or fax orders to 1-859-305-6464.

Examkrackers.com

Osote.com

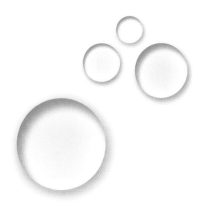

PHOTOCOPYING & DISTRIBUTION POLICY

The illustrations and all other content in this book are copyrighted material owned by Osote Publishing. Please do not reproduce any of the content, illustrations, charts, graphs, photos, etc., on email lists or websites.

Photocopying the pages so that the book can then be resold is a violation of copyright.

Schools and co-ops MAY NOT PHOTOCOPY any portion of this book. For more information, please contact Osote Publishing: email: support@examkrackers.com or phone 1.888.KRACKEM.

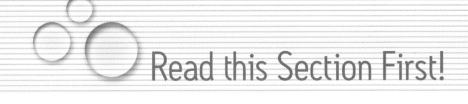
Introduction to the Examkrackers Manuals

The Examkrackers manuals are designed to give you exactly the information you need to do well on the MCAT® while limiting extraneous information that will not be tested. This manual organizes all of the psychology and sociology tested on the MCAT® conceptually. Concepts make the content both simple and portable for optimal application to MCAT® questions. Mastery of the psychology and sociology covered in this manual will increase your confidence and allow you to succeed with seemingly difficult passages that are designed to intimidate. The MCAT® rewards your ability to read complex passages and questions through the lens of basic concepts.

An in-depth introduction to the MCAT® is located in the Reasoning Skills manual. Read this introduction first to start thinking like the MCAT® and to learn critical mathematical skills. The second lecture of the Reasoning Skills manual addresses the research methods needed for success on 20% of questions on the science and psychology sections of the MCAT®. Research questions are the most difficult on the MCAT® and are the questions that help students beat the mean and get a high score. Once you have read those lectures, return to this manual to begin your review of the psychology and sociology you will need to excel on the MCAT®.

How to Use This Manual

Examkrackers MCAT® manuals can be used with the Examkrackers Comprehensive MCAT® Course or as a tool for independent MCAT® study. Examkrackers MCAT® preparation experience has shown that you will get the most out of these manuals when you structure your studying as follows. If you are taking the Examkrackers Comprehensive MCAT® Course, read each lecture twice before the class lecture. During the first reading, you should not write in the book. Instead, read purely for enjoyment. During the second reading, highlight and take notes in the margins. Complete the twenty-four questions in each lecture during the second reading before coming to class. Do not look at the In-Class Exams before class. Immediately after class, read the lecture again, slowly and thoroughly.

If you are studying independently, read each lecture twice (as described above), completing the in-lecture questions during the second reading. Take the In-Class Exam, then read the lecture once more, slowly and thoroughly.

The In-Class Exams are designed to educate. They are similar to an MCAT® section, but are shortened and have most of the easy questions removed. We believe that you can answer most of the easy questions without too much help from us, so the best way to raise your score is to focus on the more difficult questions. The In-Class Exams are designed to help you prepare for test day when you will be faced with an intensity that is difficult to simulate. Technically, the Examkrackers In-Class Exams are timed to take as long as 35 minutes to complete. By practicing with a few minutes less, you will be ready for the pressure and pace of the real exam, and MCAT® day will feel more manageable. These methods are some of the reasons for the rapid and celebrated success of the Examkrackers prep course and products.

With each In-Class Exam you should see the number of questions you answer correctly increase. Do not be discouraged by poor performance on these exams; they are not meant to predict your performance on the real MCAT®. **The questions that you get wrong (or even guess correctly) are the most important ones. They represent your potential score increase.** When you get a question wrong or have to guess, determine why. If content was the problem, target those areas for review. If the issue was your approach to the question, make a commitment to a different approach for the next practice test. As you learn to think like the MCAT®, you will see your score increase.

In order to study most efficiently, it is essential to know what topics are and are not tested directly in MCAT® questions. This manual uses the following conventions to make the distinction. Any topic listed in the AAMC's guide to the MCAT® is printed in red, bold type. You must thoroughly understand all topics printed in red, bold type. Any formula that must be memorized is also printed in red, bold type.

If a topic is not printed in bold and red, it may still be important. Understanding these topics may be helpful for putting other terms in context. Topics and equations that are not explicitly tested but are still useful to know are printed in *italics*. Knowledge of content printed in *italics* will enhance your ability to answer passage-based MCAT® questions, as MCAT® passages may cover topics beyond the AAMC's list of tested topics on the MCAT®.

Features of the Examkrackers Manuals

The Examkrackers manuals include several features to help you retain and integrate information for the MCAT®. Take advantage of these features to get the most out of your study time.

- **The 3 Keys** – The Three Keys unlock the material and the MCAT® by highlighting the most important things to remember from each chapter. The Three Keys are listed at the beginning and end of each lecture with reminders from Salty throughout the text. Examine the Three Keys before and after reading each lecture to make sure you have absorbed the most important messages. As you read, continue to develop your own key concepts that will guide your studying and performance

- **Signposts** – The MCAT® is fully integrated, asking you to apply the biological, physical, and social sciences simultaneously. The signposts alongside the text in this manual will help you build mental connections between topics and disciplines. This mental map will lead you to a high score on the MCAT®. The post of each sign "brackets" the paragraph to which it refers. When you see a signpost next to a topic, stop and consider how the topics are related. Soon you will begin making your own connections between concepts and topics within and between disciplines. This is an MCAT® skill that will improve your score. When answering questions, these connections give you multiple routes to find your way to the answer.

- **MCAT® Think** – These sidebars invite deeper consideration of certain topics. They provide helpful context for topics that are tested and will challenge you just like tough MCAT® passages. While MCAT® Think topics and their level of detail may not be explicitly tested on the MCAT®, read and consider each MCAT® Think to sharpen your MCAT® skills. The MCAT® Think sidebars provide essential practice in managing seemingly complex and unfamiliar content, as you will need to do for passages on MCAT® day.

I'm Salty the Kracker. Where you see purple text, that's me. I will show you why the content makes sense and help you develop your MCAT® intuition. My job is to make sure you 1. stay awake and 2. really understand and remember what you're reading. If you think I am funny, tell the boss. I could use a raise. If you get the munchies, reconsider... you'll want me around.

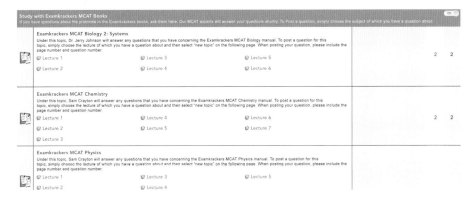

Additional Resources

If you find yourself struggling with the science or you want more practice, take advantage of the additional Examkrackers resources that are available.

Examkrackers offers a 9-week Comprehensive MCAT® Course to help you achieve a high score on the MCAT®. Whether in person or online, the course includes up to 120 hours with expert instructors, a unique course format, and regular full-length MCAT® exams. Each class includes lecture, a practice exam, and review, designed to help you develop essential MCAT® skills. For locations and registration please visit Examkrackers.com or call 1.888.KRACKEM.

EK-Tests® are Examkrackers full-length, online simulated MCAT® exams that match the AAMC MCAT® in style, content, and skills tested. Written by educators, high-scoring medical students, and physicians, EK-Tests® provide the best MCAT® practice available. To purchase EK-Tests®, please visit Examkrackers.com.

Your purchase of this book new will also give you access to the **Examkrackers Forums** at Examkrackers.com/mcat/forum. These bulletin boards allow you to discuss any MCAT® question with an MCAT® expert at Examkrackers. All discussions are kept on file so you can refer back to previous discussions on any question in this book. Once you have purchased the books you can take advantage of this resource by calling 1.888.KRACKEM to register for the forums.

Although we make every effort to ensure the accuracy of our books, the occasional error does occur. Corrections are posted on the Examkrackers Books Errata Forum, also at Examkrackers.com/mcat/forum. If you believe that you have found a mistake, please post an inquiry on the Study with Examkrackers MCAT® Books Forum, which is likewise found at Examkrackers.com/mcat/forum. As the leaders in MCAT® preparation, we are committed to providing you with the most up-to-date, accurate information possible.

Study diligently, trust this book to guide you, and you will reach your MCAT® goals.

Table of Contents

LECTURE

1 The Biopsychosocial Model, Society and Culture   1

1.1 Introduction 1

    Why a Psychosocial Section on the MCAT®? 2

1.2 The Biopsychosocial Approach 3

1.3 The Examkrackers Approach 5

1.4 Models and Theories 6

1.5 Studying Social Processes 7

1.6 Culture 12

    The Evolution of Culture 13

1.7 Society, Systems and Structures 14

1.8 Demographics of Society 18

1.9 Social Inequality 23

    Social Class 24

    Disparities in Health and Healthcare 26

LECTURE

2 Relationships and Behavior   31

2.1 Introduction 31

2.2 Learning 32

    Classical Conditioning 32

    Operant Conditioning 34

    Observational Learning 36

2.3 Behavior in a Biological Context 38

2.4 Behavior in a Social Context 39

    Elements of Social Interaction 39

    Social Processes that Influence Behavior 42

2.5 Behavior in a Cultural Context 46

    Socialization 46

    Culture 48

2.6 Prejudice, Bias, and Discrimination 49

LECTURE

3 Identity and the Individual   55

3.1 Introduction 55

3.2 Personality Theories: One View
of the Individual 56

3.3 Identity: Another View
of the Individual 61

    Influence of Social Factors on Identity Formation 62

    Influence of Personal Factors on Identity Formation 64

3.4 Theories of Development 68

3.5 From Individual Identity to
Beliefs about Others 72

3.6 Disorders: The Intersection of Psychological
and Social Factors 76

    Revisiting the Biomedical and
Biopsychosocial Models 78

    Somatoform Disorders 79

    Anxiety Disorders 79

    Obsessive-Compulsive Disorders 80

    Trauma- and Stressor-Related Disorders 80

    Depressive Disorders 81

    Bipolar Disorders 82

    Schizophrenia 82

    Dissociative Disorders 84

    Personality Disorders 84

LECTURE 4 — Thought and Emotion 89

4.1 Introduction......................................89

4.2 Cognition.......................................90

    Piaget's Theory of Cognitive Development............91

    Culture and Cognitive Development.................92

4.3 Language.......................................93

    Influence of Language on Thought..................94

    Neural Basis of Language.........................95

4.4 Intellectual Functioning.........................97

    Multiple Definitions of Intelligence.................97

    Emotional Intelligence...........................98

    Influence of Heredity and Environment
    on Cognition and Intelligence.....................98

4.5 Problem Solving.................................99

    Approaches to Problem Solving....................99

    Barriers to Effective Problem Solving..............100

4.6 Emotion.......................................101

    The Biology of Emotion.........................102

    Major Theories of Emotion:......................103

    Emotions: Universal and Adaptive.................104

4.7 Motivation and Attitudes.......................106

    Theories of Motivation.........................106

    Regulation and Interaction of
    Motivational Processes.........................107

    Attitudes....................................107

    Theories Behind Attitude and Behavior Change.......109

    Factors Affecting Attitude Change.................110

4.8 Stress...111

    Stress Responses and Outcomes...................111

    Stress Management...........................112

LECTURE 5 — Biological Correlates of Psychology 117

5.1 Introduction....................................117

5.2 Genetics, Environment,
and Behavior...................................118

5.3 Sensation......................................119

    Attention....................................121

5.4 Perception.....................................123

    Visual Processing From a Neurological Perspective.....125

5.5 Consciousness..................................125

    Hypnosis and Meditation........................128

    Consciousness-Altering Drugs.....................128

5.6 Memory: Storage and Encoding..................131

5.7 The Biology of Memory Formation...............133

5.8 Memory Retrieval and Forgetting...............134

    Forgetting of Memories.........................136

5.9 Neurologic Dysfunctions........................138

30-Minute In-Class Exams   141

In-Class Exam for Lecture 1 141
In-Class Exam for Lecture 2 149
In-Class Exam for Lecture 3 157
In-Class Exam for Lecture 4 165
In-Class Exam for Lecture 5 173

Answers & Explanations to In-Class Exams   181

Answer Table for In-Class Exams 182
Explanations to In-Class Exam for Lecture 1 183
Explanations to In-Class Exam for Lecture 2 187
Explanations to In-Class Exam for Lecture 3 191
Explanations to In-Class Exam for Lecture 4 195
Explanations to In-Class Exam for Lecture 5 199

Answers & Explanations to Questions in the Lectures   205

Answers to Questions in the Lectures 206
Explanations to Questions in Lecture 1 207
Explanations to Questions in Lecture 2 210
Explanations to Questions in Lecture 3 214
Explanations to Questions in Lecture 4 217
Explanations to Questions in Lecture 5 221

Photo Credits   225

Index   227

The Biopsychosocial Model, Society, and Culture

1.1 Introduction
1.2 The Biopsychosocial Approach
1.3 The Examkrackers Approach
1.4 Models and Theories
1.5 Studying Social Processes
1.6 Culture
1.7 Society, Systems, and Structures
1.8 Demographics of Society
1.9 Social Inequality

1.1 Introduction

This manual provides the MCAT® student with a guide to navigate the newest addition to the test: a section testing psychological and sociological concepts. This first lecture will start by introducing the nuts and bolts of the section and addressing the question that may be on some students' minds: why add a psychosocial section to the MCAT®?

Next the lecture presents the Examkrackers approach to mastering the material for this section of the MCAT®. A conceptual discussion of the major ideas of psychology and sociology is provided as an orienting and organizing framework. Understanding the relationship between psychological, sociological, and biological factors and health (or illness) will be critical for MCAT® success.

The lecture will go on to examine the macro level of social phenomena: the larger forces and structures that influence social processes and individual lives.

THE 3 KEYS

1. The psychosocial section tests the ability to consider biological, psychological, and social factors simultaneously and to think flexibly about theories.

2. Culture and social institutions organize society on a large scale.

3. Social inequality exists in many forms and affects access to resources, including healthcare.

Why a Psychosocial Section on the MCAT®?

The MCAT® has long been in the business of testing students' conceptual understanding and logical skills in the natural sciences, as well as the interpretation of verbal passages. With the introduction of the psychosocial section, the MCAT® is now testing students' understanding of psychological and social factors that play a critical role in human health and illness. A few of the AAMC's Core Competencies for Entering Medical Students demonstrate the importance of thought and behavior in medicine: 1. social skills, including the ability to interpret the behaviors of other people (such as patients and fellow physicians); 2. cultural competence; and 3. the ability to apply knowledge of human behavior to clinical and professional encounters. These competencies come into play in a multitude of situations within medical practice, including listening to and interpreting a patient history to make an accurate diagnosis, working with patients toward improved health-related behaviors, and communicating effectively. Students are now asked to demonstrate basic knowledge of these concepts before entering medical school.

The MCAT® assesses skills that help students succeed in medical school and as physicians—the psychosocial section included. An understanding of the social and psychological factors that affect health, illness, and outcomes allows physicians to make more accurate diagnoses and to create more effective treatment plans.

The psychosocial section tests the student's ability to apply concepts taught in introductory-level psychology, sociology, and biology courses. Psychology topics are tested most heavily, while biology topics are lightly tested in this section. Topics from these disciplines are not tested in isolation, but rather are likely to appear as cofactors in passages addressing health-related topics.

Psychology is most fundamentally the study of people: how people think and act, mental processes, and how individuals interact with their environments. Psychology covers an enormous number of topics and overlaps with many other fields of study, particularly biology and sociology. Like psychology, sociology is a field that studies how humans think and behave, but sociology is more concerned with behavior in groups and larger social settings. The two fields often study the same topics from different perspectives.

The fields of biology, psychology, and sociology fall along a continuum of the study of human life. Biology and sociology are on opposite ends, while psychology includes elements of each as well as its own unique way of studying the world. Each of these fields influences the others, and each has an effect on human health. No singular view is sufficient to fully understand all of the factors that affect health.

> Master the concepts tested on the psychosocial section to do well on the MCAT®. You will develop further insight into these topics throughout medical school and your career.

> Passages in the psychosocial section will integrate psychological, sociological, and biological concepts. A typical passage will discuss a health-related topic, perhaps with reference to biological influences, in the context of psychological and/or social functioning. For example, a passage might discuss a study investigating the relationship between a chronic health condition and a social factor, like socioeconomic status, or a psychological factor, like self-esteem.

Biology   Psychology   **Sociology**

1.2 The Biopsychosocial Approach

The biopsychosocial approach to health and illness provides a valuable framework to guide the study of concepts tested in the psychosocial section. It illuminates the importance of psychological and sociological study for success in medical school and in the practice of medicine. The biopsychosocial (BPS) approach expands upon the traditional biomedical approach, which focuses narrowly on the physical aspects of illness. This section will introduce the BPS approach as it applies to health and wellness. The following section will describe how this approach guides the rest of this manual and the tools that are used in this book to draw connections between the fields tested in the psychosocial section.

According to the BPS approach, illness cannot be understood by only examining biological factors. The two main claims of the BPS approach are as follows. First, illness is determined by a variety of influences, rather than a single cause. Second, the causes and effects of illness can be examined at multiple levels in the life of an individual. The multiple factors that together determine the course of illness exist at more than one level simultaneously, and no single level provides the whole picture (see Figure 1.1). The use of multiple levels of analysis is distinct from the biomedical approach, where disease is studied by examining only the biological factors of illness, neglecting the contributing factors of psychological life and sociological context.

The psychological and social factors that contribute to illness and wellness can be integrated into the scientific process of medical diagnosis. Higher-level processes in the life of the patient are tied to knowledge about the biological state, so collecting information about psychosocial context is key to the understanding of physical health and illness. This connection is immediately evident in that patients often start the process of diagnosis by presenting their narrative of how their symptoms developed. Psychological processes also affect how the individual interprets and translates biological processes. An individual exists at the intersection of the social and biological: a person is both the largest unit of the organism and the smallest unit of society, as demonstrated in Figure 1.1.

By leaving out the non-biological factors that play into both the development of illness and how it is studied, the biomedical approach leaves important variables unexplained and unexamined. The BPS approach was developed to allow for a more complete and accurate understanding of patients and their medical conditions.

> Biological Correlates
> ☰ PSYCH & SOC

The traditional biomedical model only considers the biological aspects of a patient. In this model, a patient with a liver condition, such as cirrhosis, might as well just be a liver. The treatment plan would most likely involve the treatment of the liver through pharmaceutical or surgical means. But patients have psychological and social lives that are just as significant as their functioning on the level of organs or tissues. Under a biopsychosocial model, if the cirrhosis is associated with alcoholism, the patient's alcohol consumption would need to be addressed and treatment would involve attention to the related psychosocial factors, such as the patient's housing situation and stress level. The biopsychosocial model provides us with the tools needed to understand the interacting systems that influence the outcome of the illness.

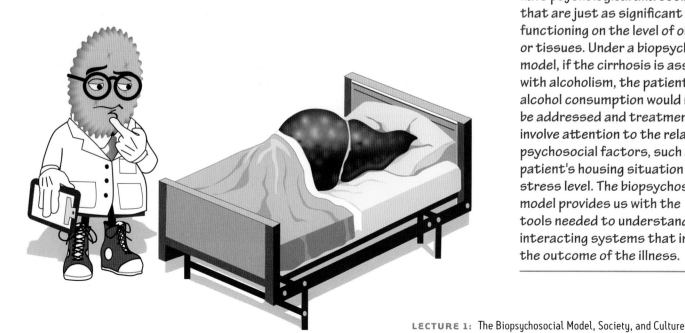

FIGURE 1.1 The Biopsychosocial Approach: Levels of Organization

Levels of Organization

Biosphere

Society - Nation

Culture - Subculture

Community

Family

Two - Person

Person (experience & behavior)

Organs/ Organ systems

Tissues

Cells

Organelles

Molecules

Atoms

Subatomic Particles

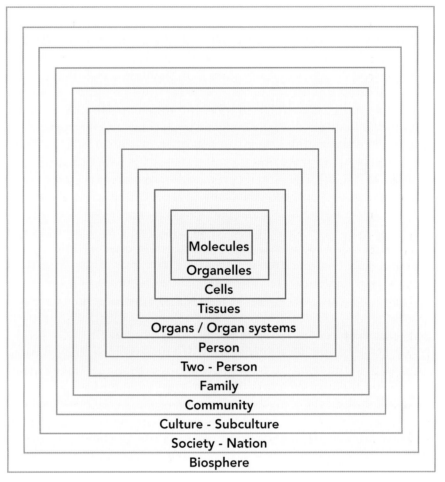

Engel, GL "The Clinical Application of the Biopsychosocial Model" *Am J Psychiatry* 13:5 May 1980

The system of different levels described by the biopsychosocial model may seem complex, but it's not that different from other ideas that you have seen in your premedical courses. To understand chemical reactions, you must understand how atoms combine to create molecules, which then form compounds. The idea of multiple levels can also be applied to biology. You would never try to understand the whole nervous system just by learning about neurons. You would not be able to grasp the larger divisions of the nervous system without including the study of how neurons communicate with each other and with their effectors. Similarly, a disease process and its resolution cannot be fully understood by reducing one's focus to only the smallest level within the individual and ignoring the influences of psychological and social life.

MCAT® passages in the psycho-social section will present health issues and require you to apply the BPS approach in order to interpret the passage.

Biological processes   Person   Society

1.3 The Examkrackers Approach

This manual will help you gain the skills necessary to master the psychosocial section on the MCAT®. Although this section is somewhat different in its content from the other MCAT® sections, the skills taught in the other Examkrackers manuals, particularly *Reasoning Skills*, *Biology 1: Molecules*, and *Biology 2: Systems*, will contribute to your success. The Examkrackers approach to the psychosocial section includes particular strategies as well as tools used in this manual to support development of the necessary skills.

Recall the importance of attending to the main idea—the author's opinion—when approaching passages in the CARS section. This skill is crucial for the psychosocial section as well. Although questions may delve into the detailed vocabulary discussed in the passage, they will also require an understanding of the writer's concerns and how the ideas that are presented relate to each other. A passage about cardiovascular health, for example, may address biological, psychological, and social factors and require an understanding of how these factors relate to health outcomes.

The psychosocial section is also reminiscent of the CARS section in that patterns of certain answer choices may appear. Most significantly, questions in the psychosocial section may tempt the test taker with answer choices that are overly simple. If an answer choice stands out relative to the others by offering a simplistic explanation for a complex phenomenon, it is likely to be incorrect. A good example would be an answer choice claiming that a given situation can be explained by either a purely genetic or purely environmental cause. In this case, a choice that acknowledges the interaction between genetics and environment (or "nature and nurture") would be a far better MCAT® answer. Just as a physician must consider the multiple aspects of a patient's life that contribute to health or illness, a successful MCAT® student examines passages in the psychosocial section for the many factors that are simultaneously at work on the psychological, social, and biological levels.

Unlike the CARS section, the psychosocial section does require the student to bring and apply knowledge of basic content and vocabulary. The skills that are key to success on the physical and biological sections are also necessary for success on the psychosocial section. You must be able to interpret the scientific data and information presented, assess research methodologies, and recall basic conceptual knowledge. The psychosocial section also requires you to determine whether a question calls for insight from the passage or independent knowledge.

This manual is organized by the continuum of phenomena studied in the fields of sociology, psychology, and biology. It starts with an overview of the social structures within which individuals develop, setting the stage for the consideration of social, psychological, and biological processes that are described in the remaining lectures. Within each lecture, signposts signal connections to ideas discussed in other lectures and manuals. This book emphasizes connections between psychological and sociological ideas and correlated biological processes. Each lecture describes health applications for some of the concepts introduced, demonstrating the way these topics could be applied in MCAT® passages.

Terms that are directly tested by the MCAT® are written in red, bold type. Terms that are unlikely to be directly tested on the MCAT® but are useful as background knowledge or could be seen in a passage appear in *italics*. The *Psychology & Sociology* manual differs from the others in that the bolded terms may seem familiar to the student from everyday life. For example, in the next part of this lecture, 'age' and 'gender' will both appear as bolded terms. You may wonder why they would be tested by the MCAT®. The fields of psychology and sociology have particular ways of understanding and studying these topics. Be careful of your intuitive feeling for these terms, as the technical definitions may differ from the

This manual speaks from the combined perspectives of biology, psychology, and sociology.

One more similarity between the psychosocial section and the CARS section: both may try to tempt you to apply outside knowledge or your own preconceptions. It's pretty hard for a physics passage to provoke bias, but a psychosocial passage might. Remember to read with fresh eyes and leave your past experiences at the door when you approach the psychosocial section.

colloquial definitions. It is important to understand these terms as they are defined within these fields, as they will be tested by the MCAT® accordingly.

The psychosocial section bridges the science sections and the CARS section of the MCAT®. It draws upon skills that are required for each. You can use the tools that you have been working hard to develop for those sections to dominate the psychosocial section!

Research Skills
REASONING SKILLS

1.4 | Models and Theories

Part of the study of psychology and sociology is learning to consider varied ways of studying and understanding the world. Scientific research involves the use of models and theories to organize and conceptualize the topics under study. The MCAT® rewards the ability to reason flexibly among competing models and theories. While studying, critically consider their strengths and weaknesses, rather than just memorizing and accepting them as fact. *Models* provide an approximation—a physical or conceptual representation of a scientific phenomenon that cannot be observed directly. Studies of a model are often helpful for drawing conclusions about the phenomenon itself. The biopsychosocial approach, sometimes called the biopsychosocial model, is a multi-factorial framework of the levels that together make up a person. This model is an organizational tool that helps healthcare providers consider the multitude of factors interacting to affect health or illness. Another example of a model, one used in psychology, is the structure of mental life put forth by Freud, which frames a flow of psychic energy between the id, ego, and superego. While these structures may correlate with neurological structures, they do not literally exist in our minds.

Apply Key 1: The MCAT® tests the ability to consider the three perspectives of the biopsychosocial model together. Remember, all models are simplifications. On the MCAT®, pick the best choice even if it is not a perfect answer.

Theories have a similar function to models and are crucial to the development of scientific research. Theories can be formed or modified to explain the results of studies; they also guide the design of new studies. A theory provides the conceptual framework for understanding objects of study, such as how people behave in groups and why they behave the way they do. The validity of a theory can be supported or undermined by the results of research. A theory can also be evaluated in terms of how well it contributes to the development of new research and practical applications.

Models and theories may seem abstract, but they are used in all of the sciences—physical, biological, and social. Chemistry provides many familiar examples, such as the shapes assigned to subshells. These shapes are a convenient way to represent mathematical probability but are not based in physical reality. For example, students learn to associate the p subshell with a dumbbell shape, but there is no physical subshell in existence. The shape does not describe the actual position of any given electron at any particular point in time. However, modeling the subshell in this way allows useful and accurate predictions about the formation of ions and bonds between atoms.

Because models and theories are constructed by scientists to organize their research and perspectives on naturally occurring phenomena, they are prone to change over time along with trends in scientific thought. In the field of psychology, multiple competing viewpoints have waxed and waned in popularity and

Hopefully no one who subscribes to the BPS model literally believes that people are made up of a series of concentric circles! The model provides a concrete way to think about abstract ideas. Models are a representation of reality, not the reality itself.

clinical acceptance over time. The psychoanalytic school of thought has declined while cognitive theories have gained popularity. That said, each of the various schools continues to be studied and modified, and no single theory dominates psychology. The historical development of differing perspectives does not reflect objective changes in the phenomena studied, but rather in ways of thinking and organizing knowledge. The MCAT® requires the ability to evaluate and apply differing models and theories. For some concepts, such as personality, the test taker is required to master multiple perspectives that have been used as explanatory models over time.

Don't get hung up on the differences between models and theories. The words are often used interchangeably. Just understand that people who study psychology and sociology, as in the other sciences, are often guided by differing theoretical representations of their object of study. In other words, models and theories are the stories that we tell about the things that we study.

1.5 | Studying Social Processes

This section will consider major theoretical approaches on how society functions. These approaches provide another demonstration of how representative models and theories can be used to organize and conceptualize scientific thought within a field. Each can be thought of as an evaluative lens for social phenomena. These sociological approaches demonstrate how theories complement one another and use varying levels of analysis. The major theories covered here differ in the following ways: the extent to which they assume that individuals can influence society, the level of society studied, the degree of harmony or discord in social relations, and their strengths and weaknesses.

Social constructionism adds to the idea of scientific models as representations of reality. According to social constructionism, human actors construct or create "reality," rather than discovering a reality that has inherent validity. In this view, the beliefs and shared understandings of individuals create social realities. Some social constructionists contend that all reality, including what many would consider to be objective natural phenomena, has no inherent meaning beyond human beliefs. Others take a more moderate view and divide reality into two categories: brute facts and institutional facts. Brute facts are physical realities that exist outside of human input, whereas institutional facts only exist as a function of society's structures and beliefs. Consider the concept of gravity. It is a brute fact that objects seem to fall to the Earth's surface when dropped from above. However, the concept of a gravitational force involving the larger planet is an institutional fact. It can be mathematically modeled and used to understand other occurrences in the natural world, but it is not an observable fact.

On the MCAT®, social constructionism could be tested in the context of understanding illness. The diagnosis of an illness requires an agreed upon set of criteria; there is a gap between the biological or physiological reality of the medical condition and the societally created meaning of the diagnosis. This is particularly evident in the context of the *Diagnostic and Statistical Manual of Mental Disorders*, in which the diagnostic categories and the disorders themselves are periodically revised according to new research and changing conceptualizations of mental illness.

The perspective of symbolic interactionism is related to social constructionism in that it allows for social determination of shared realities. However, symbolic interactionism focuses on a smaller scale of interaction between individuals and in small groups. While social constructionism would be interested in the social creation of shared meanings of health and illness, symbolic interactionism could be applied to a single interaction between a patient and physician or between two physicians. This perspective says that through social interactions, individuals develop shared meanings and labels for various symbols – terms, concepts, or items that represent specific meanings by accepted convention. One example would be the label of "drug addict," which has a variety of socially determined symbolic meanings, ranging from criminal tendencies to clinical mental illness.

Shared symbols allow for smooth societal interactions by permitting reasonable expectations of how other people will behave and what constitutes appropriate responses. This is particularly true in the case of social roles, symbols that have a large effect on behavior and identity. Symbolic interactionism says that people actively create meaning through their social interactions, allowing for human agency in creating and changing meaning. Within a single interaction, the meaning of a symbol can change, and the individuals involved may come up with different, even opposing, symbolic interpretations of an environmental stimulus or social situation. For instance, a particular symptom could have changing meanings within a doctor/patient consultation. A symptom could initially have meaning as a warning sign to the patient but then be re-understood as a harmless experience based on information provided by the physician.

Symbolic interactionism is particularly useful for examining social functioning at the level of interpersonal interactions, but it has been criticized for leaving out larger societal forces that undeniably have an effect on people's lives. Two other major theoretical perspectives, functionalism and conflict theory, attempt to understand social functioning by looking at the larger levels of society that are described in detail later in this lecture.

According to functionalism, factions of society work together to maintain stability. Functionalism claims that society, like an organism, is a system that consists of different components working together. An organism contains distinct organ systems that each have roles in the body; a society contains distinct institutions that contribute to functioning. Much like organ systems within the body, these institutions and social structures work together to maintain equilibrium in the face of environmental demands. When disruptions occur, the interacting systems respond as needed to get back to the previous state, acting like homeostatic mechanisms in the body. The actions of individuals and groups in a society can be analyzed by asking how they contribute to long-term societal stability.

Conflict theory takes a different approach from functionalism by viewing society in terms of competing groups that act according to their own self-interests, rather than according to the need for societal equilibrium. Social groups naturally come into conflict as their interests collide, and society changes over time due to continual competition for resources and power. Conflict theory views human actions in terms of larger forces of inequality but leaves the motivations and choices of individuals unexamined. Feminist theory is a closely related perspective that examines societal inequities between men and women. Feminist theory can be considered a particular type of conflict theory. Many researchers use feminist theory in combination with other sociological approaches.

Imagine two people talking about a stray dog. At different points in the conversation, both individuals might see the dog as a friendly potential pet or a dangerous wild animal, or they may disagree in their interpretation. If the dog suddenly starts foaming at the mouth, it is likely that both people will quickly come to see it as a symbol of danger and disease!

Conflict theory provides a useful perspective on health inequalities, which are discussed in detail later in this lecture. When healthcare resources are limited, access is determined by imbalances of power between social groups: more powerful groups have greater access to healthcare.

Functionalism and conflict theory each provide a method of studying large-scale forces in society. Unlike symbolic interactionism, they cannot explain social life on the micro scale. The fundamental differences between sociological theories result in complementary strengths and weaknesses. Functionalism provides a useful perspective for considering processes that contribute to social stability, but it cannot explain societal changes. It assumes that stability is always the ideal. Conflict theory argues that stability is undesirable for the social groups that are oppressed by the self-interests of the powerful, and that change will inevitably occur. Conflict theory can explain how societies change over time, but fails to recognize that society exhibits stability as well as change. It does not leave room for the types of social agreement and collaboration between individuals and groups that are addressed by symbolic interactionism and functionalism.

Most sociological theories can be placed in two broad categories. Macrosociology focuses on broad social structures that affect society. Social constructionism, functionalism, conflict theory, and feminist theory are macrosociological perspectives. Microsociology focuses on the smaller scale of social interactions between individuals. Symbolic interactionism is a microsociological perspective.

Some theories cannot be neatly categorized as macrosociological or microsociological. Rational choice theory assumes that people's actions are dictated by a rational consideration of alternatives. Individuals choose the action that is most likely to bring some type of profit. Exchange theory applies the basic principles of rational choice theory to social interactions, arguing that behaviors within relationships are determined by individuals' expectations of reward or punishment. Rational choice and exchange theory consider decision making at the scale of individuals and their relationships, a microsociological viewpoint. These perspectives also assume that large societal structures are ultimately built from these small-scale rational decisions, a macrosociological phenomenon. Rational choice and exchange theory are useful for considering how people make decisions and how such decisions contribute to the structure of society, but they cannot explain why people sometimes choose to do things that are not in their own best interest or appear to be irrational.

The MCAT® could ask you to interpret a given scenario in terms of the social theories described in this section. Here's the take-home message: symbolic interactionism deals with small-scale interactions (microsociology), while social constructionism, functionalism, conflict theory, and feminist theory focus on larger scale interactions (macrosociology). Functionalism and social constructionism share some fundamental similarities with symbolic interactionism but look at social institutions rather than individuals. Conflict and feminist theory are the only perspectives that focus on social disruption. Rational choice and exchange theory relate to both small scale interactions and societal institutions.

Any scientist worth his or her microscope can think critically about these theories and grasp the strengths and weaknesses of each.

Questions 1-8 are NOT based on a descriptive passage.

Question 1

A healthcare provider who subscribes to the biomedical model and one who is invested in the biopsychosocial model disagree about the treatment of a patient who presents with symptoms of a psychological disorder. Which feature of the traditional biomedical model would likely contribute to this disagreement?

- ○ **A.** The biomedical model would start with the assumption that psychological disorders are associated with other non-psychological medical disorders.
- ○ **B.** According to the biomedical model, no treatment is warranted for psychological disorders, since they are not based in a physical pathology.
- ○ **C.** The biomedical model would reduce the patient's symptoms to biological underpinnings such as neurotransmitter imbalances.
- ○ **D.** The biomedical model would consider a multitude of possible contributors to the disorder.

Question 2

A researcher who takes a biopsychosocial perspective and a researcher who takes a sociological perspective collaborate on a study about the causes of obesity. How would each of these researchers most likely approach the project?

- ○ **A.** The biopsychosocial researcher would focus on the biological factors that influence social contributors to malnutrition. The sociological researcher would de-emphasize biology in favor of considering mental life.
- ○ **B.** The biopsychosocial researcher would focus on the interaction between genetics and interpersonal influences. The sociological researcher would focus only on interpersonal influences.
- ○ **C.** The biopsychosocial researcher would examine causal factors in different realms of personal functioning. The sociological researcher would focus on addressing large-scale social inequalities that contribute to obesity.
- ○ **D.** Both researchers would reject a biomedical perspective that would reduce obesity to its physical manifestations and would not differ significantly in their theoretical perspectives.

Question 3

Two acquaintances glare at one another while passing on the street, which they both interpret as a continuation of an earlier disagreement. This incident is most consistent with which sociological perspective?

- ○ **A.** Functionalism
- ○ **B.** Conflict theory
- ○ **C.** Symbolic interactionism
- ○ **D.** Social constructionism

Question 4

Which perspective would be most relevant to the study of how interpretations of natural phenomena come to be widely shared and perceived as scientific truth?

- ○ **A.** Functionalism
- ○ **B.** Social constructionism
- ○ **C.** Symbolic interactionism
- ○ **D.** Conflict theory

Question 5

A sociological researcher who is interested in how different societal institutions work to maintain consistency and stability would most likely adopt which of the following perspectives?

- ○ **A.** Conflict theory
- ○ **B.** Social constructionism
- ○ **C.** Symbolic interactionism
- ○ **D.** Functionalism

Question 6

How might a social constructionist and a symbolic interactionist differ in their examinations of the development of knowledge about a specific pathological condition?

- ○ **A.** A social constructionist would focus on how the understanding of the condition comes to be shared as society's reality of the condition. A symbolic interactionist would focus on individual interactions that establish shared interpretations of the condition.
- ○ **B.** A social constructionist would examine how people in power consciously create an understanding that others must accept as reality. A symbolic interactionist would focus on the interactions between groups that debate the meaning of the condition.
- ○ **C.** A social constructionist would examine how people with the condition are systematically excluded from societal privileges. A symbolic interactionist would study how individuals discriminate against people with the condition.
- ○ **D.** The theories are so similar that there is no way to predict a difference in how they would approach this topic.

Question 7

Which of the following best describes the relative strengths of conflict theory and functionalism in describing social phenomena?

- ○ **A.** Depending on the phenomenon under study, one or the other will yield a better understanding.
- ○ **B.** The theories are equally useful for describing a broad variety of social phenomena.
- ○ **C.** Although both theories have merit, conflict theory is ultimately more useful.
- ○ **D.** Either theory may be used according to the situation, but functionalism will provide more relevant information.

Question 8

Which sociological perspective(s) would be relevant to the study of how medical schools and hospitals develop shared meanings and knowledge systems that allow individuals and the institutions themselves to work together toward the goal of promoting health?

    I.   Social constructionism
   II.   Symbolic interactionism
  III.   Functionalism

- ○ **A.** I only
- ○ **B.** I and II only
- ○ **C.** III only
- ○ **D.** I, II and III

1.6 | Culture

The perspectives described in the previous section provide a general framework for more specific theories about society and culture. This framework is necessary because an understanding of culture and society is key to the study of sociology. Just as cells work together to form tissues, tissues comprise organs, and organs work together to perform all of the functions of the body, people operate as the smallest functional units of society. The remainder of this lecture will delve into the broadest levels of social organization in sociology. Later lectures will focus on human behavior, covering group interactions and individual motivation all the way down to biological influences on individual behavior. Just as the BPS approach considers social factors to be integral to functioning at the level of individual biology, the lectures take social forces as a starting point and continue to consider psychological and biological processes.

The following sections will explore how the overarching structures of human organization, society, and culture operate and propagate so that culture can be passed down through generations. Studying the structure of society and culture provides an overview of how humans organize into groups, as well as a foundation for understanding how group dynamics influence individual behavior.

A culture can be thought of as all of the beliefs, assumptions, objects, behaviors, and processes that make up a shared way of life. While people who share a culture have individual differences, they tend to share common values, learned behaviors, and approaches to life. Culture has a pervasive effect on worldview. When people are immersed in a culture, they may assume that their culture's way of doing things is normal and natural. Through interactions with other cultures, people can learn about their own cultural assumptions. The meanings ascribed to the same behaviors can differ between cultures. For instance, hugging and kissing as a form of greeting is acceptable in certain cultures, while in others it is considered an invasion of personal space. Similarly, in the U.S. decorating houses with lights at Christmas time is a widespread practice that is generally interpreted as celebratory and cheerful, but in many parts of the world, this practice is viewed as wasteful. Differing perspectives and reactions are often due to cultural differences.

Perhaps you've had a shocking experience after encountering a new way of doing things. These experiences can arise out of studying abroad, moving across the country, or joining a new social group. Experiencing shock or discomfort when first encountering a new culture is common and can be a catalyst for growth and reflection. The discomfort and the ensuing re-evaluation of personal cultural assumptions is referred to as culture shock.

Culture can be divided into the categories of material and non-material culture. Material culture refers to the objects involved in a certain way of life. It includes products manufactured, tools used, art made, and every object that supports or enriches a lifestyle, from nuts and bolts to teacups and toys. Material culture comprises all of the things that an archaeologist might uncover and study. Non-material culture, by contrast, encompasses the elements of culture that are not physical. Non-material culture is comprised of the shared ideas, knowledge, assumptions, values, and beliefs that unify a group of people. Examples of non-material culture include religions and superstitions. Non-material culture is usually studied by living among people of another culture, as in the case of ethnographers, or through the medium of language, as in the case of historians.

Shared cultural experiences are often related to geographical area or country of origin. The formation of culture also relates to shared experiences that transcend geography. Social interactions help to define a culture by establishing social norms, expectations that govern what behavior is acceptable within a group. Sanctions are social expressions of approval for conforming to norms or disapproval for failing to conform. An approving smile from a pedestrian in response to seeing someone helping an elderly person cross the street would be a positive sanction. A glare directed toward someone who cuts in front of a line would be a negative sanction. Both of these are examples of folkways, or norms governing casual interactions. The violation of a folkway is not punished harshly. Folkways are distinct from mores, norms enforcing the moral standards of a society. Violations of mores lead to serious negative sanctions. A person who commits murder has violated a societal more. At the most extreme end of disapproval is a taboo. The violation of a taboo is considered not just immoral but also repulsive. Cannibalism is an example of a taboo in many societies.

Expectations and norms differ between groups, so identification with social groups influences the culture or cultures that a person experiences. Narrowly defined, a social group is a subset of a population that maintains social interactions. A social group can also be defined more broadly as a group identity among a set of individuals created by a collection of shared experiences. Members of a certain socioeconomic status may have shared experiences that establish them as part of a community and make them feel connected to other members of that group, even when they do not directly interact. Group identity helps bind people together and builds shared cultural expectations.

An understanding of culture is important because cultural differences influence interpretations, reactions, and understandings of the behavior of others. Knowing that people's underlying beliefs about the world are varied makes it easier to understand why human behavior is variable.

Keep the concept of culture in mind as you read the remaining lectures. Culture affects the psychological and biological processes discussed throughout this manual.

The Evolution of Culture

Humans are social animals. We live in groups and feel the need to connect with those around us. Through these interactions, we establish norms of behavior, define social expectations, exchange ideas, and, eventually, build culture. Humans are part of the order of primates. Compared to other animals, primates have a large ratio of brain to body size, and in humans, this ratio is taken to the extreme. Human intelligence allows for the development of culture to an unparalleled extent in the animal kingdom.

The human lineage split from that of other apes approximately 8 million years ago, setting humans on a separate path. Human ancestors gradually learned tool production and learned to manipulate fire, affording them greater control over their environments. During the last ice age, and leading up to the present, humans

One experience can take on different meanings in different cultures. Western medicine considers epilepsy to be a disease. However, in several cultures epileptic symptoms are considered a spiritual experience, and those who exhibit symptoms are revered for their spiritual giftedness.

Take the example of the doctor's office: the material culture of a doctor's office includes all of the medical objects and instruments, from a stethoscope to throat swabs. The non-material culture of a doctor's office consists of the ideas about disease and treatment that underlie the field of medicine. These ideas include germ theory and the practice of western medication as the standard treatment of disease. In some cultures, the material culture of a doctor's office might include various herbal powders or massage instruments, while the non-material culture might consist of homeopathic beliefs.

Some examples of culture have been observed among other animals. For instance, chimpanzees use tools and teach survival skills to their offspring. However, the degree to which human beings display a capacity for innovation, communication, and cultural variability is unique.

A thumbs-up is an example of a symbolic gesture that does not have inherent meaning, but has a socially understood meaning.

Thought and Emotion
PSYCH & SOC

Culture and society are connected but not synonymous. Loosely speaking, culture is a shared set of beliefs and lifestyles, while a society is a group of people who share a culture. A society can sometimes encompass multiple cultures. The United States is a society in which members share elements of identity and culture by virtue of being American. However, the U.S. is also multicultural in that people practice different religions, speak different languages, and emigrate from many parts of the world.

experienced an explosion of cultural changes. Cave art, metal working, agriculture, urban lifestyle, the steam engine, and the Internet are just a few of the many innovations human culture has introduced to the world in the last 40,000 years.

In addition to technological advancement, the development of symbolic culture sets human culture apart from that of other species. Symbolic culture is a type of non-material culture that consists of the elements of culture that have meaning only in the mind. Symbolic culture is based on a shared system of collective beliefs in the form of symbols. The meanings ascribed to symbols are determined by social norms and cultural values. Symbolic culture includes the meanings ascribed to rituals (formal, ceremonial behaviors with specific purpose and significance), gestures, and objects. For example, a handshake, an arbitrary bodily movement, can convey trust and greeting because of the symbolic meaning we ascribe to that movement. The extended hand would mean nothing without the set of expectations gained from shared symbolic culture.

It is possible for the same symbol to have different meanings to different people. The swastika, or hooked cross, has been considered a sacred symbol of good fortune among eastern religions for thousands of years. Since World War II, however, it has symbolized Adolf Hitler's Nazi regime. Symbolic culture provides a basis for and is reinforced by symbolic interaction. The meanings people assign based on symbolic culture affect behavior and how individuals see the world. Symbolic meanings are culturally situated and are determined by experiences and social interactions.

One of the most important aspects of symbolic culture is the development of language. Language, or the use of symbols to represent ideas, allows one person's thoughts to be transferred to the mind of a second person through symbols, speech, or writing. The advent of language marks an enormous milestone in the evolution of human culture. Language also shapes other aspects of human evolution by allowing for cooperation and the exchange of information. Language plays an important role in individual growth and learning by enabling the transfer of shared ideas and knowledge throughout development.

Symbols are all around us. $, %, =, and ? all convey particular meanings. The letters, words, and sentences that make up this text are symbols that represent sounds, objects, and ideas. The human mind has the capacity to store an enormous repertoire of symbols and the ability to use them to communicate and find meaning.

1.7 | Society, Systems, and Structures

A society is defined as two or more individuals living together in a community and/or sharing elements of culture. One way to make sense of the organization of a society is to examine its social institutions. Social institutions are hierarchical systems that bring order to interpersonal interactions, structuring society. Social institutions address a specific purpose or set of tasks. Common examples of social institutions include:

1. Government and economy: Government provides order to society through the services it provides and the making and enforcement of law. The economy is an institution that distributes goods and services to meet the needs of a society. These institutions exist on a local, state, national, and international level. They provide a framework and rules to structure society. Both the government and the economy are organized by power and authority. According to sociologist *Max Weber*, power allows individuals or groups to exert their will even when they are opposed by others. Authority is a type of power that is viewed

as legitimate by the population. A government wielding authority can maintain stability and carry out its ends without having to resort to force.

Authority can be enacted through tradition, bureaucracy, or charisma. *Traditional authority* depends on a population's respect for cultural patterns that have existed for a long time. The bureaucratic type, called *rational-legal authority*, describes power maintained by rules and regulations such as traffic laws. Personal qualities that inspire devotion allow individuals or groups to have *charismatic authority*. This type of authority is the least stable and must eventually transform into one or a blend of the other two types.

In addition to the overall concept of economy and government, the MCAT® requires knowledge of comparative economic and political systems. The most important distinction is between capitalism and socialism. In capitalism, resources and the means to produce goods and services are privately controlled by individuals and organizations. The desire for profit drives commercial activity. Socialism is a system in which resources and the means of producing goods and services are managed collectively. A socialist economy relies on government regulation to match productive output to the demands of consumers. Capitalist societies are considerably more productive and tend to enjoy a greater degree of political freedom. Socialist societies tend to generate less per capita income but also have decreased wealth disparity.

One trend of economic modernization is the division of labor, in which an increasing number of individuals engage in work that is highly specific. This trend contrasts with traditional labor frameworks in which all members of society engage in more or less the same daily activities. As a result of the division of labor, members of a society must rely on one another to meet their daily needs.

2. Education: Most places in the world have some type of formalized education. The purpose of education is generally two-fold within a society. Education provides a formal structure during childhood and the transition to adulthood and an opportunity to instruct youth on the social norms, expectations for behavior, knowledge, and skills that they will need to operate within a society. In other words, education is a transfer of cultural knowledge. By creating a formal space for learning, education encourages technological advancement, innovation, and discovery.

The effects of educational systems are not always explicit. The hidden curriculum in schools transmits cultural ideals beyond the stated goals of the institution. It encompasses the unspoken aims of education, such as teaching children to conform to social expectations. Students' education and school experiences are also affected by teacher expectancy, where teachers treat students differently according to preconceived ideas about their capabilities. This treatment, in turn, influences students' achievement.

Social forces also affect educational outcomes. Segregation is the separation of groups according to socially constructed characteristics such as gender or race. Communities are often racially segregated, with minority communities enjoying fewer socioeconomic resources. Segregation affects educational outcomes because communities with greater socioeconomic resources can spend more on education. The result of educational segregation is that students in disadvantaged groups receive a lower quality education than more privileged students. Educational stratification refers to the separation of students into groups on the basis of academic achievement. This process begins early on in education and creates a snowball effect that influences opportunities later in life.

3. Religion: Religion is a system of beliefs that affects how people make sense of their experiences and provides a framework for questions about life, death, and the purpose of existence. As a social institution, religion is an organized structure of behaviors and social interactions that addresses the spiritual needs of

"Family" can come in a diversity of forms and can have different meanings to different people.

Despite laws banning racial segregation in schools, integration is still far from the norm. School systems that were integrated in the 1960s have gradually become resegregated due to socioeconomic pressures and racism dividing neighborhoods based on race. As a result, underprivileged communities of color have fewer educational opportunities. Educational stratification can worsen the impact of educational segregation, leaving the children who are behind to fall even further behind. As these children age, they have decreased access to college and job opportunities.

Demographic categories such as race, gender, ethnicity, and sexual orientation are not only useful in understanding a society but are also important constructs in forming self-identity, as discussed in the Identity and the Individual Lecture. The difference between these two ways of discussing the same categories hinges on perspective. Demographics has to do with understanding the makeup of a group by classifying people into different categories. Identity depends on how you categorize yourself as belonging or not belonging to these various demographic categories.

You may have strong opinions or emotions about some of the topics covered in the psychosocial section. This makes sense— often the topics address who we are as people and how we see the world. You must answer the questions based on the information presented in the passage and your knowledge of psychology and sociology without being influenced by the prior assumptions and biases that we all possess.

Other important relationship terms to know are *monogamy* (having just one romantic or sexual partner at a given time) and *polyamory* (having more than one romantic or sexual partner at a given time).

society. **Religiosity** is the extent to which religion is important to an individual or community.

There are a multitude of religions worldwide. Currently the most practiced religions are Christianity, Islam, Hinduism, and Buddhism. Religions that espouse the existence of one god are *monotheistic*, while those that express belief in many gods are *polytheistic*. Three major **types of religious organizations** can be described based on how fully they are integrated into society at large. A church is a religious organization that is well established in the larger society. A sect is a more radical group that forms by breaking away from the established norms or beliefs of a mainstream church. A cult has views or practices that situate it outside the traditions of mainstream society and, unlike a sect, tends to form outside of any pre-existing religion. These organizations exist on a continuum. After growing over time, a cult or sect may eventually become more mainstream and transition into a church. Cults and sects are likely to have living founders, but by the time religious organizations become churches, they have typically gone through several generations of leadership.

The words "cult" and "church" are used differently in sociology than in everyday language. A church can mean any mainstream religion and is not necessarily associated with Christianity. A cult is not defined by extreme practices like brainwashing. Remember to leave behind outside biases!

Since society and religion are interrelated, there is an important relationship between **religion and social change**. Modernization has made it possible for individuals to access information about many types of religious practice, especially through the Internet. As a result, people are exposed to diverse challenges to their religious identities. Today it is much easier than it was in the past for religious ideas to spread across the globe. Religion has also been affected by **secularization**, or decreasing devotion to religious doctrines and practices. People who identify as "culturally Jewish" provide an example of this trend. These individuals view Judaism as part of their cultural identification, but they may not engage in traditional Jewish customs. **Fundamentalism** is the opposite tendency, which entails a strictly literal interpretation of sacred writings. A limited tolerance for other religions often accompanies this ideology.

4. Family: Families consist of bonds of kin and marriage and make up a major organizing institution of society. **Kinship** describes the social bonds that unite individuals into families. There are three main **forms of kinship**: bloodline, marriage, and adoption. In most societies, the institution of family creates a social group in which to procreate, rear children, pass on cultural knowledge, and cooperate to better meet life's challenges. In the United States' recent history, the most common concept of family has been one man and one woman living together with their children. This structure is known as the *nuclear family*. However, other groups of related individuals or families are possible. **Diversity in family forms** can manifest in many ways. Two heterosexual parents might be considered a traditional form, but there has always been diversity in family structure, including one-parent families, couples that have no children, and gay and lesbian families. In many places, multiple generations of a family will dwell together in an *extended family* model. Other family types include *polygyny* (more than one woman married to a man) and *polyandry* (more than one man married to a woman). The term *polygamy* encompasses both of these possibilities. American ideas about family are shifting. Rising rates of divorce, blended families, single-parenting, unmarried cohabitation, and same-sex marriage are leading to a more inclusive idea of what constitutes a family.

While families are a source of financial and emotional support for many people, for others the family can be dangerous. **Violence in the family** comes in many forms and includes emotional, physical, or sexual abuse. Victims of violence are usually non-dominant members of the family such as elders, females, or children. It is important to remember that males can be victims of domestic violence. Victims may find it difficult to leave their abusers due to dependence on the family for resources. The risk of family violence increases with some types of substance abuse, particularly alcohol.

5. **Health and medicine:** The social institution of medicine fulfills the need for healthcare in an organized manner. Beliefs about disease and approaches to healing vary between societies and cultures. In Western societies, science-based medicine (the biomedical approach) is more prevalent than holistic medicine, which focuses on the wellness of a whole person – body, mind, and spirit. (The biopsychosocial approach is more consistent with the holistic approach.)

Delivery of health care refers to the mechanisms by which a society provides health care to individuals. Health care can be delivered at several levels. Personal health care services for individuals are available at clinics, neighborhood centers, offices, or homes. On a larger scale, public health services are required to maintain a healthy environment in order to prevent disease spread and other health conditions in the population. Examples include the control of water and food supplies as well as safety and drug regulations. The advancement of medical knowledge and education of new health care providers is another critical component of healthcare that bears on the prevention, detection, and treatment of disease. Education occurs in schools or private businesses, including pharmaceutical companies. Health care delivery also involves finances and payment mechanisms, most notably health insurance.

Medicalization is the effort to describe a type of behavior as a symptom of an underlying illness that should be treated by a doctor. This process has been criticized as an attempt on the part of the powerful to control behaviors that are inconsistent with societal demands. One example of medicalization is that a student displaying disruptive behavior in a classroom may be diagnosed with attention-deficit/hyperactive disorder and given treatment with the goal of making the student conform to classroom expectations.

Individuals who are diagnosed with illnesses may assume the **sick role**, exhibiting the expected behaviors for an ill person. The nature of the sick role varies according to culture and socioeconomic status, but there are some common features. It is understood that serious illness exempts individuals from normal responsibilities such as going to work or school. It is also expected that the ill person wants to be healed and will seek medical help of his or her own accord. While the sick role refers to outward behaviors, the term **illness experience** describes how an individual adjusts to interruptions to their health. "Illness" refers to the definition of health problems in popular consciousness, while "disease" refers to an expert or medical definition of wellness. These terms create the possibility that a person can be ill without having a disease, or can have a disease without being ill. Two people with the same disease can have markedly different illness experiences.

Understanding Key 2: Overarching social structures such as culture and institutions influence our lives. We are constantly subjected to social forces much larger than us!

Demographics of Society

Another way to understand the attributes of a population is through the study of demographics. **Demographics** are statistics used to examine the nature of a specific population by quantifying subsets of that population. Commonly quantified demographic parameters include age, gender, *nationality*, race, ethnicity, sexual orientation, socioeconomic status, immigration status, and *education level*. Sensitivity to these differences among people is essential for understanding and establishing trust with patients. Demographic information is useful for organizations such as government and businesses because of the relationship between demographic group and behavior. For instance, young American voters rate the importance of environmental issues more highly than do voters who are senior citizens. Elected representatives who want to reach younger constituencies may need to place more emphasis on environmental legislation in order to be re-elected. In this scenario, a demographic parameter, age, can be used as a predictor of how much the average person will care about the environment, and the age distribution of the targeted population can be used as an indicator of how the legislator should act. Demographics are useful for making sense of the organization of a population and predicting behavior based on membership in overlapping categories. Important demographic categories include:

1. Gender: Gender is a social and psychological phenomenon best described by the intersection of three related concepts: sex, gender identity, and gender expression. **Sex** is assigned at birth based on the infant's genitalia. **Gender identity**, by contrast, is an individual's internal sense of self as male, female, both, or neither. The term gender also encompasses an individual's outward appearance and behaviors, collectively known as gender expression. It is important to realize that gender and sex are distinct and that gender identity does not always align with the sex assigned at birth. According to the theory of the **social construction of gender**, the development of gender is subject to cultural influences and depends on social interactions. The range of accepted gender presentations and identities varies between societies.

2. Race and ethnicity: The **social construction of race** is the process by which racial categories are created through social forces. **Racialization** is the imposition of a racial identity on a particular group. In the present day and over the course of history, racialization has been used to support the domination of less powerful groups. **Racial formation theory** states that race is a social construct, with no basis in actual genetic differences, and emphasizes how a variety of social factors interact to construct definitions, expectations, and experiences of race.

3. Immigration status: With regard to **patterns of immigration**, some of the largest groups of immigrants to the United States are from Mexico, Caribbean nations, and India. Immigrants face many barriers to integration, including a lack of knowledge of the new society as well as prevailing negative attitudes of the existing citizenry. **Intersections with race and ethnicity with immigration status** often lead to prejudice and discrimination.

4. Age: *Gerontology* is the study of **aging and the life course**. The process of aging involves the need for continued learning. As an example, eyesight worsens with age, and an individual who was once independent may need to rely on others for transportation and learn new ways to navigate the environment. One way to study aging is to create **age cohorts**, which are groups of people categorized by age range. Popular age cohorts correspond to generations in which individuals share common experiences. Examples include the Baby Boomer Generation, Generation X, and the Millennial Generation.

The notion of the **social significance of aging** emphasizes the idea that aging is more complicated than simply the measured time since birth. Despite being

---

The increased population density associated with urbanization, along with the increased interactions between cultures associated with globalization pose risks and challenges to public health. These shifts must be considered when combating the spread of diseases, assessing health risks, and planning access to healthcare.

Ethnicity and race are related but distinct terms. An ethnic group is defined by shared cultural aspects, such as religion, and may include people of multiple races. Racial groups are not assigned based on genetic differences; they are socially defined according to physical characteristics. Both racial and ethnic groups can be targets of discrimination.

Often immigrants come to a new country due to economic hardship in their countries of origin. This can cause the original inhabitants to unfairly characterize immigrants as being dependent on handouts, leading to racist beliefs toward immigrants and people of the same racial and ethnic groups as immigrants.

affected by the same biological process, characteristics of the life course can vary from culture to culture. The difference between elders in Asia and those in the United States provides one example. In Asian societies, elders are more integrated into society than their counterparts in the United States, where it is more socially acceptable for the elderly to live in segregated communities.

Demographics are a statistical snapshot of a particular point in time, so they do not capture the changing nature of society. Multiple factors can affect changes in societal composition. Birth rate is affected by **fertility**, meaning the production of offspring within a population. Fertility rates can be measured either by following a subset of a population over time (*cohort study*) or by examining the number of offspring produced during a specific time period (*period study*). Three different types of fertility rate can be described. **Total birth rate (or total fertility rate)** describes the average number of children that one woman is expected to have over her lifetime. **Crude birth rate** describes the number of live births in a year for every thousand people. Crude birth rate is often used as a measure of a particular group's fertility. **Age-specific birth rate** refers to the fertility of women who are a specific age or fall within a range of ages.

Mortality, the death rate within a population, also affects population size. It is measured through the *mortality rate*. The most common measure is the **crude death rate**, the number of deaths per year for every thousand people in a population. **Infant mortality rate** measures how many people less than one year old die per every thousand live births in a given year. An increase in population size is typically caused by a decline in death rate, rather than an increase in birth rate.

Mortality and fertility rates provide insight into the health of a population. The introduction of factors such as disease treatment, maternal care, and immunizations influence survival rates. Certain **patterns in fertility and mortality** occur throughout the world. Birth rates typically fall as a society's economy develops, as has been seen in the United States. The economy can also drive population growth in developing countries, such as many African nations. Healthcare advances can lead to a decline in mortality rates. In the United States, the decreased birth rate and decreased mortality rate have led to an increase in the average age. The decrease in birth and death rates as a society becomes industrialized is one type of **demographic transition**, which refers to a change in demographics over time. **Population projections** predict changes in populations by examining current data. A **population pyramid** graphs a population's sex and age cohorts.

The distribution of a population pyramid gives information to social scientists about the fertility and mortality rates of the analyzed population. This information can enable social scientists to predict future trends and better understand current health needs.

FIGURE 1.2 United States Population Pyramid – 2010

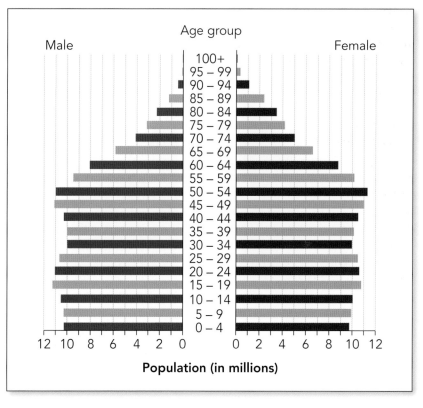

Population size is also influenced by migration, the relocation of people from one place to another. *Immigration*, the influx of new people to a specific area, leads to increased population size and density, while *emigration*, the outflow of people to other areas, leads to reduced population size and density. Push and pull factors in migration describe distinct motivations for migrating. Push factors are reasons to leave the location where an individual currently resides. Examples include natural disasters or a lack of jobs. Pull factors are reasons to move to a specific location. Job opportunities are a common reason for relocation.

Theories of demographic change attempt to explain the causes and results of population growth. Malthusian theory suggests that starvation is the inevitable result of population growth because the population increases at a geometric rate while food supply can only increase arithmetically. Demographic transition theory links population growth to the society's use of technology, describing sequential stages of change in birth and death rates. This theory suggests that technology is what keeps the population size in check, but it fails to consider other factors that limit population growth. For example, while medical technologies have led to increased reproductive success, many families are choosing to have fewer children.

TABLE 1.1 > Four Stages of Demographic Transition Theory

Stage	Birth rate	Death rate
Preindustrial	High	High
Onset of industrialization	High	Low
Industrial economy	Declining	Low
Postindustrial economy	Low	Steady

The demographic makeup of society can be used to better understand social change, such as in the context of social movements. A social movement describes a group of people who share an ideology and work together toward a specified set of goals. Examining the demographic groups involved in various social movements grants insight into the beliefs, values, and goals of the population at a particular time. Social movements often arise among people who experience deprivation or alienation. Relative deprivation refers to the feeling of disadvantage that arises when individuals compare themselves to others of similar status and feel that they possesses relatively fewer resources and privileges. This feeling of inequality can spur the creation of social movements designed to promote a more equal society.

The organization of social movements tends to have a characteristic sequence. First, emergence is the period of discontent before any organizing power arises. During *coalescence*, dissatisfaction becomes more focused through an understanding of how the factors causing discontent can be overcome. In this step, leaders come forward and specific strategies for the social movement are developed. A strategy is a general plan describing the goals of the movement, while tactics describe how the movement implements a strategy. If the movement achieves success and grows, a period of *bureaucratization* begins to meet the organization's need for coordinating procedures. Finally, after either successfully or unsuccessfully working toward the movements' goals, there is a stage of decline.

In a social movement, strategy is the "what" and tactics are the "how."

Urbanization and globalization are modern trends best studied through demographics. Urbanization is the increase in the proportion of people living in specified urban areas. Historically there has been a strong relationship between industrialization and urban growth. As the development of industry generates rapid growth, trade with and travel to centralized locations increases, and cities grow. Additionally, the demands of large-scale manufacturing encourage urban growth. As cities become larger, commerce increases even more, resulting in additional urban growth. There is an analogous relationship between suburbanization and urban decline. Suburbanization refers to the process of large-scale movement from cities to suburbs, which are communities located just beyond an official city boundary. This trend leads to a decline in the standard of living in urban areas. As families leave and property values in urban areas fall, less property tax can be collected. The subsequent decline in commerce in the city leads to higher unemployment and crime. Urban renewal refers to attempts to improve urban conditions through the restoration of buildings and public infrastructure. Gentrification is a specific urban renewal pattern in which middle- and upper-class people move to areas of a city with cheap buildings that are in need of restoration. As more individuals and families purchase inexpensive properties, the quality of life in the area improves and property values increase. Rising property values increase the economic strain on the neighborhood's poor, which results in tension between the new and old inhabitants. The less affluent original inhabitants are often driven out of the neighborhood to seek cheaper housing.

Globalization describes the increased contact between individuals on an international scale. This contact is enacted through the exchange of ideas, products, services, and information. A variety of factors contributing to globalization have been identified. Communication technologies allow an unprecedented type of interaction unbound by spatial constraints. These technologies significantly reduce the extent to which distance limits interactions. It also makes communication much more economically feasible. Globalization demands a revised interpretation of what constitutes a social group because it connects people who may not otherwise have face-to-face interactions. Economic interdependence contributes to globalization, as corporations often conduct operations across multiple continents. Manufacturing typically occurs in less economically developed nations, while the goods that are produced are sold across the world.

A variety of perspectives on globalization attempt to describe the nature and effects of increased globalization. The *hyper-globalist perspective* argues that globalization entails a movement away from individual nations toward a single global society. Some hyper-globalists believe this movement is beneficial, while others see it as problematic. A *skeptical perspective* takes a more critical stance on globalization, emphasizing that national borders are still important because individual nations are not being equally integrated into the global economy. A third perspective, known as the *transformationalist perspective*, argues that globalization causes new patterns of interdependent interactions but the outcomes cannot be predicted with any certainty. There are some problematic social changes in globalization. It has fostered international terrorism, meaning the use of violence to coerce countries and governments in order to achieve political or ideological ends. Additionally, globalization concentrates wealth into fewer hands. As a result, globalization can lead to increased civil unrest, or disorder caused by a group of people in public, due to a perceived injustice over how resources are distributed.

As an increasing proportion of the global population lives in cities and the surrounding areas, the effects of urbanization on society and health must be considered.

Questions 9-16 are NOT based on a descriptive passage.

Question 9

An archaeologist unearths six 5,000-year-old ceramic bowls and finds that the bowls were produced with kiln technology that originated approximately 7,000 years ago at a site 1,000 miles away. Which of the following is LEAST relevant to this finding?

- **A.** Material culture can change over time.
- **B.** Exchange of non-material culture can affect the production of material culture.
- **C.** Non-material culture is more location-specific than material culture.
- **D.** Material culture is more easily studied through archaeology than non-material culture.

Question 10

A college professor asks each student in his class to spend an afternoon walking inside the local mall carrying an open umbrella and to write a report about the experience. Many of the students reported feeling discomfort and embarrassment. These feelings likely result from the fact that:

- **A.** students are experiencing culture shock.
- **B.** students are violating social norms.
- **C.** students are interacting outside of their social group.
- **D.** students are practicing obedience.

Question 11

Which of the following is true regarding the evolution of human culture?

- **A.** Aptitude for culture is partially dependent on intelligence.
- **B.** Among the animal kingdom, only humans display evidence of culture.
- **C.** The spread of culture is dependent on verbal communication.
- **D.** Development of human culture peaked approximately 40,000 years ago.

Question 12

Although languages vary by culture, the presence of language is a universal human trait. Linguists argue that the number of words a language has to describe a single concept is correlated with that culture's perception of the complexity and nuance of the concept in question. Language itself can best be described as an example of:

- **A.** cultural relativism.
- **B.** a system of cultural values.
- **C.** material culture.
- **D.** symbolic culture.

Question 13

Which of the following is NOT true regarding society and culture?

- **A.** A society shares elements of cultural identity.
- **B.** A society consists of people, whereas a culture consists of beliefs and practices.
- **C.** In many situations, society and culture can be discussed interchangeably.
- **D.** A society can be multicultural.

Question 14

Which of the following is NOT true regarding social institutions?

- **A.** They are implemented in the same ways across different cultures.
- **B.** They address specific purposes.
- **C.** They are hierarchical.
- **D.** They bring order to society.

Question 15

Every 10 years, the U.S. government conducts a census that collects and analyzes information, including the age, race, and marital status of all people within each geographic area of the country. This practice can best be described as:

- **A.** demographic information being collected by a culture.
- **B.** cultural information being collected by a society.
- **C.** demographic information being collected by a social institution.
- **D.** non-material culture being collected to illustrate demographic transition.

Question 16

Assuming that urbanization most often takes place in response to pressures of over-population, which of the following is most likely to result in higher rates of urbanization?

- **A.** High fertility; high mortality
- **B.** High fertility; low mortality
- **C.** Low fertility; high mortality
- **D.** Low fertility; low mortality

STOP

1.9 | Social Inequality

No society treats all of its members equally. In the United States, no one under the age of 18 is allowed to vote. Under the Jim Crow laws in the U.S. and under apartheid in South Africa, racial segregation of public facilities was encoded in the law. In some places, women are not afforded the same legal and social rights as men.

All of these are examples of how factors such as age, race, and gender affect the way an individual experiences a society. Social inequality is the unequal distribution of opportunities or treatment of individuals within a society based on various demographic categories. Social inequality can be structural, such as a law that determines voting age, but can also exist through discrimination. One way that social inequality manifests in society is through the development of spatial inequality. Spatial inequality is the unequal access to resources and variable quality of life due to the geographical distribution of a population and its resources. Spatial inequality can be affected by income, unemployment, and unequal access to resources such as education and clean water. Spatial inequality influences health by affecting access to doctors, diagnostic equipment, and options for treatment.

Social inequality can exist on a global, national, or local level. Global inequalities are evident in the disparities between regions and nations in aspects such as gross national product, natural resources, access to healthcare, and types or amounts of work available. During the American Industrial Revolution, most employment in urban centers relied on factory work. It has now become cheaper for companies to outsource factory work to other nations. This shift toward a global market for labor changed the face of the employment landscape in the U.S. and abroad, affecting the types of employment available, expectations, and earning potential.

Lack of environmental justice—the equal treatment of all people regardless of race, gender, or other social grouping with regard to prevention and relief from environmental and health hazards—is another example of how spatial inequality acts as system of geographical hierarchy. For instance, extinguishing a fire in a rural area, where volunteer firefighters must cover large geographical districts and hydrants are scarce, poses greater challenges than urban firefighting, where there is a hydrant on every block. The reality is that people are not given equal treatment in the face of environmental hazards or natural disasters. Instead situational responses are affected by the relative resources in a geographical area and the value a society places on the people who live there.

> Inequality can be related to biological factors. Aging, for example, is a biological process that has social consequences determined by cultural beliefs and biases. Aging professionals may face hiring discrimination.

Due to a wide variety of factors, global inequalities exist in health and healthcare. Bangladesh was one of the last countries to eliminate smallpox from its population with the help of the World Health Organization (WHO) in the 1970s.

MCAT® THINK

The government's disaster relief response to Hurricane Katrina in 2005 received mass criticism because the places that were hit hardest—lower SES, African American neighborhoods—were assisted the least. To consider whether environmental justice was served, compare the disaster relief efforts in New Orleans after Hurricane Katrina with those in the affluent greater New York area following Hurricane Sandy in 2012.

Residential segregation often takes place based on socioeconomic status, leading to disparity in neighborhood resources.

Residential segregation is an instance of social inequality on the local scale. The separation of demographic groups into different neighborhoods comprises residential segregation. Location affects access to transportation, quality of education, availability of goods, health hazards, and levels of crime or feelings of personal safety. In U.S. cities, residential segregation often involves race and/or income level. Many marginalized racial groups and low-income individuals have less access to resources and opportunities.

Areas where it is difficult to find affordable, healthy food options are known as food deserts. In the U.S., food deserts are more common in low-income neighborhoods where there are fewer grocery stores and where residents may have fewer transportation options to seek out other food sources. Nutrition is fundamental to health and wellness, so food deserts pose a significant threat to health outcomes in affected populations.

Social Class

Of all the demographic categories of social inequality discussed in this section, one with some of the most far-reaching effects (and the one most likely to be seen on the MCAT®) is social class. Social class is a system of stratification that groups members of society according to similarities in social standing. Class is multifaceted and tied to status within a community and power, or influence over that community. Social class is often associated with *socioeconomic status (SES),* which defines the economic and social position of a person in terms of *income* (assets earned), *wealth* (assets already owned), education, and occupation.

Social class is related to privilege and prestige. Someone in a position of privilege has advantages of power and opportunity over those who lack privilege. The advantages of privilege may extend to not having to consider societal hierarchy, or the ability to consider personal identity as the norm. Racial privilege in the U.S. allows white individuals to form identities without reference to race in a way that is not possible for non-white individuals. Non-white individuals are "racialized" while whiteness often remains unexamined.

Within a society, social class is related to prestige, the relative value assigned to something within a particular society. The prestige associated with higher social classes varies between cultures. It may include holding aristocratic titles, maintaining a respected occupation, or conspicuous consumption of luxury goods.

Defining divisions between classes varies by particular societies. The class structure of a society generally includes an upper class, a middle class, and a lower class. The *upper class* consists of the wealthy and/or those born into "prominent" families. Among the upper class, wealth, a prestigious family name, and, in many countries, aristocratic titles are often passed down from generation to generation. Members of the upper class may receive greater educational opportunities, work in high-paying careers, and influence cultural and political affairs.

The *middle class* describes members of a society who are financially stable but not extremely wealthy. *White-collar work,* a term that is used to describe jobs that are professional, administrative, or managerial, characterizes the middle class. In the U.S. the middle class is broadly defined to include many people in *blue-collar jobs* (occupations that require skilled or unskilled manual labor), which might otherwise be considered the working class. Members of the middle class generally have access to educational opportunities. In the U.S., college degrees and post-graduate degrees are common among the middle-class. Members of the middle class are often active in the public school system and local government.

People in higher social classes tend to have the three big Ps: more Power, more Privilege, more Prestige.

The *lower class* is characterized by economic hardship or uncertainty. Members of the lower class include lower-paid wage workers, the unemployed or under-employed, recipients of welfare benefits, and the homeless. Members of the lower class may lack professional development and/or educational opportunities to stabilize their economic status. Higher education is less accessible to members of the lower class.

A class system includes fluidity, unlike a *caste system*, in which the hierarchy of society is strictly defined, position is inherited, and movement or marriage between castes is prohibited. In other words, it is possible for individuals of all classes to move up or down the class hierarchy. Moving up the class system is known as upward mobility and is achieved through education, marriage, career, or financial success. The reverse is also possible. Downward mobility, or moving lower within the class system, can result from unemployment or underemployment, reduced household income due to divorce, lack of education, or health issues.

Movement within the class system can take place within an individual's lifetime. If a young person from limited means invents a new technology and becomes wealthy, achieving the "American Dream," he or she rises to a new social class. Such instances exemplify intragenerational mobility. Upward or downward mobility may also happen over a longer period. Immigrant families moving to the U.S. may lack formal education, professional skills, or mastery of the English language. However, their children or grandchildren may become doctors, lawyers, and senators through greater access to resources gained over the generations. This kind of movement through the class system is known as intergenerational mobility.

Many Americans would like to think that individuals who work hard are rewarded with economic success and that upward mobility is the product of merit. The reality is that America is not a true meritocracy, a society in which advancement is based solely on the abilities and achievements of the individual. Wealth is passed down from parents to children, and the opportunities available to those children depend on the socioeconomic environment in which they are born. Non-monetary factors involved in upbringing affect social mobility potential and tend to maintain systems of social inequality. Cultural capital refers to the set of non-monetary social factors that contribute to social mobility. These factors influence how an individual "fits in" with or "sticks out" from a specific social context. Examples of cultural capital include dress, accent, vernacular, manners, education, cultural knowledge, and intellectual pursuits. Social capital refers to an individual's social networks and connections that may confer economic and/or personal benefits.

The essence of social capital is that "who you know" matters. Inherited wealth and the difference in cultural and social capital between classes contribute to the maintenance of a stratified society. This transmission of social inequality from one generation to the next is known as social reproduction.

Due to the factors described above, those born lower class are more likely to be lower class adults than people born into wealth. Within the lower class, poverty can produce detrimental effects. Poverty is an insufficiency of material goods, monetary wealth, and access to resources. In many less affluent nations, poverty is widespread. Even though the U.S. is one of the most prosperous nations in the world, poverty still exists. People in poverty often have fewer options compared to those with greater financial resources. This lack of access is termed isolation or social exclusion to denote how impoverished people are often excluded from opportunities available to others.

Class is a nuanced concept involving status, education, economics, and influence. There are many ways of dividing a society into classes and subclasses. For instance, members of the upper class often place importance on the distinction between "old money," those families that have long been wealthy, and "new money," or those who have newly acquired wealth. In the lower class, many people distinguish between the working poor and those who are unemployed.

Not all members of a social class have the same experiences. The effects of class intersect with the effects of other factors such as age, gender, and race to produce a complex hierarchy of power and privilege. In many societies, the dynamics of power favor the old over the very young, men over women, and non-Hispanic white people over other racial identifications. Consider how other factors may influence and change class dynamics when approaching questions about social class on the MCAT®.

If America were a true meritocracy, people would have to get rid of all of the money earned during their lifetimes after death rather than passing it on to their children. Each child would start on a level playing field and gain success through his or her own merits. Because of cultural ideas about ownership and family in America, this particular move toward a meritocracy is unlikely to happen anytime in the near future.

To understand how cultural capital matters, consider two candidates in competition for the same promotion in a prestigious consulting firm. While getting to know the candidates, the vice president of the company takes each candidate to play tennis and then out for drinks at an expensive wine bar. One candidate grew up with a tennis court on his parents' property and keeps a wine cellar in his home. The other grew up playing football and drinks beer on the weekends. Assuming otherwise identical qualifications, we may expect that the first candidate will make a better impression on the vice president because he has the cultural capital to prepare him for the situation. The type of cultural capital we possess is an influential factor in our ability to move in different circles of society.

Poverty can be divided into two major categories: absolute poverty and relative poverty. Absolute poverty describes a lack of essential resources such as food, shelter, clothing, and hygiene. Relative poverty, by contrast, describes social inequality in which people are relatively poor compared to other members of the society in which they live. Absolute poverty is more extreme and can be life-threatening, but relative poverty also has profound effects on lifestyle and livelihood.

Social theorist *Karl Marx* argued that poverty and class inequality could be remedied through political struggle. Marx argued that for this to happen the lower class must first come to understand itself as a class—a group with shared needs and interests. Marx called this collective awareness a class consciousness. According to Marx, in the absence of collective self-awareness based on class, the lower class would be divided by differences and would not act as a class. Marx's theory led to criticism of those who blame poverty on the failings of the poor themselves. The failure to recognize poverty as the product of an oppressive class system has been called a false consciousness.

Disparities in Health and Healthcare

Health disparity (or health inequity) refers to differences in health and healthcare that occur between groups of people. These differences can occur according to demographic categories such as age, race, gender, class, and sexual orientation and can affect the prevalence and prognosis of disease. In the United States, health disparities between racial groups are well-documented, with white Americans experiencing a lower incidence of chronic illness and poor health outcomes than Americans in other racial groups. For example, Native Americans, African Americans, and Latino Americans are approximately twice as likely as their non-Hispanic white counterparts to have undiagnosed diabetes. Much like race, class has a significant impact on health and health care access. The notion that socioeconomic status can influence health is called the socioeconomic gradient in health. People with higher socioeconomic status often have better overall health due to a variety of factors, including differences in exposure to environmental hazards, stress, amount of leisure time, and quality of diet. Social characteristics such as race, class, and gender create a complex landscape of health disparity.

Social epidemiology considers how social factors affect the health of a population. Health outcomes correlate with race, class, gender, and age. For example, mortality differs between the sexes. In most countries, women tend to live longer than men. This disparity in lifespan is often attributed to hormones and physiology as well as the prevalence of men's participation in high-risk behaviors. In countries where women have lower social status than men or where there is a high incidence of mortality from childbirth, the sex gap in lifespan decreases.

The problem of differences in health between demographic categories is compounded by disparities in access to and quality of healthcare. The administration of healthcare in the U.S. is unequitable in a number of ways. Those of high socioeconomic status are often able to afford more specialized healthcare than lower socioeconomic status individuals, who are often uninsured or under-insured. These differences have more subtle manifestations as well. A homosexual man living in a community with a high incidence of homophobia may be reluctant to discuss his sexual orientation with his healthcare provider. Lack of disclosure may preclude screenings for STIs such as HIV, which are more prevalent in the gay male community. In some communities, women are less likely to seek out health treatment because they are not allowed to see male doctors or travel to a clinic on their own.

The individual needs of each patient must be considered in order to provide equitable and sufficient healthcare. When a patient only speaks Spanish, and an exam or explanation of results is conducted in English, the patient's understanding will suffer. To improve care, a Spanish-speaking physician or a translator is necessary. Healthcare providers with an understanding of gender, class, and racial disparities in health and healthcare and a sensitivity to differences in lifestyle and culture are better able to address health problems and find health solutions that fit individual patients.

You don't need to know the details and examples in this section, but you are likely to see passages and questions about healthcare disparities on the MCAT®.

Consider Key 3: Disadvantaged social groups have access to fewer resources, resulting in decreased health and wellbeing. Socioeconomic status matters for health.

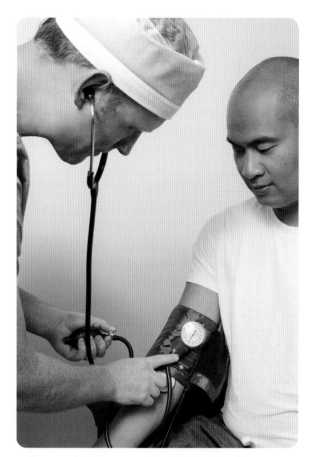

Doctors who strive to understand social influences on patients' behaviors are better equipped to take steps toward decreasing healthcare disparity and increasing the effectiveness of treatment.

Questions 17-24 are NOT based on a descriptive passage.

Question 17

A researcher wishes to design a study to examine evidence of spatial inequality within the city of Chicago. Which element of study design is most important to addressing the research question?

- ○ **A.** Also sampling residents of cities other than Chicago for comparison
- ○ **B.** Sampling residents from different neighborhoods of Chicago
- ○ **C.** Ensuring that each sampling group has similar distributions of age and sex
- ○ **D.** Including racial diversity in each sampling group

Question 18

Social scientists gather information on the gross domestic product, per-capita income, most common types of occupations, exploitation of natural resources, access to education, access to healthcare, and yearly inflation of 120 countries. This data set can most easily be applied to the study of which of the following?

- ○ **A.** Spatial inequality
- ○ **B.** Demographic composition
- ○ **C.** Global inequality
- ○ **D.** International composition

Question 19

Which of the following scenarios presents the LEAST threat to environmental justice?

- ○ **A.** In a rural town with a high rate of obesity, a company opens a chain of gyms for women only.
- ○ **B.** In the suburbs, landfills are preferentially located in the poorest neighborhoods.
- ○ **C.** In a large city, there is residential segregation by race.
- ○ **D.** After a heavy snowfall, affluent neighborhoods are plowed before less-affluent neighborhoods.

Question 20

An individual's social class is LEAST likely to be affected by:

- ○ **A.** being elected to state legislature.
- ○ **B.** inheriting a large sum of money.
- ○ **C.** attaining a higher level of education.
- ○ **D.** starting volunteer work in a homeless shelter.

Question 21

Which of the following does NOT describe a feature of a caste system that differs from a class system?

- ○ **A.** In a caste system, social position is strictly inherited.
- ○ **B.** In a caste system, the social hierarchy includes unequal opportunities.
- ○ **C.** In a caste system, upward mobility is not possible.
- ○ **D.** In a caste system, marriage between individuals of different castes is prohibited.

Question 22

A researcher wishes to study rates of intergenerational and intragenerational mobility of immigrants to different countries. Which of the following is NOT strictly necessary to explore the research question?

- ○ **A.** Recording original SES factors of an individual before immigration
- ○ **B.** Recording data regarding SES from multiple generations
- ○ **C.** Recording data regarding SES from multiple times within an individual's life
- ○ **D.** Recording the country of origin of each immigrant

Question 23

Which of the following is the best example of the importance of cultural capital?

- ○ **A.** A candidate is elected to Congress because he is able to raise 300% more money than his opponent.
- ○ **B.** A worker is given a promotion because he uses the same idioms and patterns of speech as his boss.
- ○ **C.** A couple is admitted to an exclusive country club because many of their friends are already members.
- ○ **D.** A college graduate is hired for a job because he is the best qualified candidate for the position.

Question 24

Which of the following would likely be of LEAST interest to someone concerned with health disparities?

- ○ **A.** Native Americans are underrepresented among graduates of medical and nursing schools.
- ○ **B.** Members of gay and lesbian communities are less likely than their heterosexual peers to seek out preventative healthcare measures.
- ○ **C.** Non-white Americans tend to experience greater levels of environmental hazards than white Americans.
- ○ **D.** People with higher SES tend to receive more comprehensive healthcare.

Absolute poverty
Age
Age cohorts
Age-specific birth rate
Aging and the life course
Authority
Beliefs
Biomedical approach
Biopsychosocial approach
Capitalism
Church
Civil unrest
Class consciousness
Comparative economic and political systems
Communication theories
Conflict theory
Crude birth rate
Crude death rate
Cult
Cultural capital
Culture
Delivery of health care
Demographic transition
Demographic transition theory
Demographics
Diversity in family forms
Division of labor
Downward mobility
Economic interdependence
Education
Educational segregation
Educational stratification
Environmental justice
Ethnicity
Exchange theory
Factors contributing to globalization
False consciousness
Family
Feminist theory
Fertility
Folkways
Forms of kinship
Functionalism
Fundamentalism
Gender

Gentrification
Global inequalities
Globalization
Government and economy
Health and medicine
Health disparity (health inequity)
Hidden curriculum
Illness experience
Immigration status
Industrialization and urban growth
Infant mortality rate
Intergenerational mobility
Intersections with race and ethnicity
Intragenerational mobility
Isolation (social exclusion)
Kinship
Language
Macrosociology
Malthusian theory
Material culture
Medicalization
Meritocracy
Microsociology
Migration
Modernization
Mores
Mortality
Non-material culture
Organization of social movements
Patterns in fertility and mortality
Patterns of immigration
Perspectives on globalization
Population projections
Population pyramid
Poverty
Power
Prestige
Privilege
Push and pull factors in migration
Race
Racial formation theory
Racialization
Rational choice theory
Relative deprivation
Relative poverty
Religion

Religion and social change
Religiosity
Residential segregation
Rituals
Sanctions
Sect
Secularization
Sex
Sexual orientation
Sick role
Social capital
Social changes in globalization
Social class
Social construction of gender
Social constructionism
Social epidemiology
Social group
Social inequality
Social institutions
Social movement
Social norms
Social reproduction
Social significance of aging
Socialism
Socioeconomic gradient in health
Society
Spatial inequality
Status
Strategy
Suburbanization and urban decline
Symbolic culture
Symbolic interactionism
Symbols
Taboo
Tactic
Teacher expectancy
Terrorism
The social construction of race
Theories of demographic change
Total birth rate (total fertility rate)
Types of religious organizations
Upward mobility
Urban renewal
Urbanization
Values
Violence in the family

DON'T FORGET YOUR KEYS

1. The psychosocial section tests the ability to consider biological, psychological, and social factors simultaneously and to think flexibly about different theories.

2. Culture and social institutions organize society on a large scale.

3. Social inequality exists in many forms and affects access to resources, including healthcare.

Relationships and Behavior

2.1 Introduction
2.2 Learning
2.3 Behavior in a Biological Context
2.4 Behavior in a Social Context
2.5 Behavior in a Cultural Context
2.6 Prejudice, Bias, and Discrimination

2.1 Introduction

Standards of behavior and interaction make the establishment of society and culture possible. The organization of large groups of people into the systems of society and culture, described in the previous lecture, depends on the interactions of individuals within the group. Success on the Psychosocial section of the MCAT® requires an understanding of human interactions on both the larger scale of group dynamics in society and the smaller scale of personal behavior. This lecture examines the motivations, effects, and social influences of human behavior as well as the process through which behavioral patterns are learned, changed, or reinforced.

THE 3 KEYS

1. A stimulus that increases a behavior is a reinforcement; a stimulus that decreases a behavior is a punishment.

2. Individuals tend to imitate other members of their group (conformity) and follow the orders of an authority (obedience).

3. The mentality of in-group versus out-group underlies prejudice, bias, and discrimination.

2.2 | Learning

Behavior is the foundation of social interaction. It is central to understanding humans as social animals. An understanding of how behavior is acquired is necessary for the examination of social consequences of behavior. This section will discuss theories about how individuals learn to produce certain behaviors, while later sections will consider the importance of behavior in societal interactions. Through behavioral learning, an individual determines what behaviors are culturally appropriate and how behaviors result in specific outcomes. Learning can result in modifications of behavior in order to optimize the results.

The psychological field of behaviorism, which is the study of external observable behaviors rather than internal motivations and thoughts, has influenced much of the research about learning. People who study behavior often focus on learning that involves associations between certain stimuli and specific responses. This type of learning is called associative learning or conditioning. Two types of conditioning are likely to appear on the MCAT®: classical conditioning and operant conditioning.

Classical Conditioning

Any student who has heard of Pavlov's dogs is already familiar with classical conditioning, where a test subject develops a response to a previously neutral stimulus by associating the stimulus with another stimulus that already elicited that response. Ivan Pavlov theorized the process of classical conditioning during his studies of salivation in dogs. The dogs salivated when they were presented with food. Pavlov called the food an unconditioned stimulus and the resulting salivation an unconditioned response because the salivation was innate, taking place without the need for learning. Eventually the dogs began to salivate during the normal feeding routine before the food had been presented. The dogs had come to associate the appearance of the food bowl or the person who normally fed them with the process of eating and began salivating. The sight of a food bowl, which was previously a neutral stimulus (a stimulus eliciting no response), was associated with the act of receiving food and had become a conditioned stimulus. A conditioned stimulus, which has been associated with an unconditioned stimulus, elicits a learned or conditioned response which is similar to the original, unconditioned response (in this case, salivation). Pavlov's research showed that many neutral stimuli can eventually become conditioned stimuli if they are regularly presented immediately before an unconditioned stimulus. Dogs accustomed to hearing a bell ring before feeding time would salivate whenever the bell was rung, whether or not food was then presented.

Pavlov's studies showed that dogs are capable of learning a new behavior through association of one stimulus with another. Such associations take time. The stage of learning over which a conditioned response to a new stimulus is established is called acquisition. Learned behaviors that are not reinforced can be unlearned. If a dog is accustomed to being fed after a bell rings every night, he will learn to salivate in response to the sound of the bell. If one night the bell is repeatedly rung and no food is delivered, the dog will eventually stop salivating in response to the bell. However, the learned behavior does not disappear immediately. If the bell rings the next night, the dog may begin salivating again. If the bell is rung night after night and no food is provided, the dog will eventually learn to disassociate the stimulus of the bell from the delivery of food and extinction, or disappearance of the conditioned response, will occur. The reappearance of the conditioned response after a period of extinction is called spontaneous recovery. Repeated cycles of extinction and spontaneous recovery can occur, but the strength of the conditioned response in the spontaneous recovery decreases with each cycle.

Recall Key 1: ReINforcements INcrease behaviors while punishments decrease behaviors.

Ivan Pavlov's experiments on salivation in dogs provided the foundation for the theory of classical conditioning.

FIGURE 2.1 Classical Conditioning

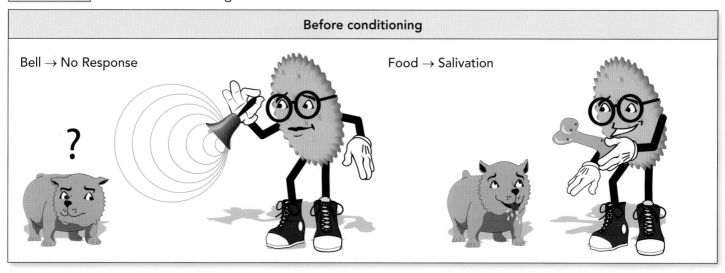

Before conditioning

Bell → No Response

Food → Salivation

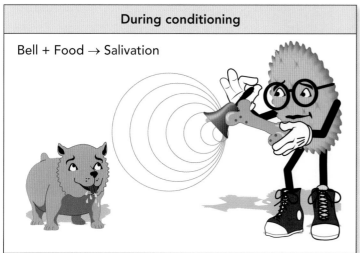 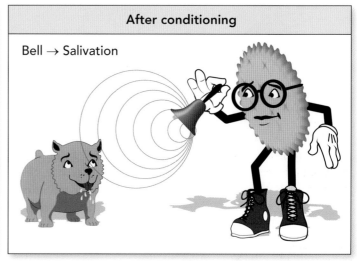

During conditioning

Bell + Food → Salivation

After conditioning

Bell → Salivation

Once a test subject has learned to respond to a conditioned stimulus, similar stimuli may also elicit the same conditioned response. A dog that has learned to salivate in response to the sound of an American crow's call, for example, may also salivate when exposed to the call of another species known as the western raven. The tendency to respond to stimuli that are similar to the conditioned stimulus is known as **stimulus generalization**. If the dog is repeatedly exposed to the call of the American crow and then presented with food, while also being exposed to the call of the western raven without being presented with food, he will eventually learn to differentiate between the two noises and will only salivate to the sound of the American crow. The learned lack of response to a stimulus similar to the conditioned stimulus is known as **stimulus discrimination**.

Classical conditioning can play an important role in how humans interact. It affects likes and dislikes, fears, and behaviors. A child who contracts a stomach virus right after eating ice cream may associate the ice cream with the sickness and end up disliking ice cream for the rest of his life. The power of associative learning is harnessed by advertisers who use every resource from celebrity appearances to calming music to encourage consumers to build positive associations with their products. Classical conditioning has been presented in this lecture in a simplified way, but it can have wide-reaching effects on complex human behaviors. One application is the treatment of phobias, where the feared stimulus is presented with no negative consequences. After the person is repeatedly exposed to the source of the phobia and sees that the feared consequences do not occur, the fear response is extinguished.

Associative learning is a useful part of the human experience. It allows us to anticipate appropriate responses to new situations and gives us "intuitive feelings" with which to make gut decisions. However, associations that go unexamined can become problematic to interpersonal interactions and the fabric of society. Following the attacks of September 11, 2001, some Americans came to associate these specific attacks with the religion of Islam in general. Such associations can lead to both discrimination and prejudice, topics that will be discussed in greater detail later in this lecture.

Operant Conditioning

Operant conditioning is a type of associative learning in which an individual becomes more or less likely to carry out a certain behavior based on its consequences. The study of operant conditioning is often associated with the experiments of B. F. Skinner. Skinner studied animals using a *Skinner box*, also called an operant conditioning chamber, which included an area for dispensing food. Food was only dispensed to rats placed in the Skinner box when the rats carried out a specific behavior, such as stepping on a lever. The rats learned that their behavior had consequences and began to step on the lever with greater frequency to obtain more food. In some cases the Skinner box could also deliver unpleasant stimuli. A Skinner box with an electrified floor could deliver a shock to a rat exhibiting a particular behavior, such as entering a certain area of the box. Rats would learn to avoid that area because of the consequences of stepping on the floor.

Operant conditioning involves learning the consequences of behaviors and adjusting the frequencies of those behaviors in response to the consequences. A consequence that increases the likelihood of a behavior (such as the delivery of food) is called a **reinforcement**, while a stimulus that decreases the likelihood of a behavior (such as the delivery of a shock) is called a **punishment**.

Reinforcement and punishment of behavior in operant conditioning can be either positive or negative. In this context, the terms positive and negative have nothing to do with whether the procedure is pleasant or unpleasant. Instead the terms indicate whether something is added to or taken away from the situation. A **positive reinforcement** is the introduction of a reinforcing stimulus in response to a desired behavior. A **negative reinforcement** is the removal of an unpleasant stimulus in response to a desired behavior. Suppose a teenager's parents want him to take out the trash. If the teenager takes out the trash and in response receives an allowance, the allowance is a positive reinforcement. If the teenager takes out the trash and in response his parents stop nagging him about taking out the trash, the cessation of the nagging is a negative reinforcement. Punishment can also be positive or negative. Suppose the same teenager stays out past curfew one night. If his parents reprimand him when he gets home, they are delivering a **positive punishment**. If his parents instead decided to take away their son's cell phone for a week, they would be delivering a **negative punishment**.

Reinforcement and punishment both work to shape behavior, but studies indicate that positive reinforcement is a much more effective tool than punishment for establishing desirable behavior patterns. If you want to teach Fido to sit, you should reward him with a treat immediately after he sits, rather than chiding him for standing up.

TABLE 2.1 > **Consequences of Operant Conditioning**

	Reinforcement	Punishment
Positive	Adding something to increase a behavior	Adding something to decrease a behavior
Negative	Removing something to increase a behavior	Removing something to decrease a behavior

Types of reinforcement and punishment can be classified as either primary or secondary. Primary reinforcers and punishers are those that relate to a physiological need. Delivery of food is an example of a **primary reinforcer**, while exposure to extreme temperatures is an example of a **primary punisher**. Primary reinforcers and punishers harness physiological needs and the drive for survival. They do not require learning to increase the likelihood of a response. Secondary reinforcers and punishers do require learning and social context to affect behavioral decisions, but once learned, they can be just as effective at controlling behavior as primary reinforcers and punishers. Examples of **secondary reinforcers** (or **conditioned reinforcers**) include money, praise, prestige, and good grades, while examples of secondary punishers include fines, scolding, ostracism, and bad grades.

People generally try to avoid stimuli that are painful or unpleasant, so punishment can be an effective way to make the occurrence of a behavior less likely. One branch of operant conditioning explores how subjects learn to evade unpleasant situations. Imagine a mouse in a cage with a floor capable of delivering electric shocks. If the half of the floor where the mouse is located becomes electrified, the mouse will learn to move to the other side of the cage in order to stop being shocked. This type of learning is called escape conditioning because the learned behavior allows the subject to escape the unpleasant stimulus. In a similar scenario, suppose the researcher blew a whistle directly before electrifying one half of the floor of the mouse's cage. Eventually the mouse would learn to move to the other side of the cage in response to the whistle. This type of learning is called avoidance conditioning because the learned behavior allows the subject to avoid the unpleasant stimulus altogether by employing a specific response.

Responses that have been established through operant conditioning, like those established through classical conditioning, can undergo extinction when the reinforcers of the behavior are no longer employed. In operant conditioning, the disappearance of a behavior through extinction is affected by the reinforcement schedule that was used to establish the behavior. A reinforcement schedule describes how often and under what conditions a behavior is reinforced. Suppose a researcher is training a mouse to press a lever. If the researcher rewards the mouse every time it presses the lever, the mouse is receiving continuous reinforcement. If the mouse is only rewarded some of the times that it stands up, the researcher is employing partial reinforcement (or intermittent reinforcement). The types of partial reinforcement schedules are shown in Table 2.2.

TABLE 2.2 > Schedules of Partial Reinforcement

Type	Description	Example
Fixed-ratio	Rewards are provided after a specified number of responses.	A reward is given after every third time a mouse presses a lever.
Variable-ratio	Rewards are provided after an unpredictable number of responses.	A reward is given after a mouse presses a lever 3 times, then after 5 times, then after 2 times, etc.
Fixed-interval	Rewards to a response are provided after a specified time interval has passed.	A reward is given 20 seconds after the first time a mouse presses a lever.
Variable-interval	Rewards to a response are provided after an unpredictable time interval has passed.	A reward is given 3 minutes after the first time a mouse presses a lever, then 2 minutes after, etc.

Continuous reinforcement is usually the most rapid way to first establish a response. However, once learned, behaviors that were established with a partial reinforcement schedule are much more resistant to extinction. Gambling provides an example of this effect. Even though gamblers only rarely earn big rewards for the risks they take, the unpredictability of the reward schedule maintains the hope for the reward and keeps gamblers coming back for more.

The purpose of operant conditioning is to make behaviors either more or less likely by controlling the consequences of those behaviors. It is easy to provide rewards that increase the frequency of behaviors that occur naturally. If a scientist gave a piece of banana to a monkey every time the monkey climbed the side of his cage, the monkey would likely increase the amount of time spent climbing. What if the scientist wanted to train the monkey to complete a task outside the realm of its normal behavior, such as opening a door? The scientist might start by rewarding the monkey for just looking toward the door. Once this behavior was

Keep the terms straight: the goal of reinforcement is always to make a behavior more likely to occur, while that of punishment is to make a behavior less frequent. The term positive refers to the addition of a reinforcement or punishment, and the term negative refers to the removal of a reinforcement or punishment.

Knowledge about operant conditioning is a useful tool for parenting. The rewards and punishments doled out by parents influence their children's behavior. Psychologists often advise parents to avoid rewarding children with their attention when the children are exhibiting bad behaviors such as throwing tantrums, because the reward will only increase the incidence of the behaviors. Parents must proceed with caution; consistency is key! Once ignoring the tantrums has started, rewarding a tantrum with attention even once creates a partial reinforcement schedule, and the bad behavior will take even longer to reach extinction.

established, the scientist could move on to giving rewards for moving toward the door, then placing a hand on the doorknob, etc. This type of operant conditioning is called **shaping** because it shapes behavior toward a certain response by reinforcing *successive approximations* toward the desired behavior.

Many new behaviors can be established using techniques of shaping even if they do not normally occur. Behavioral patterns may naturally change as animals mature and develop or may change in response to experiences (learning). Some behaviors are **innate behaviors**, which means that they are developmentally fixed. Innate behaviors are heavily influenced by the physiology and genetic inheritance of the organism and are difficult or impossible to change through learning. For example, male sticklebacks (a type of fish) are very territorial and have red bellies. Male sticklebacks will instinctively attack anything red, an innate behavior based on the biological imperative of protecting their territory from other males. Animals carry out many behaviors by instinct because the behaviors serve important functions in the survival and reproduction of the species. Appropriate **cognitive processes** are necessary for the associative learning of non-instinctual behaviors. The animal must have sufficient higher level brain function to recognize the connection between cause and effect and then choose a new course of behavior. The animal must also have the cognitive and physical abilities to perform the new behavior asked of it. Learning new behaviors is possible up to a point through both classical conditioning and operant conditioning, but the activities of any animal are always prone to biological constraints.

Observational Learning

Many complex chains of human behavior are learned by observing the actions of others, rather than through the rewards and punishments of conditioning. **Observational learning** is based on **modeling**, which consists of witnessing another person's actions, retaining information on that person's behavior, and later re-enacting what was learned through that observation in one's own behavior. Observational learning helps explain patterns of individual behavior. For example, a young boy may learn how to prepare a meal without ever being taught by observing his parent making dinner. Observational learning can be task-oriented, as in the previous example, or it can have a more general influence on an individual's behavior. Studies have shown that children who are shown a video of aggressive behavior are more likely to be aggressive or violent in their playtime immediately following the video than are children who were not shown the video. Observational learning takes place in all stages of life, but it is especially important in childhood. As children develop an understanding of what behaviors are socially acceptable, they often learn to model their behavior after that of their parents and other prominent adults in their lives.

Observational learning occurs across many species, but certain biological processes are necessary for observational learning to be possible. The learner must have the intelligence necessary to recognize a novel behavior in others, to remember the behavior, and to apply it to his own life in appropriate situations. Learning by example helps people benefit from being introduced to new skills and techniques. It also allows people to learn from the mistakes of others to avoid making the same mistakes. Observational learning is such a powerful tool in the struggle to survive and thrive that humans and many other animals have a particular process in the brain that facilitates learning by example. Specialized nerve cells, called **mirror neurons**, fire both when a person is completing an action and when the person observes someone else completing the same action. It has been suggested that mirror neurons help humans understand the actions of others and learn by imitation. The observer must have at least some neural capacity for experiencing **vicarious emotions** - feeling the emotions of others as though they are one's own - in order to learn from the successes and mistakes of others through observation.

For the MCAT®, know that learned behaviors can be modified through experience, while innate behaviors are fixed. It usually is not correct to say that biology IS destiny, but in many cases biology certainly constrains destiny.

Humans have remarkable aptitude to learn by watching the behavior of other people. Many skills are passed from one person to the next through observational learning and imitation.

Question 25

Suppose that a penguin is fed a fish whenever it waves its fin at an experimenter. Over time, the penguin increases the frequency of fin waving. This situation is best described as which of the following?

- **A.** Classical conditioning
- **B.** Punishment
- **C.** Reinforcement
- **D.** Observational learning

Questions 26–28 are based on the following experiment:

In an associative learning experiment, researchers simultaneously present a macaque with a startling noise and briefly illuminate a green light. Prior to experimental intervention, the green light elicited no response from the macaque. The macaque reliably reacts to the startling noise by producing a fear vocalization. After repeated simultaneous exposures, the green light alone leads to the production of the fear vocalization by the macaque.

Question 26

This experiment best demonstrates which of the following principles?

- **A.** Classical conditioning
- **B.** Operant conditioning
- **C.** Aversive conditioning
- **D.** Observational learning

Question 27

The green light, prior to simultaneous presentation with the startling noise, is considered to be which of the following?

- **A.** An unconditioned stimulus
- **B.** A neutral stimulus
- **C.** A conditioned stimulus
- **D.** A primary reinforcer

Question 28

Suppose that in a follow-up experiment, a blue light elicits a fear vocalization from the macaque. This finding demonstrates which of the following principles?

- **A.** Acquisition
- **B.** Spontaneous recovery
- **C.** Stimulus generalization
- **D.** Stimulus discrimination

Question 29

A female capuchin monkey notices that the alpha male becomes more aggressive towards her after engaging in an aggressive encounter with another capuchin. The female learns to flee the territorial area whenever the alpha engages in such an aggressive encounter. Which type of learning best describes the female's behavior?

- **A.** Escape conditioning
- **B.** Avoidance conditioning
- **C.** Aversive conditioning
- **D.** Classical conditioning

Question 30

A parent is attempting to potty-train her child by rewarding her for using the bathroom. Sometimes she provides these rewards immediately after her daughter uses the bathroom, and sometimes she provides them half an hour afterwards. The parent is making use of which type of reinforcement schedule?

- **A.** Fixed-ratio
- **B.** Variable-ratio
- **C.** Fixed-interval
- **D.** Variable-interval

Question 31

Which of the following situations best describes the use of shaping in teaching a dog how to roll over?

- **A.** Physically rolling the dog to teach it the desired action pattern
- **B.** Punishing the dog whenever it does not perform the desired trick
- **C.** Providing consistent rewards whenever the dog successfully performs the trick
- **D.** Initially rewarding the dog for rolling onto its back, then for rolling around completely

Question 32

Mirror neurons would be most active during which of the following activities?

- **A.** A pitcher observing an image of him- or herself
- **B.** A pitcher watching another pitcher throw a knuckleball
- **C.** A pitcher imagining the process of throwing a pitch
- **D.** A pitcher learning how to throw a pitch

2.3 Behavior in a Biological Context

The study of learned responses to specific stimuli in the laboratory has its place in psychology, but understanding behavior as a whole is much more complex and multifaceted. Behavior can be defined as the sum coordinated responses of organisms to the internal and external stimuli that they experience. Behavior is partially influenced by the biology of the organism. Genetic inheritance and neural connections can predispose organisms toward certain behavioral patterns, while hormones from the endocrine system can influence behavioral changes in a relatively direct and immediate manner. Natural selection will select for behavior in the same way that it selects for other fitness traits. An individual displaying inappropriate and maladaptive behavior will be less likely to reproduce and pass on his or her genes.

The Cell
BIOLOGY 2

Biological influences affect behavioral patterns and communication between members of a species. The ability to communicate is of great importance to human societies and cultures. The verbal communication exhibited by humans confers a wide variety of evolutionary advantages. People can use verbal communication to transfer knowledge and ideas from one individual to the next with a high level of precision. However, much of the communication between people is nonverbal. Nonverbal communication consists of all communication between people that does not involve words. It includes body language, touch, appearance, and facial expressions. Other animals also use nonverbal methods to communicate. Animal signals can consist of vocalizations (such as distress calls) or the use of visual stimuli, touch, and smell for communication.

Communication between members of a species is crucial to survival because it allows most animals to engage in a wide variety of social behavior. Social behavior is broadly defined as all interactions taking place between members of the same species. Prominent examples of social behavior that should be known for the MCAT® include attraction (factors that draw members of a species together), aggression (conflict and competition between individuals), attachment (forming relationships between individuals), and social support (finding help through social connections). Social behavior is built into the biological makeup of many species because a wide variety of social behaviors can confer evolutionary advantages.

Foraging behavior (the set of behaviors through which animals obtain food) is a type of social behavior that can be observed in many species. Animals optimize foraging behavior to maximize the energy available through food and to minimize the energy expenditure involved in obtaining it. Social behavior can increase foraging efficiency by allowing knowledge of effective techniques to be passed from individual to individual or by allowing the community to achieve what an individual alone could not. Consider that tribes of ice-age humans were successful at hunting mammoths when working in teams, but such kills would be challenging for an individual. Teamwork makes foraging behavior more efficient and gives individuals within the group a higher return on their energetic investments in food-seeking.

Social behavior also includes mating behavior, the behavior surrounding propagation of a species through reproduction. Because success at reproduction determines whether or not an individual's genes survive in the population, natural selection plays a role in mating behaviors. Natural selection is particularly influential in the process by which one member of a species chooses another individual with which to reproduce. Mate choice is determined by a number of factors, including attempts to judge the genetic qualities, overall health, and potential parenting skills of prospective mates.

Another significant type of social behavior is altruism. Altruism consists of behaviors that are disadvantageous to the individual acting, but confer benefits to other members of its social group. Many theories have been proposed to explain the existence of altruism. At first glance, altruism appears to have no evolution-

Social behavior may seem so commonplace that it's hard to imagine life without it. But why does it seem so natural? Why don't humans (and many other animals) lead solitary lives? For the MCAT®, familiarize yourself with biological explanations of how various social behaviors provide evolutionary advantages.

ary benefit. If helping others is detrimental to an individual's survival, one would assume that genes contributing to such behaviors would quickly be eliminated from a population. However, altruism persists and has been observed in a wide variety of species. One compelling explanation of altruism from an evolutionary perspective includes the concept of inclusive fitness. Inclusive fitness describes overall fitness (an individual's level of success at passing on its genes) by considering not only the individual's own progeny, but also the offspring of its close relatives. Lemurs have often been observed to care for offspring that are not their own. This altruistic behavior diverts the helper lemur's time and energy away from the creation of its own offspring. However, such altruism is often directed toward assisting close relatives that share much of the same genetic makeup. If the helper lemur aids her sister in successfully rearing more offspring to adulthood than either lemur would on her own, the helper is promoting the success of the genes she shares in common with her sister (and her sister's offspring). When the concept of fitness is expanded to include the offspring of relatives, the evolutionary benefit of altruism becomes apparent.

Many scientists apply game theory to understand and model the decision making processes that govern competition, altruism, and other social behaviors. Game theory is the use of mathematical models to represent complex decision making in which the actions of other group members must be taken into account. Interactions between organisms can be modeled as a multiplayer game in which each player carries out competitive or cooperative strategies that maximize evolutionary success (i.e. fitness). The success of an individual depends not only on his or her own strategy but also on the strategies and decisions of the other "players." Game theory presupposes that the most successful strategies result in greater fitness and will be favored by natural selection. A common application of game theory is in the "prisoner's dilemma," where two prisoners have the option of staying silent or betraying each other by confessing. If both stay silent, they both have shorter prison sentences. If one confesses and the other stays silent, the betrayer goes free, and the silent person has a longer sentence. If they both confess, they both receive a prison sentence of a length in between the short and long sentences. The best overall outcome occurs if the prisoners remain silent. In practice, participants in scenarios based on the prisoner's dilemma tend to confess in hopes of achieving the best personal outcome or at least preventing the worst personal outcome.

In societies of ring-tailed lemurs, group members help with infant care through a process called alloparenting. In addition to giving the mother time to rest and forage, this altruistic behavior increases the inclusive fitness of lemurs closely related to the infant by boosting the infant's chance of survival.

2.4 | Behavior in a Social Context

This section will discuss social interaction and how social processes influence behavior. While the previous section addressed the importance of social behavior as a biological imperative to survival and fitness, this one will examine how the nature of being social affects the construction of behavioral choices and norms.

Elements of Social Interaction

Social interaction often revolves around communication and cooperation, but it can also involve group dynamics and power differences. Social interactions can take place on many levels, including between individuals or within groups of people. (Recall from Lecture 1 that the field of sociology defines a group as a set of individuals who interact with each other and share some elements of identity.) The two smallest groups are a dyad, or two people, and a triad, or three people. These are the simplest groups, and they can be studied from microsociological perspectives. A group can be further classified as a primary group or a secondary group based on its level of intimacy. A primary group is characterized by relatively permanent intimate relationships among a small number of people. Examples include families and close friends. Dyads and triads tend to be primary groups. A secondary group is characterized by impersonal relationships among larger groups of people. Compared to primary groups, they tend to be more goal-oriented and less permanent. Examples include sports teams and groups formed in order to complete projects at school and work.

Outside of group-specific interactions, people are also connected into large social networks through webs of weaker social interactions, such as friends of friends. A collection of individuals joining together to coordinate their interactions toward a specific purpose is known as an organization. Official organizations with specific rules and guidelines are known as formal organizations. A bureaucracy, one type of formal organization, has a particular focus on efficiency and effectiveness to accomplish the goals of the organization. *Max Weber* identified several characteristics of an ideal bureaucracy, all of which are aimed at increasing efficiency. An ideal bureaucracy is specialized and organized in a clear hierarchy. There are written rules and regulation with thorough record keeping. To prevent distraction from organization's goals, an ideal bureaucracy is impersonal and impartial.

There are a couple of sociological perspectives on bureaucracy that are important to keep in mind for the MCAT®. The iron law of oligarchy criticizes the hierarchal nature of bureaucracy, stating that people at the top of the hierarchy will inevitably come to value their power over the purpose of the organization. As a result, the leadership will focus more on staying in power than on achieving the bureaucracy's goal. McDonaldization extends the concept of bureaucracy to the effect of chain stores and restaurants on consumerism and society as a whole. Chains are predictable, uniform, efficient, and automated. While these characteristics align with those of an ideal bureaucracy, the perspective of McDonaldization points out that such homogenization leads to a loss of originality and creativity.

Groups, networks, and organizations often display various aspects of collective behavior. A particular social pattern that large groups follow for a long period of time is called a *fashion*, while a fad is a novel social pattern that has a quick rise and fall in popularity. Mass hysteria, also known as moral panic, refers to a collective behavior in which groups of people feel a real or imagined threat to social order and respond in a hysteric manner. Dramatized reporting by mass media can exacerbate moral panic. Mass hysteria can progress to a riot, where the group that is feeling threatened grows frustrated to the point of violence and destruction.

All of these types of social interactions are governed by various social norms. The role that a person plays in a social interaction is defined by his or her expected behavior in a particular situation. An individual's roles can lead to role conflict or role strain. Role conflict occurs when two or more roles that an individual plays have conflicting requirements. If a boss is friends with one of her employees, a role conflict may arise if she needs to fire her friend. As a boss, she needs to fire him, but as a friend, she does not want to hurt him. In role strain, the demands of a single role become overwhelming. A boss may have many responsibilities to juggle, including management, innovation, and organizing events. Both role conflict and role strain can potentially lead to role exit, where an individual stops identifying with a particular role. The boss may become so frustrated with all of her responsibilities or the need to fire her friend that she quits her job.

Often a single individual will play distinct roles in different groups or situations, depending on that person's status, or social position, within the group, network, or organization. There are two types of status a person can have. An ascribed status is one that is assigned to a person, either at birth or later in life. Examples include gender, race, and socioeconomic status. An achieved status is one that a person intentionally earns, such as a professional athlete, doctor, and boss.

Interacting with others requires detecting the meanings and intentions of other people. At the same time, it is necessary to manage others' impressions of one's own meanings and intentions. The abilities to express emotion and detect emotions in others are key to engaging in successful social interactions. Factors such as gender and culture greatly influence the portrayal and interpretation of emo-

When colleagues work on a project together, the person who takes the role of group leader often fulfills that position because of his or her status as the person with the most experience in the field. Newer members might serve in supporting, administrative, or observational roles until they become more familiar with the project. If someone who had never taken organic chemistry joined your MCAT® study group and tried to lead the discussion on organic chemistry, your study group partners would notice that he has stepped outside his role as an inexperienced member of the group because his behavior is outside what is expected.

tion. Cultural influences on social interactions will be examined in greater detail later in this lecture.

In their interactions with others, humans modify their behavior to affect their self-presentation, or how they are perceived. The process of consciously making behavioral choices in order to create a specific impression in the minds of others is called impression management. In the age of technology, many people use social media as a form of impression management to project their desired self-presentation. One theory of impression management takes a dramaturgical approach, using a metaphor from the theater to help explain human behavioral patterns in social situations. The dramaturgical approach proposes that impression management takes place in all aspects of human interaction. A person's behavior is an ongoing performance of self that changes according to the situation. This theory implies that the self is not a fixed, unchangeable entity, but rather can be formed and reformed through interactions with others. In the theater metaphor, a person has both a front stage and back stage self for various social situations. The front stage self encompasses the behavior that a player (person) performs in front of an audience (usually society, or some subset of society). A person performs her front stage self when she knows she is being watched and that her behavior is subject to judgment by an audience. She carries out behavioral conventions that are meaningful to the audience in an attempt to give them a certain perception of her behavior. The back stage self, by contrast, is employed when players are together, but no audience is present. The back stage is still a region of performance, but the players can let go of conventions necessary for the front stage self. Players perform a different self for each other than they do for the audience. Performance of the back stage self can include behavior that would be unacceptable when performed in front of the audience.

To better understand the difference between front stage and back stage self, consider the behavioral patterns of a physician. When a doctor is with a patient (the audience), her behavioral performance follows the specific conventions expected for that interaction. The physician's back stage behavior that takes place with colleagues at the hospital may be quite different, perhaps including behavior that would be unacceptable in front of patients, such as joking or complaining about "difficult" patients that she has seen that day.

Social Processes that Influence Behavior

Social influences are strong determinants of individual behavior. Individuals act differently in groups than they do when they are alone. Often these differences in behavior can contribute to a functional, effective group that makes use of the strengths of its individuals. However, changes in individual behavior induced by group membership can also be coercive or even dangerous. The behaviors of people within groups depend not only on individual desires and intentions, but also on dynamics of the group structure.

Group dynamics are particularly important in the context of decision-making. When when a group works together smoothly, the members may agree with each other so much that they exclude alternative possibilities, considerations, and decisions. Groupthink is the phenomenon where a group's members tend to think alike and agree for the sake of group harmony. When groupthink occurs, members may self-censor ideas or opinions that go against group norms or may be pressured by other group members to keep silent on such opinions. The suppression of dissenting opinions creates the illusion that the group is unanimous in its actions, which may lead group members to believe that, because the group is unanimous, its decisions must be correct. Groupthink can be adaptive because it allows groups to make decisions quickly and efficiently, but it has also historically led to many disastrous outcomes. For that reason, many U.S. presidents have intentionally included advisors and cabinet members in their administrations who challenge their ideas and express minority perspectives.

Group dynamics can also lead to group polarization, an effect similar to groupthink. Group polarization occurs when, through the interactions and discussions of the group, the attitude of the group as a whole toward a particular issue becomes stronger than the attitudes of its individual members. Suppose a group of neighbors who own condominiums in the same building meet to discuss regulations for the external appearance of the building. Most owners arrive with vague ideas about wanting the building to look tasteful. Through discussion, the group's about regulation become more and more extreme, and the owners conclude by signing an agreement to ban all paint color choices except black, white, gray, and

navy blue. This example of group polarization demonstrates that group decisions tend not to be the average of individual desires, instead reflecting those desires taken to an extreme.

Even in the absence of participation in a formalized group environment, the presence of others affects individual behavior. Everyday life provides plentiful examples of how people alter their behavior in response to the influence of others. Peer pressure is the social influence exerted by one's peers to act in a way that is acceptable or similar to their own behaviors. For example, a person who wants to chat and play games may be motivated to sit still and study when surrounded by hard-working students in the library. Peer pressure can be an extremely powerful motivator and is connected to the desire for social acceptance.

Sometimes people are motivated to perform better than they normally would when they have an audience for their actions. After reaching record-breaking times, some Olympic athletes have reported that hearing the crowd cheer for them while approaching the end of a race pushed them to do better than they ever had in practice. Social facilitation is the tendency to perform better when a person knows he is being watched. It is usually most pronounced for tasks at which the performer is highly practiced or skilled. When carrying out new or uncomfortable tasks, an individual often performs worse in front of an audience that he would on his own.

A major factor in how the presence of others affects individual behavior is *diffusion of responsibility*, where people in a large, anonymous crowd are less likely to feel accountable for the outcome of a situation or to feel responsibility to take action. In other words, the sense of responsibility is diffused among the many people present. Diffusion of responsibility is responsible for many behavior changes associated with close proximity to others. One such change is the bystander effect, where onlookers in a crowd fail to offer assistance to a person who is in trouble because they assume that someone else will help. The bystander effect encompasses the fact that when fewer people are present, it is more likely that any one person will help another in distress.

In the bystander effect, the diffusion of responsibility caused by the presence of others makes people feel that their individual action is not as critical as it otherwise would be because there are others present to carry out necessary tasks. Diffusion of responsibility also makes people feel that their inaction is excusable because other people in the same situation similarly did not take action. In groups of people focused on completing a specific task, diffusion of responsibility often takes the form of social loafing. Social loafing occurs when members of a group decrease the pace or intensity of their own work with the intention of letting other group members work harder. Through social loafing, group members attempt to do less work and in essence gain a "free ride" off the work of their teammates. Social loafing is particularly common when individuals are not accountable for their own portions of the greater project. Group members are much less likely to participate in social loafing when they feel that other people are not available, willing, or able to complete necessary work. As with the bystander effect, social loafing demonstrates how the presence of more people encourages individuals to do less than they would with fewer people in proximity to share responsibilities.

The examples above illustrate how the diffusion of responsibility that can occur as part of group dynamics can lead to different behavior than individuals would carry out in isolation. An extreme example of this type of change occurs when immersion in a group overrides a person's sense of self. Deindividuation occurs when people lose awareness of their individuality and instead immerse themselves in the mood or activities of a crowd. This phenomenon can lead to actions that would otherwise go against individuals' moral principles. Such lapses in decision making can occur because individuals no longer feel responsible for their own behavior.

As you probably know from experience, being watched by an audience doesn't always result in better performance on a task. The occurrence of social facilitation depends on a variety of factors including mood, situation, and differences in personality factors such as levels of anxiety, extroversion, and self-esteem.

The bystander effect may seem counterintuitive. Why would a person be LESS likely to receive help when there are MORE people around? However, studies have repeatedly shown this to be true. If a person is running on an isolated wooded trail and discovers another runner who has sprained her ankle and can't walk, the person is far more likely to stop and offer assistance than if he had seen her sprain her ankle on a crowded city street.

Deindividuation is sometimes desirable. Uniforms are often used to encourage deindividuation in situations where taking on the mindset of the group is important. Uniforms, masks, and other methods of minimizing individual identity within a larger group help people conform to the social norms and expectations of group membership. However, profound and sometimes destructive effects can result when people fail to consider the repercussions of their actions. Many heinous acts of violence, such as genocide, have occurred not because all of the perpetrators were monsters, but because they went along with the group and were following orders. Mob mentality is another example of deindividuation gone awry. After a sporting event with an undesirable outcome, huge groups of upset fans may participate in acts of vandalism and violence that they would not condone under normal circumstances.

Deindividuation is closely linked to the "mob mentality" that can develop due to the loss of self-awareness in a group. Most sports fans, for example, are not involved in looting, beatings, or setting objects on fire in their everyday lives. But when riots following sports games occur, fans sometimes lose themselves in the mood of the crowd. The sense of anonymity in the group frees them from feeling personal responsibility for their actions, leading them to carry out destructive actions that they normally would not do alone.

Question 33

Which of the following is not generally thought of as a feature of behavior?

- **A.** It occurs in response to both internal and external stimuli.
- **B.** It is partially biologically influenced.
- **C.** It involves an emotional component.
- **D.** It is influenced by neural connections.

Question 34

Which of the following does not necessarily constitute social behavior?

- **A.** Nonverbal communication
- **B.** Mating behavior
- **C.** Learning behavior
- **D.** Aggressive behavior

Question 35

A woman notices a stranger drowning in a lake while walking through a park and dives into the water, placing herself in danger, to save the person. This situation demonstrates:

- **A.** altruism.
- **B.** inclusive fitness.
- **C.** game theory.
- **D.** self-interest.

Question 36

Game theory would NOT be well suited to which of the following situations?

- **A.** Deciding the optimal bidding strategy at an auction
- **B.** Choosing the ideal car purchase given a matrix of advantages and disadvantages for each
- **C.** Determining foreign policy decisions
- **D.** Selecting the best play to run in a football game

Question 37

Several friends embark on a road trip and the driver starts playing country music. She asks the other passengers if they are happy with the music selection and they all agree, even though the majority of them dislike country music. This situation best demonstrates which of the following principles?

- **A.** Diffusion of responsibility
- **B.** Group polarization
- **C.** Group dynamics
- **D.** Groupthink

Question 38

An acting troupe performs better in front of a crowd than during rehearsals. This is most likely due to:

- **A.** the dramaturgical approach.
- **B.** peer pressure.
- **C.** deindividuation.
- **D.** social facilitation.

Question 39

Which of the following situations best exemplifies social loafing?

- **A.** An employee working on a team project fails to contribute, believing that other team members will pick up the slack.
- **B.** A depressed individual cannot find the energy to socially interact with others.
- **C.** A person loses her sense of individuality when part of the crowd, performing actions that she otherwise would not have.
- **D.** An elderly man is loath to socially interact with members of the younger generation.

Question 40

First aid providers are taught to specifically instruct one person to call 911, rather than issuing a request to the crowd as a whole. Which phenomenon does this procedure combat?

- **A.** Group dynamics
- **B.** Group polarization
- **C.** Social facilitation
- **D.** Bystander effect

Behavior in a Cultural Context

The previous sections discussed how individual patterns of behavior are learned and how those patterns can be altered through social interactions and membership in social groups. Culture can also have a significant effect on behavior. Cultural experiences help people determine what behaviors are acceptable and in which contexts they are appropriate. It is also through culture that people gain a sense of group identity and belonging, which influence individual behavioral choices.

Socialization

Different practices are considered acceptable and normal in different cultures, as discussed in the previous lecture. In one culture, hosting house guests might be considered burdensome after more than a few days, while in another culture, planning a stay with friends that is shorter than a month or two may seem rude. Of course, individuals are not born with an innate knowledge of what practices and behaviors are acceptable and encouraged in their particular culture. The process by which people learn customs and values of their culture is called socialization. Socialization begins very early in childhood and continues to develop and evolve over a lifetime. Through socialization, the members of a culture learn what customs and ideologies are valued and encouraged among their communities. People also gain an understanding of social norms, the rules that community members are expected to follow. Socialization occurs through observational learning and also through operant conditioning in which "proper" behaviors are rewarded and unacceptable behaviors are met with criticism or punishment.

A variety of methods and interactions with other people contribute to the socialization of a developing individual. The agents of socialization are comprised of the groups and people who influence personal attitudes, beliefs, and behaviors. Agents of socialization include people such as family, friends, and neighbors, social institutions such as religion or school, consumption of mass media, and environments that include interactions with other people such as sports teams and the workplace. Through these interactions, individuals learn what actions are acceptable by observing both the behaviors of others and the reactions of others to their own behaviors. Social control is a more direct form of socialization in which one group or individual imposes a set of rules to control the behavior of others. This can be informal, as with parents disciplining their children, or formal, as with the creation of laws to control citizens.

Socialization helps members of a culture understand the social norms of the group and the expectations placed on them as members. The better an individual understands social norms, the more pressure he or she feels to conform to those norms. Conformity, or the tendency of individuals to change their attitudes, opinions, and behaviors to align with group norms, is a normal phenomenon for social animals. To a certain extent, conformity is necessary for the smooth functioning of social communities. As was illustrated in the phenomenon of group-think, individuals will sometimes go against their own best judgment in order to be in agreement with their peers. Conformity can be demonstrated in a controlled laboratory setting, but it is also apparent throughout all aspects of everyday life, from driving on the correct side of the road to dressing in a certain style to fit in with friends or coworkers.

Obedience is the term used to describe behavioral changes made in response to a command by an authority figure, in contrast to conformity, which involves the influence of one's peers and culture. One of the most well-known studies in the field of psychology is Stanley Milgram's study of obedience. Subjects were told that they were participating in a study on learning and that they were to act as the teacher. An authority figure (a person in a white coat) directed the teacher (research participant) to administer electrical shocks of increasing intensity to

> Socialization and conformity are related but not the same. Socialization is the process by which a person learns the rules and expectations of a group, while conformity involves changes in behavior to comply with those rules and expectations.

another person, the learner, when he or she produced incorrect answers to questions. In reality, the "learner" was an actor and did not actually receive any electrical shocks. Milgram wanted to determine whether people would adopt behavior that went against their own ethical codes if an authority figure instructed them to do so. The results of the study were startling. Every participant administered at least some level of shock to the learner, and approximately two-thirds of participants delivered shocks up to the maximum, life-threatening level. Many study participants followed the instructions reluctantly and were clearly distressed about the pain that they believed they were inflicting on another person. However, most obeyed the instructions to continue with the experiment, despite their distress. Milgram's experiments showed that behavior is sometimes more the function of a situation than of the personal qualities of the participants, and they demonstrated the power of authority or perceived authority in commanding obedience.

Although conformity and obedience can lead to negative outcomes, such as in Milgram's experiments, the failure to conform to social norms can also have dire consequences for an individual or for a society. When a person is unable to recognize social norms or chooses not to follow them, that individual is practicing **deviance**, behavior that violates social expectations. A society in which rules are no longer followed can quickly become chaotic. Imagine how dangerous it would be to drive if people decided to no longer stop at stoplights, or how difficult it would be to run a business if customers decided not to pay for the products they took. Deviant behavior is often met with disapproval because of the societal importance of maintaining rules. Behavior that defies social norms is often associated with **stigma**, a negative social label that changes a person's social identity by classifying the labeled person as abnormal or tainted in some respect. Stigma, ostracism, and other forms of escalated social punishment are societal tools used to keep members within the confines of acceptable behavior. Stigma can have negative effects, such as when stigma towards people with mental illness prevents individuals from seeking mental health treatment.

Sociological **perspectives on deviance** attempt to explain the role of deviance in society. According to **strain theory**, deviance arises when there is a conflict between societal expectations and the socially condoned methods of achieving those expectations. Strain theory is commonly used to explain the motivation for crime. An individual under pressure because he is unable to achieve the societal expectation of economic success may decide to deviate from the socially acceptable way of gaining wealth. The experience of strain can lead to **anomie**, in which individuals lose their moral guidance due to the pressures of pursuing societal expectations.

Remember Key 2: We tend to conform to our group and follow authorities.

Conformity and obedience both relate to the power of social influence. They differ from each other in the following ways: conformity involves acquiescing to the norms of the group; obedience involves following explicit instructions. Conformity happens in response to pressure from one's peers; obedience happens in response to pressure from someone in a position of authority. The drive toward conformity involves social acceptance and the need to fit in; the drive toward obedience involves relenting to social power and the desire to avoid punishment or other undesirable consequences.

Differential association theory suggests that deviance arises from social learning. If the predominant behavior of a group deviates from societal norms, individuals who are socialized by that group will learn to be deviant. In the same way that community rules are learned by observation, the breaking of rules can be learned. Labeling theory, by contrast, proposes that particular behaviors are societally defined as deviant based on the group that carries out those behaviors. The label of deviant is ascribed to a person who is part of a group that the community views as deviant, and once a person or group is identified as deviant, their actions are also considered deviant.

Culture

Rather than being universal guidelines, the definitions of acceptable behavior differ between cultures. (The basic concepts about culture that must be known for the MCAT® were covered in greater detail in the previous lecture.) Culture can be spread between groups in many ways. The passage of culture from one generation to another is called transmission. The spread of culture from one population to another, such as when one country adopts cultural aspects of another country, is called diffusion. Methods of transmission and diffusion have evolved from oral communication to writing. Technologies such as air travel, Internet-based communication, and other instruments of globalization have increased the pace of cultural diffusion throughout the world.

After moving from one culture to another, it takes time to learn a new set of cultural norms and acceptable behaviors. The process by which an individual or group becomes part of a new culture is called assimilation. Assimilation occurs through a variety of means, including language acquisition and gaining knowledge about the social roles and rules of the newly adopted culture. Before assimilation takes place, individuals often experience culture shock. Culture shock is the feeling of disorientation that occurs due to an encounter with an unfamiliar culture. There are four stages of culture shock: the honeymoon phase, negotiation phase, adjustment phase, and mastery phase. The *honeymoon phase* is an initial period of excitement, which then turns into the *negotiation phase*. Problems such as language barriers and homesickness may arise during this period. Finally, assimilation takes place over the course of the *adjustment* and *mastery* phases. *Reverse culture shock* can also occur when someone returns to their original culture after adapting to a new culture. Also known as re-entry shock or own culture shock, reverse culture shock refers to the feeling of otherness due to the changes an individual underwent while immersed in a new culture.

Variation in behavioral expectations and social norms can also exist within a single culture. A subculture is a culture that is shared by a smaller group of people who are also part of a larger culture but have specific cultural attributes that set them apart from the larger group. The United States contains many overlapping subcultures that contribute to the overall population, such as skateboarders, the Amish, and the Deaf community. The U.S. can be considered a national culture because Americans tend to share certain beliefs and experiences as a result of living in the same country. However, the United States is also a multicultural country, meaning that it contains many cultures within one larger culture. The presence of so many subcultures within the U.S. has led to the rise of multiculturalism, the practice of valuing and respecting differences in culture. Multiculturalism includes the belief that the harmonious coexistence of separate cultures is a valuable goal, rather than encouraging all cultures to blend together through assimilation.

Although many variations exist within a single culture, the most widespread cultural patterns of a society are known as popular culture. Popular culture designates the most widespread cultural patterns of a society. In the United States, big-budget Hollywood movies and Top-40 radio songs are prominent examples. Popular culture is transmitted via mass media, defined as any means of delivering standardized messages to a large audience, such as television. Mass media has been criticized for exposing consumers to violence and reinforcing stereotypes about race and gender. When mass media first emerged, only a few sources were able to reach large numbers of people. These sources of mass media had a huge influence on the culture of large groups. The advancement of technology has created many more outlets for mass media and the spread of popular culture. While increasing the number of sources of media influence has had positive effects, it has also led to reduced regulation of content, leading to increased spread of false information. **Countercultures** are groups whose members adopt cultural patterns in opposition to the larger culture and tend to acquire cultural messages from sources that are less mainstream than mass media.

Cultural lag refers to the time culture takes to adjust to technological innovations. This is particularly evident with the development of new medical technologies. Genetic technologies are quickly advancing, for example, and it is possible that soon the concept of a "designer baby" will become a reality. In the coming years, each culture will have to decide where it stands on this issue and other medical advancements.

The Hippie movement in the 1960s is a good example of a counterculture.

2.6 | Prejudice, Bias, and Discrimination

The goal of multiculturalism, that a variety of cultures can coexist and interact productively and peacefully, is not always achieved within societies. It is normal for people to feel a sense of identity with their culture and an attachment to their own way of life, sometimes to the point of criticism of other cultures. **Ethnocentrism** is the belief that one's group is of central importance and includes the tendency to judge the practices of other groups by one's own cultural standards. The opposite of ethnocentrism is **cultural relativism**, the practice of trying to understand a culture on its own terms and to judge a culture by its own standards. The ways in which people think about social groupings have substantial effects on interactions and behaviors.

Jehovah's Witnesses oppose receiving blood transfusions on religious grounds. Imagine an injured patient who is a Jehovah's Witness and might die without a blood transfusion. A physician from another religious tradition who takes an ethnocentric viewpoint might consider the patient to be stubborn or foolish for rejecting a possibly life-saving procedure. A physician approaching the situation from the perspective of cultural relativism might instead try to understand why such a procedure is objectionable to the patient and would try to explore other possibilities that are acceptable within the patient's faith.

Consider Key 3: We tend to favor our in-group over groups we are not part of. This tendency shapes how we think about and act toward other groups.

Identity and the Individual
PSYCH & SOC

Society and Culture
PSYCH & SOC

Racial profiling is an example of discrimination, involving stereotypes based on some combination of race, ethnicity, ancestry, and religious affiliation. This practice sometimes occurs in law enforcement and security protocols. Many people argue that racial profiling creates a division between law enforcement and the communities that it is meant to serve. Racial profiling is also said to be unjust, immoral, and possibly unconstitutional. Proponents of racial profiling argue that it is a necessary tool for the prevention of terrorism and other crimes.

Ethnocentrism can contribute to the establishment of a sense of identity, but taken to extremes, it can result in misunderstanding and conflict. It encourages people to define themselves in terms of social groupings, often establishing a mental dichotomy between an in-group and an out-group. An in-group is a group with which an individual shares identity and toward which she feels loyalty, while out out-group is a group with which she does not identify and toward which she may feel competition or hostility. In-groups and out-groups will be further discussed in the context of the formation of social identity in Lecture 3 of this manual.

The establishment of mental divisions and comparisons between in-groups and out-groups can lead to bias, where the individual favors the in-group and devalues out-groups. A strengthened in-group identity can lead to misunderstandings or unjustified generalizations about people who are not part of the in-group. Such strict generalizations about other groups or categories of people are called prejudices and often underlie antagonistic feelings or conflict. While prejudice is primarily founded on the "us" and "them" mentality that helps form group identity, there are many processes that contribute to prejudice. Many of the concepts discussed in the first lecture of this manual, such as power, prestige, and class, contribute to the effect that prejudice has on the lives and opportunities of individuals as well as the structure of social institutions. Emotion and cognition, which will be discussed in greater detail in Lecture 4 of this manual, also contribute to prejudice through the development of schemas. *Schemas* are organizing patterns of thought that are used to categorize and interpret information, thus shaping individual attitudes and perspectives.

One particular type of schema, known as a stereotype, is closely associated with prejudice. A stereotype is a concept about a group or category of people that includes the belief that all members of that group share certain characteristics. Unlike prejudices, which are typically negative, stereotypes can be positive, negative, or neutral. An often-studied subject in social psychology is stereotype threat, which refers to the anxiety and resulting impaired performance that a person may experience when confronted with a negative stereotype about a group to which he belongs or when he feels his performance may confirm a negative stereotype about his group. Stereotype threat can cause stereotypes to become self-fulfilling prophecies, where the stress and lowered expectations accompanying negative stereotypes contribute to making stereotypical beliefs into reality. The reverse can also be true, where exposure to a positive stereotype leads to improved performance. Stereotyping provides a useful mental shortcut when a person must make quick decisions based on incomplete information. However, stereotyping is often ill-advised because generalizations about large groups of people are not accurate for each individual member and ignore the breadth of human experience. Such generalizations can lead to misjudgment of others, misunderstanding, and conflict.

The ideas and impressions that make up prejudice and stereotypes can lead to very real effects on actions and behaviors. Prejudice often leads to discrimination, meaning unfair treatment of others based on their membership in a specific social group. The effects of discrimination, like those of prejudice, are mediated by factors such as power, prestige, and class. An individual in a powerful social position can generally inflict more damage on the quality of life and opportunities available to a person in a less powerful position than vice versa. This power differential is important to keep in mind in the field of medicine because prejudices against particular races or sexual identities can cause the targeted groups to have decreased access to medical care.

Discrimination exists at different levels of society. Individual discrimination occurs when one person behaves negatively toward another because of that person's membership in a specific social group or category. Institutional discrimination, by contrast, takes place at the level of social institutions when they employ policies that differentiate between people based on social grouping. A landlord's refusal to rent the houses on his property to women would be an example of individual discrimination, while the fact that many religions bar women from becoming high-ranking members or leaders of the clergy is an example of institutional discrimination. Discrimination is influenced by biological, social, and cultural factors and is a learned behavior that can be passed down through the generations.

> Prejudice and discrimination are similar and closely related concepts, but they are not synonymous. Remember that prejudice is based in ideas and attitudes, while discrimination describes actions and behaviors.

> You are likely to encounter questions that relate to bias, prejudice, stereotypes, and discrimination on the MCAT®. When reasoning about the answer choices to such questions, take care to consider the confluence of biological, social, and cultural elements that contribute to any behavior.

Questions 41-48 are NOT based on a descriptive passage.

Question 41

Which of the following does not necessarily constitute an agent of socialization?

- O **A.** The media that one consumes
- O **B.** One's religion
- O **C.** The school that one attends
- O **D.** The works of an influential philosopher

Question 42

A blacksmith apprentice notices that all other blacksmith apprentices wear their aprons untied, so she decides to leave her own apron untied. Which of the following phenomena does this situation best demonstrate?

- O **A.** Conformity
- O **B.** Obedience
- O **C.** Compliance
- O **D.** Assimilation

Question 43

Which of the following scenarios best exemplifies institutional discrimination?

- O **A.** A bouncer denies entry only to those with red hair.
- O **B.** A talk radio host slanders organizations with which she disagrees.
- O **C.** Standardized college admission tests are biased toward test-takers from certain cultures.
- O **D.** A police officer is more likely to give a ticket to an African American driver than a Hispanic driver guilty of the same traffic infraction.

Question 44

A European tourist, upon learning about the cultural practices of Native Americans, expresses the belief that allowing adolescents to smoke tobacco in tribal ceremonies is dangerous and that Native Americans are irresponsible parents. This situation demonstrates which of the following?

-   I.   Ethnocentrism
-   II. Cultural relativism
- III. Prejudice

- O **A.** I only
- O **B.** II and III only
- O **C.** I and III only
- O **D.** I, II, and III

Question 45

Members of a fraternity share housing and participate in social activities, including expressions of pride in their fraternity. The fraternity is LEAST likely to be considered:

- O **A.** an in-group.
- O **B.** a subculture.
- O **C.** an agent of socialization.
- O **D.** a social group.

Question 46

Suppose there is a stereotype that people with hazel eyes are less skilled athletes. Which of the following is the most likely outcome in a test of athletic ability in a high school gym class?

- O **A.** Hazel-eyed students would perform worse than students with other eye colors.
- O **B.** Hazel-eyed students would perform better than students with other eye colors.
- O **C.** Hazel-eyed students would perform worse than students with other eye colors only when reminded of this stereotype.
- O **D.** Hazel-eyed students would perform better than students with other eye colors only when reminded of this stereotype.

Question 47

A former college athlete who currently works in advertising demonstrates a preference for hiring athletic people. This could be construed as:

- O **A.** bias.
- O **B.** prejudice.
- O **C.** stereotyping.
- O **D.** nepotism.

Question 48

Which of the following scenarios is most consistent with the concept of a self-fulfilling prophecy?

- O **A.** A motivational speaker instructs her audience to recite, "I am happy."
- O **B.** A number of people are concerned that there will be a stock market crash, so they cash out their stocks. In doing so, they cause the stock market to crash.
- O **C.** A lawyer presumes that her client is guilty, so she does not advocate as passionately on her client's behalf as she would if she thought the client was innocent.
- O **D.** A mother is angry with her son, causing her son to become angry with her in return.

Achieved status
Acquisition
Agents of socialization
Aggression
Altruism
Animal signals
Anomie
Ascribed status
Aspects of collective behavior
Assimilation
Associative learning (conditioning)
Attachment
Attraction
Avoidance conditioning
Back stage self
Behavior
Bias
Bureaucracy
Bystander effect
Characteristics of an ideal bureaucracy
Class
Classical conditioning
Cognitive processes
Conditioned reinforcers
Conditioned response
Conditioned stimulus
Conformity
Countercultures
Cultural lag
Cultural relativism
Culture
Culture shock
Deindividuation
Detecting emotions in others
Deviance
Differential association theory
Diffusion
Discrimination
Dramaturgical approach
Dyad
Escape conditioning
Ethnocentrism
Expressing emotion
Extinction

Fad
Foraging behavior
Formal organization
Front stage self
Game theory
Gender
Group
Group polarization
Groupthink
Impression management
Inclusive fitness
Individual discrimination
In-group
Innate behaviors
Institutional discrimination
Intermittent reinforcement
Iron law of oligarchy
Labeling theory
Learning
Mass hysteria
Mass media
Mate choice
Mating behavior
McDonaldization
Mirror neurons
Modeling
Multiculturalism
Negative punishment
Negative reinforcement
Networks
Neutral stimulus
Nonverbal communication
Obedience
Observational learning
Operant conditioning
Organization
Out-group
Partial reinforcement
Peer pressure
Perspectives on bureaucracy
Perspectives on deviance
Popular culture
Positive punishment
Positive reinforcement

Power
Prejudices
Prestige
Primary group
Primary punisher
Primary reinforcer
Processes that contribute to prejudice
Punishment
Reinforcement
Reinforcement schedule
Riot
Role
Role conflict
Role exit
Role strain
Secondary group
Secondary reinforcers
Self-fulfilling prophecies
Self-presentation
Shaping
Social behavior
Social control
Social facilitation
Social loafing
Social norms
Social support
Socialization
Spontaneous recovery
Status
Stereotype
Stereotype threat
Stigma
Stimulus discrimination
Stimulus generalization
Strain theory
Subculture
Transmission
Triad
Types of status
Unconditioned response
Unconditioned stimulus
Verbal communication
Vicarious emotions

DON'T FORGET YOUR KEYS

1. A stimulus that increases a behavior is a reinforcement; a stimulus that decreases a behavior is a punishment.

2. Individuals tend to imitate other members of their group (conformity) and follow the orders of an authority (obedience).

3. The mentality of in-group versus out-group underlies prejudice, bias, and discrimination.

Identity and the Individual

3.1 Introduction

3.2 Personality Theories: One View of the Individual

3.3 Identity: Another View of the Individual

3.4 Theories of Development

3.5 From Individual Identity to Beliefs about Others

3.6 Disorders: The Intersection of Psychological and Social Factors

THE 3 KEYS

1. Personality is made up of internal characteristics that influence behavior.

2. Identity is one's view of self in relation to the world.

3. Psychological disorders are culturally defined and occur in the context of social, biological, and psychological factors.

3.1 | Introduction

This lecture will consider how people become unique individuals with characteristic patterns of behavior and social interaction. It covers the concepts of identity, personality, understanding of others, and psychological disorders, all of which are important not only for the MCAT® but also for medical practice. Recall that the Psychosocial section is intended to test students' ability to understand and reason about aspects of psychology and sociology that affect health outcomes. The factors that make each individual unique influence how patients and doctors interact with each other, as well as the effectiveness of medical interventions. For example, personal identity can affect a patient's response to a diagnosis, as described later in this lecture.

As with many of the other concepts discussed in this manual, growth and formation of the individual occur on several interrelated levels. On the level of the cell, genetically directed differentiation leads cells to develop into their mature form. On the level of the body, maturation into the adult form occurs during puberty. At the level of psychological and social functioning, the developing person eventually forms a distinct sense of self.

Every person can be described by two interrelated but separate concepts: personality and identity. For the purposes of the MCAT®, the most significant aspect of personality is how it contributes to behavior. Multiple theories of personality, each with its own ideas about how personality develops and correlates with behavior, will be considered. The lecture will then cover identity, with an emphasis on both personal and social aspects of identity, since identity and social interaction are closely related such that each influences the other. This relationship will be discussed in the context of identity formation and as a factor in attribution theory, which concerns how people view other people's qualities and actions. Finally, the lecture will conclude by discussing psychological disorders, which are influenced by individual characteristics and environmental factors.

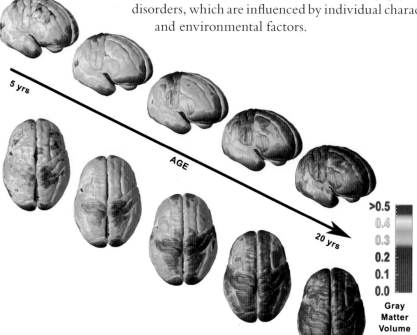

5 yrs

AGE

20 yrs

>0.5
0.4
0.3
0.2
0.1
0.0

Gray Matter Volume

On the left, MRI scans of children and adolescents from 5 years to 20 years of age show how gray matter volume in the cortex decreases during development, a necessary part of brain maturation.

Research Skills
REASONING SKILLS

3.2 Personality Theories: One View of the Individual

Consider Key 1: Personality is determined by intrinsic characteristics that shape behavior. Several theories of personality development have been proposed, but the key is that personality varies between individuals and can be used to predict behavior.

Personality is most fundamentally the collection of lasting characteristics that makes a person unique. There are many theories about how personality develops and affects behavior. The major distinctions between the theories have to do with how personality is formed, whether personality remains stable over a lifetime, and the extent to which people can influence their own personalities. This section will consider the key features and unique contribution of each theoretical approach.

The trait theory of personality is what most people probably think of when they define personality. It says that personality consists of a set of traits, which are characteristics that vary between people and are stable over the course of the lifetime, regardless of environmental factors. Traits are not either/or qualities, but rather allow for variation in degree. In other words, they are continuous variables rather than categorical. A person might be extremely friendly, extremely unfriendly, or somewhere in the middle. A large portion of research in the area of trait theory has concerned the search for a set of traits that can capture the full range of personality features and reliably distinguish between people.

The idea of a trait is useful because it allows for quantifiable comparisons between individuals. Measuring an individual's level of a certain trait allows for predictions about their behavior. If a trait is a characteristic that persists over time and does not change according to the situation, it should be a reliable predictor of how people will behave. Behavior may deviate occasionally, but according to trait theorists, people's actions will align with their traits the majority of the time.

The popular five-factor ("Big 5") model organizes a multitude of possible personality traits into five broader trait categories: Openness to experience, Conscientiousness, Extraversion, Agreeableness, and Neuroticism (OCEAN). Neuroticism has been particularly well-studied as a contributor to psychological disorders. Individuals fall along a continuum, where high neuroticism corresponds to high levels of emotional instability, anxiety, and moodiness. Unsurprisingly, high neuroticism has been linked to an elevated risk of mental illness, particularly depression.

MCAT® THINK

The five-factor model provides a useful way to examine health-related behaviors and traits. One study, by Courneya and Hellsten (1998), looked at the relationship between the Big 5 traits and exercise. The results showed that levels of extraversion and conscientiousness had positive correlations with certain exercise behaviors. By contrast, level of neuroticism was negatively correlated with exercise adherence. The five traits were also related to various psychological factors, such as perceived barriers to exercise. This study is only one example of the variety of possible relationships between personality and health that can be examined using the five-factor model.

The biological theory of personality focuses on biological contributions to certain traits. This theory assumes that a person's genome contributes to the formation of personality, and that personality traits differ in the extent to which they are influenced by **heredity** (genetic inheritance) versus environmental factors. As will be discussed in Lecture 5, infants are thought to start life with a certain temperament, an innate, genetically influenced "baseline" of personality that includes the infant's tendency towards certain patterns of emotion and social interaction. Temperament is then modified by environmental influences throughout life.

Twin studies are particularly useful in separating the effects of genetics and the environment by building a picture of which traits are more closely tied to genetics than others. Monozygotic twins have virtually identical genomes, while dizygotic twins are no more related to each other than any other biological siblings. Elevated similarity between monozygotic twins relative to dizygotic twins indicates a genetic influence on a given personality trait. Studies that compare twins separated at birth can further tease out the effects of genetic and environmental influences by eliminating the effects of a shared environment. Genes can be thought to influence a personality trait if identical twins (who share all of their genes) raised in different environments are more similar to each other on that trait than nonidentical twins (who share half of their genes) raised in different environments.

It is difficult to truly separate genetic and environmental influences on personality traits because genetic expression is heavily influenced by the environment. Genes interact with the environment to determine whether and how a personality trait is displayed. In many cases, genetic inheritance has been found to confer a vulnerability or potential that requires the influence of certain environmental factors for the development of a psychological disorder or personality trait.

A related area of study within the biological theory of personality attempts to explain personality traits in terms of their evolutionary usefulness. The genes associated with personality traits that improve an individual's chances for successful reproduction tend to be conserved. This assertion is central to the field of *evolutionary psychology*. Many evolutionary psychologists theorize that men and women have basic differences in personality traits because different behaviors led to reproductive success.

Psychoanalytic theory, pioneered by Sigmund Freud, proposes a universal personality structure that contributes both to behavior and to differences between people. Psychoanalytic theory stands in contrast to trait theories and biological theories, which do not focus on the mental processes that shape personality and translate personality traits into behaviors. In Freud's model, personality is deter-

Biological Correlates
PSYCH & SOC

Monozygotic (MZ): same genes, same environment

Dizygotic (DZ): different genes, same environment

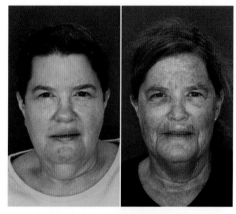
Differences between identical twins indicate the influence of environmental factors. The monozygotic twins shown in the photo above have virtually identical genomes, but due to differing levels of sun exposure, they differ significantly in appearance.

mined by the flow of psychic energy between three systems that reside in different levels of consciousness: the id, the superego, and the ego. The *id* is the most primitive part of personality, which seeks instant gratification with no consideration for morality or social norms. It is present from birth and is motivated by the desire to achieve immediate gratification and avoid pain. The *superego* develops later in life through internalization of society's rules for moral behavior, learned primarily through interactions with caregivers. Finally, the *ego* is the part of personality that is forced to direct behavior in a way that balances the demands of the id and the superego. The ego forces the delay of gratification of the id's desires until a socially acceptable method of gratification is found. The development of a healthy personality requires a balancing act between the id, superego, and ego. Mental life and the development of personality take place according to a process of continual conflict between components of the mind.

The most important feature of psychoanalytic theory is the assumption that crucial personality processes take place outside of conscious awareness. Though the dynamics of the three personality structures determine the characteristics and behaviors of an individual, the conflict does not take place in the individual's conscious awareness. Many of Freud's ideas have been discredited, in part because they are essentially impossible to prove or disprove scientifically. However, many mental processes are thought to take place outside of conscious awareness. Another important aspect of psychoanalytic theory is the assumption that early experiences can have lasting effects on the individual throughout life. Freud's influential theory of childhood developmental stages will be described later in this lecture.

Freud

Nervous System
BIOLOGY 2

Trait theory and psychoanalytic theory can be compared to two different ways of studying a machine. Trait theory is only interested in the ability to predict what the machine will do, whereas the psychoanalytic perspective is interested in the hidden internal workings of the machine and how they produce the machine's function. If you see psychoanalytic theory on the MCAT®, think about subconscious mental life.

The metaphor of a "black box" is sometimes used to describe behaviorism: behavior is understood as an output that follows certain inputs, but internal mental life is assumed to be unknowable. This idea is in sharp contrast to psychoanalytic theory, which focuses on internal mental dynamics.

The behaviorist theory states that personality is constructed by a series of learning experiences that occur through interactions between the individual and their environment. Like the other theories considered so far, this perspective takes a deterministic view of personality development. However, here it is the environment that shapes personality rather than biological factors or inherent psychological drives. Behaviorist theorists are more interested in external behaviors than internal factors. The essence of the behaviorist perspective is that individuals have learning experiences throughout their lifetimes that lead to predictable behaviors, which make up personality.

The remaining perspectives on personality take a different approach by assuming that individuals are able to actively participate in the formation of their own personalities. Social cognitive theory, like the behaviorist theory, focuses on learning experiences and observable behaviors. However, it differs in that it considers the contributions of an individual's mental life and personal choices. Although learning interactions between the individual and environment are still central, social cognitive theory explores how thought and emotion affect both the learning process and the experiences and surroundings that people choose for themselves. Social cognitive theory includes the process of observational learning, in which people learn from the experiences of others and apply the lessons of previous experiences to new situations. Developing individuals also form models of their own expected behavior.

A key concept in social cognitive theory is *reciprocal causation*, which states that behavior, personal factors, and the environment continually interact and influence each other. James and Jones (1980) examined reciprocal causation as an explanatory model for job satisfaction and job perceptions. They found that aspects of the job environment and personal characteristics, such as motivation, contribute to individuals' perceptions of their jobs. Job perception and job satisfaction influence each other and cause changes in behavior. Behavior can also influence job perception to cause further changes in job satisfaction. This process of interacting situational and personal influences can lead to changes in features of personality.

The humanistic theory says that people continually seek experiences that make them better, more fulfilled individuals. Central to the humanistic theory is the concept of self-actualization. Self-actualization is the development and realization of one's full potential in life. Self-actualization will be discussed again in Lecture 4 in the context of Maslow's Hierarchy of Needs. Like social cognitive theory, the humanistic perspective on personality points to the role of an individual in shaping his or her own personality. According to humanistic theory, conscious decisions, rather than stable, uncontrollable traits or unconscious impulses, make people who they are. The involvement of self-concept in personality formation is central to the ideas of *Carl Rogers*, an influential humanistic psychologist. According to Rogers, an individual has a healthy personality when his or her actual self, ideal self, and perceived self (self-concept) overlap (Figure 3.2). Psychological distress results when these selves are different from one another, or incongruous. Self-concept will be described further in the next section of this lecture.

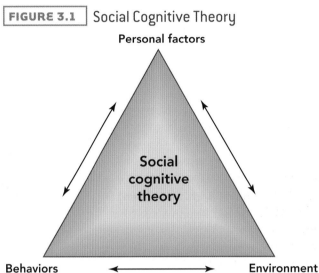

FIGURE 3.1 | Social Cognitive Theory

Personal factors

Social cognitive theory

Behaviors

Environment

Note that the humanistic and social-cognitive theories distinguish themselves from other theories of personality in their consideration of an individual's views of self. These perspectives relate to the concept of identity, which will be addressed in the next section. The key difference between these two theories is in their focus. The humanistic theory focuses on the conscious decisions people make to become their best selves or reach self-actualization. The social-cognitive theory focuses on the interaction between behavior, thoughts, and the environment. An individual may interpret the environment in a unique way based on his or her beliefs and previous experiences, which then influences how the person will respond to that environment.

FIGURE 3.2 | Humanistic Theory

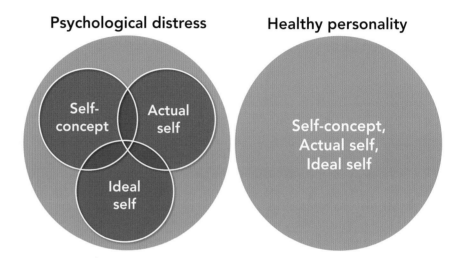

Think of the situational approach as an "if-then" theory. Although people can't be counted on to act the same across different situations, if they interpret a situation in a particular way, they will respond with a certain behavior. The fact that people tend toward certain interpretations adds an element of stability even though situations differ.

Before moving on to identity, it is important to acknowledge a challenge to the trait-based personality theories: the situational approach to explaining behavior. According to this perspective, the concept of enduring personality traits is fatally flawed because of the variations in behavior that occur across different situations. The situational approach shifts the focus from internal, stable traits to external, changing circumstances. However, it still allows for stability in personality because people behave according to their interpretations of situations. Individuals apply their own characteristic patterns of interpretation to a changing array of circumstances and situations. Environmental influences dominate when the situation requires particular behaviors, but individual personality differences have a greater effect in less constricting environments.

Although there are multiple theories about how personality develops and affects behavior, it seems clear that personality characteristics can influence the quality of interactions between physicians and patients. Attempts to explain connections between patient satisfaction and the personality features of physicians and patients make up an exciting area of research. Duberstein et al. (2007), for example, investigated the relationship between two big 5 personality traits, conscientiousness and openness to experience, and patient satisfaction. Patients were most satisfied with long-term primary care physicians who demonstrated high levels of openness to experience and average levels of conscientiousness. Such results have the potential to influence medical education, as medical students can be encouraged to foster certain desirable traits early in their training.

TABLE 3.1 > **Personality Theories**

Personality theory	Explanation of behavior	Amount of personal control over personality
Trait	Stable traits	Very little
Biological	Genetically influenced traits	Very little
Psychoanalytic	Interplay between id, ego, and superego	Very little
Behaviorist	Learned reactions to situations	Very little
Social cognitive	Reciprocal interaction between personal and environmental factors	Some (by choosing experiences)
Humanistic	Seeking betterment of self	Free will

This chart sums up the main differences between personality theories that are necessary to know for the MCAT®. Make sure you know the fundamental explanation for behavior offered by each theory.

3.3 | Identity: Another View of the Individual

Understanding Key 2: Identity is a person's view of self in relation to the world. Cultural factors such as socialization and imitation contribute to one's sense of identity. Internal factors including self-esteem, self-efficacy, and locus of control are involved in identity as well.

Identity can be thought of as a person's view of who they are in terms of both internal factors, including personality traits, and social or external factors, like group membership. The development of personality is an important part of what makes each person who they are, and personality structure has a significant effect on how people behave from day to day. However, personality does not capture all of the aspects that make an individual unique. Identity differs from personality by placing a larger emphasis on the individual's own perception of self. This section describes the internal and social processes that are involved in identity, including the psychological characteristics that shape identity. The following sections will focus on the processes that shape identity over the course of a lifetime.

Identity allows individuals to see themselves as constant, but it also maintains enough flexibility to change in response to experience, such as a career change. (Recall that by contrast, personality is generally thought of as a part of the individual's psychological makeup that stays constant over time.) Although identity is an internal concept, a person's identity includes a model of how he or she generally behaves in social settings. Identity can be understood best by examining two components: the personal and the social.

Self-concept is the most personal aspect of identity. It is the knowledge of oneself as a person both separate from other people and constant throughout changing situations. It can be thought of as a person's view of his or her own personality. Self-concept is developed and refined through interactions with others, as will be described in more detail. Once a person has a well-developed self-concept, he or she will intentionally act in ways that uphold that self-concept and may have a strong emotional response to circumstances that threaten its validity.

While views of one's personal characteristics are critical to identity, developing individuals must also situate themselves in society by constructing a social identity. Social identity is the perception of oneself as a member of certain social groups. Characteristics that are associated with the group come to be seen as a part of the self, thus influencing the individual's personal sense of identity. Like self-concept, social identity involves a cognitive and emotional component. The cognitive component is the categorization of oneself into a certain group. The emotional component of social identity comes from an individual's emotional attachment to the groups with which they identify. Social identity is a flexible concept. While it remains a fairly stable part of the self, it also allows for variation across different social contexts and levels of society. The same individual may enact one facet of their social identity while interacting with a sports team, but will probably demonstrate a different aspect of their identity at a dinner with their extended family.

The aspects of identity described in this section can all contribute to the development of different types of identities such as race/ethnicity, gender, age, sexual orientation, and class. Recall that these groupings were discussed in Lecture 1 as demographics. These characteristics are used by researchers to understand society as a whole, but they also have personal and social meaning as different aspects of an individual's identity. Just as small group membership contributes to social identity, perceiving oneself as part of a larger social group has implications for identity and behavior.

MCAT® THINK

Long-term health issues can lead to a disruption of identity. This is especially true when illness interferes with an individual's ability to carry out social functions that the person sees as part of their identity. Illness may also conflict with an individual's ideas about their own personal characteristics, such as strength and healthiness. Thus, illness can interrupt both personal and social aspects of identity.

Influence of Social Factors on Identity Formation

The process of identity formation has long been of interest to theorists and researchers. Internal characteristics, pre-existing societal structures, and personal interactions combine to shape identity throughout development. This section will describe how societal and cultural factors guide identity development. It will then discuss the interpersonal and group interactions that allow these forces to play out in the lives of individuals.

The influence of culture and socialization is a critical factor in identity development. Culture and society are structures that exist long before individuals are born. Although people can themselves influence the surrounding social environment, they are inevitably shaped by it as well. As discussed in the previous lecture, socialization is the process by which developing individuals learn the values, norms, and appropriate behaviors of their society, continuing throughout the lifespan. It can also be defined as the way that children learn the culture into which they have been born. In other words, culture is the guiding force of socialization. In this way the interrelated forces of socialization and culture facilitate identity formation as individuals gain an awareness of themselves as functioning members of society.

Relationships and Behavior
PSYCH & SOC

Of course, people socialized in the same culture still develop very different identities. Interactions between individuals can be thought of as the smallest unit of socialization. They are both a method of socialization and a source of variation among people. In this way, the influence of individuals is involved in both socialization and identity formation. Young children are primarily socialized by interactions with the individuals most immediately available to them, namely their parents and close family members. While the larger social environment is too complex for these children to grasp, they are able to observe and learn from the behavior of their parents and other individuals. Children then engage in imitation of the behaviors that they observe.

Imitation contributes to identity formation in two related ways. First, it allows the child to view himself or herself as similar to the imitated person. When a child imitates the gendered behavior of a parent, for example, they are recognizing their similarity to the parent and engaging in their own gender identity formation. Second, imitation allows children to engage in role-taking. Role-taking means adopting the role of another person, either by imitating behaviors associated with specific social roles or by taking the other person's point of view in a social interaction. Both types of role-taking allow children to develop a sense of who they are in relation to other people, encouraging the formation of identity.

Role-taking is related to the theory of symbolic interactionism in that it requires the ability to use and understand symbols. Imitating the roles of adults involves a symbolic representation of their behaviors as reflections of particular social roles. Taking the perspective of others to help inform identity is itself a symbolic act. From this perspective, identity can be seen as each person's symbolic representation of who they are.

MCAT® THINK

Part of role-taking is the idea of the looking-glass self: that identity develops through the mirror of social interactions. In a two person interaction, each takes the perspective of the other (role-taking) for the purpose of self-evaluation. In other words, if I am in a conversation with someone, taking their viewpoint provides me with a mirror that I can use to see myself. This is part of my identity formation process.

Role-taking and imitation both involve mimicking the behavior of other individuals in an attempt to "try out" their behaviors and roles, but identity formation also involves the perception of self as different from others. *Social comparison*, or evaluating oneself by contrast with others, facilitates the development of a distinct sense of self in terms of similarity with and difference from other people. The effects of social comparison on personal aspects of identity (discussed in the next section) depend to some extent on whom an individual chooses as their point of comparison. Individuals will draw different conclusions about their abilities depending on whether they compare themselves to an expert or a novice, and the resulting impact on self-perception will differ accordingly.

Group interactions also affect identity formation, particularly as children get older and participate in widening social circles. Recall from the previous section that group membership is part of social identity. An individual's reference group is a group that provides him or her with a model for appropriate actions, values, and worldviews. For a group to serve as a person's reference group, the individual must either be or aspire to be a member of that group. In other words, the person must identify with the group and its members, making the group an in-group for that person. An out-group, by contrast, is one with which the individual does not identify. Identification with a reference group allows the person to incorporate the group's way of perceiving and interacting with society into his or her own identity. Notice how identity and reference groups each influence the other: people tend to choose reference groups that align with their own identities, and the groups then exert their own influence on the individual's identity.

Relationships and Behavior
PSYCH & SOC

FIGURE 3.3 | Levels of Social Influences on Identity Formation

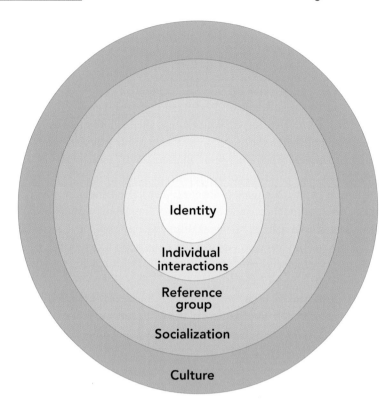

It's easy to remember what a reference group is if you remember that people REFER to their REFERence group for guidance in behavior. Notice that reference groups relate to the types of identity described in the previous section. For example, you could use the racial group with which you identify as a reference group.

In-groups and out-groups have a lot to do with ethnocentrism, as discussed in Lecture 2 of this manual.

Influence of Personal Factors on Identity Formation

The previous section discussed social factors that facilitate identity development, but personal attributes are involved as well. Identity formation involves the interplay between the individual's internal life and environment. The major psychological characteristics that influence identity and self-concept are those that concern an individual's perception of his or her capabilities and control over personal circumstances. This section will describe the three interrelated qualities that are most important to identity formation for the purposes of the MCAT®.

Self-esteem refers to a person's overall value judgment of him- or herself. Children generally have very high self-esteem that tends to level out and become more tied to reality over the course of development, although individuals still tend to judge themselves more positively and less negatively than they do others. Self-esteem acts as a mediating factor between self-concept and experience by shaping interpretations of events, which then influence self-concept. A changing self-concept can in turn modify self-esteem.

Just as self-esteem and self-concept influence each other, self-esteem and social identity can feed into each other. When an individual identifies as part of a certain social group, his or her positive or negative evaluation of that group circles back to influence self-esteem. On the other hand, the desire for heightened self-esteem can itself be a motive for identifying with a social group, so self-esteem also plays a role in the formation of social identity.

Someone who has high self-esteem has a positive self-concept. Someone with low self-esteem has a negative self-concept.

Self-concept ⟷ Self-esteem ⟷ Social identity

Self-efficacy is the feeling of being able to carry out an action successfully. This concept is more specific than self-esteem, which is a global judgment of self. Self-efficacy affects the types of experiences that people choose and how well they perform. The influence of self-efficacy on experience has a corresponding effect on identity and self-concept, since experiences lead to changes in the perception of self. Self-efficacy is also implicated in the social cognitive theory of personality, since it is a personal characteristic that affects the behaviors and interactions with the environment that shape personality.

Finally, locus of control is a person's belief about the extent to which internal or external factors play a role in shaping his or her life. An individual with a completely internal locus of control believes that he or she has complete control over their behavior and events. Someone with an external locus of control believes that external factors, such as other people, the environment, and luck, determine outcomes. Most people fall somewhere between these two extremes. Locus of control is similar to self-esteem and self-efficacy, and interacts with them to influence self-concept and identity.

Internal locus of control

External locus of control

My overall feeling of self-efficacy affects whether or not I think I can succeed at football, which then determines whether or not I try it out. If I do try and discover that I am good at it, being a talented football player may become an important part of my identity.

MCAT® THINK

The locus of control can be used to predict many behaviors. Some studies suggest that an internal locus of control is associated with increased adherence to medications and lifestyle modifications that reduce disease, such as exercising to prevent heart disease and healthy eating to prevent diabetes. Numerous studies also cite improved quality of life in people with internal locus of control living with debilitating medical conditions.

Questions 49–56 are NOT based on a descriptive passage.

Question 49

In general, personality can be thought of as:

- ○ **A.** the internal mental life of an individual.
- ○ **B.** the characteristics that make a person different from others and may be predictive of behaviors.
- ○ **C.** the behaviors and attributes that develop over a lifetime without the influence of the genome.
- ○ **D.** a set of baseline tendencies towards certain behaviors and characteristics that is present at birth.

Question 50

The purpose of a twin study is usually to:

- ○ **A.** compare monozygotic and dizygotic twins to their non-twin siblings.
- ○ **B.** randomly assign twins to certain environmental conditions to separate the effect of genetics and environment.
- ○ **C.** examine whether genetic or environmental factors are responsible for the presence or absence of a trait.
- ○ **D.** determine the degree to which genetic inheritance influences a trait.

Question 51

Which of the following claims would most likely be made by a proponent of the behaviorist theory of personality?

- ○ **A.** By selecting certain behaviors and life experiences, individuals can shape their own personality development.
- ○ **B.** Personality development occurs through a continual interaction between genetics and behaviors.
- ○ **C.** Mental life, social influences, and learning experiences combine to influence personality development.
- ○ **D.** Similar to how people learn certain behaviors based on environmental consequences, personality development occurs as people become more likely to carry out certain behaviors based on input from the environment.

Question 52

According to the situational approach to personality:

- ○ **A.** rather than being fixed characteristics, personality traits vary according to the situation.
- ○ **B.** personality is best understood as the tendency to respond to certain situational interpretations in certain ways.
- ○ **C.** an individual's response to a given situation cannot be predicted.
- ○ **D.** the experience of different situations over the course of a lifetime leads to the development of a stable personality.

Question 53

A researcher studying personality from the psychoanalytic perspective would most likely ask participants to:

- ○ **A.** participate in role-playing activities that involve choosing between impulse gratification and societally appropriate behaviors.
- ○ **B.** complete questionnaires about how they would behave in morally complex situations.
- ○ **C.** describe their personal experiences with the conflict between following their own desires and following the "rules" for how to behave in public.
- ○ **D.** answer questions about the principles for social behavior that they learned from observing caregivers.

Question 54

Sexual orientation and gender can best be described as examples of which of the following?

- ○ **A.** Social categorizations imposed by researchers
- ○ **B.** Agents of socialization that allow developing individuals to understand their culture
- ○ **C.** Identity categories that have personal and group meaning but can also be used for demographic research
- ○ **D.** Individual characteristics that are not influenced by social factors

Question 55

Which of the following is an influence on identity formation that is similar to Freud's theory of how the superego develops?

- ○ **A.** Self-efficacy
- ○ **B.** Socialization
- ○ **C.** Peer pressure
- ○ **D.** Looking-glass self

Question 56

A researcher asks participants about an instance in which they failed to accomplish a goal, how this experience influenced their perception of their ability to meet future goals, and how their overall perception of self was affected. This study is investigating the effect of:

- ○ **A.** self-esteem on self-efficacy.
- ○ **B.** self-esteem on self-concept.
- ○ **C.** self-efficacy on self-esteem.
- ○ **D.** self-efficacy on self-concept.

Theories of Development

Many researchers and theorists have attempted to divide the formation of identity and personality into a series of concrete, universal stages. This section will present four theories of development that must be known for the MCAT®. Notice that each theory takes a unique approach by placing emphasis on different factors involved in development, including social and mental processes.

Freud's theory of developmental stages proposed a sequential series of psychosexual stages in early childhood. Because Freud saw the id's urges as an important part of personality, he framed the stages of development in terms of the impulses of the id. Each stage presents a challenge to be navigated. If a child gets too much or too little satisfaction of the urge associated with a particular stage, they may fail to move on to the next stage. Freud called this phenomenon a *fixation*, a permanent aspect of the individual's personality that is related to that urge. Freud believed that fixations could cause problems for people later in their lives.

The earliest psychosexual stage is the *oral stage*, which takes place in infancy. Children in the oral stage are preoccupied with oral processes, such as sucking and biting. Successful weaning leads to the development of trust and the capacity for delayed gratification. The *anal stage* poses a conflict between the young child and his or her parents, as children wish to control their bowel movements while parents impose toilet-training. Successful toilet training allows the development of self-control. Next is the *phallic stage*, perhaps the most controversial Freudian stage. According to Freud, children in the phallic stage develop sexual and gender identity by focusing their sexual impulses on the opposite-sex parent and identifying with the same-sex parent. Through this identification, the individual begins to internalize society's rules, and thus begins to develop the superego. This dramatic stage is followed by a period of calm, the *latent period*, during which sexual impulses are suppressed and children can focus on other developmental tasks. Finally, the *genital stage*, starting in adolescence, is characterized by the return of sexual urges that lead to the achievement of adult sexuality.

> It is unlikely that the MCAT® would require you to recognize specific stages of each theory, but it is important to at least be familiar with them. Know the most important ideas of each theory, as well as how the perspectives differ from each other.

TABLE 3.2 > **Psychosexual Stages of Development**

Developmental stage	Age	Characteristics
Oral	1st year	Nursing, other oral stimulation
Anal	2nd year	Toilet training
Phallic	3-6	Gender and sexual identification
Latent	7-12	Social development
Genital	Adolescence and older	Sexual maturation

Like Freud, **Erik Erikson** was part of the psychoanalytic tradition, but he re-envisioned the psychosexual stages as psychosocial ones. Erikson's psychosocial stages involve the interaction between self and society that is experienced across the lifespan. Each stage presents a crisis that must be resolved, similar to Freud's conception of stages that can lead to fixations if not resolved. The dilemma is between two opposite ways of viewing the world, one of which is more psychologically healthy than the other. If the crisis is successfully navigated, the individual develops a perspective somewhere along a spectrum between the two opposites, with a greater emphasis on the healthier alternative. Each crisis contributes to the identity formation of the individual.

Stage 1, in the first year of life, presents the crisis of *trust vs. mistrust*. In this stage, the infant develops lasting ideas about trust according to the actions of his or her parents. Stage 2 concerns *autonomy vs. shame and doubt*, centering on the child's growing sense of whether he or she is competent to carry out self-care. In the third stage, *initiative vs. guilt*, children attempt to develop the ability to execute a plan, such as in play activities. Stage 4, *industry vs. inferiority*, takes place when children are immersed in the more complex social environment of school. It entails the crisis of whether or not a child views him- or herself as capable of mastering skills that are societally valued. Notice that stages 2-4 are all related to the personal attributes involved in identity formation, described in the previous section. For example, Erikson's idea of industry, or the ability to learn new tasks, is closely tied to the concept of self-efficacy.

Stage 5, *identity vs. role confusion*, is the one most explicitly concerned with identity formation. This is a complex stage in which adolescents explore different possibilities for their roles in society, as well as their personal beliefs and goals. The ideal outcome of this crisis is the formation of a stable sense of identity. The alternative is role confusion, meaning the lack of clear ideas about self and social belonging. This important stage is followed by stage 6, *intimacy vs. isolation*, which occurs in young adulthood and involves the ability to form emotionally signifi-cant relationships with others. In middle adulthood, the crisis of *generativity vs. stagnation* requires individuals to determine the extent to which they wish to "put back" energy into family, work, and community (generativity) or simply care for their own needs (stagnation). Finally, during old age people face the dilemma of *integrity vs. despair* as they evaluate their lifetimes and develop a sense of how well they have lived.

FIGURE 3.4 | Relationship Between Freud's and Erikson's Developmental Stages

Erikson's Developmental Stages

Stage	1	2	3	4	5	6	7	8
Oral	Trust vs. mistrust							
Anal		Autonomy vs. shame, doubt						
Phallic			Initiative vs. guilt					
Latent				Industry vs. inferiority				
Genital					Identity vs. role confusion			
Young Adulthood						Intimacy vs. isolation		
Adulthood							Generativity vs. stagnation	
Maturity								Integrity vs. despair

(Freud's Developmental Stages — vertical axis label)

James Marcia furthered Erikson's work by proposing four different types of identity status that describe an individual's progress in the stage 5 identity crisis (the process of freely exploring identity alternatives). Identity diffusion, like Erik-son's role confusion, describes a state in which a person has no sense of identity or motivation to engage in identity exploration. Identity moratorium describes an adolescent in the midst of identity crisis actively attempting to develop a unique set of values and an understanding of self in society. By contrast, a person in iden-

Note that the last three rows occur after Freud's stages are complete.

TABLE 3.3 > Marcia's Stage

Stage	Identity exploration	Identity commitment
Identity diffusion	No	No
Identity moratorium	Yes	No
Identity foreclosure	No	Yes
Identity achievement	No	Yes

MCAT® THINK

Interestingly, Adams and Shea (1979) found a correlation between the extent of internal locus of control and level of identity achievement according to Marcia's stages: internal locus of control is associated with identity achievement, while external locus of control is associated with identity diffusion. Since an internal locus of control assumes the presences of a coherent self that can influence outcomes, it makes sense that it is associated with the achievement of a strong identity.

Notice that Vygotsky points to the importance of social interaction in learning and cognitive development. This should sound familiar! Recall that social interaction is a key part of the socialization that shapes identity formation.

tity foreclosure has a sense of identity but has failed to undergo an identity crisis, instead choosing to unquestioningly adopt the values and expectations of others. Finally, identity achievement describes the successful resolution of the identity crisis with a strong sense of identity after exploring multiple possible identities; this is the opposite state from identity diffusion. Although Erikson did not present these stages of identity status, they are commonly associated with him because they are based directly on his work.

Though Erikson's psychosocial stages account for the interaction between self and the social environment, Lev Vygotsky proposed a theory that goes further in explicitly recognizing the involvement of social and cultural factors in development. The most important element of his theory is that learning takes place through interactions with others that promote the acquisition of culturally valued behaviors and beliefs. (This approach contrasts with Jean Piaget's theory of universal stages of cognitive development, discussed in the next lecture.) Vygotsky's work inspired the sociocultural approach to identity, which emphasizes socialization and the learning experiences that facilitate identity formation.

Unlike Freud and Erikson, Vygotsky did not propose a series of sequential developmental stages. Instead he focused on the process by which children attain higher levels of development with the guidance of adults and peers. Vygotsky proposed that the development of a child can be defined in terms of the child's current and potential levels of achievement at any point in time. The *current developmental level* consists of those tasks that a child can perform without help from others. By contrast, *the potential developmental level* represents the most advanced tasks that a child can do with guidance from more knowledgeable people. The range of activities between the current and potential developmental levels is referred to as the *zone of proximal development*, meaning all of the skills that can be accomplished with help. Development is fostered when the demands of the activity fall within the child's zone of proximal development, rather than within the current developmental level or beyond the child's current potential. A more knowledgeable person provides guidance by making their thought processes explicit so that they can be internalized by the learning child. As children learn new skills, what used to be their potential developmental level becomes their current developmental level. This process continues and repeats itself throughout development.

FIGURE 3.5 | Vygotsky's Levels of Development

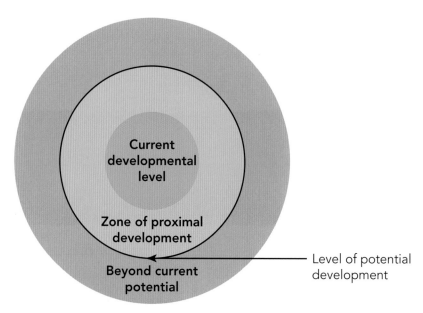

Vygotsky related learning to identity by pointing out that identity formation involves the performance of social roles, requiring the individual to exert self-control in selecting socially appropriate actions. In his view, this type of self-regulation had to be learned just like any other behavior. Although Vygotsky primarily focused on cognitive development, his theory of learning is closely tied to identity formation in its emphasis on socialization and social interaction. The sociocultural approach to identity formation builds upon Vygotsky's insights into the interactions between learning, culture, and identity.

The final theory of developmental stages that must be known for the MCAT® is Kohlberg's theory of moral development. Kohlberg proposed that developing children progress through a predictable sequence of stages of moral reasoning. This sequence parallels Piaget's stages of general cognitive development.

> According to Vygotsky, children learn about culturally valued worldviews and behavior with the assistance of others. The result is that they develop the ability to fill social roles, as well as a sense of self in relation to society. In other words, they form identities in collaboration with others in their environment.

| FIGURE 3.6 | Kohlberg's Levels and Stages of Moral Reasoning |

Level I - Preconventional Morality
Stage 1 - Punishment
Stage 2 - Reward

Level II - Conventional Morality
Stage 3 - Social disapproval
Stage 4 - Rule following

Level III - Postconventional Morality
Stage 5 - Social contract
Stage 6 - Universal ethics

Kohlberg's theory includes three general levels of moral reasoning: the preconventional, conventional, and postconventional levels. The preconventional level describes moral judgments that are based solely on consideration of the anticipated consequences of behavior. The first stage within this level involves a concern with punishment. In the second stage, moral judgments are motivated by reward. The preconventional level is focused on the consequences for the individual who carries out a certain action. By contrast, the conventional level takes into account social judgments. Within this level, the third stage of moral reasoning focuses on the potential for disapproval by others who find out about one's behavior. The fourth stage is characterized by a desire to obey rules and laws. A person in this stage will refrain from breaking a law that protects the rights of others not because it is the right thing to do, but because it is the law established by society. Finally, the postconventional level advances beyond personal and interpersonal considerations, rising to the level of universal principles and fully-developed ideas about right and wrong. Within stage five, moral reasoning is guided by the recognition of a social contract that is in place for the good of society as a whole. Stage six, the highest possible type of morality, is characterized by the belief in a set of universal ethical principles. Individuals who have reached stage six will have their own beliefs about what is right or wrong, but they share a commitment to these principles above and beyond considerations of consequences and the disapproval of others.

According to Kohlberg, advances in moral reasoning are a fundamental part of development. Kohlberg described the preconventional level as characteristic of childhood, with conventional reasoning developing in adolescence and, for most people, continuing through adulthood. Kohlberg and Gilligan (1971) also proposed that moral development is intertwined with and parallel to identity development. In particular, the transition between conventional and postconventional reasoning involves the same kind of questioning of self and society that are necessary for the development of identity. In Eriksonian terms, this transition is associated with identity moratorium: the state of active identity crisis. Those who remain in the conventional level are more likely to be in identity foreclosure, accepting societal and parental guidelines in matters of both identity and morality. Kohlberg also theorized a relationship between identity achievement and the post-conventional level, in that those who have reached the postconventional level are likely to have a well-established identity. However, not all individuals who reach identity achievement have necessarily reached postconventional moral reasoning.

One of Kohlberg's classic questions was whether or not you should steal a gratuitously expensive drug from a pharmacist to save your dying spouse. If you're in the preconventional level, you might reason that you shouldn't steal the drug because you might get caught and arrested, which would be unpleasant. However, you might also reason that you should steal the drug because you would be upset by the loss of your spouse. If you're in the conventional level, you might decide not to do it because it's against the law and people will think less of you if you get caught. You might instead decide to do it because you think that people would judge you for not taking action to save your spouse. Finally, if you're in the postconventional level, you might choose not to steal the drug because you believe that it is always wrong to steal from other people, no matter what the circumstances. Alternatively, you might steal because you think it is morally wrong for a dying person to be denied medication. Notice that, as in this example, the levels are defined by the type of reasoning used to make a decision rather than what decision is made.

3.5 | From Individual Identity to Beliefs about Others

So far this lecture has been concerned with how each individual develops a personality and concept of self over the course of a lifetime. To function in everyday life, we also make decisions about the characteristics of other people. Of course, this process is complicated by the fact that the thoughts and feelings of others are less accessible than our own. This section discusses the psychological and social processes involved in evaluating the actions and characteristics of other people, as well as the mediating factors of self-perception and perception of environmental circumstances.

MCAT® THINK

Kohlberg's theory of moral development has received some criticism. Some argue that Kohlberg's model places too much value on a Western, male morality of individual rights and justice. In other words, rather than being universal, Kohlberg's theory may reflect his own cultural biases.

Endocrine System
BIOLOGY 2

MCAT® THINK

The developmental stages of Erikson and Kohlberg point to the adolescent stage as a period of significant growth in identity and the related process of moral development. The timing of puberty, which varies significantly, often has an impact on the timing and quality of identity formation. Early puberty can have negative effects, particularly for girls, and may force young adolescents to start the process of identity formation before they are psychologically ready. The consequences of the timing of puberty are mediated by social factors, as physical maturation elicits responses from adults and peers.

Attribution theory, a line of research into the causes that people use to explain the observed behaviors of others, is a major source of ideas about how we understand people in social interactions. Conclusions that are drawn about the causes for other people's behavior then influence the subsequent behavioral response. According to attribution theory, conscious and unconscious processes both contribute to the formation of ideas about what caused another person to behave in a particular way. Attribution theory overlaps significantly with locus of control, but these theories are historically independent. Locus of control focuses on how the individual explains his or her own behavior, whereas attribution theory focuses on how people explain the behavior of others.

The most fundamental task in attributing a cause to an action is deciding whether the behavior was due to an internal quality of the person or external factors outside of the person's control. Assigning the cause to an inherent quality or desire is known as a dispositional attribution, while deciding that environmental forces were in control is called a situational attribution. Note the similarity of these attributions to the internal versus external locus of control discussed in the context of identity formation. A dispositional attribution is comparable to assigning an internal locus of control to another person, while a situational attribution is comparable to assigning them an external locus of control.

The inherent constraints on our ability to accurately judge the causes of behavior when we have incomplete information about the other person's mental processes and life circumstances manifests in the fundamental attribution error. This error is the tendency to automatically favor dispositional attributions over situational ones when judging other people. In other words, the fundamental attribution error is the inclination to assume that another person commits an action because of their personal qualities and not because of environmental influences. It is fundamental in that it is thought to occur across a wide variety of individuals and situations. The persistence of this effect can be understood by examining the process by which attributions are formed. A dispositional attribution happens quickly and sometimes outside of conscious awareness, or when information about another person's external circumstances is lacking. It is followed by the slower, conscious, more effortful process of taking environmental influences into account to form a situational attribution. The fundamental attribution error results from the fact that dispositional attributions simply require less information, time, and attention than situational attributions.

If a driver cuts me off and I assume that it's because he is rude and inconsiderate, I have made a dispositional attribution. If I assume that he's rushing due to an emergency, I have made a situational attribution. In the absence of additional information, I am more likely to make a dispositional attribution.

Individuals also make attributions about their own behaviors, particularly those that involve success or failure. The self-serving bias is the tendency to attribute one's success to internal factors while attributing one's failures to external (environmental) factors. Like the fundamental attribution error, the self-serving bias involves the attempt to attribute a situation to either internal or external factors. However, as the name suggests, the self-serving bias functions to support self-esteem by allowing individuals to believe that they control their successes while blaming failures on factors beyond their control. (See the Thought and Emotion Lecture for more about biases and how they affect decision-making.)

Note that by influencing self-esteem, the self-serving bias links attribution theory and identity formation.

Of course, attributions of motives and characteristics of ourselves and others do not occur in a vacuum. To fully understand attribution theory, it is necessary to consider how culture affects attributions. Recall that a society's culture provides an over-arching influence on the way of life of its inhabitants, including widespread beliefs and values. It is no surprise that different cultural patterns of thought would affect the process of attribution. However, the fact that the original studies on attribution theory were conducted with subjects in Western nations means that the development of this theory and the methods used to assess it were inherently biased towards a Western cultural perspective.

Society and Culture
≡ PSYCH & SOC

MCAT® THINK

The fundamental attribution error and other aspects of attribution theory are relevant to important issues in healthcare in the United States. In particular, the tendency to assign internal causes contributes to a tendency to place the blame on individuals following harmful mistakes in healthcare delivery, rather than considering organizational and institutional influences. Unfortunately, the lack of attention to situational factors inhibits the large-scale interventions that would be more effective than individual punishment.

Some evidence, as presented by Mason and Morris (2010), indicates that the fundamental attribution error is characteristic of a Western viewpoint rather than being truly "fundamental," or universal. Because the fundamental attribution error involves seeing the individual, rather than the situation, as central to events, it reflects an individualistic perspective that is typical of Western nations. Studies comparing Western and East Asian subjects have demonstrated that East Asians tend to pay more attention to situational factors than Western subjects. In tasks typically used to assess the fundamental attribution error, Western and East Asian subjects make similar attributions. When the experimental setup is altered to place greater emphasis on situational influences, East Asian subjects show a lower bias towards dispositional attributions than do Western subjects. Members of individualistic cultures are also more likely to invoke the self-serving bias. This phenomenon may be due to differences in the more automatic stage of attribution or the following effortful stage. In other words, cultural differences may affect unconscious cognitive processing, conscious attempts to consider situational influences, or both.

The influence of our self-perceptions and perceptions of the environment also affect our attributions and perceptions of other people. One of the most salient examples of the importance of self-perceptions is the influence of group identity. Recall reference groups, discussed earlier in this lecture, which provide their members with a set of values and beliefs. The ideas imparted by a reference group can include particular viewpoints on other people and groups. Perceiving oneself as part of a particular group may result in the adoption of that group's perceptions of others. In-group identification also leads to comparisons between in-group and out-group members, where in-group members are viewed more positively and are thought to have greater variability on assorted personality traits than out-group members.

Like self-perceptions, perceptions of one's surroundings can affect perceptions and beliefs about others. For instance, perceptions of the environment can influence conscious or unconscious stereotype activation. One study by Schaller et al. (2003) found that dark surroundings, which indicated the possibility of danger, led to subconscious activation of danger-related stereotypes in participants who were shown images of black men. In other words, the perception of the environment as dangerous led to the perception of other people as dangerous which, in this case, involved the activation of related stereotypes.

Questions 57-64 are NOT based on a descriptive passage.

Question 57

A student argues that college students under age 21 should not drink alcohol because it is against the law. Which stage of Kohlberg's theory of moral development does this reasoning represent?

- A. Preconventional level
- B. Conventional level
- C. Postconventional level
- D. Obedience level

Question 58

Vygotsky's theory of development is best described as a theory of how children:

- A. learn to follow social norms in accordance with their in-groups.
- B. achieve each potential developmental level of identity formation.
- C. master stages of social learning sequentially.
- D. learn new abilities and social roles with the guidance of others.

Question 59

Which of the following accurately describes a major difference between the theories of development proposed by Freud and Erikson?

- A. Freud posits distinct stages of development, while Erikson's theory involves continuous development.
- B. Freud focuses on early life, while Erikson examines the entire lifespan.
- C. Freud emphasizes only internal psychological factors, while Erikson posits that only social influences are significant.
- D. Freud's theory is based on psychosocial development, while Erikson's theory is based on psychosexual development.

Question 60

A child is presented with a hypothetical moral dilemma in which a person must decide whether or not to lie in order to get something that she wants. The child says that the person should not lie because she might get in trouble. This child is most likely in which of Kohlberg's levels of moral reasoning?

- A. Preconventional
- B. Conventional
- C. Post-conventional
- D. Super-conventional

Question 61

A person who expresses a clear set of personal values that she has developed over the course of exploring different value systems, including beliefs that are different from those of her parents, is most likely to be in which developmental stages?

- A. Identity moratorium and the preconventional level of moral reasoning
- B. Identity achievement and the preconventional level of moral reasoning
- C. Identity achievement and the postconventional level of moral reasoning
- D. Identity diffusion and the postconventional level of moral reasoning

Question 62

The field of attribution theory focuses on the study of:

- A. how people subconsciously develop beliefs about the factors that motivate actions by others.
- B. how each individual develops unique identity attributes.
- C. how people consciously and unconsciously form ideas about the causal factors behind the behaviors of others.
- D. how people reason about the causal factors behind their own behaviors.

Question 63

An individual who believes which of the following is committing the fundamental attribution error?

- A. A classmate who did well on a test must have done so because she received tutoring.
- B. A classmate from another culture who did poorly on a test must have done so due to a cultural bias in the test.
- C. A classmate who did poorly on a test must have personal problems that prevented her from studying.
- D. A classmate who did poorly on a test must have done so because she is not intelligent.

Question 64

In an experimental setup designed to elicit either situational or dispositional attributions for others' behaviors, the experimenter varied whether or not participants' social identities were made salient and evaluated the effect on their attributions. Which of the following is the independent variable in this experiment?

- A. Perceptions of self
- B. Perceptions of the environment
- C. Perceptions of the self-serving bias
- D. Perceptions of culture

3.6 Disorders: The Intersection of Psychological and Social Factors

Applying Key 3: The diagnostic criteria for psychological disorders are determined within a given cultural context. In the United States, auditory hallucinations are considered a symptom of schizophrenia. In some other cultures, auditory hallucinations are not considered pathological, so the same individual would not be diagnosed with schizophrenia. Psychological disorders are caused by complex interactions between biological, psychological, and social factors. Whether someone with a biological predisposition actually develops a psychological disorder is determined by the interaction of psychological and social factors in that individual's life.

Biological predispositions, psychological characteristics, and environmental influences (including social factors) can combine to cause an individual to develop a psychological disorder. This section will discuss the conceptual understandings and diagnostic processes associated with the study and treatment of psychological disorders. The next section will revisit the contrast between the biomedical and biopsychosocial models in the context of psychological disorders. Finally, the sections that follow will consider the defining features of all of the psychological disorders that must be known for the MCAT®.

Psychological disorders could be defined simply as sets of psychological abnormalities that are maladaptive to the individual. However, characterizing mental illness is actually very complex. Part of the difficulty is that psychological disorders fall on the extreme end of the spectrum of typical human experience and behavior. Statistical guidelines can be used to establish cutoffs for the level of a given trait or behavior that is "abnormally" low or high, but the question of where to draw that line is ultimately arbitrary. The statistical approach does not speak to the meaning of abnormality. An individual who barely exceeds the statistical threshold of abnormality on a given trait is not qualitatively very different from someone who falls just below that threshold. Yet one is considered "abnormal" while the other is not. The statistical approach imposes categories on traits that exist on a continuum.

FIGURE 3.7 | Bell Curve for Trait Level: Anxiety

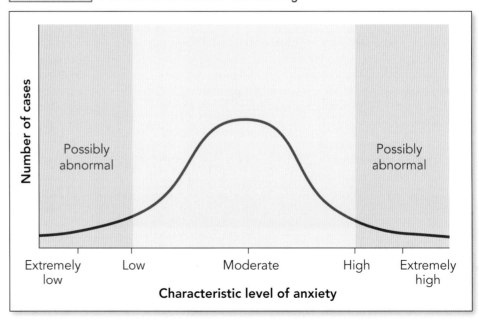

What if the individual's personal distress and functioning are taken into account? One might argue that the diagnosis of a psychological disorder is warranted if an individual is suffering and not adapting well to life circumstances and societal demands. It is also possible for an individual to not experience distress as a result of their psychological disorder, though. This is often the case when individuals with bipolar disorder experience of episodes of mania. It is equally possible that external cultural conditions could be the culprit when distress and impairment of function do exist, rather than the internal psychological conditions themselves. It is important to understand that culture plays a significant role in definitions of mental illness. The act of declaring a psychological condition to be abnormal and indicative of a disorder is inherently socially-influenced; it depends on certain cultural beliefs, values, and norms.

The MCAT® requires an understanding of the general features of the standard classification of psychological disorders. *The Diagnostic and Statistical Manual of Mental Disorders, Fifth Edition (DSM-5)* is the most recent edition of the guidebook used by mental health professionals, including psychiatrists, for the diagnosis of patients, communication with other professionals, and collection of data on psychological disorders. The DSM-5 provides a standardized system for diagnosing and discussing psychological disorders, including sets of specific symptoms that are characteristic of each disorder. Each disorder is characterized by a particular set of psychological factors, both observable by the clinician and described by the patient, that differ from the symptoms seen in other disorders. There is significant overlap in the symptoms of the disorders that will be discussed below. Recent estimates suggest that almost half of those diagnosed with a psychological disorder could be diagnosed with at least one other psychological disorder. This overlap can make it difficult to diagnose and treat patients with these conditions.

The classification of psychological disorders in the DSM-5 is tied to cultural ideas, much like the division of behavior and mental processes into categories of normal and abnormal. Some psychological disorders seem to exist only in certain cultures, and some are tied to the cultural standards of a given time. A prominent example is that homosexuality was classified as a psychological disorder in earlier editions of the DSM, and was not removed until 1973. Each new version of the DSM reevaluates the list of psychological disorders it will include based on the most recent research and cultural understandings of mental illness.

MCAT® THINK

An example of the difficulties that can be posed in the diagnosis of psychological disorders is the challenge of differentiating between depression and the "normal" process of grieving for the death of a loved one. The DSM-5 reverses the advice of earlier editions not to diagnose depression in those who have experienced bereavement in the last two months. This guideline was problematic in its arbitrariness; grief does not turn into depression at two months and one day. By allowing depression to be diagnosed at any time following bereavement, while also including strong guidelines for distinguishing between depression and grief, the DSM-5 hopes to provide more room in the provision of necessary mental health services for those who are truly experiencing depression. However, clinical judgment will become even more important for distinguishing between depression and grief.

The DSM is NOT meant to be a cookbook, where you simply read a list of symptoms (ingredients) and get a definite diagnosis (the final product, such as a cake). It has to be used with clinical and scientific judgment that take into account the whole picture of the patient's life circumstances and current functioning. Once a diagnostic label has been applied, the clinician can't lose sight of the unique individual factors that play into treatment and outcomes.

Revisiting the Biomedical and Biopsychosocial Models

Defining and classifying psychological disorders is an important and challenging task. Translation of these natural phenomena into scientific language provides an organizational structure for psychiatrists and psychologists to conduct research and discuss diagnoses in a systematic way. Psychological disorders can themselves be thought of as models that allow scientists and clinicians to usefully describe the huge range of psychological functioning human beings experience. The Biopsychosocial and biomedical approaches described in Lecture 1 offer competing perspectives for the understanding of psychological disorders.

George Engel developed original formulation of the Biopsychosocial (BPS) model in reaction to the dominance of the biomedical model in psychiatry. Recall that the biomedical model assumes that illness can be fully explained by biological processes. The biomedical model attributes psychological disorders to biological causes, with an emphasis on genetics and neurological functioning. The BPS model presents an alternative to the reductionism of the biomedical model. It rejects the idea that biological, psychological, and social processes can be neatly divided. According to the BPS model, biology alone cannot account for the intricacies of disease progression in an individual patient, even in cases where biology underlies the development of a psychological condition.

Psychiatry is perhaps the medical specialty that faced the greatest difficulties at the hands of the strict biomedical approach. The field eventually welcomed the alternative of the BPS model, yet the issue is far from settled. There are advantages and disadvantages to both perspectives. While greater attention is now given to the psychological and social factors that affect mental health, the search for biomedical explanations for psychological disorders has remained an important area of research. In the following sections, keep both the Biopsychosocial and biomedical perspectives in mind, and consider how each might be helpful in trying to understand the psychological disorders that are discussed.

The final sections of this lecture describe the major categories of psychological disorders that are required knowledge for the MCAT®. Each category has one or more defining characteristics that are shared by all disorders in that group. Consider the interplay between biological and psychological symptoms for each disorder. Recall that culture plays a role in the diagnosis of psychological disorders, as the clinician must draw upon cultural beliefs in determining whether certain psychological experiences are outside the norm.

Don't try to remember every detail! The MCAT® does not expect you to walk in with the advanced knowledge of a psychiatrist. You could see detailed information in a passage, but you just need to understand the major features of each category of psychological disorders. If a simplified description of a patient's symptoms is presented, practice the skill of selecting the corresponding type of disorder. Alternatively, a passage might present extra information about a specific disorder that is then used to test your understanding of associated mental and emotional processes that are required knowledge for the MCAT®.

Somatoform Disorders

Somatic symptom and related disorders demonstrate the advantages of an approach that incorporates psychological, biological, and social conditions. Somatoform disorders are characterized by bodily symptoms, such as pain, fatigue, and motor problems, along with associated psychological symptoms that cause significant problems for the individual. The disorders that fall under this category differ from other psychological disorders in that they are often first seen by clinicians who do not specialize in psychiatric care. The defining feature of somatic disorders is the psychological impairment that accompanies bodily symptoms, rather than the nature of the bodily experience. This is the new, modern understanding of somatic disorders. By contrast, the traditional approach emphasized the determination that biological causes could not explain the somatic symptoms. In general it is risky to diagnose a psychological disorder simply because a biological explanation cannot be found. One can imagine that the development of a new medical test could "cure" a patient's mental illness by diagnosing a physical illness! The traditional approach also neglected the psychological distress that can accompany somatic symptoms even when a biological cause can be found. The new approach puts the patient's experience of their illness at the forefront. Shifting focus to the presence of psychological symptoms increases the clarity of diagnoses and allows a better understanding of the relationship between biological and psychological factors.

Somatoform disorders include *Somatic Symptom Disorder, Illness Anxiety Disorder, Conversion Disorder,* and *Factitious Disorder,* among others. It is not necessary to memorize each of these disorders, but comfort with these terms may facilitate understanding of MCAT® passages. Somatic symptom disorder is characterized by a somatic symptom, such as pain, as well as significant anxiety about or preoccupation with that symptom. Illness anxiety disorder is similar but does not require a somatic symptom. Instead, this disorder is associated with excessive preoccupation with developing a serious illness or disorder. Conversion disorder is characterized by impairment in sensory or motor function that is not consistent with nerve damage. Although the symptoms are not neurological, they are not under the patient's conscious control and the patient experiences them as real. Factitious disorder is unlike the other disorders in this category in that the patient consciously fabricates symptoms.

Somatoform disorders can be difficult to identify and treat, particularly if clinicians believe in a rigid separation between body and mind. The new understanding of these disorders in the DSM-5 is intended to minimize counter-productive arguments about whether a patient's symptoms are caused by biological or psychological processes. A biomedical model only allows for a one-directional relationship between biology and psychology, where a biological disease leads to psychological effects, but the Biopsychosocial model allows for psychology and biology to each influence each other, as in somatoform disorders.

Anxiety Disorders

Anxiety disorders are defined by the experience of unwarranted fear and anxiety, physiological tension, and behaviors associated with the emotional and physical experience of anxiety. Anxiety is commonly connected to worries about future and hypothetical circumstances, rather than actual events in the present. It is often experienced in response to stress, which will be described in the following lecture. Somatoform disorders are the only type of psychological disorder defined by the presence of somatic symptoms, but other psychological disorders also have characteristic patterns of bodily symptoms. Anxiety disorders manifest physically

Nervous System
BIOLOGY 2

Endocrine System
BIOLOGY 2

as excessive sympathetic nervous system (SNS) activation, meaning that the body prepares for a "fight-or-flight" situation in the absence of an immediate threat. It is important to recognize that anxiety itself is not considered a disorder. Anxiety is a normal response to stress and can be advantageous in many instances. Only when anxiety becomes uncontrollable and unwarranted does a person have an anxiety disorder.

Anxiety disorders are categorized according to the type of stimulus that causes the emotional and physical symptoms. Knowledge of individual anxiety disorders is not required for the MCAT®, but it may be helpful to be aware of some that could appear in a passage. In *generalized anxiety disorder*, as the name implies, excessive, persistent anxiety is triggered by a wide variety of stimuli. *Panic disorder* involves the experience of frequent panic attacks, short-lived instances of overwhelming SNS activation and fear. During a panic attack, the physical symptoms may be so severe that the individual fears they will die. *Phobias* are characterized by excessive fear of a specific object or situation, as well as active attempts to avoid that stimulus.

Relationships and Behavior
PSYCH & SOC

Obsessive-Compulsive Disorders

Obsessive-compulsive disorder (OCD) is characterized by obsessions and compulsions. Obsessions are recurrent, intrusive thoughts. Compulsions are ritualistic or repetitive behaviors that serve the purpose of reducing anxiety associated with the obsessions. Individuals with OCD often recognize these behaviors as unreasonable and excessive. A common example of OCD is an obsession about germs and the resultant compulsive cleaning. In this example, the diagnosis of OCD is only warranted if the symptoms interfere with daily functioning. A doctor who washes his or her hands before and after seeing a patient does not have OCD, but a woman who is late to work every morning because she spends hours washing her hands likely does have OCD. OCD is usually responsive to treatment with medications and therapy.

It is important to distinguish OCD from obsessive-compulsive personality disorder (OCPD). OCPD is characterized by a preoccupation with lists, organization, and details. People with OCPD are often not distressed by their symptoms, though their symptoms may cause difficulties at work or in social interactions. In contrast, people with OCD experience significant anxiety about their symptoms.

Several other disorders fall under the same category as obsessive-compulsive disorder in the DSM 5: *body dysmorphic disorder, hoarding disorder, trichotillomania, and excoriation disorder.* Body dysmorphic disorder is characterized by a preoccupation with a perceived physical flaw, even though the individual looks relatively normal to others. Individuals with body dysmorphic disorder may seek plastic surgery to fix their perceived flaw, but they are rarely satisfied even after surgery. Hoarding disorder is characterized by a persistent difficulty disposing of belongings, regardless of their value. Belongings will often accumulate until living areas are cluttered and even unsafe. Trichotillomania and excoriation disorder are preoccupations with hair pulling and skin picking, respectively. These acts are often performed to relieve anxiety.

Nervous System
BIOLOGY 2

Trauma- and Stressor-Related Disorders

Posttraumatic stress disorder (PTSD) is a relatively common psychological disorder with an incidence of roughly 5%. Although frequently associated with a history of military combat, PTSD can be caused by exposure to any life-threatening or traumatic event. The event may be experienced, witnessed, or learned about through a third party. PTSD is associated with re-experiencing of the event through dreams, flashbacks, and even hallucinations. To avoid distress, people with PTSD may avoid certain "triggers" that are associated with the event. PTSD is thought to be an over-activation of the sympathetic nervous system and is often associated with symptoms of hyperarousal. These symptoms may include difficulty sleeping, hypervigilance, exaggerated startle response, and irritability.

Also under the category of trauma- and stressor-related disorders are *acute stress disorder and adjustment disorder.* Acute stress disorder is similar to PTSD, but the symptoms occur within a month of exposure to a trauma. Symptoms of acute stress disorder include extreme anxiety and dissociative symptoms. Adjustment disorder is the experience of extreme distress associated with a major life event or change, such as loss of a loved one.

Depressive Disorders

Mood disorders are a category of psychological disorders that deal with disruptions in emotion that influence personal functioning, much like anxiety disorders. However, depressive disorders are defined by two extremes, or poles, along the spectrum of emotional experience: extreme sadness and despair (depression) versus excitement so intense that it is detrimental to well-being (mania). Mood disorders are divided into two categories based on these two poles. Depressive disorders do not involve the manic end of the spectrum while bipolar disorders do.

Depressive disorders, which commonly share the name of depression, are defined by pervasive feelings of sadness and hopelessness and/or the loss of interest in activities that an individual usually enjoys. These core features of depression lead to lowered functioning in various spheres of everyday life. Although depression is defined by the emotional experience, a person who is depressed also experiences physical and cognitive symptoms, such as disruptions in sleep and eating, thoughts of suicide, and inability to concentrate. The severity and duration of the symptoms determine the actual diagnosis. *Major depressive disorder* is associated with more severe symptoms for a shorter period of time and is considered an episodic disorder. *Persistent depressive disorder* is associated with less severe symptoms, but they persist for longer periods of time, minimally two years.

Although social, emotional, and cognitive factors play a crucial role, much research has focused on identifying a biological basis of depression for the purpose of refining medical treatment of the disorder. Family studies have indicated the role of genetics, demonstrating a large increase in risk of depression when a first-degree relative has had it. The heritability of depression is found to be about 40%. Genetic inheritance appears to have a strong influence on depression (although the genetics seem to play a more significant role in the bipolar disorders and schizophrenia). This is not to say that genes have a deterministic effect. The genetic contribution to depression involves multiple genes, unlike the case of dominant-recessive disorders such as Huntington's disease, which involves a single genetic locus. This type of polygenetic influence is common to many psychological disorders. An individual may have higher or lower risk of depression depending on the array of genes they inherited. Some (but not all) of the genetic contribution to depression is mediated by the heredity of personality features, particularly neuroticism.

The biological malfunctioning found in depression involves the brain, as one might expect. Multiple areas of the brain have been found to have altered functioning in depression. Two ideas about neurological function and depression have been particularly influential. One is the *monoamine hypothesis*, which involves the monoamine neurotransmitters (serotonin, norepinephrine or noradrenaline, and dopamine). The monoamine hypothesis states that a deficiency in the availability or potency of monoamines in the synapses contributes to depression. Recall the multitude of processes that are involved in the transmission of an action potential. A misstep at any stage, such as reuptake or number of available receptors, can alter the amount of neurotransmitter in the synapse and its ability to carry out the desired effect on the post-synaptic neuron.

The monoamine hypothesis is was developed in response to the first successful pharmaceutical treatment of depression: monoamine oxidase inhibitors,

Even though anxiety disorders and depression have features in common and may be found in the same person, you can keep them straight by thinking of the disorders in terms of energy. Anxiety involves a hyper-alert state (think SNS activation!) while depression is characterized by a flattening of emotion and the feeling that normal tasks require extra effort.

Genetics
≡ BIOLOGY 1

Nervous System
≡ BIOLOGY 2

which inhibit the breakdown of monoamines, thereby increasing the availability of monoamines in the brain. Belmaker and Agam (2008) offer further support for the proposed involvement of monoamines on the development of depression. They found monoamine activity in widespread areas of the brain, including those that contribute to processes impacted by depression, such as thought and emotion. However, monoamine deficiency is not the only biological contributor to depression.

Another promising area of research involves the *hypothalamic-pituitary-adrenal (HPA) axis*. As described in the Endocrine System Lecture in the *Biology 2: Systems* manual, the nervous and endocrine systems interact to produce the body's response to stress. Recall that the hypothalamus releases a hormone that causes the anterior pituitary to release the hormone ACTH, which then triggers the release of cortisol by the adrenal cortex. The interactive process carried out by this group of structures is referred to as the HPA axis. Numerous studies have demonstrated elevated levels of one or more of the hormones involved in the HPA axis in individuals with depression, indicating that over-activation of this stress response system may contribute to the development of the disorder.

Bipolar Disorders

The bipolar disorders are characterized by episodes of mania and usually involve episodes of depression as well. Manic episodes may include uncontrollable impulses and reckless decisions. In addition, mania often involves a distortion of self-concept, where the self is viewed in an exaggeratedly positive light. In other words, self-esteem is hugely elevated. The individual's self-concept and other ideas may become distorted to the point of delusions, which are more commonly associated with psychotic disorders. *Psychotic disorders* are characterized by a loss of connection with reality, such as delusions or hallucinations. The bipolar disorders share features with both psychotic disorders and depressive disorders, but are classified as a distinct diagnostic category in the DSM-5.

There are two types of bipolar disorders: Bipolar I and Bipolar II. *Bipolar I disorder* is associated with mania that occurs in episodes lasting at least one week. When the mania is not present, a person may have a normal mood or may experience depression. *Bipolar II disorder* is associated with hypomania which is very similar to mania but does not cause impairment in functioning. A person with mania is often so detached from reality that he or she needs to be hospitalized. This is not common in hypomania. Like bipolar I disorder, bipolar II disorder may be mixed with periods of depression.

Schizophrenia

Schizophrenia is a debilitating and rare disorder that can have a wide variety of clinical presentations but is fundamentally characterized by psychosis, an impaired connection with reality. A patient with schizophrenia experiences at least one of the following core symptoms: hallucinations, delusions, and disorganized speech. A hallucination is a sensory perception that does not correspond to an actual event or object in the outside world. Hallucinations are most commonly auditory, and although they do not result from actual stimuli, they are correlated with neural activity in brain areas associated with hearing and language. A delusion also involves a disconnect from reality, but rather than a sensory experience, it is an unrealistic and unreasonable belief. Note that clinical judgment with attention to differing cultural norms is required to establish what constitutes a delusion. Someone who is delusional will hold onto their belief even in the face of strong evidence to the contrary. Finally, disorganized speech describes the inability to effectively communicate due to nonsensical trains of thought, responding inappropriately to others' speech, or other disruptions.

All of the symptoms described above are referred to as positive symptoms, meaning they are disturbances that add to or modify the individual's normal psy-

The question of what biological processes relate to depression is still very much a source of debate. The MCAT® may ask you to think critically about different hypotheses presented in a passage. Remember, no one biological factor is responsible for depression.

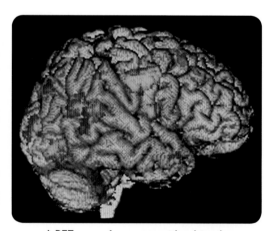

A PET scan of a person with schizophrenia who is experiencing auditory and visual hallucinations shows that the areas involved in processing sight and hearing are activated, just as they would be if the sensations were based on actual stimuli.

chological function (perception, belief, or communication). Schizophrenia also involves negative symptoms, which, in contrast, are characterized by absence. Negative symptoms often consist of lack of emotion, motivation, and enjoyment of activities. The presence and severity of negative symptoms predict poorer outcomes for individuals with schizophrenia.

Keep in mind the question of correlation versus causation. When differences in neurological functioning are observed in people with depression (or any other psychological disorder), you can't immediately jump to the conclusion that these abnormalities actually cause the disorder. Both the disorder and the altered neurological functioning could come from a common cause, or the disorder could cause the changes in the brain, rather than the other way around. Using experimental methods such as animal models of psychological disorders can help establish causality.

The biological basis of schizophrenia has been studied extensively. Genetic vulnerability is clearly a contributing factor, as the risk of schizophrenia is sharply elevated among close relatives compared to the general population. The level of risk is correlated to the degree of relatedness; siblings are at greater risk than cousins, for instance. Like depression, schizophrenia cannot be pinpointed to a single, specific genetic cause. Evidence suggests that many genes, each with a small effect, influence the development of schizophrenia. Some of the genetic alleles that have been associated with schizophrenia have also been implicated in bipolar disorder, indicating a genetic overlap between the disorders in addition to the symptomatic link described previously.

Note that genetic vulnerability to schizophrenia interacts with environmental influences. For example, certain complications in pregnancy can raise the likelihood of the development of schizophrenia for an individual who is genetically at risk.

The role of neurotransmitters in the development and experience of schizophrenia is the topic of much research. Although multiple neurotransmitters have been studied, dopamine has received the most attention. The study of neurotransmitter involvement in schizophrenia has been partly guided by the mechanism of drugs that are effective in treating the disorder. Drugs that block the receptors for dopamine were found to be useful as anti-psychotics, which inspired research on the possible involvement of dopamine in the disorder. Because dopamine levels are affected by anti-psychotics, dopamine is more closely associated to the positive symptoms of schizophrenia than the negative ones. Elevated dopamine is involved in the abnormalities in perception and thought that are associated with certain recreational drugs, providing further support for the role of dopamine in schizophrenia.

As described by Walker et al. (2003), schizophrenia has also been associated with significant structural abnormalities in the brain. In particular, multiple structures in the brains of people with schizophrenia are, on average, smaller than normal, perhaps indicating an inability to generate new neurons. Imaging studies have indicated that the atrophy of the brain exists prior to the onset of schizophrenia and continues to worsen over the course of the disorder.

A multitude of biological factors associated with schizophrenia have been studied- we could easily write a whole book about it! Schizophrenia is a complex disorder with a wide variety of symptomatic presentations that are associated with different genetic risk factors and neurological abnormalities. For the MCAT®, just remember the factors presented here: genetics, excess dopamine activity, and brain atrophy. Also realize that the development of schizophrenia involves an interaction between genetic predisposition and environmental factors.

Dissociative Disorders

The dissociative disorders are defined by the experience of dissociation: a split between different aspects of psychological functioning. Dissociation is experienced as a disruption in identity, memory, or consciousness. *Dissociative amnesia* occurs when a person forgets about past events. It is often associated with a traumatic experience. Like schizophrenia, the experience of dissociation can be understood in terms of positive and negative symptoms. The example of dissociative amnesia involves a negative symptom: the loss of a psychological function that is intact in healthy individuals (in this case, memory). Negative symptoms may go unnoticed to the individual with the disorder. By contrast, a positive symptom is an abnormal psychological experience that is disruptive to the individual. *Depersonalization/derealization disorder* is characterized by feelings that either the self or the surroundings are unreal and disconnected from the individual. This is a positive symptom. People with dissociative disorders have often had some type of traumatic experience, suggesting that dissociation serves the function of allowing the person to gain psychological distance from the trauma. For example, an individual with dissociative amnesia might lose conscious memory of a car wreck or the death of a parent.

One type of dissociative disorder that has been the subject of controversy is *dissociative identity disorder* (once called *multiple personality disorder)*. As both names suggest, dissociative identity disorder (DID) involves a significant disruption of stable identity. The individual experiences or displays evidence of multiple distinct personalities that can differ significantly in terms of traits and behaviors. Each different personality may also lack awareness of the other personalities. As described by Elzinga et al. (1998), following increased public awareness of the disorder in the late twentieth century, there were dramatic increases in both reported numbers of cases and the average number of personalities per patient, causing speculation that the disorder was being over diagnosed or even produced by the therapy itself. The sensational stories of recovered memories as patients become aware of their multiple personalities have also caused skepticism. Although dissociation has been associated with trauma, the extreme nature of the experiences described by DID patients has raised the question of whether the memories have been induced by therapists. This suspicion is bolstered by research that demonstrates that it is possible to cause people to form and believe in false memories. It seems likely that while the disorder may be valid, clinicians must exercise extreme caution to avoid inadvertently encouraging patients to develop symptoms of DID.

Personality Disorders

All of the disorders previously discussed are considered to be temporary states of psychological dysfunction, though in many cases they are chronic or recurring. By contrast, personality disorders, like personality itself, are defined by their tendency to endure across different situations and over the course of a lifetime. Personality disorders involve the development of personality traits that cause psychological and social dysfunction. Just as personality and identity development is particularly associated with adolescence, personality disorders are often first noticeable during that stage.

As the name suggests, the fundamental feature of all personality disorders is that some aspect of personality is psychologically unhealthy for the individual. However, multiple specific personality disorders have been defined according to the type of personality dysfunction. These disorders are not required knowledge for the MCAT®, although they could be described in a passage. This traditional method of categorically dividing personality disorders into clusters of specific characteristics, including disruptions in thought, emotion, and behavior associated with unhealthy personality functioning, may be revised in the future. The DSM-5 includes discussion of an alternative view of personality disorders, where they would be understood in a continuous rather than categorical way. Under this

---

It is important to realize that (as with all of the psychological disorders discussed!) culture must be considered in diagnosing dissociative disorders. Cultural norms and beliefs can affect both the presentation and diagnosis of dissociative disorders. For example, the reported experience of possession can be considered appropriate and typical in some cultures. In the United States, it can instead be taken as evidence for DID.

model, clinicians would come to a diagnosis by considering the specific pathological traits that characterize the individual, the specific types of personal and interpersonal functioning that are affected, and the severity of each. This diagnostic scheme could be more valid than the current method of strictly separating different personality disorders, since a large proportion of patients who meet the criteria for one disorder also have characteristics of other personality disorders. While this method was judged to be too complex for clinical usefulness, it may inspire a re-thinking of personality disorders in the future.

The changing ideas about personality disorders demonstrate once again the use of scientific models. Ongoing research and experience allow the evolution of models of psychological disorders, which have a practical significance for clinicians' decision-making.

Have a sense of these rates for the MCAT®. Think about it like MCAT® math. You won't be asked to decide whether 9.5% or 10.5% of Americans 18 and older experience a mood disorder in a given year, but you could be asked to choose between 3%, 10%, 30%, and 50%. Remember, the rates are drawn from studies that examine samples of the population, so they are not exact! Notice how rare schizophrenia is compared to the other disorders- partly because it is a single disorder, rather than a group such as the mood disorders.

TABLE 3.4 > Approximate 1-Year Prevalences of Psychological Disorders Among Americans 18 Years or Older

Disorder	Rate
Anxiety disorders	18%
Mood disorders	9.5%
Schizophrenia	1%
Personality disorders	9%

Question 65

Anxiety disorders are LEAST characterized by which of the following traits?

○ A. The experience of unwarranted fear
○ B. Worries about one's present circumstances
○ C. A physical manifestation of excessive sympathetic nervous system activation
○ D. The frequent experience of excessive responses to stress

Question 66

Which of the following psychological disorders is LEAST prevalent among Americans 18 years or older?

○ A. Anxiety disorders
○ B. Mood disorders
○ C. Schizophrenia
○ D. Personality disorders

Question 67

Somatic symptom and related disorders are best defined as:

○ A. psychiatric conditions defined by the psychological response to bodily symptoms.
○ B. mental illnesses that produce physical ailments.
○ C. disorders treated by clinicians that do not specialize in psychiatric care.
○ D. mental disorders presenting in situations that pose physical challenges.

Question 68

Which of the following is NOT true of depression?

○ A. It is considered a mood disorder.
○ B. It is associated with physical symptoms.
○ C. It is associated with altered neural functioning.
○ D. It is a heritable recessive phenotype.

Question 69

Which of the following psychological disorders has the strongest genetic component?

○ A. Schizophrenia
○ B. Generalized anxiety disorder
○ C. Depressive disorders
○ D. Dissociative identity disorder

Question 70

Which of the following statements is (are) true regarding schizophrenia?

    I. Expression of schizophrenia involves an interaction between genotype and environment.

    II. In order to be diagnosed with schizophrenia, one must exhibit hallucinations, delusions, or disorganized speech.

    III. Schizophrenia is associated with excess dopamine activity.

○ A. I only
○ B. II only
○ C. II and III
○ D. I, II, and III

Question 71

Which of the following is NOT considered a negative symptom?

○ A. Lack of motivation
○ B. Feeling out of touch with others
○ C. Hallucinations
○ D. Having little emotion

Question 72

Which of the following are psychiatric conditions that are defined by their tendency to endure temporally and across different situations?

○ A. Psychological disorders
○ B. Personality disorders
○ C. Dissociative disorders
○ D. Somatoform disorders

Age

Anxiety disorders

Attribution theory

Behaviorist theory

Biological basis of depression

Biological basis of schizophrenia

Biological theory

Biomedical

Biopsychosocial

Bipolar disorders

Class

Classification of psychological disorders

Conventional level

Culture

Demographics

Depression

Depressive disorders

Different types of identities

Dispositional attribution

Dissociative disorders

Erik Erikson

Freud's theory of developmental stages

Fundamental attribution error

Gender

Heredity

How culture affects attributions

Humanistic theory

Identity

Imitation

In-group

Influence of culture and socialization

Influence of individuals

Kohlberg's theory of moral development

Lev Vygotsky

Locus of control

Mood disorders

Observational learning

Obsessive-compulsive disorder

Out-group

Perceptions of the environment

Personality

Personality disorders

Postconventional level

Psychoanalytic theory

Psychological disorders

Preconventional level

Post-traumatic stress disorder (PTSD)

Race/ethnicity

Reference group

Role-taking

Schizophrenia

Self-actualization

Self-concept

Self-efficacy

Self-esteem

Self-serving bias

Sexual orientation

Situational approach to explaining behavior

Situational attribution

Social cognitive theory

Social groups

Social identity

Socialization

Somatic symptom and related disorders

Stress

Temperament

The influence of our self-perceptions

Trait theory

Traits

Trauma and Stressor related disorders

Twin studies

DON'T FORGET YOUR KEYS

1. Personality is made up of internal characteristics that influence behavior.

2. Identity is one's view of self in relation to the world.

3. Psychological disorders are culturally defined and occur in the context of social, biological, and psychological factors.

Thought and Emotion

4.1 Introduction

4.2 Cognition

4.3 Language

4.4 Intellectual Functioning

4.5 Problem Solving

4.6 Emotion

4.7 Motivation and Attitudes

4.8 Stress

THE 3 KEYS

1. Thought and emotion are internal processes of mental life that affect observable external behaviors.

2. Motivation uses thought and emotion to translate need into behavior.

3. Attitudes and behavior each influence the other and are crucial entry points for change.

4.1 | Introduction

This lecture will discuss several major psychological processes as they affect behavior: cognition, emotion, motivation, and attitudes. Beginning with an examination of cognitive development, the lecture will explore the biological, cultural, and individual factors that influence the development of cognitive abilities and intelligence. The MCAT® emphasizes the confluence and interplay of these factors. The lecture will then consider the cognitive and problem solving strategies that people employ, as well as common barriers to effective problem solving and decision making. This section will show that all human problem solving strategies have strengths and weaknesses—there is no perfect system. An understanding of these strategies (and the mistakes associated with them) is essential to exploring decision making by patients and physicians in the medical environment. The next portion of the lecture will focus on emotion, including its relationship with biology and cognition. Motivation and attitudes will be considered as they are influenced by thought and emotion. The MCAT® will focus on the link between motivation, attitudes, and health behaviors. Finally, the lecture will conclude with a look at stress as both adaptive and maladaptive, that is to say, both helpful and harmful.

The concepts discussed in this lecture are crucial to the practice of medicine, which requires constant examination of a patient's internal state and external environment. Understanding the patient's world and then offering an empathic and sensitive response are critical to good doctoring. Both diagnosis and treatment depend on an understanding of symptoms as they are embedded in the context of social systems, habits of mind, and ways of living. Patients' physical and emotional lives are inseparable. It is essential for doctors to understand thought and emotion in order to interpret and respond to each case effectively.

Consider Key 1: Cognition is an internal process that affects behavior. Cognition is an ability present in humans and only a few other mammals. Our brains are uniquely able to use cognitive processes to analyze information about the environment and decide the best way to respond. Cognitive skills allow you to power through MCAT® questions!

Some people argue that cognition is a form of behavior. But for the sake of the MCAT®, think of cognition (and emotion) as internal processes that influence external behavior. Use your intuitive understanding of thought to understand cognition: thought and cognition are roughly the same thing.

The next lecture will discuss serial and parallel processing in the context of perception, and will also consider an information processing model of memory.

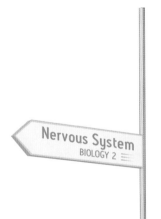

Roughly speaking, the front half of the cortex (the frontal lobe) sends motor instructions and other types of output to the body, while the back half (the other three lobes) receives sensory input from the body and sends it to the frontal lobe for further processing.

4.2 | Cognition

How do people come to understand their surroundings? How do they make decisions and solve problems? This section will consider the development and application of various types of cognition. Cognition refers to a wide range of internal mental activities, such as analyzing information, generating ideas, and problem solving. While perception refers to the organization and identification of sensory inputs, cognition refers to higher-level processes like language and logical reasoning.

A cognitive psychological perspective views the mind as a computer. For both minds and computers, input and processing can be viewed as the two steps that determine output. The brain receives a stimulus input, processes the stimulus, and selects an output function. Along the way, people can draw on prior knowledge, including stored memories, to make decisions and solve problems. Computer-like models of cognitive functioning are called information-processing models. Information-processing models focus on input-output functions and distinguish between serial and parallel processing of information: as the name implies, serial processing considers each input one at a time, while parallel processing devotes cognitive resources to multiple inputs at once.

The computer analogy is also relevant in that the brain employs different areas for processing different types of information. Information processing takes place in the cerebral cortex, which is the most recently evolved part of the brain. The cerebral cortex can be divided into four lobes: from the front of the brain to the back, the frontal, parietal, occipital, and temporal lobes. The frontal lobe is associated with motor control, decision making, and long-term memory storage. The other three lobes carry out various types of sensory processing: tactile information in the parietal lobe, which contains the somatosensory cortex; visual information in the occipital lobe; and auditory and olfactory information in the temporal lobe. The temporal lobe is also associated with emotion and language, as discussed later in this lecture, and memory formation, which will be discussed in the following lecture.

FIGURE 4.1 | Lobes of the Cerebral Cortex

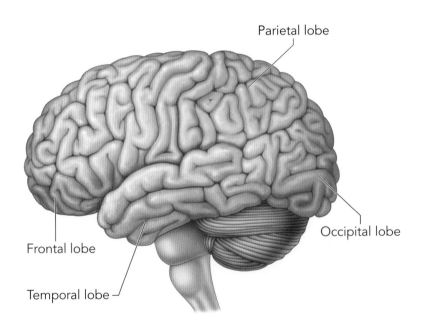

It is important to remember that the computer analogy for information processing is only a *model*. Recall from Lecture 1 that models enable simplified discussion of complex processes but are not perfect representations.

There is a vast body of literature on the various algorithms and strategies that people employ (both consciously and unconsciously) to understand the environment, make decisions, and solve problems. First, take a step back and think about how humans develop their capacity for complex thought. Just like identity, discussed in the previous lecture, cognition develops over the course of a lifetime. At the most basic level, it is obvious that infants do not think the same way that adults do. So what happens to enable the development of understanding, logical information processing, and adult cognition?

Piaget's Theory of Cognitive Development

The field of *developmental psychology* examines psychological and behavioral change across the human lifespan. Early developmental psychology was based on a supposed dichotomy of *nature versus nurture*. Some psychologists argued that children's personality and cognitive abilities were innate and predetermined (*nature*), while other psychologists believed that children's experiences with environmental factors such as parenting and community shaped children's development (*nurture*). Jean Piaget was one of the first developmental psychologists to reconcile these two previously opposing ideas into an integrated theory of child development.

Piaget observed that children developed cognitively by experimenting with their environment. The "results" of experimentation can then be fitted by the child into preexisting *schemas*, mental representations or frameworks of the world, in a process he called *assimilation*. Alternatively, if the new information does not fit into any previously held schemas, the child's schemas are changed in response to the new information, which Piaget called *accommodation*. To Piaget, the goal of this process is to develop accurate mental representations of the world.

The *nature versus nurture* debate extends across multiple disciplines. In medicine, we discuss the interaction between innate genetic inheritance (*nature*) and environmental factors (*nurture*). To what extent do genetic traits and sun exposure account for a patient's development of skin cancer? As in psychology, genetic predisposition and environmental contributions both play a role.

For some of his early study of infant development, Piaget used his own three children as research subjects. As you can imagine, his findings may have been compromised as a result: the sample size was tiny; he may have inadvertently conditioned his children to perform his tasks "correctly"; as the children's parent, he had enormous influence on their behavior and lacked the perspective of an empirical researcher; and his subjects were genetically and experientially similar to each other. All of these potential confounds raise issues about the validity of his data and the generalizability of his findings.

Research Skills
REASONING SKILLS

While you might think you learned the law of conservation of mass from chemistry, your brain gained the ability to understand this concept sometime during the concrete operational stage. Piaget demonstrated conservation by having children pour water from a tall, thin glass into a shorter, wider glass. Children who say that there is more water in the taller, thinner glass don't yet understand conservation.

Perhaps Piaget's most notable contribution to developmental psychology is his theory of four universal stages of cognitive development. Piaget proposed that all children pass through the same set of discrete cognitive developmental stages, including particular milestone achievements, at the same ages on their way to maturity. This *stage theory* perspective is in contrast to *continuous theories* that view development as constant and gradual, such as Vygotsky's theory of development (discussed further in the following section).

Recent work has shown that young children are more capable cognitively than Piaget believed and that the stages are not uniform across different cultures. However, Piaget contributed an important framework upon which later developmental psychologists could build. Piaget's four stages are:

1. Sensorimotor (birth to 2 years): Children learn to separate themselves from objects. They recognize their ability to act on and affect the outside world, and learn that things continue to exist even when they are out of sight—this understanding is called *object permanence.*

2. Preoperational (2 to 7 years): Children learn to use language while they continue to think very literally. They maintain an *egocentric* (self-centered) world-view and have difficulty taking the perspective of others.

3. Concrete Operational (7 to 11 years): Children become more logical in concrete thinking. They develop *inductive reasoning*, meaning that they can reason from specific situations to general concepts. (The reverse, *deductive reasoning*, is not yet developed.) They come to understand the idea of *conservation*—the concept that a quantity remains the same despite changes in its shape or container.

4. Formal Operational (11 years and older): Children develop the ability to think logically in the abstract. They develop *deductive reasoning* skills—the ability to apply general concepts in specific situations—and they learn to think theoretically and philosophically. Children and adolescents who have reached the formal operational stage are capable of achieving what Kohlberg referred to as post-conventional moral reasoning. Recall from Lecture 3 that this means they are able to help others and/or act morally despite danger or consequences. In fact, Kohlberg intentionally drew upon and expanded Piaget's work in his own development of a theory of moral stages.

On the MCAT® and in your medical career, being able to draw from multiple competing theories may allow you to find a useful approach to a situation. A pediatrician may use a stage theory perspective to quickly check if a child has reached age-appropriate milestones during a check-up. A continuous approach would allow the physician to consider both the child's growth across time and the rate of improvement in a more thorough and focused exam of cognitive progress.

Culture and Cognitive Development

While Piaget initially presented his four stages as universal—as though ALL typically-developing children passed through these milestones at specific ages—critics of his theory asserted that expectations and cultural context affected children's performance on his experimental tasks. Piaget later revised his theory to allow for some contextual effects.

As discussed in Lecture 3, the psychologist Lev Vygotsky proposed a contrasting theory to Piaget's, asserting that societal factors, such as parents, peers, and cultural beliefs, are essential factors in children's developmental progress. Piaget thought that children's curiosity and discoveries were largely *self*-initiated; Vygotsky pointed to the importance of social learning through caregivers and peers. Sociocultural theories like that of Vygotsky emphasize that development is more complex than the singular, internally driven process originally presented by Piaget.

A classic example of the role of culture in cognitive development emerges in the way that children think about objects. Children in Western cultures are generally object-focused, while those raised in Eastern cultures are more relationally focused. When asked to describe a fish tank, Western children will spend their time talking about the one brightly colored fish in the tank, while Eastern children tend to discuss the fish in relation to the tank, the water, and the room around the tank. As demonstrated by this example, cognitive processes have a cultural context, where assumptions and expectations are embedded in culturally normative thought.

Think about cross cultural differences as analogous to the differences between traditional Eastern and Western medicine. Traditionally, Eastern medicine is holistic and emphasizes the relationship of mind and body as co-factors of health, while Western medicine takes a more concrete, symptom-based, compartmentalized approach.

 ## Language

As children develop an inner understanding of the world around them, they simultaneously develop a way to express themselves through language. The way in which people develop language across time is universal. However, there is debate about how people acquire syntax rules and grammar. Three major theories attempt to explain this process. Each theory approaches language development from a different place on the continuum of nature versus nurture. Learning theorists emphasize environmental factors, nativists describe language as part of human nature, and interactionists take a middle ground.

1. The learning theory of language development (also known as the *behaviorist theory*) argues that language is a form of behavior and is learned through operant conditioning. According to this theory, put forth by B. F. Skinner, children receive reinforcement such as excitement and kisses when they make correct vocalizations, like saying "ma" to their mother, and punishment, like less maternal attention, when they do not. As language development advances, the behaviors that are reinforced or punished become increasingly specific. Learning theory assumes that language develops through continuing interaction with environmental reinforcement, rather than focusing on innate ability.

2. The nativist theory of language development emphasizes innate biological mechanisms and was developed in the context of criticism of the behaviorist explanation. The linguist Noam Chomsky, who developed the nativist theory, pointed out that children developed language even without systematic feedback from parents, as in orphanages where children had significantly less adult contact or in homes where parents did not speak the dominant language. Instead, nativist theorists propose that language development is innately human, and that all people have a neural cognitive system, the *language acquisition device*, which allows for learning of syntax and grammar.

3. The interactionist theory emphasizes the role of social interaction in language acquisition. The interactionist theory argues that the human brain develops so that it can be receptive to new language input and development, and children are motivated to practice and expand their language base in order to communicate and socialize.

Strong language skills are essential to your medical career. Your ability to understand and communicate with patients determines success in one of the first and most fundamental arts you will learn in medical school—taking a patient history. To further emphasize the importance of language in your future career, the AAMC has named oral communication as one of its core competencies.

Relationships and Behavior
PSYCH & SOC

Influence of Language on Thought

Research has shown that people who speak different languages have distinct thought patterns. Language provides a tool for organizing and manipulating thought, affecting aspects of cognition that include the following: specificity versus generality of thought about certain concepts, how and whether abstract ideas are understood, and how social connections and structures are understood. Language both determines and limits how we experience and view the world.

Certain languages allow more or less specificity in various domains, which in turn influences how people think about and frame their knowledge and experience of the world. For example, several Inuit and Scandinavian dialects have many words for "snow." As a result, snow can be discussed and thought about in a very specific manner, according to the different types of snow that can be named in that language. Further, language allows for the understanding, expression, and discussion of abstract concepts. It would be impossible for disciplines such as philosophy or psychology to exist without language as an intellectual and emotional medium. Finally, language influences social interaction by framing thought about ourselves and others. Differences in the use of personal pronouns, such as whether or not words like "I" and "me" are used, lead to differences in social relationships. Language is one medium that allows for the development of meaningful social connection and empathy.

> The fact that distinct languages lead to distinct patterns in thinking is similar to the effect of culture on cognition, discussed previously. However, there is an important difference: it is the structure of language patterns rather than features of the associated culture, that influences thought processes.

FIGURE 4.2 | Interdependence of Language and Thought

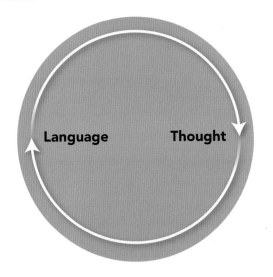

MCAT® THINK

Recall the discussion of the Diagnostic and Statistical Manual (DSM) in the previous lecture. The names of the psychological disorders affect how they are thought of by physicians and patients. More generally, the negative language of "*ill*ness" and "*dis*order" perpetuates a certain way of thinking about and experiencing mental and physical health issues. Simple linguistic changes like using person-first language—a "person diagnosed with schizophrenia" rather than "a schizophrenic"—can potentially ease the stigma associated with mental illness. Some cultures use very different language to describe health issues, including terms that suggest spiritually elevated states rather than disordered conditions.

Neural Basis of Language

Language can be localized to specific areas in the brain. Most of the brain's language processing occurs in the left hemisphere of the cerebral cortex. There are two significant areas associated with language:

1. **Broca's area** is located in the frontal lobe, and is primarily involved in speech production. When patients experience damage to this area, they have difficulty enunciating and speaking fluently, but their ability to understand the language of others is unaffected – a condition known as *Broca's aphasia* or *expressive aphasia*. A person with Broca's aphasia would be able to follow commands but would have trouble producing speech.

2. **Wernicke's area** is found in the temporal lobe, and contributes primarily to the understanding of language. Patients with damage to Wernicke's area can hear words and repeat them back, but cannot understand the words' meaning. This condition is called *Wernicke's aphasia* or *receptive aphasia*. A person with Wernicke's aphasia would not be able to follow commands, and although he or she could produce words, they would sound like nonsense sentences with no comprehensible meaning.

Both the understanding and production of speech are critical to effective verbal communication.

| FIGURE 4.3 | Language Areas of the Brain

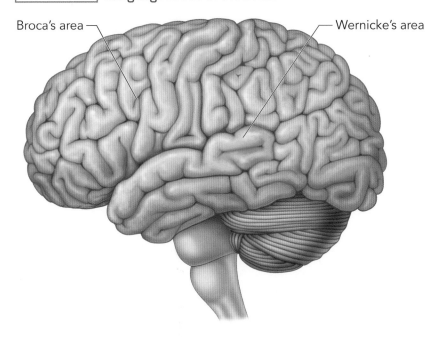

Broca's area — Wernicke's area

These "language areas" were initially discovered by studying patients with brain damage, and then performing autopsies following their deaths. Only recently have brain functions been localized in vivo using techniques such as fMRI.

Question 73

Engaging in conversation involves which of the following?

- ○ **A.** Cognition only
- ○ **B.** Perception only
- ○ **C.** Both cognition and perception
- ○ **D.** Neither cognition nor perception

Question 74

Which of the following best represents the sequential activation of brain regions involved as a student views a piece of artwork, formulates an opinion about it, and then delivers an oral presentation about this opinion?

- ○ **A.** Occipital lobe, frontal lobe, frontal lobe
- ○ **B.** Parietal lobe, occipital lobe, frontal lobe
- ○ **C.** Occipital lobe, frontal lobe, occipital lobe
- ○ **D.** Frontal lobe, occipital lobe, parietal lobe

Question 75

A child playing in the sink empties a short, wide glass of water into a tall, thin glass of equal volume. Questioning revealed that the child believed the tall glass contained more water. This indicates that she has not yet reached which of Piaget's stages?

- ○ **A.** Sensorimotor
- ○ **B.** Preoperational
- ○ **C.** Concrete operational
- ○ **D.** Logical operational

Question 76

A scientist states that a child's brain develops in a way that facilitates social reinforcement of language skills. This assertion most closely represents which theory of language development?

- ○ **A.** The learning theory
- ○ **B.** The cognitive theory
- ○ **C.** The nativist theory
- ○ **D.** The interactionist theory

Question 77

Which of the following LEAST demonstrates a way in which language affects cognition?

- ○ **A.** A new language is developed that only contains gender-neutral pronouns.
- ○ **B.** Speakers of a language with a highly developed vocabulary for blue colors have enhanced recall of the particular shade of various blue colored objects.
- ○ **C.** A vocabulary for a new field of ethics makes ethical constructs easier to understand.
- ○ **D.** The Australian language Guugu Yimithirr lacks relative directions (e.g. left, ahead); speakers of this language express all spatial relationships in terms of cardinal directions (e.g. North, West).

Question 78

A stroke patient presents with the inability to produce and understand speech, but can produce and process other auditory cues. The patient most likely has lesions in which of the following region(s)?

- ○ **A.** Broca's area only
- ○ **B.** Wernicke's area only
- ○ **C.** Both Broca's area and Wernicke's area
- ○ **D.** Neither Broca's area nor Wernicke's area

Question 79

Which of the following best describes a serial information processing model of cognition?

- ○ **A.** A child simultaneously hears a dinner bell and recognizes that it is dinner time, decides to walk home, and then walks home.
- ○ **B.** A child hears a dinner bell, recognizes that the bell signifies that dinner is to be served, and then walks home.
- ○ **C.** A child hears a dinner bell and then walks home.
- ○ **D.** A child thinks of cereal and then walks home.

4.4 | Intellectual Functioning

What does it mean to be intelligent? Is intelligence synonymous with high academic achievement? With creativity? Psychologists have not come to a consensus on a single definition of intelligence, but an examination of the various arguments can demonstrate how intelligence has been studied and quantified.

Multiple Definitions of Intelligence

Intelligence can be defined as the ability to understand and reason with complex ideas, adapt effectively to the environment, and learn from experience. The commonly-employed *Wechsler Adult Intelligence Scale*, which evolved from the earlier *Stanford-Binet* scale, contains a verbal scale and a performance scale. Scores from the two scales are synthesized to yield one IQ (intelligence quotient) score. The intent of IQ is to predict school performance, so it correlates strongly with school-related skills, like math and verbal skills, but has lower correlations with other skills such as art and design. The average IQ is defined as 100, and every 15 points above or below this average score represents one standard deviation above or below the mean. IQ scores in the population fall along a continuum, and a below-average IQ is said to represent a *general learning disability*.

There are some distinct advantages to using the conventional IQ test: it is relatively simple to administer, provides scores that are easy to compare, and has proven to correlate with academic performance. However, it is less useful in predicting later career success or advancement. There are also distinct weaknesses to the IQ test. Standard IQ tests show a cultural bias, so minorities tend to score lower than their white counterparts. Furthermore, the single number score can be misleading when the test is used to diagnose learning disability, either by unnecessarily labeling someone as "not intelligent" and thereby harming confidence and intellectual drive, or by not accurately depicting the needs of a child in order for them to qualify for special education or government aid.

Some psychologists posit that every individual has a set level of intelligence that applies to all of their intellectual pursuits and determines performance on various types of intelligence tests, regardless of the specific subscales. This construct has been termed g, or *general intelligence factor*. The g factor is most frequently associated with Charles Spearman, although others have advanced the construct. General intelligence can be divided into two types of intelligence. *Fluid intelligence* is the ability to think logically without the need for previously learned knowledge (e.g., detecting visual patterns); it peaks in young adulthood and then declines. *Crystallized intelligence* is the ability to think logically using specific, previously learned knowledge (facts, vocabulary, etc.), which remains stable throughout adulthood.

Howard Gardner's *theory of multiple intelligences* argues in direct opposition to the notion of g. Gardner proposed that everyone has a variety of intelligences that are used in combination to solve problems and perform tasks. According to Gardner, each individual has a different level of intelligence for each of the following domains: *linguistic intelligence*, *musical intelligence*, *logical-mathematical intelligence*, *spatial intelligence*, *bodily-kinesthetic intelligence*, and *interpersonal intelligence*.

Sternberg's triarchic theory provides an alternative view of multiple intelligences, stating that thought processes, experience, and cultural environment interact to yield a person's intelligence. Specifically, he believed that intelligence emerges from a person's adaptive abilities, and he provided three factors that he believed comprised intelligence: *analytical intelligence*, which refers to problem solving abilities; *creative intelligence*, which describes the ability to handle new situations using existing skills and experiences; and *practical intelligence*, which involves the ability to respond to environmental changes.

> Keep in mind that the construct of "intelligence" can be defined in different ways depending on the usefulness of each definition in a given situation. Some theories take a singular, specific approach (as with g and traditional IQ testing), while others stress the significance of multiple factors (notably Gardner and Sternberg). Flexibility in your ability to think about concepts like intelligence will be rewarded on the MCAT®.

Effective doctoring depends on emotional intelligence. The ability to perceive and understand one's own emotions and the emotions of others allows for effective communication and treatment.

Emotional Intelligence

Emotional intelligence, distinct from the types of intelligence considered above, has emerged in recent years as an important correlate of psychological and physical health. Emotional intelligence is understood to have four components:

1. *Perceiving emotions*: Recognizing others' emotions via body language or situational cues and identifying one's own emotions, such as recognizing chronic physiological arousal as a sign of anxiety.

2. *Using and reasoning with emotions*: The ability to employ emotions for cognitive ends.

3. *Understanding emotions*: The ability to correctly attribute emotions, both one's own and those of others, to a particular source.

4. *Managing emotions*: Regulating emotion by knowing when and to what degree to react in an emotionally-charged situation.

Emotional intelligence is essential to effective doctoring. Physicians must be able to identify the emotion and affect of patients, while remaining attuned to their own emotional states which have the potential to impact their behavior. Doctors need to be able to determine the root causes of their emotions, and most importantly, they must be able to manage their emotions in the often emotionally-charged environment of the hospital. The study of emotional intelligence illustrates the necessity of strong psychological skills for a career in medicine.

Influence of Heredity and Environment on Cognition and Intelligence

As mentioned earlier in the discussion of *nature versus nurture*, both heredity and the environment influence cognitive development and intellectual ability. Twin studies, described in Lecture 3, allow researchers to tease apart the individual effects of genetics and environment. Multiple twin studies have found that identical twins raised in the same home have highly correlated IQs. The IQs of identical twins raised in different homes are somewhat less correlated, and the IQs of fraternal twins raised in the same home are even less correlated. This research highlights the genetic component of IQ, as it indicates that identical twins with the same genes raised in different environments tend to have greater similarity in IQ scores than fraternal twins with different genes who were raised in the same home environment. However, it also demonstrates environmental effects in that identical twins raised in the same home have more highly correlated IQs than those raised in different homes.

Hereditary Influences: In some cases of below-average IQ, the general learning disability can be traced to a genetic disorder. One example is phenylketonuria, in which children are unable to metabolize phenylalanine, causing a damaging build-up in the body and brain. Even when a trait has high heritability, change is still possible. When children with phenylketonuria are provided a diet without foods containing phenylalanine until maturity, intellectual development is normal. Some chromosomal disorders, such as Down syndrome and Fragile X syndrome, also affect IQ. Finally, as demonstrated by the twin study described above, IQ is a highly heritable trait.

Environmental Influences: The prenatal (in utero) environment can have a lasting impact on cognitive and intellectual abilities. Both acute and chronic conditions affecting a pregnant woman can lead to general learning disability in the child. Examples include the acute contraction of rubella, herpes, or syphilis, or the chronic conditions of diabetes or high blood pressure. Maternal drug use or alcohol consumption can contribute to intellectual impairment.

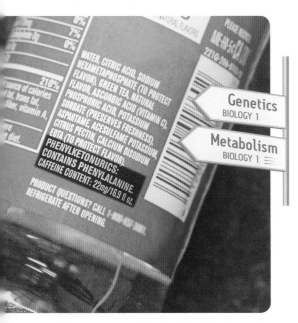

Children with phenylketonuria have to avoid the amino acid phenylalanine in order to prevent brain damage.

Of course, postnatal factors contribute as well. Childhood socioeconomic status (SES) significantly influences children's cognitive development. According to a 1997 study by Drs. Stipek & Ryan, children from disadvantaged families are less academically skilled than their more economically privileged peers from when they first enter school, and they often lag cognitively and academically throughout their education. There are many factors that potentially contribute to the effect of low SES on IQ, including increased lead exposure, poorly funded schools, racial tensions, and less parental involvement in children's education.

4.5 | Problem Solving

A primary purpose of thinking is to guide behavior. The vast cognitive abilities of humans are often applied through complex decision making and strategies for problem solving, processes that are among the executive functions associated with the frontal lobe. The MCAT® will test knowledge of both successful problem solving strategies and common errors in problem solving and decision making.

Approaches to Problem Solving

Problem solving strategies can be divided into two major categories—those that are exhaustive but not necessarily efficient, and those that are efficient mental "short-cuts" but may not yield the complete spectrum of potential solutions. Factors like emotion and confidence level affect the ways that people approach problems and arrive at solutions. Several prominent problem solving strategies and potential hindrances to effective problem solving are outlined below.

One strategy is the use of an algorithm, which is a step-by-step procedure that leads to a definite solution. Due to the exhaustive nature of this technique, it is not always the most efficient. The quadratic formula is an algorithm that will always lead to the correct solution of x, while factoring is a simpler method but cannot always produce the answer.

Analogies allow a new problem to be reduced to a previously known problem, where prior knowledge of how to determine the solution can be applied. An analogical problem solving method reduces a new, complex problem to a set of simpler problems that can be solved by familiar methods.

The trial and error method of problem solving is characterized by repeated, unsystematic attempts to solve a problem until the desired outcome is achieved. This method will eventually be successful but is very inefficient.

Heuristics are mental shortcuts or "rules of thumb" that often lead to a solution (but not always!). They can be helpful and timesaving. However, heuristics can potentially lead problem solving efforts astray.

The use of intuition in problem solving is based on personal perception or feeling rather than logic. Consider the "mind as a computer" information processing model: intuition does not follow this kind of stepwise, logical process. Rather, it is the "gut feeling" that leads to a quick but potentially flawed solution, much like a heuristic. Researchers have suggested that intuition is neurologically algorithmic, but not at a conscious level.

The problem solving techniques described above have interesting applications in the world of medical diagnosis. When a patient presents with a certain set of symptoms, an exhaustive set of tests may be used to rule out alternative diagnoses and to arrive at a definitive diagnosis. This process is an example of an algorithmic strategy. However, in some cases physicians may decide they cannot wait for a battery of tests to be completed. They can employ a similarity heuristic, such as prescribing immediate antibiotic therapy if the symptoms resemble a serious infection, in order to halt an infection's progression, and then work through the full differential diagnosis more closely.

Trying all possible combinations on a locker until you guess the correct one will take a lot longer than cutting the lock!

By employing the similarity heuristic, you can decide if you will like a new book based on whether you have enjoyed similar books in the past.

Barriers to Effective Problem Solving

The downside of a heuristic is that it may lead to overgeneralization. Consider the example of the *representativeness heuristic*, which is used to make an educated guess about the probability of an event or characteristic based on prior knowledge. The following description illustrates the potentially misleading nature of the representativeness heuristic: *Maggie is very knowledgeable about gourmet food and wine. She hosts elaborate dinner parties for friends and colleagues, and is known to be strongly opinionated.* When asked whether Maggie is a food critic or a teacher, the majority of people would say food critic because the qualities described are representative of the "food critic" category. However, teachers so greatly outnumber food critics that the probability of Maggie being a teacher is actually much higher, despite the existence of qualities that are similar to those of a food critic.

> ## MCAT® THINK
>
> In his book *How Doctors Think*, Dr. Jerome Groopman argues that heuristics play an important role in medical decision-making and diagnosis but can also lead to faulty problem solving. He points to the example of the *availability heuristic*, where a person, in this case a physician, assigns high likelihood to an event or characteristic simply because it is highly "available" to conscious thought. In the medical setting, the availability heuristic can show itself as a physician's increased likelihood of making a particular diagnosis that he or she has seen many times recently, even if another (unavailable) diagnosis is more likely to be correct. A growing body of literature considers the cognitive processes of doctoring, to prevent medical errors and improve care. Dr. Atul Gawande has written about ways to compensate for cognitive errors in patient care.

Cognitive biases are various tendencies to think in particular ways, which can be helpful but can also inhibit problem solving abilities. *Functional fixedness*, a tendency to view objects as having only a single function, can be useful but can also stifle creativity, depending on the context. For example, it is almost always helpful to think of the primary function of a hammer and nails when faced with a picture frame that needs to be hung. However, this functional fixedness makes it difficult to think of other potential uses for the objects when faced with a less traditional problem.

Another type of bias is the *confirmation bias*: people tend to value new information that supports a belief they already hold, while they often disregard information that goes against their preconceived notions. This is related to the phenomenon of belief perseverance, in which people hold on to their initial beliefs, even when rational argument would suggest that they are incorrect.

Overconfidence can be an example of belief perseverance: in this case, information that should logically undermine confidence to some extent is overlooked. There is a tipping point at which overconfidence can lead to negative outcomes, including faulty problem solving. That said, confidence in one's own abilities is generally a positive trait. Due to *response expectancy*, confidence can serve as a self-fulfilling prophecy. There is some truth to the "fake it till you make it" strategy. Some evolutionary psychologists have argued that confidence is evolutionarily advantageous. Overall, the benefits of confidence fall along a confidence curve, where a medium level of confidence is most beneficial and extremely low or high confidence may be harmful.

Another bias to be aware of is *causation bias*, which is the tendency to assume a cause and effect relationship. As discussed in the Research and Reasoning Skills Lecture, correlation does not necessarily mean causation. When taking a patient

---

The optimal level of confidence is analogous to biological homeostasis. For many physiological factors, a hormone brings the system back to its set point. Too much OR too little is maladaptive; too much OR too little confidence is also maladaptive.

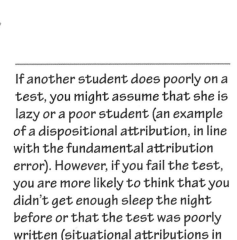

I believe that I am an ideal romantic partner, so I dismiss relationship foibles and failures that conflict with this belief as a fluke—in other words, I experience belief perseverance. Because I disregard evidence of my flaws that contradicts my belief, I am overconfident and miss important opportunities to improve.

history, it is important to be able to think critically about multiple symptoms that emerge concurrently or immediately following patients' behavioral changes or life events. The symptoms may or may not be related to one another and/or to the external factor, but causation bias can lead to premature assumptions of a causal relationship. Faulty decision making and problem solving often occur as a result of fundamental attribution error. As described in the previous lecture, this is a tendency to attribute others' actions to internal factors like personality, rather than external circumstances. In a related effect, we tend to attribute our own actions to external circumstances according to the self-serving bias. These two types of bias often work in tandem, leading to faulty judgment.

Emotions can also pose a barrier to effective problem solving. Decision making and problem solving abilities can be affected by one's emotional state at the time of the decision or by the anticipation of certain emotions that may come about as a result of the outcome of that decision. Being able to predict an emotional response to a particular solution or outcome can be positive in many situations. However, negative emotions can interfere with cognitive abilities and problem solving efficiency and effectiveness.

In medicine, emotion and decision making are inseparable. For example, families who are faced with difficult end-of-life decisions, such as taking a loved one off life support or initiating the organ donation process, may experience grief, anger, disbelief, and confusion. It is important for physicians to communicate with patients and families in order to remain aware of how emotion may impact decision making, both by the physician and the patient or family.

If another student does poorly on a test, you might assume that she is lazy or a poor student (an example of a dispositional attribution, in line with the fundamental attribution error). However, if you fail the test, you are more likely to think that you didn't get enough sleep the night before or that the test was poorly written (situational attributions in line with the self-serving bias).

4.6 | Emotion

Emotion is a multifaceted experience that is connected to thought, physiology, and behavior. As demonstrated in the example of emotion's effect on decision making, thought is never fully disconnected from feelings and emotional states. The brain-as-computer is a model that accounts for cognitive processes; here we consider how these processes interact with emotion.

Emotion can be divided into three components:

1. Cognitive: Emotion includes a personal assessment of the significance of a particular situation. This assessment leads to the *subjective experience* of the emotion—that is, the feeling that results from cognitive appraisal.

2. Physiological: Emotions are often associated with activation of the autonomic nervous system. For example, a racing heartbeat and sweaty palms may be a manifestation of fear or anxiety.

3. Behavioral: Emotion can lead to urges to act in a certain way and thereby lead to actions. If provoked in an argument, for instance, one may feel the behavioral urge to retaliate physically.

Keep in mind that the three components of emotion are not necessarily sequential as listed. Each can be the trigger that leads to the others. While an emotional experience might begin with anxious thoughts about an upcoming test, which could then lead to physiological arousal and an eventual decision to act and begin studying, instead the emotional experience could begin with a pounding heartbeat and shortness of breath, from which one might conclude that one is experiencing anxiety. Just as the mind can cue a physiological response, physiological arousal can be interpreted by the mind as representing an emotional experience.

The Biology of Emotion

Various biological processes play central roles in the perception and consequences of emotion. At the broadest level, the generation and experience of emotion involves the entire nervous system. However, the limbic system and autonomic nervous system are the two most significant players in the physiology of emotion. Within the limbic system (which connects the hypothalamus with structures in the temporal lobe), the amygdala is chiefly responsible for the emotional reactions of fear and anger. Studies have shown that the amygdala can respond to an emotion-laden stimulus without conscious awareness of the stimulus. The circuitry of the amygdala and hippocampus also allows the recollection of emotional memories when similar emotional circumstances occur. In addition to the automatic, unconscious emotional processing of the amygdala, the prefrontal cortex is involved in conscious regulation of emotional states. The prefrontal cortex is also critical in temperament and decision making. (Recall from the previous lecture that temperament relates to emotional reactivity.) As for the physiological processes associated with emotion, recall that the hypothalamus regulates the autonomic nervous system's sympathetic and parasympathetic functions, including the effects of stressors on heart rate, sweating, and arousal. Emotion can have pronounced effects on the autonomic nervous system. Emotions like fear and anger stimulate the sympathetic nervous system, which is why people experience a characteristic elevation in heart rate when watching scary movies or arguing with someone. Other physiological markers of emotion have also been identified. Activation of the sympathetic nervous system is associated with "fight or flight" physiological responses. From head to toe, the responses associated with sympathetic nervous system activation include pupillary dilation, decreased salivation, increased respiration, increased heart rate, slowed digestion, and increased concentration of glucose in the blood. The responses associated with parasympathetic nervous system activation are opposite to those of the sympathetic nervous system and are associated with "rest and digest" functions. They include pupillary constriction, increased salivation, decreased respiration, decreased heart rate, increased digestion, and decreased concentration of glucose in the blood.

Nervous System
BIOLOGY 2

As discussed in the problem solving section of this lecture, we often make decisions by anticipating the emotional state that would result from each outcome. The prefrontal cortex is responsible for emotion-based planning and for predicting in abstract the consequences of our choices.

Major Theories of Emotion:

The major theories of emotion present varied models of how emotional experience and response develop. While the James-Lange theory argues that emotion is based purely in physiological response, the Cannon-Bard and Schachter-Singer theories add layers of complexity. The theories differ in their treatment of the sequence of physiological and emotional events, as well as the extent to which they incorporate cognitive appraisal.

The **James-Lange theory** of emotion is physiologically-based. It states that an external stimulus elicits a physiological response, and that emotional experience depends on the recognition and interpretation of this physical reaction.

By contrast, the **Cannon-Bard theory** of emotion posits that emotional "feelings" and physiological reactions to stimuli are experienced simultaneously. It argues, critiquing James-Lange, that emotions cannot be determined solely by one's appraisal of physiological arousal because many physiological experiences have multiple emotional correlates. A racing heartbeat, for instance, could indicate excitement, fear, or anger.

The **Schachter-Singer theory** of emotion is a cognitive theory, also known as the *two-factor theory of emotion*. Like James-Lange, the theory states that physiological arousal is the first component of the emotional response. This theory suggests that for cognitive appraisal, that is to identify a reason for the initial arousal, one takes into account both the physiological response and situational cues. The main difference between the Schachter-Singer theory and the James-Lange theory is that the Schachter-Singer theory recognizes higher level thinking.

Think Schachter-two-factor!

Though cognition and emotion are related processes, one difference between them is the extent of bodily involvement. As the major theories of emotion demonstrate, emotion is rooted in physiology, whether as a source or effect. Cognition, by contrast, can be viewed as a mental process that is localized to the brain.

Imagine you come across a bear while hiking in the woods. According to James-Lange, you would think "Since I am trembling, I must be afraid." The Cannon-Bard theory would say that you see the bear and think "I am afraid and I am beginning to tremble." According to Schachter-Singer, you would think "I am trembling and I am also near a bear (that is, I am in a threatening situation), so my trembling must be caused by fear; I am afraid."

FIGURE 4.4 | Theories of Emotion

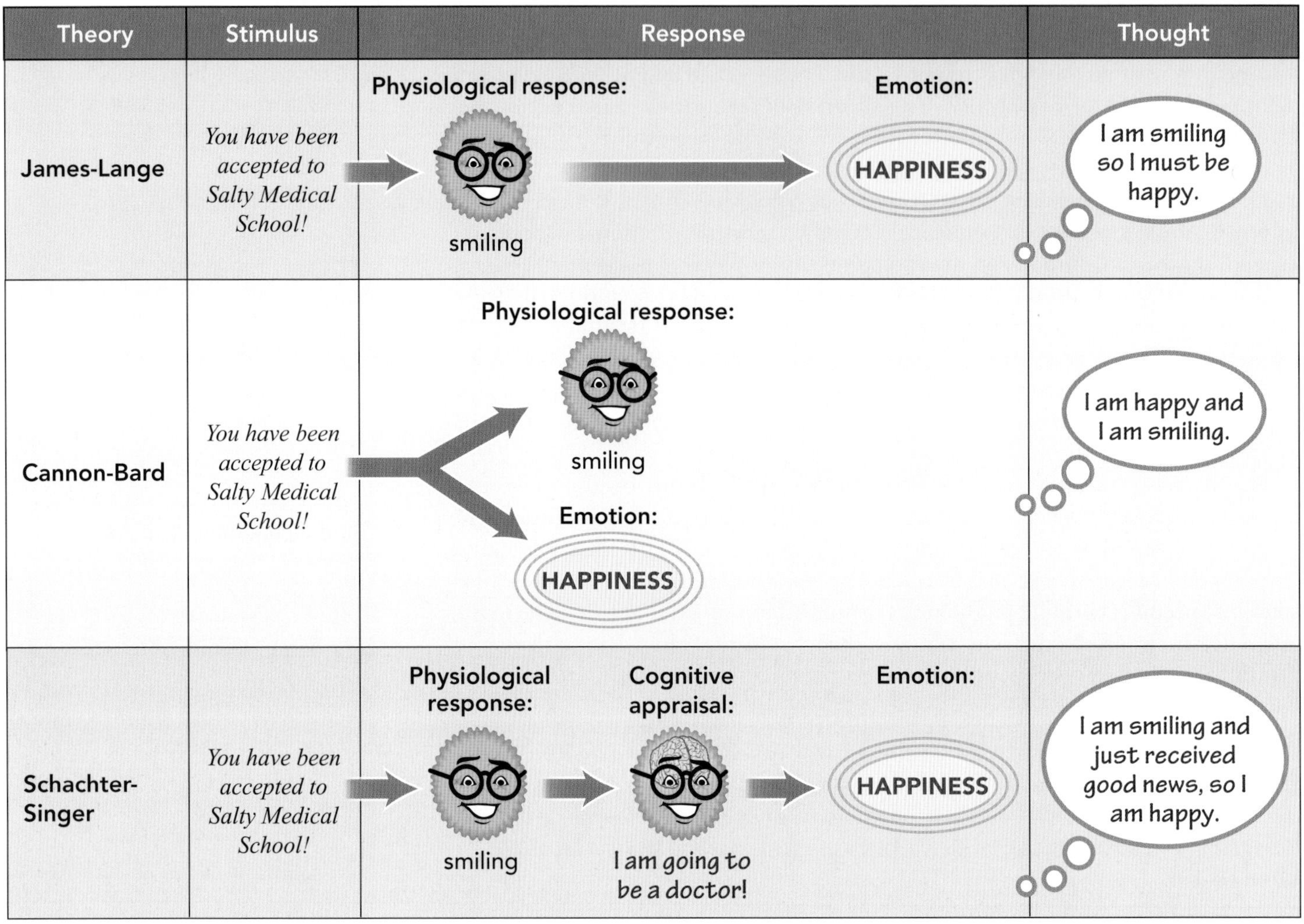

Theory	Stimulus	Response	Thought
James-Lange	*You have been accepted to Salty Medical School!*	**Physiological response:** smiling → **Emotion:** HAPPINESS	I am smiling so I must be happy.
Cannon-Bard	*You have been accepted to Salty Medical School!*	**Physiological response:** smiling / **Emotion:** HAPPINESS	I am happy and I am smiling.
Schachter-Singer	*You have been accepted to Salty Medical School!*	**Physiological response:** smiling → **Cognitive appraisal:** I am going to be a doctor! → **Emotion:** HAPPINESS	I am smiling and just received good news, so I am happy.

Emotions: Universal and Adaptive

What is the purpose of emotion for humans? Emotion enables a physical response to internal mental states; it also allows people to communicate their internal experiences and to understand the feelings and experiences of others. The most basic emotions are universal. Fear, anger, happiness, surprise, joy, disgust, and sadness appear to be recognized as distinct and meaningful emotions in all cultures.

Emotion is adaptive, meaning that it promotes the organism's ability to thrive. The universality of emotion is adaptive in that it allows interpersonal communication, including cross-cultural communication. Facial expressions conveying each of the basic emotions are distinct and universal, so a smile communicates happiness regardless of the individual or culture. Another example is that an angry facial expression, in combination with body language, can serve as a warning sign that someone is about to commit an aggressive act. In addition, emotion helps to guide behaviors that promote safety. When people experience fear, they find a way to escape or lessen the fear-inducing stimulus. These are evolved, adaptive behaviors, inspired by emotional experience.

Question 80

Which of the following is true regarding standard IQ tests?

- ○ **A.** IQ scores are predictive of later career success.
- ○ **B.** IQ scores are consistent across cultural divisions.
- ○ **C.** IQ tests are predictive of performance in a wide range of non-academic pursuits.
- ○ **D.** IQ tests demonstrate test-retest reliability.

Question 81

Which of the following does NOT accurately describe a way in which traditional IQ tests are inconsistent with the theory of multiple intelligences?

- ○ **A.** Traditional IQ tests do not assess a range of abilities.
- ○ **B.** Traditional IQ tests are used to diagnose global learning disabilities.
- ○ **C.** Performance on traditional IQ tests predicts performance on a variety of intelligence tests.
- ○ **D.** Traditional IQ tests correlate with academic performance.

Question 82

Which of the following best exemplifies algorithmic problem solving?

- ○ **A.** Comparing a problem to one solved previously
- ○ **B.** Using logical deduction to find the most efficient means of solving a problem
- ○ **C.** Following a set list of steps to solve a problem
- ○ **D.** Problem solving using perception rather than logic

Question 83

A contestant on a game show is presented with three doors, labeled A, B, and C. A large cash prize can be found behind only one of these doors, and the contestant must guess which door contains the prize. The contestant initially selects door A and does not change her guess when the game show host reveals that there is only a 20% chance that the prize is located behind door A. This situation best describes:

- ○ **A.** belief perseverance.
- ○ **B.** confirmation bias.
- ○ **C.** overconfidence.
- ○ **D.** self-serving bias.

Question 84

All of the following have been shown to influence a child's cognitive development EXCEPT:

- ○ **A.** mother's health during pregnancy.
- ○ **B.** father's health during pregnancy.
- ○ **C.** social environment.
- ○ **D.** language spoken at home.

Question 85

A referee at a soccer game notices that another referee made multiple incorrect calls and loudly criticizes the referee for being incompetent. When it is pointed out to the critical referee that she herself has made multiple incorrect calls, she blames each on poor visibility. This situation best exemplifies which of the following principles?

  I. Causation bias
 II. The fundamental attribution error
III. Self-serving bias

- ○ **A.** I only
- ○ **B.** II only
- ○ **C.** II and III only
- ○ **D.** I, II, and III

Question 86

Which of the following is not considered to be one of the three major components of emotion?

- ○ **A.** Cognitive
- ○ **B.** Neural
- ○ **C.** Physiological
- ○ **D.** Behavioral

Question 87

An experiment was performed on two groups of rats. In the experimental group, shocks were administered periodically but unpredictably over the course of 60 hours. The control group received no shocks over the same time span. The experimental group most likely had increased activation in which of the following regions?

- ○ **A.** Amygdala
- ○ **B.** Prefrontal cortex
- ○ **C.** Hippocampus
- ○ **D.** Ventral tegmental area

Question 88

Which of the following descriptions best aligns with the Cannon-Bard theory of emotion?

- ○ **A.** Someone with a fear of spiders sees a spider, feels her heart racing, then recognizes that she is feeling fearful.
- ○ **B.** A viewer of a horror film simultaneously experiences a pounding heartbeat and a feeling of fear.
- ○ **C.** A pedestrian walking home at night notices that she has a rapid heart rate. She interprets this emotional response as excitement if she is looking forward to returning home, or as fear if she is being followed home by an unknown person.
- ○ **D.** A student with a fear of public speaking thinks about a public speaking event, becomes anxious, and then experiences physical discomfort.

4.7 | Motivation and Attitudes

In order to fully understand how thought, emotion, and biology contribute to action, it is important to examine **motivation,** a psychological factor that provides a directional force or reason for behavior.

A motivation is a complex psychological and behavioral event that can be influenced by a variety of lower-level factors, such as needs, instincts, arousal, and drives. Motivations often originate from unsatisfied **needs,** which can be physiological or psychological. An **instinct** is a biological, innate tendency to perform a certain behavior that leads to the fulfillment of a need. Since instincts are not based on experience, all people share the same basic instincts. For example, infants are born with the instinct to seek out a nipple for feeding and to suck, which originates from the physiological need for nourishment.

Another major factor in the development of motivation is **arousal,** physiological and psychological tension. High arousal triggers attempts to return to an ideal and more comfortable level of arousal. **Drives** are urges to perform certain behaviors in order to resolve physiological arousal when that arousal is caused by

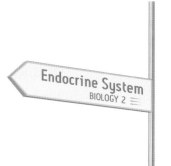

Endocrine System
BIOLOGY 2

the biological needs of the organism. Many drives contribute to maintenance of physiological homeostasis. One prominent example of a drive is thirst. Much like hormonal processes, thirst operates as a **negative feedback system.** When the body is dehydrated, thirst increases, which increases the drive to drink water in order to regulate blood osmolarity. This process is triggered by changes in blood volume and communication between the kidney and the brain. Once water intake has occurred, homeostasis is achieved, and the drive to drink is reduced.

Theories of Motivation

There are several general theories that consider how motivation contributes to human behavior. The drive reduction theory describes internal drives as the impetus for motivation, while the incentive theory focuses on external rewards. Cognitive and need-based theories emphasize the role of psychological factors such as expectations and needs.

Drive reduction theory focuses on internal factors in motivation, positing that people are motivated to take action in order to lessen the state of arousal caused by a physiological need. This theory is best applied to innate biological drives that are critical for immediate survival, such as hunger or thirst, but it is also relevant to more complex motivations like sex drive.

According to **incentive theory,** people are motivated by external rewards. Although incentives guide motivation similar to the way positive reinforcement affects behavior in operant conditioning, incentive theory is distinct in how it highlights the psychological feeling of pleasure that comes with receiving an incentive. By contrast, operant conditioning only looks at the outcomes of reinforcement and punishment, without attention to the involvement of inner processes such as emotion and motivation. An example of incentive theory is found in a person who is motivated to go to work each day because he or she enjoys receiving a paycheck, an external incentive.

Cognitive theories of emotion suggest that people behave based on their expectations. That is, people behave in a way that they predict will yield the most favorable outcome. Cognitive theories further propose that motivation can be categorized into *intrinsic* and *extrinsic* motivation. Intrinsic motivators are those that are internal, such as the reward of feeling satisfied after completing a task. Extrinsic motivation is driven by external reward, similar to incentive theory.

Relationships and Behavior
PSYCH & SOC

Studies have shown that people who consistently receive extrinsic rewards for something that they intrinsically enjoy may eventually lose the intrinsic motivation. For example, a person who loves to bake for fun might enjoy it less if they began to sell their baked goods for profit.

Need-based theories propose that people are motivated by the desire to fulfill unmet needs. According to *Abraham Maslow*, all people strive to meet a hierarchy of needs in ascending order. In other words, the most basic, physiological needs must be met before one has the motivation to achieve the next level of need.

FIGURE 4.5 | Maslow's Hierarchy of Needs

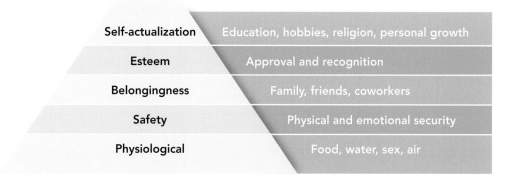

Regulation and Interaction of Motivational Processes

Motivations develop from the interaction between biological drives, external incentives, and socio-cultural factors. The various theories of motivation can be applied to particular behaviors, such as eating, sexual behavior, and drug and alcohol use. Consider the example of consuming alcohol. This behavior cannot simply be explained by drive reduction theory—people do not drink alcohol because of the biological drive for thirst. They may drink because it is socially or culturally normative. Perhaps there is an incentive, such as experiencing reduced social anxiety. Alternatively, a person who is addicted to alcohol may be motivated by physiology - the brain's dopamine reward pathway or avoidance of the symptoms of withdrawal.

> Biological Correlates
> ☰ PSYCH & SOC

Attitudes

In order to fully understand the factors that influence behavior, it is also important to examine attitudes. Attitudes are favorable or unfavorable organizations of beliefs and feelings about people, objects, or situations. The three major components of attitudes can be remembered through the *ABC model*:

1. The <u>A</u>ffective component: A person's feelings or emotions about an object, person, or event.
      Example: "I am afraid of snakes."

2. The <u>B</u>ehavioral component: The influence that attitudes have on behavior.
      Example: "I will avoid snakes and flee if I see one."

3. The <u>C</u>ognitive component: Beliefs or knowledge about a specific object of interest.
      Example: "I believe snakes can harm me."

Attitudes and behavior are bi-directional, meaning that behavioral patterns and attitudes influence one another. For instance, health behaviors, such as food choices, are constantly influenced by attitudes towards diet and overall health, which

> Understanding Key 3: Attitudes and behavior influence each other to lead to change. Attitudes have three components with varying complexities. The interplay between attitudes and behavior is important to human psychology.

> Think about your attitudes regarding the MCAT®. You feel happy when you score well on a practice test (an affective component of your attitudes). You are studying (a behavioral component) because you believe that it will help you to succeed on test day (a cognitive component and a correct attitude!).

Imagine that a friend asks you to borrow a few dollars, which you readily lend. If the friend then asks to borrow a significantly greater sum of money, you may be more likely to agree than if they had originally asked for that amount.

are in turn influenced by our own behavior, the behavior of others, and societal norms. This section will first consider the effects of behavior on attitudes and will then cover some of the ways in which attitudes can affect behavior.

The foot-in-the-door phenomenon is based on the premise that people are much more likely to agree to a large request if they first agree to a smaller one. This is a persuasive technique that uses behavior change to affect attitudes. The act of accepting an initially modest request fosters an accepting and willing attitude. One is then motivated to comply with a larger request, consistent with this newly established attitude.

Behavior can also shape attitudes through role-playing. A role is a set of norms that dictate expected behavior in a specific situation. Consider a student who has graduated from college and is starting a corporate job. While dressing professionally and joining the corporate world may feel like a forced role at first, she will eventually come to believe and feel that she is an adult contributor to the company. Similarly, the behaviors associated with a new role may feel artificial. With time, they soon seem to reflect a true self as role-consistent attitudes are adopted. Think back to the previous lecture: role-playing allows for the development of an internal self-concept and identity, as well as a set of external attitudes about the world.

On the flip side, attitudes may influence behavior. Research indicates that people are more likely to behave in accordance with an attitude when the attitude is repeatedly stated or personally meaningful, or when a significant outcome is expected (as when something is at stake to be lost or gained). In some cases, the way that messages are framed can influence people's attitudes, which then subsequently influence their behavior. According to Drs. Gallagher and Updegraff's review of multiple studies, when health messages are framed positively (i.e. exercising is good for weight loss), people develop positive attitudes about exercise, which leads them to exercise more. When the message is framed negatively (i.e. not exercising leads to weight gain), people develop negative views of exercise and are less likely to change their behavior. This pattern of behavior mirrors the effectiveness of reinforcement over punishment in learning. Positive messages encourage behavior change, and positive reinforcement fosters learning. Conversely, negatively-framed messages do not influence behavior as well, and punishment has less of an impact on learning.

MCAT® THINK

People tend to have strong attitudes about going to see their doctor. Some feel comforted by frequent consultation with a physician, while others feel intimidated or skeptical and rarely choose to visit their primary care physician. These attitudes not only influence behavior that affects the patients' immediate and long term health, but can have widespread policy and economic implications. If a patient believes his annual check-up is useless, he may not benefit from the early detection of disease. This attitude and its resultant behavior or lack thereof may lead to advanced disease, reliance upon the Emergency Room, and a need for more extensive and expensive treatment.

Cognitive dissonance theory assumes that people have a self-concept of consistency and honesty. If you don't see yourself as honest, cognitive dissonance won't cause discomfort and you will not be moved to correct the inconsistency between attitude and behavior.

It is important to note that attitudes do not always influence behavior. Negative attitudes about smoking, such as knowledge of its dangerous effects, do not always lead to smoking cessation. Cognitive dissonance refers to the conflict or inconsistency between internal attitudes and external behaviors. According to cognitive dissonance theory, people have an inherent desire to avoid the internal discomfort associated with a mismatch between attitudes and behaviors. To resolve cognitive dissonance, people either change their attitudes towards a situation, change their perception of the behavior, or modify the behavior.

Consider how smoking cigarettes could cause cognitive dissonance:

Attitude: "Smoking is unhealthy and I should not smoke."

Behavior: Smoking a cigarette.

A person with this attitude and behavior will experience cognitive dissonance because the behavior is inconsistent with the attitude. In this case, the cognitive dissonance can be mitigated in one of three ways:

1. Changing the attitude ("smoking is not actually bad for your health") or changing the behavior (quitting smoking)

2. Justifying the behavior by changing the conflicting cognition ("even though smoking is bad for your health, it's not so bad to smoke as long as it's only once in a while")

3. Justifying the behavior by adding new cognitions ("I'll work out every day to nullify the effects of smoking")

People's feelings and behaviors do not always align, but they are inextricably linked and exert constant influence on one another.

Cognitive dissonance affects decision making and can contribute to faulty decision making. In the example of smoking, notice that the resolution of cognitive dissonance can lead to changes in cognition that then feed into the decision to continue a maladaptive behavior.

Theories Behind Attitude and Behavior Change

Knowledge of the theories behind changing attitudes and behaviors is relevant to the practice of medicine due to the relationship between behavior and health. Health-related behaviors and attitudes, both positive and negative, play a role in the development and management of many chronic health conditions. Two major theories of attitude and behavior change are described below. One describes change through learning from social and environmental interactions, while the other focuses on change in response to a specific persuasive argument.

The **elaboration likelihood model** takes an information processing approach to persuasion, describing the interaction between an argument and relevant psychological factors of the person who receives the argument. According to the elaboration likelihood model, there are two routes to attitude formation and change, defined by the likelihood that the person who receives an argument will elaborate on it by generating his or her own thoughts and opinions in response.

- **Peripheral route processing** occurs when an individual does not think deeply to evaluate the argument. This can happen when a person is unable or unwilling to evaluate the situation fully or uses a heuristic method of problem solving.

- **Central route processing** occurs when an individual does think deeply and even elaborates on the argument that is presented. Central route persuasion appeals to logic and reason, and is influenced mostly by the argument itself.

People often follow the central route when they are deeply invested in a situation or have personal knowledge about it. They follow the peripheral route when they are less interested and have minimal knowledge of the issues. Studies have shown that only a strong argument will be effective in changing attitudes through the central route to persuasion, but both strong and weak arguments can be effective through the peripheral route.

Pay attention to the various factors that accompany successful and unsuccessful attitude and behavior change—these will be important to understand and identify on the MCAT®.

Imagine that you are watching a political debate. If you are deeply invested in the outcome of the election, you will probably pay close attention to the content of the debate in order to decide on your vote (central route processing). If you care less about the election, you might pay attention to superficial factors like the candidates' voices or appearances in order to make a decision (peripheral route processing).

Social-cognitive theory approaches behavior change from a social learning perspective, in contrast to the intentional persuasion described by the elaboration likelihood model, and proposes that behavior and attitudes change through a system of *reciprocal causation*, in which personal factors (such as cognition, affect, and biology), behavior, and environmental factors all influence each other. According to social-cognitive theory, behavior is not based solely on internal drives or external, environmental reward and punishment. People learn behaviors by observing others' actions and consequences as well. The theory also states that people have a strong ability to *self-regulate*; they can control behavior in the absence of rewards or punishments.

> Recall that the social-cognitive theory is also relevant to personality development.

MCAT® THINK

The *Five Stages of Change* model uses concepts of attitude and behavior change in a clinical setting to help people overcome addiction. People work through the stages from *pre-contemplation*, at which point they have no desire to change, to *contemplation*, the initial awareness that there is a problem, to *preparation*, in which they get ready for change by shifting attitudes, to *action*, the actual modification of behavior and environment, to *maintenance*, the prevention of relapse.

Factors Affecting Attitude Change

Multiple influences on attitudes have been discussed throughout this lecture, including behavior, persuasion, social learning, and the environment. Overall, the factors that may change attitudes fall into the following categories:

1. Behavior change: This includes the foot-in-the-door strategy, role-playing, and some instances of relieving cognitive dissonance.

2. Characteristics of the message: A speaker who is viewed as credible is better able to affect the attitudes of the audience. A strong and persuasive argument is generally more likely to influence attitude than a weaker one (although recall that a weak argument can be equally effective if the peripheral route to persuasion is employed).

3. Characteristics of the target: When the intended recipient of a persuasive message, sometimes called a target, has deep knowledge and is willing to engage with the argument, he or she is more likely be persuaded if the argument is strong. Such an informed target would thereby follow the central processing route. A target who is less invested will follow the peripheral processing route by paying attention to situational cues like the number of arguments, the surroundings, or the perceived credibility of the speaker. The age of the target also matters: young children are likely to respond emotionally rather than logically, which makes them particularly susceptible to attitude change and manipulation.

4. Social factors: Many social and environmental forces impact attitude and behavior change. The medium of communication has an effect. Face-to-face communication is the most successful in changing attitudes. Social factors such as in-group/out-group identification and groupthink significantly sway people's attitudes and behaviors.

MCAT® THINK

While it is important for a physician to understand how persuasion could help a patient improve health-related habits, it is equally important for the patient's opinions and preferences to be respected, especially when they are different from those of the physician.

4.8 Stress

The final topic to be examined is stress, a phenomenon that spans both the normative and pathological spectrums of the cognitive and emotional processes discussed in this lecture. Stress is the strain that is experienced when an organism's equilibrium is disrupted and it must adapt. The source of stress, or stressor, can range from daily hassles like traffic, to major personal events like going to college or the birth of a child, and cataclysmic events such as natural disasters or war.

There is great variability in how people experience and manage stress. People's cognitive appraisals, or personal interpretations of the situations that triggered stress, can account for many of these differences. According to the *appraisal view of stress*, people make two appraisals which determine their overall emotional reaction to the event:

1. *Primary appraisal:* Evaluating a situation for the presence of any potential threat. If a threat is present, a secondary appraisal is generated.

2. *Secondary appraisal:* Assessing personal ability to cope with the threat. An individual who does not believe that he or she can handle the threat well experiences a greater level of stress than someone who appraises his or her ability more highly.

If you are afraid of bugs, you might appraise a harmless spider as posing a threat, resulting in a stress response. Someone who does not share your fear would appraise the situation at a much lower threat level and would not experience stress.

Stress Responses and Outcomes

An acute stressor causes the body to prepare a physiological fight-or-flight response to the actual or imagined threat. The sympathetic division of the autonomic nervous system releases epinephrine (adrenaline) and norepinephrine (noradrenaline), followed by the release of the same chemicals as a hormonal response from the adrenal glands, which causes a longer-lasting stress responses. This pattern of hormonal and nervous system activation causes increased heart rate, blood pressure, and breathing rate. The adrenal glands also release cortisol, the primary stress hormone. Cortisol increases blood glucose, which is directed toward the body's muscles, preparing the body for fight or flight. The amount of cortisol in saliva is a commonly used measure of stress.

If the stressor does not present a long-term perceived threat (and is not compounded by additional stressors), the body quickly returns to baseline heart rate, blood pressure, and systemic functioning. However, chronic stress can lead to a host of physical ailments because the body's fight-or-flight response remains activated, maintaining high cortisol levels. Potential negative effects of long-lasting stress include digestive problems, weight gain, sleep issues, and increased risk of infection resulting from suppressed immunity.

Stress also has profound effects on psychological and behavioral functioning. The fight-or-flight response often activates the emotion of fear. Emotion and cognition serve an adaptive purpose by guiding the decision to fight or flee in a stress-provoking situation. Chronic stress, however, contributes to psychological disorders such as anxiety and depression. Acute cataclysmic events, like witnessing atrocities of war or involvement in a car accident, can spark the onset of *post-traumatic stress disorder (PTSD)*.

While stress can play a significant role in the development of psychological disorders, it interacts with other biological, genetic, cognitive, and emotional factors; it does not itself *cause* the disorders.

Stress has an evolutionary advantage: the fight-or-flight stress response evolved perfectly for dealing with a short-term stressor like an oncoming predator that requires an intensely physical response, like running. When stress is chronic (long-lasting) and the response is largely mental and emotional rather than physical, like lying in bed and worrying, stress can have negative consequences for health.

FIGURE 4.6 | Relationship Between Arousal and Performance

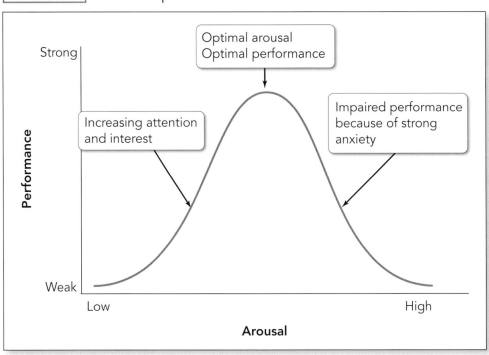

This means that if you prepare well for the MCAT®, those test day jitters you experience can actually help you!

Despite the negative effects of stress, there are some situations in which a certain amount of stress can enhance performance. Research has shown that people perform better under a mild amount of stress, particularly when they have expertise in the task at hand. However, much like the confidence curve discussed previously, the benefits of arousal follow a curved path: once stress levels exceed the optimal amount, stress can cause memory and cognitive impairment.

Stress Management

Stress can be managed through biological, psychological, and social means. Recent research has focused on the potential of exercise for effective stress management. Exercise can utilize the same physiological resources that are provided by the acute stress response, which evolved to provide increased blood flow and glucose levels for evading an acute stressor like a predator.

Spirituality can also facilitate stress relief by allowing people to achieve a sense of purpose, focus, and optimism. Studies have found that spirituality can help cancer patients reduce their stress levels throughout treatment. Spiritual practice may also aid in stress management by causing people to join churches or other organized groups that provide social support. It is important to recognize that spirituality is not synonymous with religion. Generally, spirituality is a much broader concept than religion. A person may be spiritual without being religious, but a person who is religious is also spiritual.

Meditation can be an effective mind-body technique, now promoted within the mainstream of medicine as mindfulness. This may occur through focus on the breath, guided imagery, mantra repetition, or yoga. Meditation allows for deep relaxation and focus on the present as a way to allow stressful thoughts and experience to dissipate. Recent research has found that mindfulness meditation can not only lower reported anxiety, stress, and fatigue, but also reduce the body's release of cortisol.

Yoga can be used as a method for stress relief. The man in this photo is participating in a class provided to Centers for Disease Control and Prevention (CDC) employees in order to promote their physical and mental well-being.

Think about what happens during a stress response in the absence of the physical component for which it is highly adaptive. All of the components intended to make us more comfortable while running make us uncomfortable while sitting: inhibited digestion and increased blood glucose, heart rate, and vasodilation in the extremities leave us feeling on edge. Using the body, as in exercise, allows the physical aspects of the stress response to be utilized and thereby resolved.

MCAT® THINK

Stress pervades healthcare in multiple ways. First of all, stress contributes to physical ailments that require medical treatment. Stress correlates with high cholesterol and blood pressure, both of which increase the risk of heart attack. Stress may also lead to behavioral risk factors for heart disease such as smoking and overeating. As mentioned earlier in this section, prolonged stress can lead to increased cortisol and a weakened immune response, meaning that chronically stressed people get sick more easily and more often. Secondly, stress accompanies medical procedures and conditions. Patients and their families experience stress while attempting to cope with a diagnosis, rigorous treatment plans like chemotherapy, or long rehabilitation period. It is important for physicians to talk to their patients about stress in order to understand and minimize the physical and psychological consequences of long term stress.

Questions 89-96 are NOT based on a descriptive passage.

Question 89

A parent attempts to motivate a child to eat her vegetables by stressing how good it will feel for her to know that she will grow up to be strong and healthy. Which theory of motivation is consistent with the parent's strategy?

- **A.** Drive reduction theory
- **B.** Incentive theory
- **C.** A cognitive theory
- **D.** A need-based theory

Question 90

Which of the following is not considered to be a major component of attitudes?

- **A.** A person's feelings or emotions about an object, person, or event
- **B.** The influence that attitudes have on behavior
- **C.** Beliefs or knowledge about a specific object of interest
- **D.** Synthesis of preconceived information and presented information regarding an object, person, or event

Question 91

An employee first asks the IT specialist to help her move a piece of equipment a couple of feet over. The next day, the employee asks the IT specialist to spend a significant amount of time resolving a complex technical issue, and the IT worker agrees to do it. This scenario can best be described as:

- **A.** the foot-in-the-door phenomenon.
- **B.** the door-in-the-face technique.
- **C.** compliance.
- **D.** role-playing.

Question 92

Which of the following phenomena best demonstrates how attitudes can effect a change in behavior?

- **A.** Social-cognitive theory
- **B.** Cognitive dissonance
- **C.** Central route processing
- **D.** Peripheral route processing

Question 93

Social-cognitive theory describes:

- **A.** changes in social behavior driven by thought processes.
- **B.** changes in attitudes driven by observations of the actions of others.
- **C.** behavior change driven by social learning in addition to internal and external drives.
- **D.** behavior change driven by social learning in the absence of internal and external drives.

Question 94

Which of the following is NOT a target characteristic that can influence attitude change?

- **A.** Knowledge base
- **B.** Age
- **C.** Willingness to engage with the argument
- **D.** Credibility of the speaker

Question 95

A camper recognizes that she is in the path of a deadly snake, realizes that there is no possibility of getting to a hospital in time if she is bitten, and begins to panic. This scenario best describes:

- **A.** cognitive appraisal.
- **B.** fight-or-flight response.
- **C.** a cataclysmic event.
- **D.** elaboration likelihood model.

Question 96

Someone who is chronically stressed is most likely to have elevated levels of which of the following hormones?

- **A.** Cortisol
- **B.** Epinephrine
- **C.** Norepinephrine
- **D.** Glucose

STOP

Adaptive
Affective component
Amygdala
Algorithm
Analogies
Anger
Arousal
Autonomic nervous system
Behavior change
Behavioral
Behavioral component
Belief perseverance
Biases
Broca's area
Cannon-Bard theory of emotion
Cataclysmic events
Central route processing
Cerebral cortex
Characteristics of the message
Characteristics of the target
Cognition
Cognitive
Cognitive appraisals
Cognitive component
Cognitive dissonance
Cognitive dissonance theory
Cognitive theories
Concrete operational
Cortisol
Disgust
Drive reduction theory
Drives
Elaboration likelihood model

Emotion
Environmental influences
Epinephrine (adrenaline)
Exercise
Fear
Foot-in-the-door phenomenon
Formal operational
Frontal lobe
Fundamental attribution error
Happiness
Hereditary influences
Heuristics
Hypothalamus
Incentive theory
Information processing models
Intelligence
Interactionist theory
Instinct
Intuition
IQ (intelligence quotient)
James-Lange theory of emotion
Jean Piaget
Joy
Learning theory
Limbic system
Motivation
Nativist theory
Need-based theories
Needs
Negative feedback system
Norepinephrine (noradrenaline)
Occipital lobe
Overconfidence

Parietal lobe
Perception
Peripheral route processing
Personal events
Physiological
Physiological fight-or-flight response
Physiological markers of emotion
Prefrontal cortex
Preoperational
Role
Role-playing
Role of culture in cognitive
    development
Sadness
Schachter-Singer theory of emotion
Self-serving bias
Sensorimotor
Social-cognitive theory
Social factors
Spirituality
Stages of cognitive development
Stress
Stressor
Surprise
Temperament and decision making
Temporal lobe
Theories of attitude and behavior
    change
Trial and error
Universal emotions
Wernicke's area

DON'T FORGET YOUR KEYS

1. Thought and emotion are internal processes of mental life that affect observable external behaviors.

2. Motivation uses thought and emotion to translate need into behavior.

3. Attitudes and behavior each influence the other and are crucial entry points for change.

Biological Correlates of Psychology

5.1 Introduction

5.2 Genetics, Environment, and Behavior

5.3 Sensation

5.4 Perception

5.5 Consciousness

5.6 Memory: Storage and Encoding

5.7 The Biology of Memory Formation

5.8 Memory Retrieval and Forgetting

5.9 Neurologic Dysfunctions

5.1 Introduction

This lecture will explore the biological processes that are associated with many aspects of health and mental life. This *Psychology & Sociology* manual has primarily focused on the psychological and sociological study of human behavior, as will the MCAT®. Knowledge of the biological phenomena correlated with psychological and social functioning is also required for the MCAT®. The biological topics tested in the psychosocial section of the MCAT® can be found in this lecture and the Nervous System and Endocrine lectures of the *Biology 2: Systems* manual. You will also benefit from reviewing the Genetics lecture in the *Biology 1: Molecules* manual, which relates to some of the topics discussed in this lecture.

The second half of the Nervous System Lecture, beginning with section 5.10 ("The Central Nervous System"), contains information that will likely be tested in the psychosocial section.

This lecture discusses the biological "correlates" of behavior. Remember that a correlation does not always mean causation. This manual has demonstrated that psychological, social, and biological factors are concurrent. The psychosocial section of the MCAT® requires the understanding that biology interacts with other factors as part of behavior and mental life. Isolating the cause of a given psychological or social process is difficult. In fact, such causes are generally complex and involve multiple factors. Rather than speaking of a biological "basis" of psychosocial processes, it is important to realize that biological, mental, and social factors constantly influence each other.

The biological information tested on the MCAT® falls into three general categories: biological correlates of psychology, the interaction between genetics and environment, and neuropsychological processes. Previous lectures in this manual have often pointed to biological factors in psychosocial processes. This lecture will begin with the interaction of genetics and environment that influences development and behavior. The rest of the lecture will focus on neuropsychological processes, tracing the flow of information as it is discerned and processed to allow the formation of a response. Higher-level psychological processes that affect the intake of information and are used to organize experience, such as states of consciousness and memory, will also be discussed. The lecture will conclude by examining the biology of several nervous system disorders.

The MCAT® will reward you for thinking simultaneously about psychological, sociological, and biological factors. Wrong answer choices may present biology as the "basis" or cause of behavior, while the best answer will allow for multiple influences.

> **THE 3 KEYS**
>
> 1. The environment is experienced through sensation (gathering of information) and perception (processing and interpretation of information).
>
> 2. Stages of sleep serve different functions. Early in the night, more time is spent in deep sleep; later on, more time in light sleep and REM sleep.
>
> 3. Memory involves encoding, storage, retrieval, and loss of information.

5.2 | Genetics, Environment, and Behavior

Psychological and social behaviors are correlated with the interaction of multiple genes and environmental factors; they do not follow the Mendelian genetics seen with simpler traits. This section will describe how the interaction between genetics and the environment influences individual development and behavior. It will also consider genetic inheritance at the population level.

Gene expression is influenced by environmental factors, those within the internal environment of the body and those found in the environment beyond the individual. The dynamic interaction between the environment and heredity (genetic inheritance) plays a critical role throughout psychological development, including that of behavioral traits. This process starts early in life with the development of temperament. Recall that temperament is an innate predisposition towards certain personality characteristics. Temperament demonstrates the effect of heredity on behavior, but environmental factors quickly come into play as the infant's behavior elicits certain reactions from caregivers. A baby expressing irritability is likely to receive a different response than a calm and quiet one. Environmental feedback then leads to changes in the infant's behavior.

The interaction between heredity and the environment that occurs in the case of temperament continues throughout the process of physical and psychological development. Rather than being fully predetermined, genetic inheritance provides guidelines that are then further shaped by the environment. For example, heredity and environment both affect the development of the nervous system. Although genetic instructions guide neuronal growth, the variety of stimulation available exerts a crucial influence. Hubel and Wiesel showed that the absence of certain visual features in the environment can actually cause the loss of neurons that would have been dedicated to those stimuli.

One way that the environment influences gene expression is through regulatory genes, which affect various steps from DNA to protein and can therefore alter gene expression. Gene regulation in response to the environment can promote or repress the transcription of a gene. By changing the expression of other genes, regulatory genes can indirectly affect an individual's behavior. Genetic expression and associated behaviors also change in response to the environment through *epigenetics*. Epigenetic changes can be physical alterations to the genome, such as DNA methylation and histone modification, that do not change the base pairs themselves but can still be passed down to offspring. These changes are influenced by environmental factors, providing a way for environmental influence to be "inherited" in addition to the genome itself.

The interaction between genes and the environment also plays a role at the population level. Genetically based behavioral variation in natural populations has been studied in the context of many of the social behaviors that were discussed in the Learning and Behavior Lecture, such as foraging for food. Recall from the study of evolution that the gene pool of a population is defined by the relative number of unique alleles. Genetic variation within a population is the variation of alleles between individuals in that population. When various combinations of alleles are associated with different behaviors, behavioral variation accompanies genetic variation. When the behaviors and traits associated with genotypes differ in their adaptive values, the extent to which they contribute to survival in the given environment, natural selection will result. Genetic variants leading to behavior that is adaptive to the organism's environmental conditions are selectively preserved. This leads accordingly to changes in the gene pool of the population over the course of successive generations.

Identity and the Individual
PSYCH & SOC

On the MCAT®, remember that experience interacts with genetics to produce psychology and behavior, and that behavior can in turn influence further experience. Mendelian genetics works for simple traits like plant height, but complex behaviors like those associated with personality and psychological disorders are influenced by multiple genes and environmental factors.

The Cell
BIOLOGY 2

5.3 | Sensation

Sensation and perception are psychobiological processes that allow us to understand the environment. The Nervous System Lecture in the *Biology II: Systems* manual discusses sensation and perception at the anatomical and molecular level; this lecture examines these processes from a psychobiological perspective. Sensation will be discussed in this section, followed by attention and perception.

Sensation is how we receive information from the outside world—through our senses—and perception is our interpretation of that information. More technically, **sensation** is the conversion of physical stimuli into electrical signals that are transferred through the nervous system by neurons, while **perception** is the use of sensory information and pre-existing knowledge to create a functional representation of the world. Together sensation and perception enable the detection and interpretation of environmental stimuli, providing information that can be used to formulate a response. Sensation is a physical process, while perception involves physiological and mental processing, allowing for conscious awareness of the environment. Attention determines what stimuli continue to the level of perception after being sensed.

The psychological study of sensation often examines the question of what stimuli are sufficiently intense to be sensed. Intensity is defined based on the type of stimulus involved. For example, the intensity of sound can be defined either as the rate of energy transfer of the sound wave or on the logarithmic scale (decibels), which more accurately captures the psychological experience of sound. The threshold intensity is defined by the sensory organs. Since each sense involves the detection of a different type of stimulus through types of sensory receptors, it is not surprising that thresholds differ across the senses.

The **absolute threshold** is the lowest intensity of a stimulus that can be sensed. A person's absolute threshold for sound is the softest sound, the sound of lowest intensity, that he or she can reliably hear. Sounds that are quieter than the absolute threshold cannot be detected by the auditory sensory apparatus, so they are inaccessible to perception.

> **Remember Key 1: Sensation and perception allow us to experience the environment. Sensation is the act of converting the environment into electrical signals and sending that information to the central nervous system. Perception is how the cortex of the brain decodes and interprets that information.**

Waves: Sound and Light
≡ PHYSICS

MCAT® THINK

How does this type of absolute threshold relate to the absolute threshold for the generation of an action potential, discussed in the Nervous System Lecture? It is not a coincidence that "absolute threshold" is used both to describe our conscious experience of sensation and the amount of depolarization required for the generation of an action potential in a neuron. When the absolute threshold is reached at the molecular (microscopic) level, it is also achieved at the neurological and psychological (macroscopic) level.

Because the absolute threshold for each sense reflects the physical capabilities of the associated sensory receptors in each sensory organ, it can be thought of as a biological characteristic. However, absolute thresholds can be lowered or raised psychologically based on factors such as strong emotions or the degree of subjective importance of correctly identifying the stimulus. While the biological limits of sensory receptors and synaptic summation set the absolute threshold, psychological processes can modify the threshold.

A **difference threshold,** also called a *just noticeable difference,* describes the smallest difference that is sufficient for a change in a stimulus to be noticed. In contrast to the absolute threshold, it measures a sensory system's ability to detect small changes from a previously perceived stimulus. The more sensitive the sensory system, the smaller the change that is required for detection. The difference threshold is not defined by a set value for each sense. Instead, the change

Salty, you're leaving crumbs everywhere!

Did you say something? I can't hear you right now!

From an evolutionary perspective, it makes sense that changes in stimuli of lower intensity—such as the increasing loudness of footsteps as a predator approaches—are more easily detectable than changes in intense stimuli. Our evolutionary ancestors had little need to distinguish increases in already loud noises, unless the change was substantial.

An individual can detect a change when it reaches a certain fraction of the original stimulus. The fraction is constant, but the actual amount of change required is not. Take the example of an individual whose Weber fraction for detecting a change in weight is 1/10. When one pound is added to a ten pound weight held in the hand, he or she will be able to detect the difference. If the original weight were twenty pounds, one pound would not be enough. Instead, the addition of two pounds would be required to reach the just noticeable difference.

Notice that Weber's Law, as the name implies, is considered to be a "law" in psychology. Also recall from the Research Skills Lecture of the CARS manual that social science research often focuses on describing relationships between different social and psychological variables, rather than strictly defined laws like those of natural sciences such as physics. Weber's Law is an unusual topic in the psychosocial section, because it is a law of sorts and could require calculation. If you see a calculation problem with Weber's Law, don't get bent out of shape! It's a snap compared to the MCAT® math that you have mastered for other sections.

FIGURE 5.1 Absolute Threshold

This hypothetical plot shows how a person's absolute threshold is determined: it is usually defined as the intensity level that is detected 50% of the time.

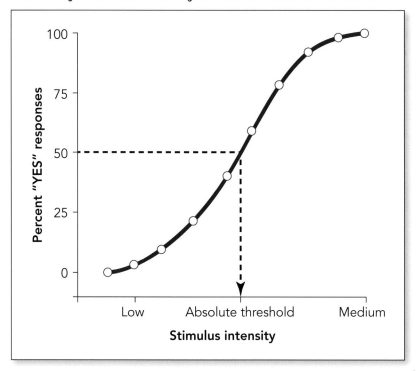

required to meet the difference threshold is dependent on the original value of the stimulus. According to **Weber's Law,** the change required to meet the difference threshold is a certain fraction (the *Weber fraction*) of the originally presented stimulus. Although the fraction is constant for each sense, Weber's Law means that the actual amount of change required to reach the difference threshold differs according to the original stimulus. To better understand Weber's law, imagine a very bright room. If the lights are turned up just a bit more, the change may not be perceived, whereas in a dimly lit room, a small increase in brightness is easily noticeable.

Weber fractions vary across the senses, because the sense organs differ in *sensitivity.* Sensitivity is the ability to detect a change from baseline, such as when the noise level in a room suddenly increases. High sensitivity is correlated with a small Weber fraction: for a more sensitive sense organ, only a small change in the stimulus is required for the change to be detected. Although each individual has a slightly different set of Weber fractions, there are general patterns found across the human species that are evolutionarily advantageous. Pitch detection is adapted to threats that would be relevant to our evolutionary ancestors, like identifying a predator. The ability to detect pitch is extremely sensitive and has a much smaller Weber fraction than that of taste.

The study of thresholds is concerned with the ability to detect any stimulus, regardless of its importance. By contrast, **signal detection theory** focuses on how an organism differentiates important or meaningful stimuli (signals) from those that are not of interest (noise) in an environment where the distinction is ambiguous. The ability to detect a meaningful stimulus in the midst of vast amounts of sensory information increases an organism's chances of survival.

Sensitivity—in this case, the ability to detect a meaningful signal in the midst of noise—can be expressed as a comparison between the false alarm rate and the hit rate. The false alarm rate is the rate at which the observer identifies a signal when there is only noise, and the hit rate is the rate at which the observer correctly recognizes the presence of a signal. If the hit rate is significantly higher than the false alarm rate, the individual is said to have high sensitivity. According to signal detection theory, there is always some amount of error in the process of distinguishing signal from noise.

Signal detection theory differs from the study of absolute thresholds, although there are similarities, in that it explicitly includes a decision-making component. Sensitivity is said to be mediated by *bias*, the individual's tendency toward or against accepting evidence of a signal. The individual consciously decides whether the evidence of a signal is sufficiently compelling. Through bias, the mind consciously filters incoming information while unconscious filtering takes place at the level of the nervous system. Individuals with the same sensitivity but differing biases can have different false alarm and hit rates. Just like absolute threshold, bias can be influenced by psychological and environmental factors. The perceived rewards of hits or the dangers of false alarms can cause people to adjust their biases. In fact, a procedure in which the relative rewards and dangers of signal detection are manipulated can be used to compare the sensitivities of individuals with very different biases.

Attention

Similar to the process by which signal detection allows the identification of a stimulus as meaningful, attention selects sensory information for perceptual processing. Sensory information that is not given attention may be unconsciously processed but will not reach conscious awareness. The gateway of attention is necessary for goal-directed behavior, since a large amount of sensory information, irrelevant to current goals, is always present and would interfere with perceiving the information that is useful and necessary.

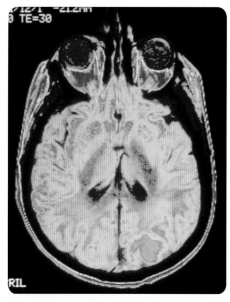

The task of a radiologist is to determine whether a meaningful signal, such as a tumor, is present in the midst of "noise" that does not convey useful information. In the MRI shown above, the bright blue blotch is a meaningful signal, indicating brain cancer in the occipital lobe.

> ## MCAT® THINK
>
> Signal detection is described in this section as a psychological process, but it is influenced by the network of sensory receptors in the eye. As described in the Nervous System Lecture, vertical and horizontal inputs allow the resolution of visual information. While bipolar cells receive information from associated photoreceptors, horizontal cells also inhibit neighboring cells. As a result, the response can be sharply focused on a particular visual stimulus.

Selective attention is an either/or process. Divided attention is a both/and process.

Selective attention refers to the focus of attention on one particular stimulus or task at the exclusion of other stimuli. It is like the narrowing of a tunnel between sensation and perception such that only certain information is allowed to proceed. A limitation of selective attention is that potentially important information, like the approach of a potential danger, may be discarded and missed. By contrast, divided attention splits perceptual resources between multiple stimuli or behaviors. It is analogous to dividing the tunnel used for selective attention into two smaller lanes. Because attentional resources are limited, divided attention causes each of the multiple stimuli to receive less attention than would be the case with selective attention. Each type of attention can be advantageous at certain times. Selective attention is beneficial when two people are having a conversation in a crowded place. Each person must filter out other stimuli in order to focus on the conversation. Divided attention is useful when two tasks must be completed at once. For example, a person may wish to watch TV and eat dinner at the same time.

Attention is often drawn to change. A stimulus that stays the same over time, like the feeling of a shirt on your back, is unlikely to provide useful information. A sudden change, like the appearance of a predator, is more relevant to survival and is given more attention.

You should use selective attention while reading this lecture!

Question 97

Although no single cause has ever been identified for schizophrenia, heredity is generally thought to be involved, especially since the disease is almost twice as common in males. Which of the following most likely explains the link between schizophrenia and genetic inheritance?

- **A.** The products of several Y-linked alleles interact with each other and lead to the attributes of schizophrenia.
- **B.** Childhood experience may lead to schizophrenia in individuals with an inherited X-linked recessive allele for a neurotransmitter transporter.
- **C.** Homozygous expression of a recessive X-linked synaptic scaffolding protein allele causes schizophrenia.
- **D.** Homozygous expression of a dominant X-linked synaptic scaffolding protein allele causes schizophrenia.

Question 98

Which of the following is NOT an example of behavioral evolution?

- **A.** An allele that causes lethal embryonic defects is eliminated from a gene pool.
- **B.** Highly successful courtship behaviors become widespread among members of a bird population over many generations.
- **C.** An allele for a dopamine receptor that contributes to empathetic behavior becomes less prevalent in a gene pool.
- **D.** Genetic variants leading to behavior that is adaptive to an organism's environmental conditions are selectively preserved.

Question 99

The conversion of physical stimuli into patterns of action potentials is known as:

- **A.** olfaction.
- **B.** perception.
- **C.** sensation.
- **D.** sensitivity.

Question 100

Which of the following is most responsible for setting an absolute sensory threshold?

- **A.** A bipolar cell in the retina
- **B.** A hair cell in the cochlea
- **C.** A neuron in the primary visual cortex
- **D.** A neuron in the auditory cortex

Question 101

A group of researchers performed an experiment to determine the difference threshold for noise frequency in mice. They calculated a Weber fraction of ¼. If the experiment began with a device playing the noise eight times every second (8 Hz), what frequency change would be required for the mice to be able to detect the change?

- **A.** 1 Hz
- **B.** 2 Hz
- **C.** 4 Hz
- **D.** 7 Hz

Question 102

Which of the following is true, according to signal detection theory?

- **A.** An individual with high sensitivity has a hit rate roughly equal to the false alarm rate.
- **B.** A false alarm occurs when an individual fails to differentiate a signal from noise.
- **C.** Individuals with the same sensitivity to a signal can be more or less adept at identifying the signal.
- **D.** Signal detection is determined solely by physical parameters like absolute thresholds.

Question 103

When video and audio recordings of a person speaking are temporally aligned, observers are better able to remember both visual and auditory information about the recordings. By contrast, misaligned recordings cause a severe decline in the ability to remember either visual or auditory information, depending on the individual. The latter finding is an example of:

- **A.** sensation.
- **B.** an absolute threshold.
- **C.** selective attention.
- **D.** divided attention.

Question 104

All of the following are examples of difference thresholds EXCEPT:

  I. the minimum intensity needed to perceive a sound.

  II. the minimum acceleration needed to perceive a change in velocity.

  III. the minimum amount of an odorant necessary to trigger firing of olfactory chemoreceptors.

- **A.** I only
- **B.** I and II only
- **C.** I and III only
- **D.** I, II, and III

5.4 | Perception

Our psychological experience of the world would be completely disorganized if sensory stimuli were simply detected and left unprocessed. Our sensory apparatuses collect and convey information about the world to the brain, but they are not equipped to interpret that data. Perception is the process by which the brain interprets incoming sensory information from the peripheral nervous system to construct an organized big-picture view of the external environment.

One of the most fundamental aspects of perception is that it involves both bottom-up and top-down processing. Bottom-up processing involves the construction of perceptions from individual pieces of information provided by sensory processing, while top-down processing brings the influence of prior knowledge into play to make perception more efficient. Much of the time, neither type of processing is sufficient on its own. Without top-down processing, it would be difficult to organize the crude information provided by sensation into a useful model: a reinvention of the wheel would be required for each new stimulus. However, without bottom-up processing, top-down processing would operate in a vacuum without moment to moment input from one's surroundings.

Top-down processing can be thought of as a pre-existing system for organizing incoming information. In fact, organization is a defining feature of perceptual processing. The rest of this section will describe the systems of perceptual organization that make sense of incoming sensory information.

When visual stimuli are first sensed, there is no intrinsic organization of the sensory information into separate objects. Our perception of the surroundings as being made up of distinct, stable objects occurs according to Gestalt principles. These principles describe the top-down processing that organizes sensory information, such as that from the visual and auditory senses, into distinct forms (objects) according to distinct regions of the sensed surroundings. When one object is recognized as a form or *figure*, the rest of the stimulus is perceived as the background or *ground*.

The Gestalt principles describe the criteria that are used to distinguish between figure and background or between objects in a group and objects out of the group. The *principle of nearness* says that clusters of objects will each be perceived as a distinct group. The *principle of similarity* points out that objects with a shared feature, such as shape, will likewise be perceived as a single group. However, both of these principles can be superseded by the *principle of common region*, which says that objects sharing a common background are perceived as a group even if they would be separated by the principles of nearness and/or similarity. According to the *principle of continuity*, the brain will perceive an ambiguous stimulus according to the simplest possible continuous form(s). In a related process, the *principle of closure* points out that we perceive whole shapes even when they are not actually present in the stimulus.

FIGURE 5.2 | Gestalt Principles

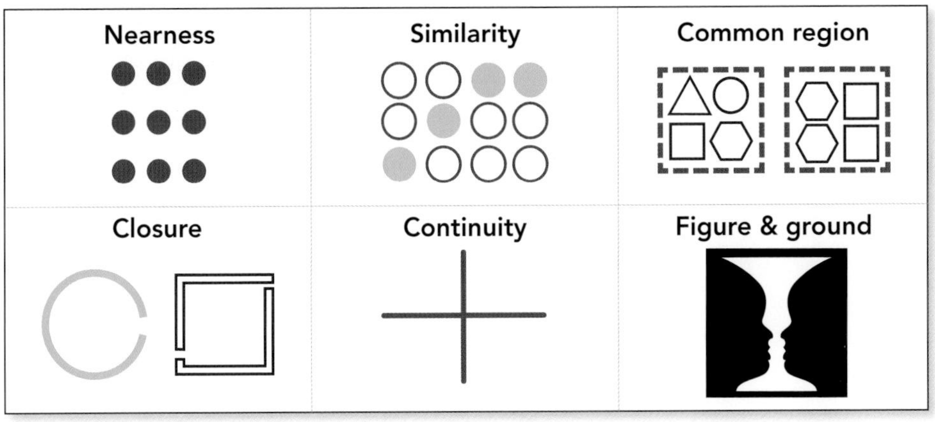

The words "sensation" and "perception" are sometimes used interchangeably. However, sensation occurs at the level of sensory organs and receptors, that is, the level at which environmental stimuli are first registered, while perception involves the higher-level processing that occurs in the brain. Sensation is the feeling of a pin pricking your finger; perception is the interpretation of the pain as meaningful information. Perception allows the pin to be interpreted as an object in the environment that should be avoided. Although perceptual processing takes place out of conscious awareness, the resulting picture of the environment is available to consciousness.

```
HHHHHHHH    SSS        SSS
HHHHHHHH    SSS       SSS
HHH         SSS     SSS
HHH         SSS   SSS
HHHHHHHH    SSSSSS
HHHHHHHH    SSSSSSS
HHH         SSS   SSS
HHH         SSS     SSS
HHHHHHHH    SSS       SSS
HHHHHHHH    SSS        SSS
```

The illustrations above are known as Navon's hierarchical letters. Interpreting the small letters relies on bottom-up processing whereas interpreting the large letters relies on top-down processing.

The influence of attention on perception can be described as its own type of top-down processing. When attentional resources are directed toward certain stimuli, others do not reach conscious awareness. In other words, top-down processing has eliminated those stimuli from the scope of perception.

Other types of perceptual organization deal with the problem of how visual phenomena that cannot be represented accurately on the retina are perceived. Consider the logistical problem of perceiving **depth** (distance). Unlike other features such as relative size, depth cannot be represented on the two dimensional surface of the retina. This means that the brain must interpret information provided by the eyes in order to represent depth in the mental model of surroundings. One of the most reliable methods is to compare the image seen by each eye. Because the eyes are in different locations, they see two versions of the same stimulus from slightly different locations. The closer the object is to the eyes, the further apart the two images are. The brain interprets the difference between the eyes' images to estimate the depth of the object being viewed. As the object's distance from the eye increases and the images produced by the eyes become closer and closer together, retinal disparity becomes less useful for depth perception, but the brain can also use other clues that do not require information from both eyes. One example is that if two objects are placed such that one partially blocks view of the other, the brain uses this information to determine that the blocked object is further away.

FIGURE 5.3 Perceiving Depth by Comparing the Eyes' Images

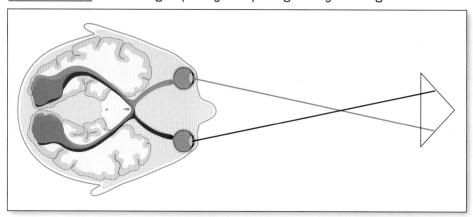

Like depth, **motion** cannot be represented by the brain based only on the pattern of information received by and represented on the retina. In this case, it is because motion does not always produce a pattern of motion on the retina, and, conversely, a moving pattern on the retina is not always due to an object's motion. If the eyes move along with a moving object, the image projected on the retina does not move. On the other hand, if the eyes move in order to view a stationary scene, the image on the retina does move while the scene does not. Despite these inconsistencies, movement or the lack of it is correctly perceived in each case. The brain's visual cortex integrates information gathered by the retina and information about eye movements in order to make correct inferences about motion.

Another type of perceptual organization is **constancy.** Much like the perception of motion, perceptual constancy deals with the problem of distinguishing between information received by the retina and changes in the surroundings. Top-down processing of perceptual systems preserves the experience of constancy when changes in retinal patterns do not reflect actual changes in the world. For example, *size constancy* allows a single object to be perceived as remaining constant in size even when it moves closer to or further from the eyes, seeming to get bigger or smaller, and causing the retinal image to change in size. Another example is *shape constancy*, when the brain perceives an object as maintaining its shape, even when it moves relative to the eyes which changes the shape of the light reflected onto the retina. In these situations, perceptual processing compensates for the change to the retinal image.

Visual Processing From a Neurological Perspective

The Nervous System Lecture introduced the neural aspects of processing visual information. This section will focus on psychological theories of visual processing. Recall that visual processing is the interpretation of otherwise raw sensory data to produce visual perception. Two types of processing take place: feature detection and parallel processing. Both are methods of bottom-up processing, in contrast to the types of top-down processing described in the previous section— Gestalt principles, depth, motion, and constancy.

As discussed in the context of information processing models, parallel processing is the use of multiple pathways to convey information about the same stimulus. It starts at the level of the bipolar and ganglion cells in the eye, which, as discussed in the Nervous System Lecture, have high sensitivities to certain areas of visual information (their *receptive fields*). Thus, information about different areas of the visual field can be processed in parallel. Through two types of ganglion cells, visual information is split into two distinct pathways: one that detects and processes information about motion, and one that is instead concerned with the form of stimuli (including shape and color). The motion and form pathways project to separate areas of the lateral geniculate nucleus (LGN) and visual cortex.

Once visual information reaches the visual cortex via parallel pathways, it is analyzed by feature detection. Just as ganglion cells are sensitive to information projected from certain areas of the visual field onto certain parts of the retina, there are cells in the visual cortex of the brain that optimally respond to particular aspects of visual stimuli, such as lines of particular orientation. These cells provide information concerning the most basic features of objects, which are integrated to produce a perception of the object as a whole. Feature detection is a type of serial processing, where increasingly complex aspects of the stimulus are processed in sequence.

> You should also review sections 2.9 and 2.10 in the *Biology 2: Systems Nervous System Lecture*, which discuss visual processing in the eye and nervous system.

> Make sure you understand that parallel processing involves multiple pieces of information about a stimulus being processed at the same time, while feature detection describes sequential processing. The details of parallel processing and feature detection, such as the names of cells involved and the exact organization of the LGN and visual cortex, are beyond the scope of the MCAT®.

5.5 | Consciousness

Consciousness can be roughly equated with awareness, such as awareness of oneself, one's surroundings, one's thoughts, and one's goals. As described in the previous section, the distinction between consciousness and unconsciousness is critical to the filtering process that sorts incoming sensory information. In fact, attention can be thought of as the gatekeeper of consciousness. Only information deemed important enough for the focus of attention comes to be perceived consciously.

Alertness can be called the "default" state of consciousness; most people are generally alert while they are awake. In a fully conscious, alert state, the brain is able to attend to tasks and carry out goal-directed processes. Alertness and wakefulness are related states but not identical, as it is possible to be awake but not alert. This has been shown in recordings of electrical activity in the brain. One of the methods used to observe brain activity is an *electroencephalogram (EEG)*, a recording at the scalp of general patterns in electrical signals (called brainwaves). EEG recordings during alertness show a particular type of brainwave, a *beta wave*, that differs from the types of brainwaves observed during sleep stages and altered consciousness.

The daily balance between wakefulness and sleep is maintained by a circadian rhythm. A circadian rhythm regulates the body's functions on a predictable schedule. By definition, a circadian rhythm cycle lasts roughly 24 hours and can refer to many processes. Sleep is the most common example of circadian rhythm in humans. The circadian rhythm of sleep and wakefulness involves opposing systems that promote each process. The drive for sleep, which is not well understood, builds up over the course of the day. However, it is opposed by the "biological clock" of the *suprachiasmatic nucleus (SCN)* located in the hypothalamus. This group of cells regulates the timing of many of the body's circadian rhythms, such

> Understanding Key 2: Sleep is necessary for humans, but its definite function is not well understood. Deep sleep occurs more early in the night and REM sleep occurs more later on. Sleep disorders lead to functional impairments and can result from abnormalities in any stage of sleep.

as body temperature. As part of the sleep-wake cycle, the SCN maintains the drive for wakefulness by inhibiting release of the hormone *melatonin* by the pineal gland. Later in the day, SCN firing decreases, which increases the release of melatonin. The drive for sleep comes to dominate, while the wakefulness drive is inhibited, and slumber is the result. Due to the regulatory influence of the SCN, transitions between sleep and wakefulness occur at predictable intervals.

Note that the SCN does not act in isolation from environmental influence. Light affects the timing of the 24 hour schedule by triggering the SCN to increase its inhibitory effect on melatonin release.

Besides the obvious distinction from everyday experience, the state of sleep differs in function from the states of alertness and wakefulness, and each state correlates with distinct patterns of brain activity. While sleep is understood to be necessary for physical and psychological functioning, it is not a time to attempt goal-oriented behaviors like studying for an exam. Some of the benefits of sleep can be inferred from the negative effects of sleep deprivation, such as difficulty with attention, impaired memory, and a variety of physical symptoms. How sleep is adaptive for the organism is not completely understood, but it may be related to the clearing of metabolic byproducts in the brain.

The stages of sleep are each associated with characteristic patterns of brainwaves. In general, as sleep becomes deeper, the wavelength of brainwaves increases. Stage 1, also called light sleep, includes *alpha waves*. Alpha waves are associated with a state of wakefulness, but one that is more relaxed than the fully alert state associated with beta waves. Stage 2 sleep is associated with bursts of brain wave activity that indicate a full transition into sleep. In stage 3 sleep, *delta waves*, much longer than alpha waves, are first seen, reflecting the transition into deep sleep. Brainwaves in stage 4 (deepest sleep) are almost entirely delta waves.

A sleeper goes through a series of sleep cycles as shown in Figure 5.4. This means that the stages are repeated throughout the night. While one might expect that the sleeper descends straight into stage 4 sleep and stays there throughout the night, this is not the case. Sleep cycles allow the distinct benefits of both light and deep sleep to be gained. The first few sleep cycles of the night include the deepest level of sleep, allowing for healing, growth, and recovery from the fatigue of the day. However, later in the night, more time is spent in the lighter stages of sleep. Understanding this requires consideration of two distinct types of sleep: rapid eye movement (REM) sleep and non-REM (NREM) sleep. REM sleep is named for the characteristic eye movements associated with it, but more importantly, it is a separate sleep stage of high brain activity. REM sleep does not occur in the first sleep cycle of the night, but makes up a significant portion of sleep in later cycles. It can be thought of as a period where the brain relives the massive amount of stimuli experienced during the day, consolidating important information into memory and discarding less important information. In contrast, during NREM sleep, the largest proportion of sleep, brain activity is much lower.

How do the functions of REM sleep occur? The answer to this question is not fully known, but dreaming appears to play an important role. Most of REM sleep is accompanied by dreaming, while most of NREM sleep is without dreaming. The purpose of dreams and the mechanism by which they are formed are still not understood. According to one theory, dreams tend to retrace daily experiences, allowing the brain to process these experiences and consolidate memory. Dreaming may also be the consequence of neurological activity during REM sleep. According to this view, random activity in lower brain centers triggers the higher brain areas involved in perception to interpret this incoming information based on past experience, as though the experience is happening to the dreamer. Either way, dreaming provides a window into the brain's functioning during REM sleep and can even be thought of as a special type of *conscious* awareness that occurs within sleep.

Sufficient sleep is necessary for both physiological and psychological health.

FIGURE 5.4 | Brainwaves During the Stages of Sleep

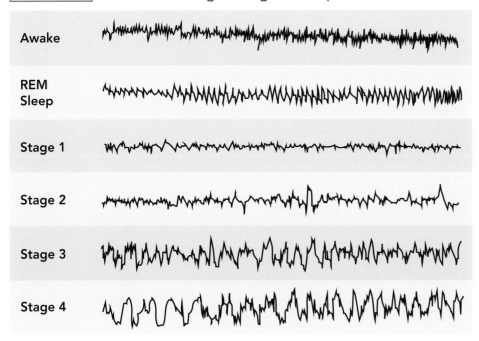

So far, this discussion of sleep has focused on the characteristics of sleep in typical people. However, some people suffer from sleep disorders, in which some aspect of sleep is abnormal, leading to negative health consequences. One of the most well-known is *insomnia,* in which falling asleep is a struggle and the quality of sleep is low. Insomnia can lead to significant impairment, due to the lost benefits of sleep. Quality of sleep is also significantly disrupted by *sleep terror disorder,* which is characterized by severe nightmare-like imagery. Sleep terrors are very different from nightmares, however, in that they occur during NREM sleep. During REM sleep the body is immobilized—consider how inconvenient it would be if dreams were acted out by the body—but the body is free to move during NREM sleep, and it may during sleep terrors. Furthermore, sleep terrors are much more psychologically disturbing than nightmares, involving a sense of total panic. Another sleep disorder, *narcolepsy,* is essentially the takeover of waking life by REM sleep that occurs without warning. Not surprisingly, narcolepsy can be dangerous and disruptive.

FIGURE 5.5 | Sleep Cycles

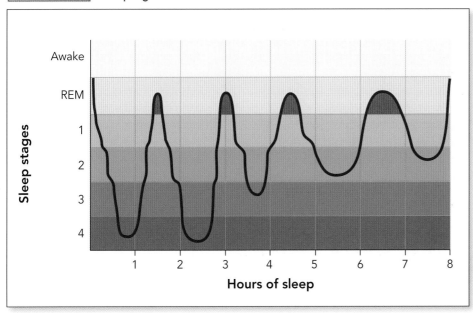

Hypnosis and Meditation

Sleep is only one of the states of consciousness that differs from the baseline state of alert wakefulness. The MCAT® also requires knowledge of two other states that can be experienced and may actively be created: meditation and hypnosis. Both involve changes in attention and in one's relationship with the surroundings. Each has been explored as a potential treatment method for difficulties in psychological functioning.

Hypnosis is a state of relaxation, focused attention and increased willingness to relinquish control over one's own actions. Rather than occurring naturally, it is induced through cooperation with a hypnotist or later as self-hypnosis. In other words, no one can be hypnotized against their will. Some have suggested that hypnosis is not actually a separate state of consciousness, but rather more of an imaginative role-playing exercise. Hypnosis appears to be useful as a treatment for the anxiety and pain associated with medical conditions.

Meditation is an intentional, self-produced state of consciousness induced by relaxing and systematically shifting attention away from day-to-day concerns. This shift can be accomplished by narrowing attention to a single focus, such as an object in the visual field or the process of breathing, or by broadening attention to sensory information. Regardless of the specific techniques used in meditation, the end result is that attention is shifted away from anxiety-provoking thoughts and stimuli. Meditation can be an effective coping mechanism for stress.

Consciousness-Altering Drugs

More dramatic alterations in our state of consciousness can be brought about through consciousness altering drugs, including some with everyday use like caffeine, some that are used medicinally, and others that are recreational. These drugs affect nervous system function and psychological characteristics, such as perception, attention, and emotion. The effects of consciousness altering drugs, including the addictive potential of some, are produced by altering structures and pathways that already exist in the brain. For example, *agonists* mimic chemically similar, naturally-occurring neurotransmitters, thus enhancing the effect of these neurotransmitters. *Antagonists* are drugs that bind to neurotransmitter receptors without activating them, blocking the binding of the associated neurotransmitter and undermining its normal effects. Other types of drugs affect the amount of neurotransmitters in the synapse. Reuptake of neurotransmitters prevents the constant stimulation of postsynaptic receptors; *reuptake inhibitors* interfere with this process so that a greater amount of neurotransmitter remains in the synapse. Drugs that are *enzyme inhibitors* prevent the breakdown of neurotransmitters; as with reuptake inhibitors, more neurotransmitters then remain in the synapse.

Although there are many different drugs that alter consciousness, they can be roughly categorized into three types: stimulants, depressants, and hallucinogens. Stimulants raise the level of activity in the central nervous system. Many stimulants act by increasing the amount of monoamine neurotransmitters, such as epinephrine and dopamine, in the synapse. The body then enters an aroused state of vigilance, with analogous psychological effects—increased feelings of alertness and energy. By contrast, depressants cause a decrease of activity in the central nervous system. Although both stimulants and depressants may produce enjoyable emotional effects, in other ways their effects are very different: depressants are associated with feelings of relaxation and decreased alertness.

Hallucinogens are a category of drugs that cannot be neatly classified as stimulants or depressants; instead, their defining feature is an alteration in sensory and perceptual experience. The type and intensity of the effects of hallucinogens can vary, from subtle changes to full-blown hallucinations. Most hallucinogens seem to exert their effects by mimicking the body's natural neurotransmitters. Some hallucinogens, for instance, bind to and activate a particular type of serotonin receptor.

Remember, epinephrine is associated with the sympathetic nervous system, "fight or flight". It makes sense that drugs associated with raised epinephrine in the synapse have a stimulating effect!

TABLE 5.1 > Example of Consciousness-Altering Drugs

Class	Example
Stimulants	Illicit drug: Methamphetamine (crystal meth) Prescription drug: Methylphenidate (Ritalin) Used to treat ADHD
Depressants	Illicit drug: Heroin Prescription drug: Alprazolam (Xanax) Used to treat anxiety
Hallucinogens	Illicit drug: LSD Prescription drug: Ketamine Used in anesthesia

MCAT® THINK

Antidepressants are not generally thought of as consciousness altering drugs, but they use the same mechanisms described here. Selective serotonin reuptake inhibitors (SSRIs), for example, increase the amount of serotonin present in the synapse. Monoamine oxidase inhibitors (MAOIs) interfere with the breakdown of monoamine neurotransmitters, including serotonin and norepinephrine.

While drugs create a multitude of effects on the nervous system, drug addiction is correlated with similar neurologic mechanisms for all types of addictive drugs. Just as consciousness-altering drugs affect biological functioning and behavior by mimicking or activating naturally occurring neural systems, the addictive power of some drugs is achieved by hijacking a system in the brain that causes feelings of pleasure and reward. The addictive potential of certain drugs is a consequence of activity in the limbic system. A particular pathway within the limbic system, sometimes called the reward pathway, is associated with both feelings of reward in day-to-day life and the feelings of pleasure that lead to cravings and addiction. By activating this pathway, addictive drugs increase levels of dopamine and feelings of reward. Ultimately, long-term drug use can alter the reward pathway to produce the characteristic features of drug addiction. When the brain is chronically exposed to an excess of dopamine due to drug use, it will try to compensate by inhibiting the synthesis and effects of dopamine. The result is that feelings of reward are harder to achieve in the absence of the drug and more of the drug is needed to achieve a feeling of reward.

Thought and Emotion
≡ PSYCH & SOC

This is not the first time you have learned about the limbic system. Recall that the limbic system is also involved in emotion, stress, and memory!

Question 105

Perception is best described as:

- A. the process by which sensory information and prior knowledge are integrated to form a representation of the environment.
- B. the process by which sensory receptors "translate" physical stimuli into electrical information.
- C. the lowest stimulus intensity that can be detected by a sensory organ.
- D. the goal-oriented focus of attention on a particular stimulus.

Question 106

One consequence of selective attention is that some stimuli must be ignored in favor of others. This process is an example of:

- A. bottom-up processing.
- B. sensitivity.
- C. sensation.
- D. top-down processing.

Question 107

Which of the following would most likely NOT be grouped, according to Gestalt principles?

- A. Three unique shapes painted in the same region of a canvas
- B. Three unique shapes painted in separate regions of a canvas
- C. Three similar shapes painted in the same region of a canvas
- D. Three similar shapes painted in separate regions of a canvas

Question 108

Which of the following could be most reasonably expected of an individual's performance on a depth discrimination task that involves identifying the closer of two objects at various distances?

- A. Performance should be worst when both objects are near the individual.
- B. Performance should be worst when both objects are far from the individual.
- C. Performance depends only on the distance between the two objects, regardless of their distance from the individual.
- D. Performance should be best when both objects are far from the individual.

Question 109

By treating neurons with excessive levels of some neurotransmitters, scientists are able to induce cell death and "ablate" specific regions of the brain. This provides a convenient but crude method of controlling certain brain functions during experiments. If a researcher was interested in generating mice incapable of identifying specific shapes in their visual fields, where would he or she most likely deposit excess dopamine?

- A. The retina
- B. The optic chiasm
- C. The lateral geniculate nucleus
- D. Layer 1 of the visual cortex

Question 110

Feature detection is best described as which of the following?

- A. Sequential processing of information from parallel pathways
- B. Parallel processing of information from sequential pathways
- C. Sequential processing of information from sequential pathways
- D. Parallel processing of information from parallel pathways

Question 111

Which of the following best describes the relationship between consciousness and attention?

- A. Consciousness and attention are separate processes that act independently.
- B. Attention ensures that all sensory information is available for conscious perception.
- C. Consciousness controls which information becomes available for analysis through attention.
- D. Attention controls the flow of information that becomes available for conscious perception.

Question 112

Which of the following would most likely be found in the blood of a sleep-deprived individual at night?

- A. High levels of melatonin
- B. Low levels of melatonin
- C. Abnormally high levels of depressants
- D. Abnormally low levels of stimulants

5.6 | Memory: Storage and Encoding

Consider Key 3: Memory involves encoding, storage, and retrieval. Each stage is important in preserving memories and a problem at any stage may lead to loss of information. Scientists are not certain how many memories our brains can hold, but the number is certainly greater than the memory of most household computers.

The study of memory—how it is formed, maintained, and brought to mind—is complex. In a way, it can be thought of as the neural correlate of learning. While learning is generally measured by the presence of certain behaviors, memory is the representation and maintenance of information by the nervous system. The MCAT® requires an understanding of both the psychological and biological perspectives on memory. The discussion of memory in this section and those that follow will demonstrate the relationships between attention, sensation, consciousness, and memory. Like many of the processes that have been discussed, memory is a tool that we use to organize information for the purpose of behavioral response. Much like perception, memory formation does not create an exact recording of surroundings or events. Instead, a representative model is created based on incoming stimuli.

Relationships and Behavior
PSYCH & SOC

It is important to realize that we are capable of many types of memory, each associated with distinct neural structures and patterns of activity. Broadly speaking, there are two types of memory. *Declarative memory* involves information that is consciously known, such as the memory of specific lifetime events and the knowledge of facts. *Non-declarative* or *procedural memory*, in contrast, refers to the unconscious ability to remember how to perform a particular task. Although both types of memory are crucial to everyday functioning, the MCAT® will focus on declarative memory.

Declarative memory involves various types of memory storage, each uniquely processing and storing information. This section will trace the progress of incoming information as it moves from one type of memory to the next. As will be shown, the process is carried out actively, not passively, as only selected information ultimately proceeds throughout the stages of memory while other information is discarded. At each stage, memory undergoes encoding, where it is transformed into the type of representation that is used by that particular form of memory storage.

FIGURE 5.6 | Encoding and Storage of Declarative Memory

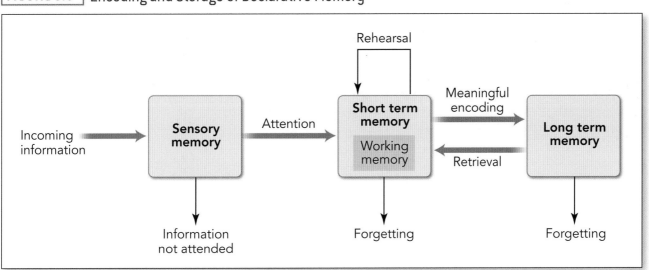

The Cell
BIOLOGY 2

The first phase in memory formation is sensory memory. Sensory memory is temporary storage for incoming sensory stimuli. At this stage, encoding is simply the process of transducing physical stimuli into electrical information that is thereby accessible to the nervous system. The encoding of sensory memory—i.e., transduction of stimuli—is largely an unconscious, neurological process, carried out via sensory receptors and dendritic summation. However, conscious processes, like the experience of fear, can affect what stimuli are encoded and the sensitivity of sense organs.

Although sensory memory can hold a large quantity of sensory data from all the senses, information remains in sensory memory for a very limited time. The next step is either short-term memory storage or the loss of the information altogether. As with sensation and perception, attention is the deciding factor. Information that receives attention gains access to short-term memory and therefore consciousness, while information that is not the focus of attention is lost. Information that has emotional significance or is related to the completion of a task is likely to receive attentional resources.

Information that makes it past sensory memory enters *short-term memory*, which holds items in conscious awareness. Information held in short-term memory can be manipulated rather than stored passively: in other words, the information can be used, applied, or elaborated, such as when answering test questions. As a component of short-term memory, this combination of memory storage and active use is called working memory. Working memory differs substantially from sensory memory in terms of encoding and storage. Information is usually encoded into working memory through an auditory representation. Consider the process of trying to remember a short string of numbers that have been read from a page. A visual representation of the numbers would appear briefly in sensory memory and, if attended to, would then move into short-term memory. Once in short-term memory, the numbers would be represented as auditory information. Working memory is more limited than sensory memory in the number of items that can be stored simultaneously. Research indicates that most people can hold only 5 to 9 (7 ± 2) pieces of information in working memory at one time.

Short-term memories tend to fade or to be pushed out by newly acquired information. Keeping items active in working memory requires effort. The following processes that aid in encoding memories are used to maintain information in working memory. Rehearsal, or the repetition of a phonetic representation, is one of these processes. Another is chunking, reorganizing a large number of items into a smaller number of "chunks." By reducing the number of items, chunking allows a larger amount of information to be maintained in working memory.

After passing from the sensory storage to short-term memory, information may enter the more durable storage of long-term memory. Information held in long-term memory is maintained outside of conscious awareness and can be called back into working memory when needed. Encoding of information into long-term memory is guided by meaning. Assigning meaning occurs by linking new information to meaningful ideas that are already held in long-term memory. Not all information reaches long-term memory, but there appears to be no limit on the amount of information that long-term memory maintains.

Working memory is what allows you to do MCAT® problems in your head!

$86.49 - $23.15 = $63.34

TABLE 5.2 > **Memory Storage**

Type of memory storage	Encoding	Storage
Sensory	Physical transduction	Unlimited
Working	Rehearsal	Limited (7 ± 2)
Long-term	Meaning	Unlimited

5.7 | The Biology of Memory Formation

The MCAT® requires an understanding of the features of the nervous system that facilitate learning and memory. At the most basic level, the formation of new memories is associated with changes in the parts of the brain that correspond to working and long-term memory. Neural plasticity allows memories to be stored as changes to networks of neurons. **Neural plasticity** is the ability of the brain's networks of neurons and their synapses to change. It is most apparent in early development, but continues to a lesser extent throughout life. Neural plasticity includes the brain's ability to reorganize in response to a traumatic brain injury or stroke, such that the functions associated with lost tissue can be taken over by unaffected areas. Without neural plasticity, adaptation to changing life circumstances and memory formation would be impossible.

The key to learning and memory formation is that when patterns of neural activity occur in response to the internal and external environment, the brain holds these patterns as changes in receptors and synapses, maintaining a physical record. Take the example of a single excitatory synapse. Every time a signal crosses that synapse—i.e., every time the presynaptic neuron releases neurotransmitter triggering an action potential in the post-synaptic neuron—the synapse is strengthened. From this perspective, the neural representation of a long-term memory is a network of neurons that is strengthened not only by the encoding but also the retrieval of that memory. Every time the memory is activated, the simultaneous firing of synapses involved in the neural network causes the neural connections to be strengthened. The strengthening of the neural network that represents a memory is called *memory consolidation*, which, as described previously, is one of the functions of sleep.

What does it mean that a connection between neurons is strengthened? Long-term potentiation is the molecular process underlying the formation of long-term memories through the strengthening of synapses. **Long-term potentiation (LTP)** describes the increase in likelihood that presynaptic input will trigger an action potential in the postsynaptic neuron. When repeated stimulation by the presynaptic neuron while the postsynaptic neuron is also active leads to an increase in the strength of the *excitatory postsynaptic potential* that is produced by similar stimulation, LTP has occurred. Considering the example of a single excitatory synapse again, the occurrence of LTP in this synapse would mean that the postsynaptic neuron became increasingly likely to fire in response to stimulation by the presynaptic neuron. Of course, in actuality an action potential usually is triggered by the combined signals of many presynaptic neurons, so LTP can take place via the additive influence of multiple inputs. The strengthening of a network of synaptic connections via long-term potentiation of excitatory synapses increases the likelihood that the corresponding memory will persist in the brain.

The detailed mechanisms of LTP and the larger process of memory formation in the brain are the focus of active research and changing models. It does seem clear that the hippocampus and adjacent areas play an important role in the initial consolidation of declarative memory. LTP in hippocampal synapses has been extensively studied. After the process of memory consolidation through LTP, communication between the hippocampal system and the prefrontal cortex establishes the storage of long-term memories in various areas of the cortex.

Neural plasticity will allow different parts of my brain to take over some of the functions associated with the damaged parts.

Cells that fire together, wire together!

"I remember the hippo
I saw on campus!"

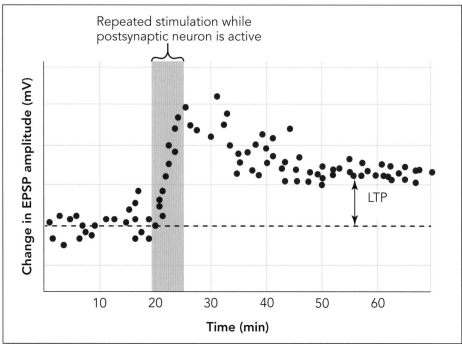

FIGURE 5.7 Long-Term Potentiation

Repeated stimulation while postsynaptic neuron is active

Change in EPSP amplitude (mV)

Time (min)

LTP

5.8 Memory Retrieval and Forgetting

The previous sections focused on the encoding and storage of memory. Next, information that has passed through these stages must be accessible in order to be useful. Memory formation involves the transfer of information from the temporary storage of working memory to long-term memory, but a defining feature of long-term memory is that information can also move in the other direction. In other words, through **retrieval**, information stored in long-term memory can return to working memory for the purpose of problem-solving and guidance of behavior.

The ability to activate a particular memory as needed depends on the presence of some form of organization of the massive amount of information stored in long-term memory. Since long-term memory is encoded according to meaning, it is not surprising that meaning also plays a role in structuring the way that mem-

FIGURE 5.8 Semantic Network of Spreading Activation

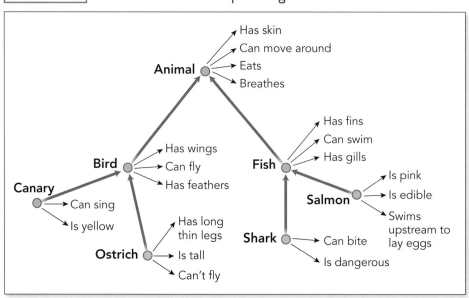

ory is stored. Long-term memory appears to make use of semantic networks, which organize information in networks of meaningfully related memories. This structure has implications for the way that long-term memories are brought to consciousness. The activation of a memory of a certain item or idea leads to the activation of other memories that are also located in or linked to the network of memory. Related memories are brought to mind through spreading activation, where one item triggers an activation of related memories.

The quality and ease of memory retrieval varies significantly according to situational characteristics. As a result, various methods of assessing retrieval have been developed. Two such methods are recall and recognition. Recall is the retrieval of a memory "from scratch," while recognition is the correct identification of information that is presented.

Both processes are enhanced by the presence of retrieval cues. Retrieval cues are environmental stimuli or pieces of information that are associated in some way with the memory being sought. Notice that the useful role of retrieval cues is consistent with the theory of semantic networks and spreading activation discussed previously. Retrieval cues are often environmental stimuli that were present at the time that the memory sought was originally formed. This type of retrieval cue is *context-dependent*. For example, suppose that a student sat in a particular room while studying for an exam. Retrieval of facts learned while studying would be improved if the student took the exam in the same room. Retrieval cues can also be internal feelings, such as anger, or specific states of consciousness, such as intoxication. This type of retrieval cue is *state-dependent*. As an example, someone who is angry is more likely to remember other times when they were angry rather than situations in which they were calm. This is evidence of the role of emotion in memory. Another type of retrieval cue is priming. Priming occurs outside of conscious awareness and causes activation of semantic networks. It makes an individual more likely to recall a memory that is similar to the retrieval cue, though the individual is not conscious of the connection. Priming is used extensively in marketing, where certain words or images are used to make consumers more likely to purchase certain products. Recognition is frequently an easier task than recall—the presence of the correct answer acts as an effective recognition cue.

The role of emotion in retrieving memories can be understood as a retrieval cue. Memory retrieval is strongest when the emotional state during retrieval is similar to that of memory formation. In other words, emotions are retrieval cues. This demonstrates the usefulness of both internal and external retrieval cues. In addition, memories that have high emotional significance or were formed in the context of strong emotions are particularly available for retrieval. That said, emotion does not always improve the ability to retrieve memories. As anyone who has taken an important exam knows, anxiety can pose a distraction that interferes with memory retrieval.

Psychologists have also studied other processes that aid in retrieval of memories. These techniques can be used to study for a test and may have applications to the diseases that impair memory. One of these processes is organization of the information. *Clustering* is the organization of information by grouping similar terms together. If asked to memorize the words, "Apple, Bear, Catastrophe, Deal, Egg, and Fox," it would be easiest to group apple and egg (food), bear and fox (animals), and catastrophe and deal (events). Another way to organize information is *temporally*. A doctor prescribing new medications may go over the doses in the order that they should be taken. Rather than saying, "Take pill X three times a day and pill Y twice a day," he or she would say, "Take pill X and pill Y in the morning. Take only pill X at lunch. Then take pill X and Y in the evening." Organizing information temporally can help the patient remember the medication regimen. Another process that can aid in retrieval of memories is the use of *mnemonics*. Mnemonic is a general word referring to any memory tool, but the term is often associated with a tool in which a word or phrase is constructed from the first letter of each term that needs to be memorized. A common mnemonic is

It's easy to remember the difference between recognition and recall. Just imagine a vocabulary test where you have to know the definitions for words. If you have to pick the definition from a bunch of choices (like on a multiple choice test), it's recognition. If you have to write in the definition, it's recall. A lifetime of test taking has probably given you the intuition that recognition is generally easier than recall.

I took French a few years ago and thought I had forgotten everything. But when I got to Paris, I picked up right where I left off!

"ROY G BIV" to remember the order of colors in the visual spectrum. Another tool that can aid in retrieval is visualization. To memorize the six words used in the first example, someone may picture a catastrophe caused by a bear eating an apple and making a deal with a fox who is eating an egg. Other processes are also important to memory retrieval. Studies have shown retrieval is maximized when a person has had sufficient sleep. Caffeine, exercise, and time of day also affect memory retrieval.

Another indicator of memory retrieval is the **relearning** of material that was previously encoded in memory. Relearning allows for the detection of long-term memories that have become inaccessible to conscious recognition or recall and as a result are experienced as lost. One can infer that a seemingly lost memory persists unconsciously when relearning requires less time or effort than a first instance of learning.

Forgetting of Memories

Memory is not immune to errors and loss. A full understanding of memory includes the study of how memories change and fade over time. The process of **decay** describes the fading of a memory: this is the fate of information in working memory that does not get encoded into long-term memory. From a neurological perspective, decay is the weakening of connections that make up the neural network that holds a memory. The strengthening of these connections prevents the decay of long-term memories.

The circumstances of encoding affect whether or not information in short-term memory is likely to decay. Consider a test of the ability to recall items presented in an ordered list. Recall is reliably strongest for items at the beginning of the list, the **primacy effect**, and items at the end of the list, the **recency effect**, while memory of items in the middle are most vulnerable to decay. This phenomenon results from the limitations of working memory. The earlier items are easily maintained in working memory through rehearsal, so they can be transferred to long-term memory. Due to the limited number of items that can be held in working memory, the middle items on the list are displaced as new items are presented. Since the items in the middle cannot be held long enough for sufficient rehearsal, they decay before entering long-term memory. The later items in the list can be maintained in working memory because, unlike the items in the middle, they are not displaced by new incoming information.

Decay usually affects working memory as well as sensory memory (as the brief representation of sensory stimuli quickly fades) whereas the forgetting of information in long-term memory is often due to problems with retrieval rather than loss of the memory altogether. A common phenomenon that prevents successful memory retrieval is **interference**, where similar information prevents the retrieval of a memory. Newly learned material that prevents successful retrieval of related older memories is called **retroactive interference**. However, the opposite effect can also occur when previously held knowledge prevents successful retrieval of more newly learned information. This problem is called **proactive interference**.

The greater the similarity between memories, the more likely it is they will interfere with one another. It is likely this is caused by the sharing of retrieval cues. Although retrieval cues improve recall, when similar retrieval cues are used for multiple memories, a given cue is likely to activate either piece of information. Consider how this affects the ability to retrieve long-term memories. Over time, the same retrieval cue comes to be associated with increasing numbers of similar memories. Older memories therefore have a greater vulnerability to interference.

Memories that are repeatedly retrieved from long-term memory are altered by the process of retrieval itself. Just as perception creates a particular representation of the world that is likely to differ from an "objective" view, memory is a construct of the mind rather than an unbiased record of events. Memories can be updated with new information and experiences, a process called **memory construction**.

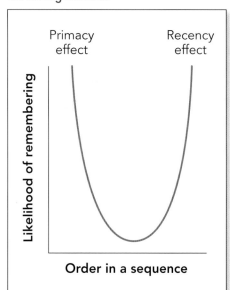

FIGURE 5.9 The Primacy and Recency Effects

Primacy effect

Recency effect

Likelihood of remembering

Order in a sequence

FIGURE 5.10 Retroactive vs. Proactive Interference

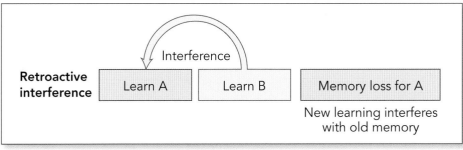

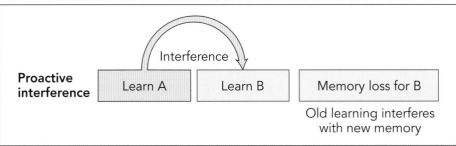

You can maintain your mental abilities by exercising your brain. Use it or lose it!

Memory construction occurs during retrieval. When we retrieve a memory, we re-activate the neural network that represents that memory. This activation provides an opportunity for changes to be made in that network and the associated memory.

Source monitoring occurs when a person attributes a memory to a particular source, correctly or not, such as recalling that a story was told by a particular person. Memory construction may follow: when a person believes that a memory comes from a particular source, they may draw conclusions based on characteristics of the source, and these inferences then come to be part of the memory. Source monitoring may also lead to the construction of memories of events that never actually occurred. An example would be the incorrect belief that an imagined event—such as the false memory that one completed a task—is a memory of a real event.

The ability to attribute a memory to the correct source is one aspect of declarative memory that sometimes declines with aging. While there is a stereotype about the relationship between aging and memory, there is in fact a great deal of variation in the amount and type of memory decline associated with aging. Severe deficits in memory are possible but not inevitable. When age-related changes do occur, either or both of the areas of the brain mentioned in the context of memory formation—the hippocampus and prefrontal cortex—can be involved. The capacity for accurate source monitoring is one of several processes whose decline seems to be tied to damage of the prefrontal cortex. Changes in the hippocampus with age also seem to be involved in memory deficits. Declining memory has been shown to accompany loss of synaptic connections in both the prefrontal cortex and hippocampus. Since memory is maintained by networks of synaptic connections, it makes sense that a decrease in the overall strength of connectivity would have a negative impact on memory.

The possibility of memory impairment is part of the broader spectrum of cognitive changes in late adulthood. In general, aging is associated with cognitive decline, where ability gained in earlier development is lessened. Many cognitive processes, including speed of thought and working memory, typically decline with age. Seemingly unrelated conditions can also lead to a decline in cognitive abilities, such as from systemic diseases like cardiovascular disease, which can reduce blood flow to the brain. Recent research has suggested that activities like completing crossword puzzles or playing bridge can help maintain cognitive ability in old age.

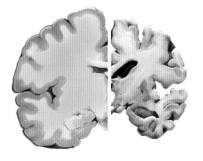

A section of a healthy brain is shown on the left in this photo. On the right is a section of the brain of a person with severe Alzheimer's disease, demonstrating marked loss of volume due to cell death.

5.9 | Neurologic Dysfunctions

Although a degree of change in memory capacity with age is normal, there are also neurological disorders that can have a more severe impact on memory. **Alzheimer's disease** is associated with aging but is not considered part of normal age-related cognitive change, and has a characteristic pattern of neurodegeneration. Symptoms typically begin with the loss of the ability to form memories of recent events. This ability is mediated by the hippocampus and surrounding areas, so it is not surprising that these structures are typically the first to be affected in Alzheimer's. There are two distinctive types of damage in the brain in Alzheimer's: *amyloid plaques*, which are extracellular protein deposits, and *neurofibrillary tangles*, which are located within neurons. As the disease progresses, the negative effects of amyloid plaques spread to a variety of structures throughout the brain and further abilities, such as language, are affected.

Korsakoff's syndrome is similar to Alzheimer's disease in how it presents as a deficit in the ability to recall recent events while older memories are relatively unaffected. Korsakoff's is caused by a nutritional deficiency rather than age-related neurodegeneration. It is almost always associated with a deficiency in *vitamin B_1*, which is often due to severe alcoholism. The pattern of neurological damage that leads to Korsakoff's syndrome is not fully understood, but appears to include damage to the frontal cortex and thalamus.

Parkinson's disease is a neurodegenerative disease, like Alzheimer's, but the associated brain damage is restricted to a specific area rather than being widely distributed. In Parkinson's, deterioration within the *substantia nigra*, located within the **midbrain**, leads to the impairment of motor abilities. Common symptoms of Parkinson's include difficulty initiating movement, tremors, and weakness of facial muscles. The affected neurons release the neurotransmitter dopamine, so Parkinson's is associated with a deficiency in dopamine in this part of the brain. As a result of neuron loss and dopamine deficiency, the substantia nigra is unable to fulfill its normal function of contributing to the initiation of movement.

Current research in the treatment of neurodegenerative conditions such as Alzheimer's and Parkinson's is using **stem cell based therapy** to regenerate neurons in the central nervous system. Stem cells are able to differentiate into a variety of different cell types. If stem cells could be introduced into areas of neurodegeneration and be induced to proliferate and differentiate into the appropriate cell type, they could potentially provide a powerful method to replace lost or damaged cells. This approach seems particularly promising for Parkinson's disease because the damage is restricted to a limited number of neurons. Stem cell therapy also has many other possible applications, including Alzheimer's disease and traumatic injury to the nervous system.

> Endocrine System
> BIOLOGY 2

If I am completely terrified, my ability to create and store memories will be impaired. When I am just slightly irritated or slightly amused, my ability to store new information that is linked with these emotions will be enhanced. And that's my job—to slightly amuse or irritate you to assist in your memory of important material for the MCAT®!

Question 113

With enough repetition, even difficult physical tasks such as performing complex surgeries or musical compositions can become easily replicable. Which of the following best explains the relative ease with which well-practiced individuals can complete these tasks?

- ○ **A.** Declarative memory
- ○ **B.** Working memory
- ○ **C.** Procedural memory
- ○ **D.** Sensory encoding

Question 114

If a scientist was interested in studying brain abnormalities in individuals with unusually high capacities for working memory, which of the following regions of the brain would she be most likely to study?

- ○ **A.** Sympathetic ganglia
- ○ **B.** Auditory cortex
- ○ **C.** Hypothalamus
- ○ **D.** Visual cortex

Question 115

A person who memorizes large segments of speeches by repeating them out loud many times is practicing which memory encoding technique?

- ○ **A.** Hypnosis
- ○ **B.** Feature recognition
- ○ **C.** Chunking
- ○ **D.** Rehearsal

Question 116

Which of the following differentiates long term memory from other forms of declarative memory?

- ○ **A.** Long term memory is less durable and persists outside of conscious awareness.
- ○ **B.** Long term memory is less durable and persists only within conscious awareness.
- ○ **C.** Long term memory is more durable and persists outside of conscious awareness.
- ○ **D.** Long term memory is more durable and persists only within conscious awareness.

Question 117

Gabapentin is a drug capable of blocking new synapse formation. Which type of memory would be LEAST affected in a patient treated with gabapentin?

- ○ **A.** Working memory
- ○ **B.** Sensory memory
- ○ **C.** Long term memory
- ○ **D.** Procedural memory

Question 118

New memories are constantly being formed, in part through long-term potentiation. The opposing process of long-term depression also constantly affects memory formation. Which of the following is most likely FALSE concerning long-term depression?

- ○ **A.** Long-term depression can be important for forgetting unused memories.
- ○ **B.** Long-term depression increases the likelihood that presynaptic input will trigger a postsynaptic action potential.
- ○ **C.** Entire networks of synapses can be affected by long-term depression.
- ○ **D.** The hippocampus is an especially active site for long-term depression.

Question 119

If a student wants to maximize her recall of material for a test, which of the following study techniques should she employ?

- ○ **A.** Studying in the same room every day
- ○ **B.** Studying in a new location every day
- ○ **C.** Studying by answering practice test questions in the same format as those seen on the test
- ○ **D.** Studying with a new group of classmates every day

Question 120

Highly similar memories can cause which of the following?

   I. Retroactive interference
  II. Spreading activation
 III. Proactive interference

- ○ **A.** II only
- ○ **B.** I and III only
- ○ **C.** II and III only
- ○ **D.** I, II, and III

Absolute threshold
Adaptive values
Aging and memory
Alertness
Alzheimer's disease
Attention
Bottom-up processing
Circadian rhythm
Cognitive changes
Consciousness
Consciousness altering drugs
Constancy
Decay
Depressants
Depth
Difference threshold
Divided attention
Dreaming
Drug addiction
Encoding
Feature detection
Forms
Genetically based behavioral
 variation
Gestalt principles
Hallucinogens
Heredity
Hypnosis
Hypothalamus

Interaction between heredity and
 environment
Interference
Korsakoff's syndrome
Long-term memory
Long-term potentiation (LTP)
Meditation
Memory
Memory construction
Midbrain
Motion
Neural plasticity
Non-REM (NREM) sleep
Parallel processing
Parkinson's disease
Perception
Primacy effect
Priming
Proactive interference
Processes that aid in visual
 processing
Rapid eye movement (REM) sleep
Recall
Recency effect
Recognition
Regulatory genes
Relearning
Retrieval
Retrieval cues
Retroactive interference

Reward pathway
Role of emotion
Selective attention
Semantic networks
Sensation
Sensory memory
Signal detection theory
Sleep
Sleep cycles
Sleep disorders
Source monitoring
Spreading activation
Stage 1
Stage 2
Stage 3
Stage 4
Stages of sleep
Stem cell based therapy
Stimulants
Top-down processing
Types of memory storage
Visual processing
Weber's law
Working memory

DON'T FORGET YOUR KEYS

1. The environment is experienced through sensation (gathering of information) and perception (processing and interpretation of information).

2. Stages of sleep serve different functions. Early in the night, more time is spent in deep sleep; later on, more time in light sleep and REM sleep.

3. Memory involves encoding, storage, retrieval, and loss of information.

STOP!

DO NOT LOOK AT THESE EXAMS UNTIL CLASS.

30-MINUTE IN-CLASS EXAM FOR LECTURE 1

Passage I (Questions 1-5)

The biopsychosocial (BPS) model has utility in the understanding and treatment of both mental and physical health problems. In a study aimed at examining biopsychosocial case complexity in an emergency room environment, patients were assessed using the INTERMED method, in which biological, psychological, social and health care-related aspects of disease are rated to give a patient profile in these four domains. Scores on the INTERMED are directly correlated with biopsychosocial complexity, and high scores predict negative outcomes such as long hospital stay and poor results in patients with diabetes. Statistical analysis revealed three clusters of ER patients, as shown in Figure 1.

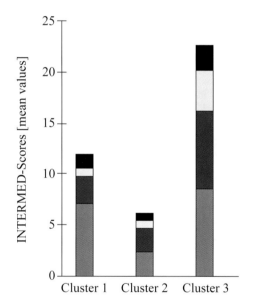

Figure 1 Description of the three clusters of patients by INTERMED domain scores summing up to total scores

The BPS model has been critiqued for failing to clarify the nature of the relationships between the components of the model. In a second study, researchers attempted to clarify the implications of the BPS model for mental disorders. They hypothesized that psychological factors, which are amenable to evidence-based therapy, mediate the effects of biological and environmental factors on mental health. Data were collected from questionnaires measuring levels of depression and anxiety as well as the key psychological processes of response style and self-blame. Statistical analysis showed that although life events and social status were significant predictors of mental health problems, the overall ability of the model to explain the data was significantly improved by the inclusion of psychological processes as mediators in the hypothesized relationship between biological factors, life events, and environmental challenges, on the one hand, and mental health on the other.

This passage was adapted from "Psychological Processes Mediate the Impact of Familial Risk, Social Circumstances and Life Events on Mental Health." Kinderman P, Schwannauer M, Pontin E, Tai S. *PLoS ONE*. 2013. 8(10) doi:10.1371/journal.pone.0076564 and "Biopsychosocial Health Care Needs at the Emergency Room: Challenge of Complexity." Matzer F, Wisiak UV, Graninger M, Söllner W, Stilling HP, Glawischnig-Goschnik M, Lueger A, Fazekas C. *PLoS ONE*. 2012. 7(8) doi:10.1371/journal.pone.0041775 for use under the terms of the Creative Commons CC BY 3.0 license (http://creativecommons.org/licenses/by/3.0/legalcode).

Question 1

Additional data from the first study described in the passage showed that compared to patients in the other two clusters, those in cluster 2 were younger and had obtained higher educational levels. This difference is best described as a difference in:

○ **A.** social class.

○ **B.** demographics.

○ **C.** social institutions.

○ **D.** material culture.

Question 2

Which conclusion is NOT consistent with the results of the second study?

○ **A.** Genetics and psychological processes have largely separate effects on the development of mental disorders.

○ **B.** Social status has a significant influence on mental health.

○ **C.** Psychological factors influence the relationship between genetics and mental health.

○ **D.** Psychological, biological, and environmental factors interact to influence the development of mental disorders.

Question 3

Lack of access to healthcare is an example of a social and environmental factor that can contribute to biopsychosocial case complexity. Which theoretical approach would likely be most useful for examining differential access to healthcare between social groups due to differing levels of power and prestige?

○ **A.** Social constructionism

○ **B.** Symbolic interactionism

○ **C.** Functionalism

○ **D.** Conflict theory

Next ▶

Question 4

A follow-up study indicated that ER patients who had been admitted multiple times in the past year, compared to those who had not, had lower levels of cultural knowledge that facilitates belongingness in one's social context. Compared to the other patients, those patients with multiple hospital admissions had lower:

○ **A.** intergenerational mobility.

○ **B.** cultural capital.

○ **C.** social capital.

○ **D.** socioeconomic status.

Question 5

Based on the results of the two studies described in the passage, which of the following interventions would likely be most effective in addressing mental health problems among emergency room patients with high biopsychosocial case complexity?

○ **A.** Improving the participants' social status

○ **B.** Directing treatment only at social factors

○ **C.** Restricting treatment to interventions in biological factors

○ **D.** Carrying out psychological interventions

Passage II (Questions 6-9)

Bullying affects the health and well-being of both perpetrators and victims. Peer-relations in adolescent schoolchildren have been shown to be significantly related to metabolic syndrome in middle age. The metabolic syndrome represents a cluster of metabolic and cardiovascular disturbances, including central obesity, dyslipidemia, high blood pressure, and disturbed glucose metabolism. The potential pathways whereby peer relations could influence the risk of metabolic syndrome in adulthood are manifold and include direct and indirect social pathways.

A study examining the prevalence of bullying and victimization among young elementary school children also examined socioeconomic disparities in bullying behavior. School neighborhood socioeconomic status (SES) was examined for its association with bullying behavior independent of family SES. School neighborhood SES was determined by linking school postal code areas with government-determined status scores for neighborhoods. Parental questionnaires were used to determine parental SES, while school-teacher questionnaires were used to determine incidence of bullying and victimization activity.

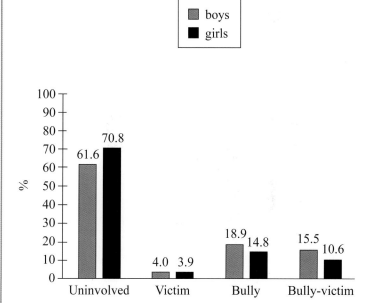

Figure 1 Prevalence of involvement in bullying and victimization in boys and girls

The results of the study showed that all indicators of low family SES and low school neighborhood SES were associated with an increased risk of being a bully or bully-victim. When family SES was controlled for, the influence of school neighborhood SES on bullying became statistically non-significant.

This passage was adapted from "Prevalence of Bullying and Victimization Among Children in Early Elementary School: Do Family and School Neighbourhood Socioeconomic Status Matter?" Jansen PW, Verlinden M, Dommisse-van Berkel A, Mieloo C, van der Ende J, Veenstra R, Verhulst FC, Jansen W, Tiemeir H. *BMC Public Health*. 2012. 12(494) doi:10.1186/1471-2458-12-494 and "Do Peer Relations in Adolescence Influence Health in Adulthood? Peer Problems in the School Setting and the Metabolic Syndrome in Middle-Age." Gustafsson PE, Janlert U, Theorell T, Westerlund H, Hammarstrom A.2012. 7(6) doi:10.1371/journal.pone.0039385. for use under the terms of the Creative Commons Attribution 4.0 License (www.biomedcentral.com/pdf/Creative_Commons_Attribtion_4.0_International_CC_BY_4.0.pdf).

Question 6

Which of the following might be expected to increase the likelihood of bullying behavior?

○ **A.** Moving a child to a higher SES school
○ **B.** Expanding the social group of the child
○ **C.** Treating bullying as a social norm
○ **D.** Eliminating residential segregation

Question 7

Which of the following is LEAST likely to be used by the government in determining SES status scores of a school's neighborhood?

○ **A.** Income levels
○ **B.** Education levels
○ **C.** Unemployment rates
○ **D.** Racial composition

Question 8

A separate study found that children from low SES families are 350% more likely than their high SES peers to have at least one parent who was also raised in low SES conditions. These findings are consistent with the idea of:

○ **A.** meritocracy.
○ **B.** social reproduction.
○ **C.** cultural capital.
○ **D.** social capital.

Question 9

Which of the following, if true, would be LEAST likely to introduce error to the findings of the study presented in the passage?

○ **A.** Teachers over-report bullying behavior of louder students.
○ **B.** Parents are experiencing relative poverty rather than absolute poverty.
○ **C.** Parents are experiencing absolute poverty rather than relative poverty.
○ **D.** School districts have been re-zoned since the government determination of status scores.

Passage III (Questions 10-14)

Although immigrants typically have improved socioeconomic profiles with increasing length of time spent in the U.S. or through successive generations, the opposite holds true for health outcomes, an effect known as unhealthy assimilation. Unhealthy assimilation, or deterioration in health status, raises questions about the social and environmental factors that are associated with the health of immigrants and their descendants.

The "healthy immigrant effect" refers to the paradox that despite often having worse socioeconomic characteristics, less access to health care services, and greater linguistic and cultural barriers related to accessing health information, immigrants tend to have better health profiles than native born Americans. Several studies have shown that this health advantage deteriorates over time and with successive generations in the U.S. This effect may be due to adoption of less healthy American lifestyles, including those related to diet, smoking, and physical activity.

In another area of the study of immigration status and health, researchers compared the treatment outcomes of documented and undocumented Hispanic immigrants with HIV in the U.S. While Hispanics represent about 16% of the total U.S. population, they represent 20% of persons newly infected with HIV. Researchers took initial counts of CD^4 cells, a type of T-cell that helps the body fight infection, and found that undocumented Hispanic patients had a lower median initial CD^4 cell count than documented Hispanic patients. Once in care, undocumented Hispanic patients did as well or better than their documented counterparts. One year after entering HIV care, rates of retention in care and HIV suppression were similar between undocumented and documented Hispanic patients.

This passage was adapted from "Treatment Outcomes in Undocumented Hispanic Immigrants with HIV Infection." Poon KK, Dang BN, Davila JA, Hartman C, Giordano TP. *PLoS ONE*. 2013. 8(3) doi: 10.1371/journal.pone.0060022 and "Change in Self-Reported Health Status among Immigrants in the United States: Associations with Measures of Acculturation." Lee S, O'Neill AH, Ihara ES, Chae DH. *PLoS ONE*. 2013. 8(10): doi:10.1371/journal.pone.0076494 for use under the terms of the Creative Commons CC BY 3.0 license (http://creativecommons.org/licenses/by/3.0/legalcode).

Question 10

Measuring which of the following would likely be LEAST helpful to researchers who want to assess the correlation between assimilation and immigrant health?

○ **A.** English language proficiency
○ **B.** Choice of occupation
○ **C.** Change in diet
○ **D.** Exposure to psychosocial stress, including racial and anti-immigrant discrimination

Question 11

All of the following could be plausible explanations of the paradox of the "healthy immigrant effect" EXCEPT:

○ **A.** U.S. culture promotes healthy behaviors compared to the native cultures of the immigrants studied.

○ **B.** individuals who are more healthy and resilient are more likely to migrate.

○ **C.** immigrants who are older or unhealthy are more likely to return to their home country.

○ **D.** culturally-specific healthy behaviors of immigrants are more influential on health outcomes than conventional risk factors such as low socioeconomic status.

Question 12

Which statement(s) is/are supported by the study presented in the passage regarding treatment of HIV?

   I. Hispanics are disproportionately at risk for HIV infection in the U.S.

  II. Hispanics are significantly more likely to enter HIV care with advanced disease than people of other races

 III. Entry into HIV care late in the disease process results in worse clinical outcomes.

○ **A.** I only

○ **B.** II only

○ **C.** I and II only

○ **D.** I and III only

Question 13

Suppose a later study finds that documented and undocumented Hispanics tend to live in separate neighborhoods, and that neighborhood location is significantly associated with access to health care resources. Which of the following conclusions is supported by this finding?

○ **A.** Differential health outcomes are partially due to documented vs. undocumented status.

○ **B.** Undocumented immigrants experience structural barriers to accessing healthcare.

○ **C.** Hispanics in the U.S. do not experience intragroup social inequality.

○ **D.** Spatial inequality contributes to differential health outcomes among Hispanic immigrants.

Question 14

According to the passage, second generation immigrants are more likely than first generation immigrants to experience all of the following EXCEPT:

○ **A.** greater prestige.

○ **B.** longer lifespan.

○ **C.** greater wealth.

○ **D.** higher educational attainment.

Passage IV (Questions 15-18)

Over the past twenty years, attention deficit hyperactivity disorder (ADHD) has been widely diagnosed in children. ADHD, like dyslexia and glue ear, can dramatically affect classroom performance and has for this reason been the focus of substantial bodies of research. A diagnosis of ADHD can help children receive specialized medical and educational services, but the medications and surgical interventions used to treat the condition can present adverse short- and long-term effects.

In his essay on medicalization processes, Conrad argued that when disorders previously viewed as non-medical are redefined as sicknesses, non-medical professionals often perform the "everyday routine work" of disseminating understanding of the new sickness. Where ADHD is concerned, the teacher's work extends beyond simply ensuring the disorder is understood by parents. Instead, the teacher also participates in the diagnosis and may broker different forms of treatment. They may even reject treatment altogether. Teachers do not broker treatment uniformly. They may have a vested interest in detecting and managing disruptive children, or they may adhere to beliefs about learning disorders which lead them to dissuade parents of the need for treatment.

Abuse of prescription drugs, including stimulants used to treat ADHD, is a major public health concern. Stimulants are often abused on college campuses and in high-stress careers in order to increase productivity and alertness. It is difficult to ascertain the prevalence of prescription drug abuse in the United States due to issues of legality. However, the culture and laws in India permit self-medication of drugs that are obtainable only by prescription in many other countries. Researchers assessed the prevalence of overall self-medication among 440 medical students in South India. The prevalence of self-medication was 78.6%. A greater proportion of females were self-medicating (81.2%) than were males (75.3%). Reasons for self-medicating are provided in Table 1.

Reason for self-medication	Percentage
Illness too trivial for consultation	70.5%
Sufficient pharmacological knowledge	45.0%
Desire to save time	19.0%
Desire to avoid the crowd	11.2%
Privacy concerns	5.2%

Table 1 Characteristics of study subjects indulging in self-medication

This passage was adapted from "Medicine goes to school: Teachers as sickness brokers for ADHD." Phillips CB. *PLoS Med.* 2006. 3(4) doi: 10.1371/journal.pmed.0030182 for use under the terms of the Creative Commons CC BY 2.0 license (http://creativecommons.org/licenses/by/2.0/legalcode) and "Perceptions and Practices of Self-Medication among Medical Students in Coastal South India." Kumar N, Kanchan T, Unnikrishnan B, Rekha T, Mithra P, et al. *PLoS ONE.* 2013. 8(8): e182. doi: 10.1371/journal.pone.0072247 for use under the terms of the Creative Commons CC BY 3.0 license (http://creativecommons.org/licenses/by/3.0/legalcode).

Question 15

Medicalization is defined as:

- ○ **A.** an attempt to control individuals by defining certain behaviors as abnormal.
- ○ **B.** the gradual characterization of behaviors as constituting disease.
- ○ **C.** the desire to obtain medication for an illness.
- ○ **D.** the need to expand medical practice to include more illnesses.

Question 16

Which of the following are important in diagnosing illnesses like ADHD?

   I. Values

   II. Norms

   III. Beliefs

- ○ **A.** I only
- ○ **B.** II only
- ○ **C.** I and II only
- ○ **D.** I, II, and III

Question 17

Students in the experiment also cited the inaccessibility of clinics as a primary reason for self-medication. Assuming students in the United States self-medicate at a far lower rate, this is an example of a(n):

- ○ **A.** health disparity and global inequality.
- ○ **B.** environmental injustice and social inequality.
- ○ **C.** healthcare disparity and spatial inequality.
- ○ **D.** globalization and healthcare transition.

Question 18

Based on the results in Table 1, students may be avoiding:

- ○ **A.** the sick role.
- ○ **B.** medicalization.
- ○ **C.** health inequity.
- ○ **D.** the illness experience.

Next ▶

Questions 19 through 23 are NOT based on a descriptive passage.

An individual lost his job and is currently homeless. His situation can best be described as:

○ **A.** isolation.

○ **B.** social exclusion.

○ **C.** relative poverty.

○ **D.** absolute poverty.

Question 20

All of the following items or gestures are examples of symbolic culture EXCEPT:

○ **A.** a thumbs up.

○ **B.** a handshake.

○ **C.** a novel.

○ **D.** a fork.

Question 21

Re-introducing ex-prisoners into the larger society is often fraught with difficulties. Economic hardship can be the biggest immediate threat to integration into society, as ex-prisoners often experience difficulty finding jobs and affordable housing. Which of the following best describes the likely outcome of such hardships?

○ **A.** Prejudice arises from socioeconomic status.

○ **B.** Prejudice arises from spatial inequality.

○ **C.** Poverty arises from social capital.

○ **D.** Poverty arises from social exclusion.

Question 22

Which of the following best describes the office of President of the United States?

○ **A.** A position of power in a meritocracy

○ **B.** A position of prestige in a social institution

○ **C.** A position of upward mobility in a social class

○ **D.** A white-collar position in a social movement

Question 23

An American equestrian lover visits the Yunnan province of China and is upset when she is served horse meat for dinner. Her experience most closely relates to which of the following processes?

○ **A.** Globalization

○ **B.** Material culture

○ **C.** Culture shock

○ **D.** Demographic transition

STOP. IF YOU FINISH BEFORE TIME IS CALLED, CHECK YOUR WORK. YOU MAY GO BACK TO ANY QUESTION IN THIS TEST BOOKLET.

30-MINUTE IN-CLASS EXAM FOR LECTURE 2

Passage I (Questions 24-27)

An emerging literature implicates psychological stress from anxiety disorders and mood disorders, both prevalent in women, as potential paths toward accelerated aging. In a study of 5,423 women, high phobic anxiety was significantly associated with lower leukocyte telomere lengths, a factor in the deterioration of immunity to disease processes. Anxiety is treatable, and any potential impacts on telomere shortening may be amenable to prevention. Studies of the mechanisms underlying anxiety disorders, including worry and fear, may be helpful in preventing such accelerated aging.

In order to investigate anxiety, specifically, how worrisome thoughts shape associative fear, researchers used electric shocks to fear condition participants with a previously neutral picture (PIC1). Shortly after acquisition, an eye-blink tracking method known as the fear potentiated startle test (FPS) was used to measure participants' fear responses after witnessing the conditioned picture. Next the "Worry" group went through a period of intense worrisome thinking induced by distressing interviews. In the PIC1 group, fear response was then measured for a second time after seeing the conditioned picture. Another group underwent the same procedure, except that the second measurement involved a neutral picture unconditioned to any other stimulus (PIC2). A control group (NW) experienced a similar procedure, but had neutral interviews that did not induce worrisome thinking. The results of the experiment are depicted in Figure 1.

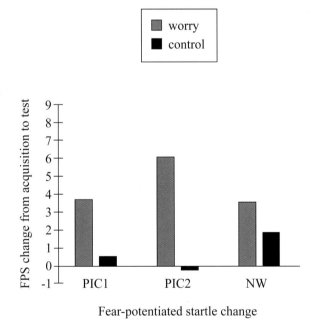

Figure 1 Change in FPS from fear acquisition to second testing in Worry and Control groups. FPS scores are standardized to an arbitrary scale, with higher numbers indicating a greater fear response

This passage was adapted from "Worrying Affects Associative Fear Learning: A Startle Fear Conditioning Study." Gazendam F, Kindt M. *PLoS ONE*. 2012. 7(4) doi: 10.1371/journal. pone.0034882 and "High Phobic Anxiety is Related to Lower Leukocyte Telomere Length in Women." Okereke OI, Prescott J, Wong JYY, Han J, Rexrode KM, De Vivo I. *PLoS ONE*. 2012. 7(7) doi: 10.1371/journal.pone.0040516 for use under the terms of the Creative Commons CC BY 3.0 license (http://creativecommons.org/licenses/by/3.0/legalcode).

Question 24

Which of the following terms best describe the "previously neutral event" and "associative fear after acquisition" described in the passage, respectively?

○ **A.** Unconditioned stimulus; unconditioned response
○ **B.** Unconditioned response; conditioned response
○ **C.** Conditioned stimulus; conditioned response
○ **D.** Conditioned stimulus; unconditioned stimulus

Question 25

There is evidence that anxiety might also interact with other types of learning. If the researchers from the passage discover a line of transgenic mice that are unable to learn new behaviors by watching other mice perform them, genes in which cell type have most likely been affected?

○ **A.** Mirror neurons
○ **B.** Empathy cells
○ **C.** Somatic motor neurons
○ **D.** Erythrocytes

Question 26

Which of the following best explains the responses to PIC1 and PIC2 after worrisome thinking seen in Figure 1?

○ **A.** Worry is driving fear extinction.
○ **B.** Worry is enhancing fear acquisition.
○ **C.** Worry is driving stimulus discrimination.
○ **D.** Worry is driving stimulus generalization.

Question 27

Suppose the researchers described in the passage wanted to use operant conditioning to ensure that participants continued to look voluntarily at the fear conditioned picture for as long as possible. Which technique should they use?

○ **A.** Offer participants a reward sporadically, with at least 15 picture views between each reward.
○ **B.** Offer participants a reward every time they view the picture for 20 views.
○ **C.** Punish participants every time they view the picture for 20 views.
○ **D.** Allow the conditioned fear to become extinct and offer no rewards or punishments.

Next ▶

Passage II (Questions 28-32)

In remote communities, geographic isolation and limited access to health services adversely affect outcomes in medical emergencies. In the absence of local paramedical services, the management of time-sensitive emergencies depends on the response of bystanders. Research on the behavior of bystanders in emergencies began with the rape and murder of Kitty Genovese in New York in 1964. Social psychologists Bibb Latané and John Darley read a report suggesting that 38 witnesses watched the murder unfold over 30 minutes– and yet failed to intervene. In order to understand why this might have happened and to gain insight into ways to minimize violent assaults in the future, Latané and Darley set out to create laboratory-based experimental analogies of the event. Their research led to the discovery of the 'bystander effect'.

A later experiment on the bystander effect used immersive virtual environments (IVE), computer-generated realities through which participants can affect responses in the virtual environment. The study participants were all supporters of the same sports team. The IVE portrayed a crowded sports pub occupied by the subject, a simulated attacker (A), and simulated victim (V). Subjects viewed a violent confrontation between A and V. In one condition, V wore a jersey and spoke enthusiastically about the team that test subjects supported. In a second condition, V wore an unaffiliated jersey and asked questions about the team without enthusiasm, displaying ambivalence about the team's prospects.

The researchers measured the number of times that participants attempted to verbally intervene during this confrontation. The "*Group*" variable was V's in-group or out-group status with respect to the participant. The "*LookAt*" variable was whether V looked towards the participant for help (On) or did not (Off). The results are shown in Table 1.

Group	LookAt		
	Off	On	All
Out-group	3.96 ± 1.4	2.06 ± 1.3	2.96 ± 1.0
In-group	6.86 ± 1.8	4.76 ± 1.9	5.86 ± 1.3
All	5.46 ± 1.2	3.46 ± 1.2	4.46 ± 0.8

Table 1 Means and standard errors of number of verbal interventions. The effect of Group was found to be significant.

This passage was adapted from "Bystander Responses to a Violent Incident in an Immersive Virtual Environment." Slater M, Rovira A, Southern R, Swapp D, Zhang JJ, Campbell C, Levine M. *PLoS ONE*. 2013. 8(1) doi:10.1371/journal.pone.0052766 and "Where There is No Paramedic: The Sachigo Lake Wilderness Emergency Response Initiative." Orkin, A, VanderBurgh D, Born K, Webster M, Strickland S, Jackson B. *PLoS Med*. 2012. 9(10) doi: 10.1371/journal.pmed. 1001322 for use under the terms of the Creative Commons CC BY 3.0 license (http://creativecommons.org/licenses/by/3.0/legalcode).

Question 28

What factor has likely most hindered contemporary researchers' attempts to replicate the conditions surrounding the murder of Kitty Genovese?

- O **A.** There are too many uncontrolled variables that could have led to the inaction of all 38 onlookers.
- O **B.** Ethical considerations prevent exposing subjects to simulated violence.
- O **C.** It would be impossible to have a control group.
- O **D.** Group effects would require a sufficiently large number of subjects to produce undesired confounding variables.

Question 29

Which of the following would most call into question the conclusions that can be drawn from this experiment?

- O **A.** Subjects reported discomfort with the presented scenario.
- O **B.** Subjects verbally intervened to different extents.
- O **C.** Subjects reported the IVE to be unrealistic.
- O **D.** Subjects reported small differences in levels of team affiliation.

Question 30

What effect would the *LookAt* condition be expected to have on the findings of this experiment?

- O **A.** It should not affect the findings of this study.
- O **B.** It strengthens the conclusions drawn about the bystander effect.
- O **C.** It should minimize the extent of the bystander effect.
- O **D.** It decreases the validity of the findings by introducing a confounding variable.

Question 31

The actions of the attacker best exemplify:

- O **A.** institutional discrimination.
- O **B.** social facilitation.
- O **C.** deviance.
- O **D.** social loafing.

Question 32

In a modification to the experiment, participants were encouraged to socially engage with other pub occupants while viewing the confrontation. As a result, study participants began to demonstrate group polarization. Which of the following scenarios best represents this effect?

- ○ **A.** Though they began with different viewpoints, members of the group converged on the decision to verbally intervene with the confrontation.
- ○ **B.** Several pub occupants suggested verbally accosting the attacker, but the group ended up physically accosting the attacker.
- ○ **C.** Members of the group felt anonymity in the crowd and began assaulting the attacker.
- ○ **D.** One group member made a compelling case for violently intervening in the confrontation, changing the opinion of the group.

Passage III (Questions 33-37)

The reduction of high risk drinking is a public health challenge, especially in countries experiencing rapid change. Substantial clinical evidence suggests that alcohol abuse suppresses both innate and adaptive immune responses leading to an increased risk for infections and cancer, and delayed recovery from trauma. Malnutrition and/or malabsorption are almost invariably associated with chronic alcohol abuse and contribute to immunosuppression and increased susceptibility to infections. To develop effective programs to reduce alcohol-related risks, psychosocial and cultural influences on drinking behavior must be better understood.

A recent study analyzed drinking habits of Chinese university students. The transition to the university environment presents a challenging situation for students as they are faced with increased Western influence, particularly when moving from more rural to more urban areas. The degree to which an individual accepts imported Western values relative to the degree to which he retains his traditional value system reflects his cultural orientation. Previous studies have indicated that a Western cultural orientation is associated with a higher probability for alcohol use whereas a local, traditional orientation is associated with a lower probability.

Cultural orientation was measured using the CCOS instrument, which contains ten subscales reflecting either Western or traditional cultural values. Based on their responses in the CCOS survey, participants were divided into four different groups: marginal, Western, traditional, and bicultural. Bicultural students identify with both Western and traditional cultures, while marginal individuals do not identify strongly with either culture. Figure 1 shows drinking habits amongst students in these groups.

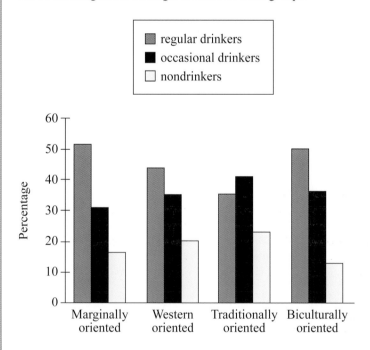

Figure 1 Drinking behavior by cultural orientation.

This passage was adapted from "The Association between Cultural Orientation and Drinking Behaviors among University Students in Wuhan, China." Tang H, Cai W, Wang H, Zhang Q, Qian L, Shell DF, Newman IM, Yin, P. *PLoS ONE*. 2013. 8(1) doi:10.1371/journal. pone.0054796 and "Community-Acquired Bacterial Meningitis in Alcoholic Patients." Weisfelt M, de Gans J, van der Ende A, van de Beek D. *PLoS ONE*. 2010. 5(2) doi:10.1371/journal.pone.0009102 for use under the terms of the Creative Commons CC BY 3.0 license (http://creativecommons.org/licenses/by/3.0/legalcode)

Next ►

Question 33

Among the Chinese university students surveyed, Western media acted as:

○ **A.** an agent of socialization.

○ **B.** a subculture.

○ **C.** a cultural assimilant.

○ **D.** a socionormative influence.

Question 34

Suppose the experiment were altered so that experimenters collected data from participants in a group setting. Which of the following phenomena would most likely alter the participants' responses?

    I. Peer pressure

    II. Groupthink

    III. Group polarization

○ **A.** I only

○ **B.** I and III only

○ **C.** II and III only

○ **D.** I, II, and III

Question 35

Later research revealed that impression management was a significant explanatory factor behind the observed trends. This finding most likely indicates that:

○ **A.** respondents omitted negative answers in order to maintain a positive self-image.

○ **B.** respondents skewed their answers in order to demonstrate more socially acceptable drinking behaviors.

○ **C.** data collectors mediated the responses of participants via preconceived notions of participants.

○ **D.** researchers framed questions that biased answers in one direction.

Question 36

How might a cultural relativist react to the differences in measured drinking habits between Western and traditional cultural orientations?

○ **A.** She would analyze the drinking habits of each culture relative to the other.

○ **B.** She would embrace the diversity of different cultural viewpoints.

○ **C.** She would recognize the inability to judge foreign cultures.

○ **D.** She would judge each drinking habit relative to the norms of each culture.

Question 37

A follow-up study was performed to assess the influence of authority figures on alcohol consumption. Which concept would best describe abstention from alcohol consumption resulting from a ban on drinking by an authority figure?

○ **A.** Obedience

○ **B.** Conformity

○ **C.** Operant conditioning

○ **D.** Self-fulfilling prophecy

Passage IV (Questions 38-41)

Poor nutrition and inadequate physical activity can result in obesity and a host of chronic diseases. Theories of environmental and health interactions have suggested that an environment may promote or prevent healthy behaviors through the physical, interpersonal, organizational, and sociocultural characteristics of a setting. Considering the potential for environments to impact health beyond the individual level, worksites may be an effective setting for efforts to promote healthy weight. Previous research has shown that demographic characteristics of workers (e.g., race and gender) and workplace size are associated with diet and activity behaviors. Behavior theories emphasize the importance of social norms, including those in the worksite, in determining health. Norms have been shown to influence obesity and other health-related behaviors.

This study explores the relationship between workplace social environment, cultural factors, diet, physical activity, and obesity in a large sample of employees from a diverse set of workplace settings across multiple metropolitan areas. Telephone interviews were conducted, and questions included demographic characteristics, workplace factors related to physical activity/diet, and obesity. There were differences in reported health behaviors and socio/organizational environment by gender, race, age, income, and worksite size, summarized in Table 1. Additionally, survey responses demonstrated that seeing coworkers eating fruits and vegetables was associated with increased reporting of eating at least one vegetable per day. Observing coworkers being active was associated with higher physical activity levels.

	Race (%)			Workplace size (%)			Income (%)		Age (%)			Sex (%)	
	White	Black	Other	0-49	50-199	200+	<$29K	≥$30K	21-44	45-54	55-65	F	M
Eat fast food 2+x/ wk (%)	41.4	58.4	35.5	59.9	43.7	46.8	51.9	44.4	51.8	46.7	38.9	45.5	46.8
Physical activity (150+ min/wk) (%)	80.2	76.3	81.0	80.3	80.9	75.5	82.4	78.4	80.6	79.7	77.3	76.1	85.6
Obesity (BMI>30) (%)	29.7	46.5	30.3	31.9	34.8	37.0	41.5	33.1	34.5	35.4	33.9	35.3	33.0
Agree that "company values health" (%)	87.3	81.4	87.4	84.2	84.0	87.8	78.7	87.1	82.6	85.3	88.8	84.5	87.7

Table 1 Selected social/organizational, diet, physical activity, and obesity variables and demographics (n = 1,338)

This passage was adapted from "Workplace Social and Organizational Environments and Healthy-Weight Behaviors." Tabak RG, Hipp JA, Marx CM, Brownson RC. 2015. *PLoS ONE*. 10(4): e0125424. doi:10.1371/journal.pone.0125424 for use under the terms of the Creative Commons CC BY 4.0 license (http://creativecommons.org/licenses/by/4.0/legalcode).

Next ▶

Question 38

Which of the following would NOT be true of an individual consuming exclusively healthy foods at work in front of their fit and active coworkers, while regularly consuming unhealthy food at home?

- ○ **A.** The individual is modifying his or her behavior to appear healthier.
- ○ **B.** This person is behaving in a way to make others believe they make healthy diet choices.
- ○ **C.** The dramaturgical approach suggests that this person's behavior at work is not his or her "true self."
- ○ **D.** This behavior may be the result of this individual fearing judgement for eating unhealthy food.

Question 39

Based on the data provided in Table 1, which of the following cohorts would perform best on a nutrition and fitness assessment?

- ○ **A.** White males in large workplace because they are more obedient
- ○ **B.** African-American males in a mid-size workplace due to peer pressure from coworkers
- ○ **C.** White males in a large workplace due to social norms in the workplace
- ○ **D.** African-American males in a large workplace due to social norms in the workplace.

Question 40

If members of an office that promotes healthy lifestyle choices believe that all individuals who do not have more than 150 minutes of physical activity per week are lazy, this is NOT an example of:

- ○ **A.** discrimination.
- ○ **B.** stigma.
- ○ **C.** prejudice.
- ○ **D.** a stereotype.

Question 41

Many members of a given company expressed prejudice against people who have a BMI>30. This prejudice is likely most detrimental if the members of this company are:

- ○ **A.** male.
- ○ **B.** African American.
- ○ **C.** wealthy.
- ○ **D.** single.

Questions 42 through 46 are NOT based on a descriptive passage.

Question 42

Patients with anxiety disorders often learn to steer clear of the neutral stimuli that trigger their anxiety attacks. This is an example of which type of learning?

- ○ **A.** Shaping
- ○ **B.** Deviance
- ○ **C.** Avoidance conditioning
- ○ **D.** Escape conditioning

Question 43

Which of the following statements is most consistent with the practice of cultural relativism?

- ○ **A.** It describes the belief that one's group is of central importance and includes the tendency to judge the practices of other groups by one's own cultural standards.
- ○ **B.** It is the opposite of ethnocentrism, which is the practice of trying to understand a culture on its own terms and to judge a culture by its own standards.
- ○ **C.** It may help promote multiculturalism within various populations.
- ○ **D.** It renounces assimilation into any new cultures.

Question 44

Which of the following is the best example of conditioning through negative punishment?

- ○ **A.** A mother begins spanking her son when he starts to throw a temper tantrum in a public place.
- ○ **B.** A father confiscates his son's favorite toy when he starts to throw a temper tantrum in a public place.
- ○ **C.** A father gives his son his favorite toy when he stops throwing a temper tantrum in a public place.
- ○ **D.** A mother stops spanking her son when he stops throwing a temper tantrum in a public place.

Question 45

After major disasters it is common for people to put themselves in potentially dangerous situations, such as crawling into unstable buildings, in order to help rescue strangers who are trapped or injured inside. This kind of behavior can best be described by which of the following concepts?

- ○ **A.** Inclusive fitness
- ○ **B.** Altruism
- ○ **C.** Foraging behavior
- ○ **D.** Game theory

Question 46

A person with a multiculturalist perspective would be most likely to agree with which of the following statements regarding immigration to the US?

○ **A.** Immigration should not be allowed.

○ **B.** Immigration should be allowed and immigrants should receive services to help them assimilate.

○ **C.** Immigrants' native cultures should be preserved and appreciated.

○ **D.** Immigrants' behavior should be judged by the cultural norms of their native culture, not of their adopted country.

STOP. IF YOU FINISH BEFORE TIME IS CALLED, CHECK YOUR WORK. YOU MAY GO BACK TO ANY QUESTION IN THIS TEST BOOKLET.

STOP

30-MINUTE IN-CLASS EXAM FOR LECTURE 3

Major depressive disorder (MDD) has been associated with deteriorating physical health. An elevated prevalence of diabetes is found amongst people with depression, although the mechanism and direction of causality of this association is not yet understood.

A large majority of MDD patients show a reduction to less than 50 percent of baseline depressive symptoms following antidepressant treatment. The minority who do not respond are said to have treatment-resistant depression. Personality traits are thought to influence the clinical outcome of antidepressant treatment. The Temperament and Character Inventory (TCI) is a psychosocial model of personality that is commonly used to study MDD. It defines four dimensions of temperament, including harm avoidance and reward dependence, and three dimensions of character, including self-directedness. In a meta-analysis of MDD study data, harm avoidance scores showed a clear negative change following antidepressant treatment. Another study showed that reward dependence in non-depressed siblings of depressed patients was significantly higher than for siblings with a history of depression. Since temperament is thought to have a strong genetic component, this finding suggests that reward dependence may be an innate protective factor against the development of depression in people who have heightened risk of developing the disorder.

In a study intended to examine possible personality risk factors for treatment-resistant MDD, the TCI was used to evaluate treatment-resistant MDD patients, remission MDD patients, and age- and gender-matched healthy controls. A depression rating scale was used to categorize the MDD patients; remission was defined as a full recovery, corresponding to a score of less than 7. The results for selected temperament and character dimensions are shown in Figure 1.

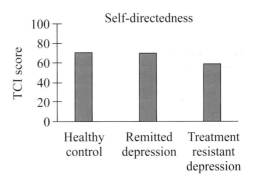

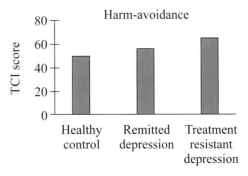

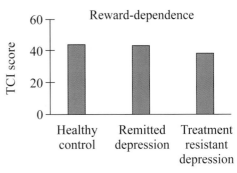

Figure 1 Scores for TCI temperament and character dimensions according to depression status

This passage was adapted from "Personality Traits as Risk Factors for Treatment-Resistant Depression." Takahashi M, Shirayama Y, Muneoka K, Suzuki M, Sato K, et al. *PLoS ONE*. 2013. 8(5) doi:10.1371/journal.pone.0063756 and "Depression, Antidepressant Use and Mortality in Later Life: The Health in Men Study." Almeida OP, Alfonso H, Hankey GJ, Flicker L. *PLoS ONE*. 2010. 5(6) doi:10.1371/journal.pone.0011266 for use under the terms of the Creative Commons CC BY 3.0 license (http://creativecommons.org/licenses/by/3.0/legalcode).

Question 47

Another researcher found that patients with treatment-resistant MDD are less likely than controls to attribute their successes to internal characteristics and their failures to external characteristics. This finding suggests that MDD affects:

○ **A.** locus of control.

○ **B.** role-taking.

○ **C.** self-concept.

○ **D.** self-serving bias.

Next ▶

Question 48

Which is the most likely mechanism of the antidepressants described in the passage?

- ○ **A.** Acting as monoamine antagonists
- ○ **B.** Decreasing the production of monoamine neurotransmitters in presynaptic neurons
- ○ **C.** Decreasing the reuptake of monoamine neurotransmitters
- ○ **D.** Increasing the reuptake of monoamine neurotransmitters

Question 49

The finding that antidepressant treatment of MDD leads to substantial decreases in harm avoidance scores in some patients is LEAST consistent with which theory of personality?

- ○ **A.** Social cognitive theory
- ○ **B.** Situational approach
- ○ **C.** Trait theory
- ○ **D.** Humanistic theory

Question 50

Which conclusion about temperament and the course of MDD is supported by the information given in the passage?

- ○ **A.** Temperament and MDD are both influenced by genetic and environmental factors.
- ○ **B.** Temperament is influenced by genetic factors only, while MDD is influenced by genetic and environmental factors.
- ○ **C.** Temperament is influenced by environmental factors only, while MDD is influenced by genetic factors only.
- ○ **D.** Both temperament and MDD are influenced by genetic factors only.

Question 51

If the TCI scores are assumed to be continuous, which change to the methods of measurement in the last study described in the passage, if any, would allow use of a correlation for statistical analysis?

- ○ **A.** No change is needed; it is already possible to use a correlation.
- ○ **B.** Dividing the subjects into low, average, and high categories for each personality dimension.
- ○ **C.** Recording numerical depression scores rather than dividing the subjects into control, remission, and treatment-resistant categories.
- ○ **D.** There is no way to alter the methods of measurement such that a correlation could be used.

Passage II (Questions 52-55)

Group identification fosters categorization of other people and ideas as in-group or out-group. Research increasingly shows that group identification can affect health choices and outcomes. Patients who self-identify as racial or ethnic minorities tend to underutilize recommended preventative health services, such as vaccinations and disease screenings. Perceived discrimination as out-group members likely contributes to this avoidance of care.

Group identification has received a great deal of research attention in the realm of politics. Social identity theory predicts that people will try to maximize distinctions between their own political party and a political out-group. In one study, researchers looked at the content and extent of moral stereotypes. They used the Moral Foundations Theory, which posits five psychological "foundations" upon which moral virtues and institutions are socially constructed. The two "individualizing" foundations are harm/care and fairness/reciprocity. The other three foundations—in-group/loyalty, authority/respect, and purity/sanctity—are called the "binding" foundations. Participants who were classified as conservatives or liberals filled out a questionnaire that asks respondents to indicate the importance of various moral concerns on a scale from 0 to 6. The subjects were randomly assigned to answer according to their own opinions, as they believed a typical liberal would answer, or as they believed a typical conservative would answer. The results are shown in Figure 1.

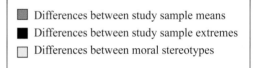

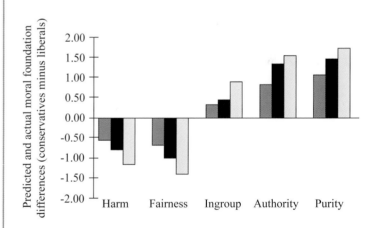

Figure 1 Comparisons of moral stereotypes to actual conservative-liberal differences in moral foundation endorsement

Another group of researchers investigated how personal political beliefs mediate religious in-group favoritism. In this experiment, participants were asked to choose how much money to donate to charities whose names indicated either a religious or secular affiliation. Compared to non-religious people, Christians donated more money to religious charities. However, within Christians, conservative Christians favored religious charities more than liberal Christians did.

This passage was adapted from "The Moral Stereotypes of Liberals and Conservatives: Exaggeration of Differences across the Political Spectrum." Graham J, Nosek BA, Haidt J. *PLoS ONE*. 2012. 7(12) doi:10.1371/journal.pone.0050092 and "When Ingroups Aren't "In": Perceived Political Belief Similarity Moderates Religious Ingroup Favoritism." Hawkins CB, Nosek BA. *PLoS ONE*. 2012. 7(12) doi:10.1371/journal.pone.0050945 and " Socially-Assigned Race, Healthcare Discrimination and Preventive Healthcare Services." MacIntosh T, Desai MM, Lewis TT, Jones BA, Nunez-Smith M. *PLoS ONE*. 2013. 8(5) doi:10.1371/journal.pone.0064522 for use under the terms of the Creative Commons CC BY 3.0 license (http://creativecommons.org/licenses/by/3.0/legalcode) and "Do 'Good' Values Lead to 'Good' Health Behaviors? Longitudinal Associations Between Young People's Values and Later Substance-Use." Young R and West P. *BMC Public Health*. 2010. 10(165) doi:10.1186/1471-2458-10-165 for use under the terms of the Creative Commons Attribution 4.0 License (www.biomedcentral.com/pdf/Creative_Commons_Attribtion_4.0_International_CC_BY_4.0.pdf)

Question 52

Which processes were most likely involved in the development of religious or non-religious identities by the study participants?

   I. Role-taking based on parental behaviors

   II. Imitating behaviors of out-group members

   III. Cultural transmission of values

○ **A.** I only

○ **B.** II only

○ **C.** I and III only

○ **D.** I, II and III

Question 53

Which of the following is most likely to be influenced by in-group/out-group identity?

○ **A.** Prejudiced behavior based on ethnocentrism

○ **B.** The creation of shared meanings in symbolic culture

○ **C.** An individual's level of extraversion and neuroticism

○ **D.** The process of operant conditioning

Question 54

The formation of political and religious identities would most likely be addressed by the work of which theorist?

○ **A.** Freud

○ **B.** Vygotsky

○ **C.** Skinner

○ **D.** Erikson

Question 55

What was the dependent variable of the second study described in the passage?

○ **A.** Participants' religious identity

○ **B.** Participants' political identity

○ **C.** The amount of money that participants donated to each charity

○ **D.** The religious or non-religious connotation of each charity

Passage III (Questions 56-60)

Personality traits and cardiorespiratory fitness in older adults are reliable predictors of health and longevity. Researchers examined the association between personality traits and energy expenditure at rest (basal metabolic rate) and during normal and maximal sustained walking. Personality traits and oxygen (VO_2) consumption were assessed in 642 participants from the Baltimore Longitudinal Study of Aging. Results indicate that personality traits were mostly unrelated to resting metabolic rate and energy expenditure at normal walking pace. However, those who scored lower on neuroticism and higher on extraversion, openness, and conscientiousness had significantly higher energy expenditure at peak walking pace. In addition to greater aerobic capacity, individuals with a more resilient personality profile walked faster and were more efficient in that they required less energy per meter walked. The associations between personality and energy expenditure were not moderated by age or sex, but were in part explained by proportion of fat mass.

Differences in personality may matter the most during more challenging activities that require cardiorespiratory fitness. These findings suggest potential pathways that link personality to health outcomes, such as obesity and longevity. This information may be applied to disease screening and prevention in at-risk individuals.

This passage was adapted from "Personality, Metabolic Rate and Aerobic Capacity." Terracciano A, Schrack JA, Sutin AR, Chan W, Simonsick EM, et al. *PLoS ONE*. 2013. 8(1): e54746. doi:10.1371/journal.pone.0054746 for use under the terms of the Creative Commons CC BY 3.0 license (http://creativecommons.org/licenses/by/3.0/legalcode).

Question 56

According to the passage, participants with low emotional instability and anxiety may:

○ **A.** have a greater aerobic capacity.

○ **B.** have more body fat.

○ **C.** have many friends.

○ D. show variability in aerobic capacity with age.

Question 57

The passage focuses on the trait theory of personality. Which of the following statements is most consistent with the biological theory of personality?

○ **A.** Personality can be described through a set of characteristics which are stable across one's lifetime.

○ **B.** Personality is controlled by specific genes on several different chromosomes.

○ **C.** The personalities of monozygotic twins are more similar than those of dizygotic twins.

○ D. The personality of a child is often a mix of the personalities of both parents.

Next ►

Question 58

Individuals with high neuroticism and low extraversion are recruited to participate in a study of aerobic capacity. All participants had low aerobic capacity just after recruitment, but a small group of them had significantly higher aerobic capacity at a five-year follow-up. This finding is most consistent with:

○ **A.** trait theory.

○ **B.** biological theory.

○ **C.** social cognitive theory.

○ **D.** humanistic theory.

Question 59

In extreme cases, some personalities are considered "disordered." How common is this condition?

○ **A.** 1% prevalence

○ **B.** 5% prevalence

○ **C.** 10% prevalence

○ **D.** 20% prevalence

Question 60

Which of the following conditions is NOT associated with high neuroticism?

○ **A.** Depression and suicide

○ **B.** Low aerobic capacity

○ **C.** Inheritance of the *Nrt* gene

○ **D.** Low self-esteem and self-efficacy

Passage IV (Questions 61-64)

Apathy is a reduction of spontaneous and goal-directed behaviors, making affected individuals less responsive and engaged in daily activities. Apathy affects behavioral, cognitive, and emotional domains. In Parkinson's disease (PD), apathy has a high prevalence, ranging from 17% to 70%. Although apathy and depression have been clearly dissociated as independent syndromes in PD, symptoms may overlap.

Detecting apathy in patients with PD has important prognostic implications, as apathy is a predictive factor for the development of dementia and cognitive dysfunction. Forty-eight patients were recruited prospectively from a cohort referred to the study by their clinicians. Based on clinical evaluation, they were classified in two groups: PD with apathy (PD-A) and PD without apathy (PD-NA). The clinical evaluation included: the Apathy Evaluation Scale-patient version, the Hamilton Depression Rating Scale-17 items, and the Unified Parkinson's Disease Rating Scale. Neuropsychological evaluation explored speed of information processing, attention, working memory, executive function, learning abilities and memory, which included several measures of recall.

Researchers hypothesize that in PD, the impaired implementation of novel cognitive strategies has a pivotal role in inefficient storing and recall of new information as well as in abstract reasoning and problem solving. This altered biological mechanism may be the sole underpinning of apathy and cognitive dysfunction in PD. Results supported this hypothesis, as PD-A and PD-NA groups did not differ in age, disease duration, treatment, or motor condition, but differed in recall and executive tasks. Depression and apathy had a weak correlation, and the depressed and non-depressed PD patients within the non-apathetic group did not differ.

This passage was adapted from "Apathy, but Not Depression, Reflects Inefficient Cognitive Strategies in Parkinson's Disease." Varanese S, Perfetti B, Ghilardi MF, Di Rocco A. *PLoS ONE.* 2011. 6(3): e17846. doi:10.1371/journal.pone.0017846 for use under the terms of the Creative Commons CC BY 3.0 license (http://creativecommons.org/licenses/by/3.0/legalcode).

Question 61

The symptoms of apathy and depression often overlap, but not everyone with detectable apathy has a clinical diagnosis of depression. While apathy can affect up to 70% of patients with PD, the prevalence of disordered mood within the broader population is:

○ **A.** 1%.

○ **B.** 10%.

○ **C.** 20%.

○ **D.** 30% .

Question 62

Based on the hypothesis presented in the passage, the researchers in this study would most likely argue that:

- ○ **A.** apathy is explained by a biomedical model that is focused on biological, psychological, and social factors.
- ○ **B.** apathy is explained by a biomedical model that is focused on genetics and neuronal functioning.
- ○ **C.** apathy is explained by a biopsychosocial model that is focused on biological, psychological, and social factors.
- ○ **D.** apathy is explained by a biopsychosocial model that is focused on genetics and neuronal functioning.

Question 63

Which of the following is NOT true about the classification of psychological disorders?

- ○ **A.** Somatoform disorders are best explained using the biopsychosocial approach.
- ○ **B.** Generalized anxiety and major depression are the two extremes on the mood disorder spectrum.
- ○ **C.** Schizophrenia typically manifests as a disconnect from reality.
- ○ **D.** Personality disorders tend to endure across the lifespan.

Question 64

In another study, researchers hypothesized that rates of depression in Parkinson's patients would exceed the rates observed in the general population. Which of the following biological mechanisms would best explain the reasoning for this hypothesis?

- ○ **A.** Depletion of neurons in the substantia nigra leads to overcompensation by monoamine neurons in other areas of the brain.
- ○ **B.** The symptoms of PD lead to difficulty performing daily activities, which causes some individuals to experience symptoms of depression.
- ○ **C.** Depletion of dopaminergic neurons leads to a decrease in monoamine transmission.
- ○ **D.** One of the side effects of the dopamine-precursor drug for PD is depressive symptoms.

Questions 65 through 69 are NOT based on a descriptive passage.

Question 65

Seeking experiences to make an individual feel better about himself or herself is characteristic of which theory of personality?

- ○ **A.** Biological theory
- ○ **B.** Humanistic theory
- ○ **C.** Trait theory
- ○ **D.** Behaviorist theory

Question 66

A classical twin study design would most likely allow researchers to:

- ○ **A.** separate the effects of genetic influences and shared environment by comparing monozygotic twins that were raised in the same household.
- ○ **B.** separate the effects of genetic influences and shared environment by comparing dizygotic twins that were raised in different households.
- ○ **C.** separate the effects of shared environment and genetic influences by comparing sets of monozygotic and dizygotic twins that were each raised in the same household.
- ○ **D.** separate the effects of non-shared environment and genetic influences by comparing sets of monozygotic and dizygotic twins that were each raised together.

Question 67

A researcher asks subjects from Western and Eastern countries to complete a task assessing the fundamental attribution error. This study will most likely find that:

- ○ **A.** Western subjects are always more biased toward situational attributions than are Eastern subjects.
- ○ **B.** Eastern subjects are always more biased toward situational attributions than are Western subjects.
- ○ **C.** Western subjects are more biased toward situational attributions than are Eastern subjects when situational factors are emphasized.
- ○ **D.** Eastern subjects are more biased toward situational attributions than are Western subjects when situational factors are emphasized.

Next ▶

Question 68

A study examined social functioning in a group of patients with a variety of psychological symptoms, including unexplained disruptions in memory and identity. Of the following psychological disorders, which would be the most likely diagnosis for a subject in this study?

○ **A.** An anxiety disorder

○ **B.** An affective disorder

○ **C.** A somatoform disorder

○ **D.** A dissociative disorder

Question 69

Which finding would be most likely in a study of neurological features in patients diagnosed with schizophrenia?

○ **A.** Enlargement of multiple structures in the brain

○ **B.** Activation of the hypothalamic-pituitary-adrenal axis

○ **C.** Unusually high dopamine levels

○ **D.** Unusually low dopamine levels

STOP. IF YOU FINISH BEFORE TIME IS CALLED, CHECK YOUR WORK. YOU MAY GO BACK TO ANY QUESTION IN THIS TEST BOOKLET.

30-MINUTE IN-CLASS EXAM FOR LECTURE 4

Passage I (Questions 70-74)

The ability to understand and connect with the emotional state and mind frame of another is referred to as empathy. Clinical empathy is associated with positive health outcomes, including higher adherence to treatment among patients. Among patients with hypertension, poor adherence to medication treatment remains a major problem. Poor adherence is associated with unnecessary over-prescription of drugs, substantial worsening of disease, and longer hospital stays. Research suggests that the current structure of medical education and the pervading model of health care delivery erode the clinician's innate predisposition to empathize.

Cognitive empathy is the conscious process of vicariously taking the perspective of another and using learned information to infer the emotional state of another. The "Reading the Mind in the Eyes" ('eyes') test measures the understanding of subtle mental states and how to recognize them in another. In this task, subjects are exposed to a series of photographs of the eye region of actors/actresses displaying different emotions and asked to select the best of four possible descriptors for the emotion depicted. This test has been verified as a measure of cognitive empathic accuracy.

In one study, subjects performed the 'eyes' test and completed two standard self-report instruments pertaining to empathy: the Interpersonal Reactivity Index (IRI) and the Empathy Quotient (EQ-60). Five participant groups were surveyed: students in their first two years of medical school (MedPhase1), students in the last two years of medical school (MedPhase2), practicing physicians (Doctors), one control group matched to the 'Doctors' group (older controls), and one control matched to the mean of the two medical student groups (younger controls). Control groups were matched for age, sex, and educational achievements.

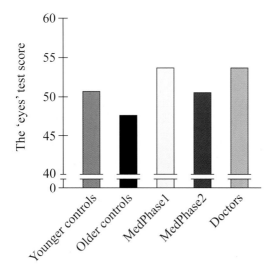

Figure 1 Mean scores for 'eyes' test for the five participant groups

This passage was adapted from "Empathy as a Function of Clinical Exposure – Reading Emotion in the Eyes." Handford C, Lemon J, Grimm MC, and Vollmer-Conna U. *PLoS ONE*. 2013. 8(6) doi:10.1371/journal.pone.0065159 and "Empathy in Clinical Practice: How Individual Dispositions, Gender, and Experience Moderate Empathic Concern, Burnout, and Emotional Distress in Physicians." Gleichgerrcht E and Decety J. *PLoS ONE*. 2013. 8(4) doi:10.1371/journal.pone.0061526 and "Determinants of Medication Adherence to Antihypertensive Medications among a Chinese Population Using Morisky Medication Adherence Scale." Lee GKY, Wang HHX, Liu KQL, Cheung Y, Morisky DE, et al. *PLoS ONE*. 2013. 8(4) doi:10.1371/journal.pone.0062775 for use under the terms of the Creative Commons CC BY 3.0 license. (http://creativecommons.org/licenses/by/3.0/legalcode).

Question 70

A separate experiment presented emotionally valent images to both a control group and an experimental group that was administered epinephrine and found that the experimental group reported heightened emotional responses. Which idea does this finding support?

○ **A.** The James-Lange theory of emotion

○ **B.** Cognitive dissonance

○ **C.** The Cannon-Bard theory of emotion

○ **D.** The fundamental attribution error

Question 71

The researchers were interested in studying international applicability of this study's findings. In a follow-up study, they administered the 'eyes' test in the Māori language to age-matched samples of Māori, an indigenous people of New Zealand. How would the results most likely compare to those of the original study?

○ **A.** An age-related decline in 'eyes' performance would be expected among Māori subjects.

○ **B.** Scores would be similar to those of the original study's control groups.

○ **C.** Scores of medicine men would most closely align with those of the 'Doctors' group.

○ **D.** There is no anticipated relationship between results acquired from the two populations.

Question 72

Which of the following would be LEAST consistent with the theory of multiple intelligences?

- ○ **A.** A subset of subjects scored among the top tenth percentile in both the IRI and on the 'eyes' task.
- ○ **B.** High scorers among the 'eyes' task also score highly on problem solving tasks.
- ○ **C.** A subject with lower empathic scores was found to be an exceptional athlete.
- ○ **D.** Performance on the 'eyes' task improved when subjects were presented with music samples corresponding to the emotion displayed.

Question 73

A physician surveyed for the study in the passage credited her empathic skill to placing an arm on a patient's shoulder whenever they shed tears. This action is an example of:

- ○ **A.** emotional appraisal.
- ○ **B.** belief persistence.
- ○ **C.** a heuristic.
- ○ **D.** social-cognitive theory.

Question 74

A lesion to which of the following regions would most likely affect performance on the 'eyes' task?

- ○ **A.** The prefrontal cortex
- ○ **B.** The occipital lobe
- ○ **C.** The hypothalamus
- ○ **D.** The ventral tegmental area

Passage II (Questions 75-78)

Specific language impairment (SLI) is a problem with speech that is not attributable to cognitive delay, anatomical abnormality, autism spectrum disorder, brain damage, or hearing loss. Children with SLI often struggle academically, but it is unclear if this difficulty is due to an inability to communicate or a deeper neurological difficulty with understanding language. Researchers aimed to determine if SLI is related to problems with memory or with grammatical knowledge, which would suggest that SLI may be a manifestation of a larger language or memory impairment.

Eleven-year-old children, either with a history of SLI or their typically developing (TD) peers, were administered sentence repetition, phonological short term memory (PSTM) and grammatical morphology tasks. Children with a history of SLI were divided into four subgroups: specific language impairment (SLI), non-specific language impairment (NSLI), low cognition with resolved language (LIQRes), and resolved (Res). Two tests were used to assess memory and grammatical knowledge, respectively: the children's test of non-word repetition (CN Rep) and the past tense morphology elicitation task (PT). The results are shown in Figure 1. Regression analyses revealed grammatical knowledge was predictive of performance for TD children and children with a history of SLI. However, memory abilities were significantly predictive of sentence repetition task performance for children with a history of SLI only.

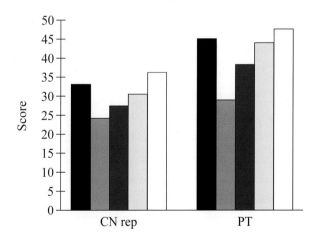

Figure 1 CNRep and PT results are raw scores (maximum 40 for CNRep, 52 for PT)

This passage was adapted from "Memory and Language in Middle Childhood in Individuals with a History of Specific Language Impairment." Hesketh A, Conti-Ramsden G. *PLoS ONE*. 2013. 8(2): e56314. doi:10.1371/journal.pone.0040298 for use under the terms of the Creative Commons CC BY 3.0 license (http://creativecommons.org/licenses/by/3.0/legalcode).

Question 75

Which feature of sensory processing may be impaired in children with SLI?

    I. Auditory sensation

    II. Auditory perception

    III. Cognition

○ **A.** I only

○ **B.** III only

○ **C.** II and III only

○ **D.** I, II and III

Question 76

Deep brain stimulation is a technique that has been successfully used to treat neurological problems, including Parkinson's disease. If researchers want to test whether deep brain stimulation has any effect of language impairment, which part of the brain should be stimulated?

○ **A.** Broca's area

○ **B.** Occipital cortex

○ **C.** Lenticular nucleus

○ **D.** Wernicke's area

Question 77

How could a theory of language development explain the impairments in the participants in the study?

○ **A.** The interactionist theory suggests that language is biologically impaired in participants.

○ **B.** The empiricist theory contradicts the interactionist theory by arguing that there is no reason to believe biology controls language development in the participants.

○ **C.** The learning theory suggests that participants were not conditioned to speak correctly.

○ **D.** The nativist theory suggests that multiple biological and environmental factors resulted in impairment.

Question 78

At which task may participants in the SLI group perform well?

○ **A.** Describing their weekend

○ **B.** Drawing a self-portrait

○ **C.** Taking a spelling test

○ **D.** Taking a college admissions test

Passage III (Questions 79-82)

Cognitive deficits have been inconsistently described for late or moderately preterm children but are consistently found in very preterm children. Researchers investigated the association between cognitive workload demands of tasks and cognitive performance in relation to gestational age at birth. Data were collected as part of a prospective geographically defined whole-population study of neonatal at-risk children. At 8 years of age, n = 1326 children (gestation range: 23–41 weeks) were assessed with the K-ABC and a Mathematics Test. Test tasks were presented to children in book form with 29 items assessing numerical estimations, reasoning, and mental rotation abilities. Item responses were scored for accuracy and subscale scores were summed into a total score. All cognitive assessments were carried out by trained assistant psychologists that were blind to children's background characteristics. Results are shown in Figure 1.

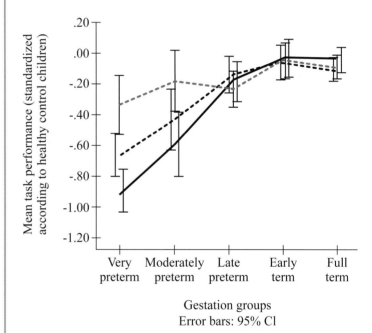

Figure 1 Task performance according to workload and gestational age

The cognitive workload model may help to explain variations of findings on the relationship of gestational age with cognitive performance in the literature. The findings have implications for routine cognitive follow-up, educational intervention, and basic research into neuroplasticity and brain reorganization after preterm birth. Researchers examined within each gestational age group how much of the variance in low, moderate, and high cognitive workload tasks could be explained by biological factors. Results are shown in Figure 2.

Next ▶

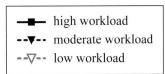

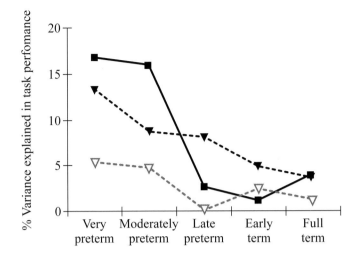

Figure 2 Variance explained by biological factors according to workload and gestational age

This passage was adapted from "Effects of Gestational Age at Birth on Cognitive Performance: A Function of Cognitive Workload Demands." Jaekel J, Baumann N, Wolke D. *PLoS ONE.* 2013. 8(5): e65219. doi:10.1371/journal.pone.0065219 for use under the terms of the Creative Commons CC BY 3.0 license (http://creativecommons.org/licenses/by/3.0/legalcode).

Question 79

Which of the following conclusions is NOT supported by Figure 1?

○ **A.** Prematurity may result in defects in formation of the temporal lobe, resulting in cognitive impairments.

○ **B.** Prematurity is associated with impairments in cognition and may be mediated by defects in the cerebral cortex.

○ **C.** Prematurity is associated with impairments in cognition that increase in severity with increased cognitive load.

○ **D.** Gestational age has an inverse correlation to cognitive impairment.

Question 80

Based on the final paragraph, why are the findings of this study relevant?

○ **A.** Pre-term children have impairments in cognition, especially at high cognitive workload.

○ **B.** Performance on cognitive tests during school age can predict success later in life.

○ **C.** Very pre-term children may be at risk for low IQ and need extra instruction in school.

○ **D.** Cognitive function may be relevant to areas other than intelligence including relationships and happiness.

Question 81

Which of the following may be a confounding variable in this study?

○ **A.** Gestational age at birth

○ **B.** Age at time of cognitive assessment

○ **C.** Cultural background

○ **D.** Genetic disorders

Question 82

How would Piaget describe the participants in the full-term group?

○ **A.** Sensorimotor cognition

○ **B.** Preoperational cognition

○ **C.** Concrete operational cognition

○ **D.** Formal operational cognition

Passage IV (Questions 83-87)

In Study 1, researchers examined the incidence of chronic stress in business executives and its relationship with cognitive performance after an acute mental stressor. Acute stress induces specific patterns of neuronal activation within the brain and stimulates excess transmission in the dopaminergic projections in the prefrontal and anterior cingulate cortices. Furthermore, acute stress stimulates the hypothalamic-pituitary-adrenal (HPA) axis, which leads to the release of higher concentrations of glucocorticoids disrupting memory formation and impairing learning because glucocorticoids can modulate these processes. 109 subjects, 75 male and 34 female, completed the Stroop Color-Word Test to evaluate cognitive performance levels. In the Stroop Color-Word Test, the subjects were instructed to identify the color of the word in which the names of colors were printed and to do so as quickly and accurately as possible. The results from this study are summarized in Figure 1.

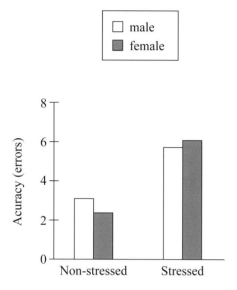

Figure 1 Accuracy of non-stressed and stressed subjects on the Stroop Color-Word Test

Previous studies have evaluated the HPA axis response to an acute psychosocial stressor in chronically stressed healthy subjects; these studies demonstrated a hyporeactivity of this system, which is an abnormal physiological stress response. The recurrent and uncontrolled activation of the HPA axis and the autonomic nervous system (ANS), as found in chronic stress, can lead to the development of a series of pathological conditions ranging from insomnia and hypertension to fatigue and heart disease. Study 2 measured the reactivity of the ANS, which is evaluated using salivary alpha-amylase (sAA) or catecholamine levels. After the acute mental stressor, the non-stressed male group showed an increase in sAA activity. This ANS reactivity was not observed in the chronically stressed male subjects, nor in either group of females.

This passage was adapted from "Chronic Stress Induces a Hyporeactivity of the Autonomic Nervous System in Response to Acute Mental Stressor and Impairs Cognitive Performance in Business Executives." Teixeira RR, Díaz MM, Santos TVS, Bernardes JTM, Peixoto LG, et al. *PLoS ONE*. 2015. 10(3): e0119025. doi:10.1371/journal.pone.0119025 for use under the terms of the Creative Commons CC BY 4.0 license (http://creativecommons.org/licenses/by/4.0/legalcode).

Question 83

The Stroop Color-Word Test in Study 1 primarily tests:

○ **A.** divided attention.

○ **B.** signal detection.

○ **C.** selective attention.

○ **D.** difference threshold.

Question 84

Given the sAA results of Study 2, male participants in the non-stressed condition are likely to experience all of the following characteristics after an acute stressor EXCEPT:

○ **A.** increased sweat production.

○ **B.** increased heart rate and contraction.

○ **C.** increased dilation of bronchioles.

○ **D.** increased blood flow to all muscles.

Question 85

The behavioral effects of stress are observed in the:

○ **A.** cognitive performance of non-stressed males on the color-word task.

○ **B.** loss of sAA responsiveness in stressed males after acute stress.

○ **C.** cognitive performance of stressed males on the color-word task.

○ **D.** elevated sAA levels in non-stressed males after acute stress.

Question 86

Which conclusion is NOT supported by Figure 1?

○ **A.** Changes in neuronal activation from chronic stress can lead to impaired performance on cognitive tasks.

○ **B.** Decreased activity of the HPA axis can disrupt attention in such a way that the performance on cognitive tasks is affected.

○ **C.** Increased ANS reactivity is the source of impaired performance on the cognitive task.

○ **D.** The physiologic changes experienced in chronic stress have effects on cognition.

Question 87

Which of the following statements about the nature of stress is supported by the study results?

○ **A.** The ANS of men and women responds similarly to strains caused by changes in equilibrium.

○ **B.** Men who have repeated exposures to stress have a blunted ANS response to further changes in environment.

○ **C.** The attention of men, but not women, is affected by disruptions to their daily lives.

○ **D.** Continuous disruptions in the lives of women, but not men, can lead to health-related repercussions.

Next ▶

Questions 88 through 92 are NOT based on a descriptive passage.

Question 88

Which statement best explains thirst in terms of negative feedback? Negative feedback occurs once:

- ○ **A.** an individual feels thirst.
- ○ **B.** hydration is returned to normal.
- ○ **C.** water intake begins.
- ○ **D.** the body is overhydrated.

Question 89

A neurosurgeon finds that her patient has suddenly lost the ability to understand speech. What portion of the brain did the surgeon most likely lesion?

- ○ **A.** Frontal lobe
- ○ **B.** Parietal lobe
- ○ **C.** Broca's area
- ○ **D.** Wernicke's area

Question 90

Children who are medically unable to produce speech, and who are therefore unable to produce speech errors, have mastered their native language. This finding best supports which theory of language development?

- ○ **A.** Learning
- ○ **B.** Nativist
- ○ **C.** Interactionist
- ○ **D.** Developmentalist

Question 91

Which of the following has the least influence on cognitive development?

- ○ **A.** A child's genetic information
- ○ **B.** A mother ate a diet of only canned tuna during pregnancy.
- ○ **C.** A mother contracts an acute case of tuberculosis during pregnancy.
- ○ **D.** A child is born into an exceptionally wealthy family.

Question 92

A patient presents with a malformed limbic system. Which of the following is most likely a symptom?

- ○ **A.** Difficulty retrieving memories
- ○ **B.** Impaired visual processing
- ○ **C.** Inability to regulate temperament
- ○ **D.** Loss of language comprehension

STOP. IF YOU FINISH BEFORE TIME IS CALLED, CHECK YOUR WORK. YOU MAY GO BACK TO ANY QUESTION IN THIS TEST BOOKLET.

30-MINUTE IN-CLASS EXAM FOR LECTURE 5

Passage I (Questions 93-97)

Restriction of sleep has many adverse effects on human physiology and health. Sleep deprivation is associated with both elevated blood pressure and type II diabetes. These are not the only consequences of sleep deprivation, however. Restriction of sleep is also known to compromise brain function, including memory formation.

Human memory is not perfectly accurate – what is retrieved from memory can substantially differ from what was originally encoded. Of particular interest are false memories, or "memories" of events that never happened, but are semantically associated with actually encoded events. The development of false memories is similar to the development of correct memories, comprising the three sub-processes of encoding, consolidation, and retrieval.

Sleep plays an active role in memory consolidation. In order to learn about the effects of sleep deprivation on false memory formation, a series of experiments was carried out.

Experiment 1

Two groups were tested in the morning on their ability to select words they had learned the night before from semantically similar non-learned words. One group slept normally after the learning task (night sleep), while the other was sleep deprived (night wake). A third group learned in the morning and was tested nine hours later, after normal daytime wakefulness (day wake).

Experiment 2

All participants completed the learning task in the evening, followed by a normal night of sleep. On the second night, one group slept normally (2nd night sleep), while the other was deprived (2nd night wake). Both groups were tested on the morning after the second night.

Experiment 3

Experiment 1 was repeated with the addition of an extra night of normal sleep for both the 1st night sleep and 1st night wake groups. All participants were tested on the morning after the second night.

Experiment 4

Participants learned in the evening, followed by a night of sleep deprivation and testing the next morning. Half of the participants were given caffeine prior to testing (night wake caffeine), while the other half were given a placebo. The results of experiments 1-4 are shown in Figure 1.

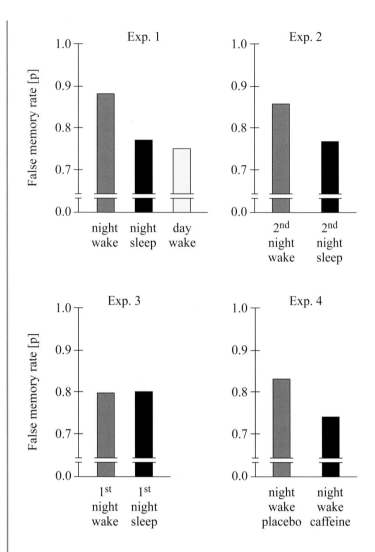

Figure 1 Effects of sleep deprivation on false memory rates

This passage was adapted from "Sleep Loss Produces False Memories." Diekelmann S, Landolt HP, Lahl O, Born J, Wagner U. *PLoS ONE*. 2008. 3(10) doi:10.1371/journal.pone.0003512 and "Partial Sleep Restriction Activates Immune Response-Related Gene Expression Pathways: Experimental and Epidemiological Studies in Humans." Aho V, Ollila HM, Rantanen V, Kronholm E, Surakka I, et al. *PLoS ONE*. 2013. 8(10) doi:10.1371/journal.pone.0077184 for use under the terms of the Creative Commons CC BY 3.0 license (http://creativecommons.org/licenses/by/3.0/legalcode).

Next ▶

Question 93

Which of the following conclusions can be drawn from Figure 1?

○ **A.** Sleep is necessary for the proper encoding of memories.
○ **B.** Sleep is necessary for proper retrieval of memories.
○ **C.** Caffeine enhances long term potentiation.
○ **D.** Caffeine has no effect on memory retrieval.

Question 94

Which stage of sleep is most important for memory consolidation?

○ **A.** Non-REM sleep
○ **B.** Stage 2 sleep
○ **C.** Stage 3 sleep
○ **D.** REM sleep

Question 95

Which of the following concepts best accounts for the strong semantic relationship between real and false memories described in the passage?

○ **A.** Primacy effect
○ **B.** Weber's Law
○ **C.** Spreading activation
○ **D.** Neural plasticity

Question 96

Which of the following techniques could the study participants have chosen to improve their recall accuracy?

○ **A.** Interference
○ **B.** Synaptic potentiation
○ **C.** Hypnosis
○ **D.** Chunking

Question 97

Given the passage information, patients with which neurological disorder would likely have the highest false memory rate?

○ **A.** Epilepsy
○ **B.** Insomnia
○ **C.** Narcolepsy
○ **D.** Schizophrenia

Passage II (Questions 98-101)

Genes expressed in the brain interact with environmental factors to affect behavior and social relationships. One example is the serotonergic system, where several genes are predictive of social behaviors that impact physical health and safety. The $5HT^{2A}$ gene, which codes for a certain type of serotonin receptor, is associated with popularity in adolescent males, an important predictor of diseases like metabolic syndrome later in life. Two alleles exist for the gene: A and G.

Aggressiveness and number of female friends are social features that also correlate with young males' popularity. Researchers investigated how different $5HT^{2A}$ genotypes affect this relationship. Survey data on aggressiveness, number of female friends, and popularity was collected from peers of genotyped adolescent males. (Figure 1)

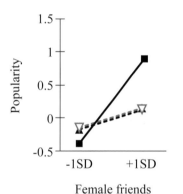
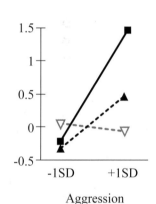

Figure 1 Relationship between number of female friends (left) or aggression (right) and popularity for three $5HT^{2A}$ genotypes (popularity scores range from -2 (least popular) to 2 (most popular); SD = standard deviation)

Variation in the serotonin transporter gene *5-HTT* is also known to correlate with behavioral phenotypes in young males, especially response to fearful stimuli. Humans have two alleles for *5-HTT*: S and L. Another group of experimenters studied how these alleles' expression correlates with an active fear response: owning a handgun for self-defense, which has been linked to increased risk of injury or death due to gun violence. Participants were surveyed on whether they owned a gun for self-defense six months before and six months after a strong fear-inducing stimulus. SS homozygotes were found to be three times less likely to purchase a gun in response to the stimulus, whereas twice as many LL homozygotes reported gun ownership in the later survey.

This passage was adapted from "The Secret Ingredient for Social Success of Young Males: A Functional Polymorphism in the *5HT^{2A}* Serotonin Receptor Gene." Dijkstra JK, Lindenberg S, Zijlstra L, Bouma E, Veenstra R. *PLoS ONE*. 2013. 8(2) doi: 10.1371/journal.pone.0054821 and "A Functional Polymorphism in a Serotonin Transporter Gene (*5-HTTLPR*) Interacts with 9/11 to Predict Gun-Carrying Behavior." Barnes JC, Beaver KM, Boutwell BB. *PLoS ONE* 2013. 8(8) doi: 10.1371/journal.pone.0070807 for use under the terms of the Creative Commons CC BY 3.0 license (http://creativecommons.org/licenses/by/3.0/legalcode).

Question 98

Suppose that over the last several million years, males in certain mammalian species have developed more aggressive patterns of behavior. Which of the following would best explain this change?

○ **A.** New social pressures that affect all phenotypes equally

○ **B.** Aggressive behavior leads to a decrease in transcription of genes associated with passive behavior.

○ **C.** Alleles leading to aggressive behavior have higher adaptive value than those leading to passive behavior.

○ **D.** Alleles leading to aggressive behavior have been artificially selected for over time.

Question 99

Which is the best explanation for the decreased probability of gun ownership in SS homozygotes after fear induction described in the passage?

○ **A.** The SS genotype leads to transcription products that are implicated in behavior and whose activity is modulated by a strong fear response.

○ **B.** The percentage of SS homozygotes in the gene pool decreased after a fearful stimulus.

○ **C.** The percentage of SS homozygotes in the gene pool increased after a fearful stimulus.

○ **D.** The SS genotype leads to an increase in active fear responses.

Question 100

Which of the following best explains the findings seen in Figure 1?

○ **A.** Heterozygous allele expression causes popularity among peers in adolescent males.

○ **B.** Homozygous allele expression causes popularity among peers in adolescent males.

○ **C.** Possessing two G alleles enhances a pre-existing relationship between popularity and number of female friends.

○ **D.** Possessing two A alleles enhances a pre-existing relationship between popularity and number of female friends.

Question 101

Which of the following is most likely responsible for the changes in gene expression indicated by the findings of the second study described in the passage?

○ **A.** Allele frequencies

○ **B.** Regulatory genes

○ **C.** Absolute thresholds

○ **D.** Tumor suppressor genes

Passage III (Questions 102-106)

Perception involves cross-talk between sensory modalities. Interactions between vision and hearing, which humans rely on for most sensory information, are of particular interest – deficits in these two systems are common and debilitating conditions. In one study, researchers investigated how deafness from early childhood affects visual sensitivity. Hearing and deaf participants focused on the center of a screen between two identical stationary patterns. One of the patterns then began slowly rotating, with participants attempting to identify which pattern was moving. Movement speed was adjusted until a threshold speed was reached at which the participant was correct on fifty percent of trials. The investigators found that the mean threshold was roughly 25 percent lower in deaf patients than in the hearing.

Conscious sensory perception is also dependent upon the coordinated activity of arousal and sensory systems in the brain. Arousal provides a basic aptitude for behavioral response to the environment and a means for optimizing behavior. In a study of the relationship between sensation, perception, and arousal, researchers measured visual sensitivity in normal and hyper-aroused states. Participants completed a discrimination task where they were presented with two white pegs at different depths in front of a black background and asked to determine which was closer. Depth difference between the pegs was adjusted until threshold values could be determined. Thresholds were defined as the difference in depth at which a participant was correct on 50 percent of trials. Half of the participants then received an arousing stimulus, while the other half received a similar non-arousing (sham) stimulus. Both groups then repeated the discrimination task. The results are shown in Figure 1.

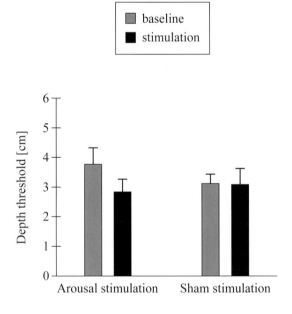

Figure 1 Depth thresholds before (baseline) and after stimulation in participants receiving an arousing or sham stimulus

This passage was adapted from "Enhancement of Visual Motion Detection Thresholds in Early Deaf People." Shiell MM, Champoux F, Zatorre RJ. *PLoS ONE*. 2013. 9(2) doi: 10.1371/journal.pone.0090498 and "Hyper-Arousal Decreases Human Visual Thresholds." Woods AJ, Philbeck JW, Wirtz P. *PLoS ONE* 2013. 8(4) doi: 10.1371/journal.pone.0061415 for use under the terms of the Creative Commons CC BY 3.0 license (http://creativecommons.org/licenses/by/3.0/legalcode).

Next ▶

Question 102

In a follow-up to the second study described in the passage, participants were shown two rotating patterns and asked to identify when one of them started to rotate faster than the other. In which of the following groups would the lowest difference thresholds be expected?

- ○ **A.** The hearing group when both patterns started at a fast speed
- ○ **B.** The deaf group when both patterns started at a fast speed
- ○ **C.** The hearing group when both patterns started at a slow speed
- ○ **D.** The deaf group when both patterns started at a slow speed

Question 103

If a participant in the first experiment has a difference threshold of 6 cm when the pegs start at 48 cm apart, how far will one peg need to be moved from the other in order for the participant to detect the difference when the initial positions are 12 cm apart?

- ○ **A.** 6 cm
- ○ **B.** $^3/_2$ cm
- ○ **C.** 2 cm
- ○ **D.** $^1/_2$ cm

Question 104

It has been reported that individuals who become deaf later in life begin integrating areas of the brain previously reserved for auditory perception into visual circuits. This process is an example of:

- ○ **A.** Gestalt principles.
- ○ **B.** selective attention.
- ○ **C.** plasticity.
- ○ **D.** divided attention.

Question 105

Which of the following conclusions is indicated by the results shown in Figure 1?

- ○ **A.** Arousal has no effect on perception.
- ○ **B.** Arousal decreases sensitivity to changes in depth.
- ○ **C.** Perception depends on both physical sensation and psychological state.
- ○ **D.** Perception depends on physical sensation alone.

Question 106

In a similar experiment, researchers tested both seeing and blind participants on their ability to discern auditory tones at several frequencies by measuring how intense each tone needed to be before the participant could hear it. What were these researchers testing?

- ○ **A.** Absolute thresholds
- ○ **B.** Difference thresholds
- ○ **C.** Weber fractions
- ○ **D.** Visual acuity

Passage IV (Questions 107-110)

Light is the most important time cue for maintaining the 24 hour period of circadian rhythms in humans. In the Arctic and Antarctic Circles, deprivation of natural light occurs in winter. Some studies suggest that these suboptimal light conditions are deleterious to health, sleep and mood. An adequate light exposure pattern may help to prevent or even reverse health problems associated with circadian disruption.

In this study, two different populations of workers were compared, one living beneath the Equator in northern Brazil and another within the Arctic Circle in northern Sweden. The hypothesis was that at an extreme latitude (Swedish workers), lack of natural light exposure affects sleep quality and may lead to depressive symptoms. Both Arctic and Equatorial workers reported the number of hours per day on average that they were exposed to natural light. Three independent indices related to sleep problems were obtained from the Karolinska Sleep Questionnaire: sleep quality, awakening problems, and sleepiness. At both sites, clinical depression was assessed using the Work Ability Index or Hamilton Depression Subscale. The workers were split according to self-reported natural light exposure into short and long light exposure groups, according to the mean within each group. The study results are shown in Figure 1.

While Arctic workers reported more sleep problems on the questionnaires, electroencephalogram (EEG) studies revealed that many Equatorial workers rarely entered REM sleep. A higher proportion of Arctic workers complained that they were depressed compared with the Equatorial workers.

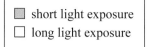

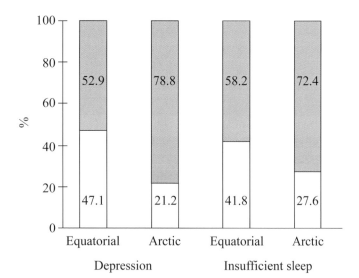

Figure 1 Percentage of workers reporting depression and insufficient sleep divided according to self-reported natural light exposure groups for Equatorial and Arctic groups

This passage was adapted from "Natural Light Exposure, Sleep and Depression among Day Workers and Shiftworkers at Arctic and Equatorial Latitudes." Marqueze EC, Vasconcelos S, Garefelt J, Skene DJ, Moreno CR, et al. *PLoS ONE*. 2015. 10(4): e0122078. doi:10.1371/journal.pone.0122078 for use under the terms of the Creative Commons CC BY 4.0 license (http://creativecommons.org/licenses/by/4.0/legalcode).

Question 107

People who have suffered an aneurysm in the diencephalon do not experience increased wakefulness based on light. This is best explained by the finding in these individuals that:

- ○ **A.** the suprachiasmatic nucleus becomes overactive in signaling to the pineal gland.
- ○ **B.** the pineal gland begins producing excess melatonin.
- ○ **C.** the optic nerve becomes more sensitive to changes in light.
- ○ **D.** the connection between the hypothalamus and pineal gland is lost.

Question 108

Based on the passage, researchers should be most concerned about Equatorial workers experiencing which type of sleep disorder?

- ○ **A.** Sleep terror disorder
- ○ **B.** Nightmares
- ○ **C.** Insomnia
- ○ **D.** Narcolepsy

Question 109

Based on the findings in the passage, if Arctic workers were given a memory test, they would:

- ○ **A.** outperform Equatorial workers because they achieve Stage 4 sleep.
- ○ **B.** underperform relative to Equatorial workers because they only achieve Stage 4 sleep.
- ○ **C.** outperform Equatorial workers because they achieve better REM sleep.
- ○ **D.** underperform relative to Equatorial workers because they only achieve better REM sleep.

Question 110

Arctic workers in this study who self-report problems awakening and daytime sleepiness show a lack of delta waves on their EEG during sleep. They are likely not achieving which stage of sleep?

- ○ **A.** Stage 1
- ○ **B.** Stage 2
- ○ **C.** Stage 3
- ○ **D.** REM

Next ▶

Questions 111 through 115 are NOT based on a descriptive passage.

Question 111

The efficacy of the class of antidepressants known as selective serotonin reuptake inhibitors in treating depression shows that:

○ **A.** neurotransmitters have an influence on mood.

○ **B.** decreased serotonin levels in the brain cause depression.

○ **C.** altered levels of neurotransmitters permanently change behavior.

○ **D.** there is a genetic basis of depression.

Question 112

Sarah listens to her mom read out their extensive grocery list. Which items is she most likely to forget?

○ **A.** Items at the top of the list

○ **B.** Items in the middle

○ **C.** Items at the end of the list

○ **D.** Random items

Question 113

Researchers are using a specialized fMRI to study the location of long-term potentiation for memory formation. Where should they expect to see these signals?

○ **A.** The thalamus and the cortex

○ **B.** The hippocampus and the cortex

○ **C.** The brainstem and the thalamus

○ **D.** The brainstem and the hippocampus

Question 114

Which component of the CNS is associated with drug addiction and gambling?

○ **A.** Mirror neurons, in the limbic system

○ **B.** Mirror neurons, in the frontal lobe

○ **C.** The reward pathway, in the frontal lobe

○ **D.** The reward pathway, in the limbic system

Question 115

A person severely deficient in water-soluble vitamins might be expected to show memory loss consistent with which neurological disorder?

○ **A.** Alzheimer's disease

○ **B.** Korsakoff's syndrome

○ **C.** Parkinson's disease

○ **D.** Hypothyroidism

STOP. IF YOU FINISH BEFORE TIME IS CALLED, CHECK YOUR WORK. YOU MAY GO BACK TO ANY QUESTION IN THIS TEST BOOKLET.

ANSWERS & EXPLANATIONS

FOR

30-MINUTE IN-CLASS EXAMINATIONS

ANSWERS TO THE 30-MINUTE IN-CLASS EXAMS

Lecture 1	Lecture 2	Lecture 3	Lecture 4	Lecture 5
1. B	24. C	47. D	70. A	93. B
2. A	25. A	48. C	71. B	94. D
3. D	26. D	49. C	72. B	95. C
4. B	27. A	50. A	73. C	96. D
5. D	28. B	51. C	74. B	97. B
6. C	29. C	52. C	75. B	98. C
7. D	30. C	53. A	76. A	99. A
8. B	31. C	54. D	77. C	100. C
9. C	32. B	55. C	78. B	101. B
10. B	33. A	56. A	79. A	102. D
11. A	34. A	57. C	80. C	103. B
12. A	35. B	58. D	81. C	104. C
13. D	36. D	59. C	82. C	105. C
14. B	37. A	60. C	83. C	106. A
15. B	38. C	61. B	84. D	107. D
16. D	39. C	62. B	85. C	108. A
17. C	40. A	63. B	86. C	109. C
18. A	41. C	64. C	87. B	110. C
19. D	42. C	65. B	88. B	111. A
20. D	43. C	66. C	89. D	112. B
21. D	44. B	67. D	90. B	113. B
22. B	45. B	68. D	91. D	114. D
23. C	46. C	69. C	92. A	115. B

SCORING

Any attempt we could make at score correlation to the MCAT® would mislead. Unlike the AAMC MCAT®, which includes easy questions, Examkrackers deliberately asks questions only of medium and high difficulty in order to optimize your practice time and maximize the increase to your MCAT® score. To accurately predict your MCAT® score, use an official AAMC MCAT® practice test.

Your goal is to see your raw score improve with each Examkrackers In-Class Exam and full-length EK-Test® you take. Look closely at each question you get wrong to find areas for review and to notice the habits that don't work. As you approach each new In-Class Exam or practice test, make commitments to replace what doesn't work with the approach you need to get questions right. Focus on the questions you get wrong to learn to think like the MCAT® and increase your score.

Toward your success!

EXPLANATIONS TO IN-CLASS EXAM FOR LECTURE 1

Passage I (Questions 1-5)

1. **B is the best answer.** This question is best answered by process of elimination. Although education may relate to social class, a difference in social class cannot be assumed on the basis of educational differences alone; choice A can be eliminated. Social institutions are aspects of society at large, not characteristics of individuals, so C can be eliminated. The information given in the question stem does not relate to material culture, ruling out choice D. Demographics are societal categories that include age and educational levels. This makes choice B the best answer.

2. **A is the best answer.** As described in the passage, the results of the study indicated that psychological factors are mediators between biological and environmental factors and mental health. Choice C is entirely consistent with these results—genetics are a type of biological factor—so it can be eliminated. Although psychological factors mediate the effects of other types of factors, the passage states that social status predicts mental health, so B can be eliminated. Choice D is consistent with the general idea of the BPS model and with the interaction between factors that is indicated in the second study, so it is a weak answer. Only choice A goes against the results of the second study: since psychological factors mediate the effect of biological factors (such as genetics) on mental health, these two types of influences cannot be separated. This makes choice A the strongest answer. You also could have taken a shortcut by noticing that answer choices A and C are opposite statements. This means that one of them is likely consistent with the results and one is likely contradictory, so one of these choices is probably the best answer.

3. **D is the best answer.** This question requires an understanding of the major theoretical approaches to the study of society. Choice B can be eliminated because symbolic interactionism is generally applied to small-scale interactions rather than larger societal forces. The other theoretical approaches do apply to the societal level. However, functionalism examines the harmonious functioning of social institutions, so it is not generally used to examine societal problems like healthcare disparity; choice C can be eliminated. Choice D is a better answer, since conflict theory addresses inequalities between social groups that have the potential to lead to societal conflict. Social constructionism could be involved in healthcare disparities, such as in the process of building our societal understanding of healthcare and illness, but is not as directly related to healthcare disparities. Choice D is the best answer.

4. **B is the best answer.** As is often the case with definition questions, process of elimination is a useful strategy. Intergenerational mobility and socioeconomic status, choices A and D, could be influenced by the kind of cultural knowledge described but are not directly related to the question stem. This means that the strongest answer will likely be choice B or choice C. Cultural and social capital are both types of knowledge that influence social success. Loosely speaking, cultural capital is what you know, while social capital is who you know. The question stem describes cultural knowledge ("what" someone knows), making choice B the best answer.

5. **D is the best answer.** Despite the fact that both studies are referenced, this question really just requires an understanding of the results of the second study. Recall that the results pointed to psychological factors as mediators of the effects of other factors on mental health. It makes sense to think that psychological interventions would be an effective method of directly influencing mental health, as described in choice D. In addition, the passage mentioned that psychological processes can be impacted by evidence-based interventions, which further supports choice D. Choices B and C do not account for the mediating effect of psychological factors, so neither is the best answer choice. In fact, choice C is reminiscent of the biomedical model, which is certainly not supported by the results of the study. Finally, choice A might be tempting because the passage indicates that social status significantly effects mental health, but changing a complex characteristic like social status is a far less realistic option than intervention in psychological processes. Choice A is wrong, and choice D is the best answer.

Passage II (Questions 6-9)

6. **C is the best answer.** Because low SES is associated with bullying, moving a child to a higher SES school should DECREASE the likelihood of bullying behavior, so choice A can be eliminated. Although social groups may have some type of involvement in bullying, the specific impact of EXPANDING the social group of a child is not covered by the passage or required background information, so B is not a good answer choice. Residential segregation, or the separation of demographic groups into different neighborhoods, may contribute to the creation of high and low SES schools. Eliminating residential segregation could raise SES in low SES areas but would also lower SES in high SES areas. The overall effects of such a change on bullying are not clear from the information in the article, so choice D can be eliminated. On the other hand, children learn to model their behavior after the social norms of their culture. Making a bullying a social norm could be expected to increase the incidence of bullying; therefore choice C is the best answer.

7. **D is the best answer.** SES describes both economic position, in terms of income and acquired wealth, and social position, in terms of factors like education and profession. Thus income levels, education levels, and unemployment rates are all involved in SES. Racial identity is considered a separate demographic category and is not a part of defining SES, so choice D is the best answer.

8. **B is the best answer.** Social reproduction, the transmission of social inequality from one generation to the next, is most relevant to the findings of the study, making choice B the best answer. In a meritocracy, social rank is based on merit only, so there should be no correlation between parent SES and child SES. Answer choice A is contradictory to the finding described in the question stem and can be eliminated. Cultural capital and social capital may contribute to the continuance of social inequality throughout the generations, but they do not apply as precisely to the findings as does social reproduction. Choice B is a better answer.

9. **C is the best answer.** If teachers over-report bullying in certain students and under-report it in others, a bias is introduced, creating error. Choice A can be eliminated. Choice D can be eliminated because a re-zoning of school districts would invalidate the school neighborhood status scores determined by the government. To distinguish between choices B and C, it is necessary to understand the difference between relative and absolute poverty. Parents experiencing relative poverty may self-report markers of lower SES in relation to those with whom they compare themselves, introducing error. By contrast, absolute poverty is not defined by comparisons with others. Parents in absolute poverty are likely to accurately recognize their lack of basic essentials for survival. Choice B can be eliminated, and C is the best answer.

Passage III (Questions 10-14)

10. **B is the best answer.** Researchers wishing to assess the relationship between assimilation and health should choose variables that can be used as proxies to measure either degree of assimilation or quality of health. It is reasonable to think that English language proficiency can be used as a measure of assimilation in U.S. society, so choice A is a weak answer. Choices C and D can directly influence physical and mental health, so they are also weak answers. While choice of occupation may influence health or indicate level of assimilation, it is not as directly related to either variable as are the other three choices, so choice B is the best answer.

11. **A is the best answer.** The passage implies that choice A is a true statement. However, the encouragement of healthy behaviors by U.S. culture does not explain the paradox of why recent immigrants to the U.S. are healthier than their native-born counterparts. This makes A the best answer. The scenarios described in choices B and C would contribute to the healthy immigrant effect by altering the health profiles and death statistics of immigrant vs. native populations. Choice D refers to culture norms (e.g. supportive family structure, healthy nutrition choices, decreased risky behavior) that may contribute to better health in spite of risk factors such as the lower socioeconomic status associated with immigration. Like choices B and C, this answer choice is a plausible explanation for the paradox referenced in the question stem.

12. **A is the best answer.** The passage states that Hispanics represent 20% of new HIV infections but make up only 16% of the general population, making them disproportionately at risk for HIV infection. Answer I is true, and choice B can be eliminated. The passage does not provide any information regarding the validity of answer II, which confirms the elimination of choice B and also eliminates choice C as a possible answer. The passage does indicate that undocumented Hispanics are more likely to enter treatment with advanced disease state than documented Hispanics, but both groups have similar treatment outcomes. This makes answer III false, eliminating choice D and leaving choice A as the best answer.

13. **D is the best answer.** Spatial inequality refers to differential access to resources based on location. Hispanics in neighborhoods with better resources may be likely to experience better health outcomes. This inequality is related to location, not documentation status; choice A is a weak answer. Choice B is wrong because the passage does not specify the attributes of either documented or undocumented immigrant neighborhoods. There is not enough information to support this choice. Choice C is not supported by the finding because the separation of Hispanic immigrants into documented and undocumented neighborhoods with different neighborhood resources means that social inequality DOES exist among Hispanic immigrants. Choice D accurately describes the implications of the finding in the question stem.

14. **B is the best answer.** The passage states that more time spent in the U.S. correlates to greater socioeconomic status. Prestige, wealth, and educational attainment are all factors that contribute to socioeconomic status. By process of elimination, choice B is the best answer. You can also identify choice B as the strongest answer because it contradicts the information presented in the passage. The passage states that more time spent in the U.S. is detrimental to immigrant health. Therefore, one might expect second generation immigrants to have shorter, not longer, lifespans.

Passage IV (Questions 15-18)

15. **B is the best answer.** Medicalization is defining a behavior as an illness that requires treatment. This is often viewed as an attempt to control people and define normal behavior, especially in psychology. However, this is biased view of medicalization that does not hold true in every circumstance. As an example, high blood pressure was not always considered to be a medical problem, but it is now diagnosed as hypertension. This change in classification represents the medicalization of high blood pressure. Since choice A ascribes a motivation to medicalization that is true in some cases, but not in others, it is likely not the best answer. Choice B describes the process of medicalization without assuming a particular motivation for it, so it is a better answer than choice A. The desire to obtain medication for a condition could contribute to defining new diseases. If a large group of people desire medication for a set of symptoms, those symptoms may be medicalized. Choice C refers to an illness, not to symptoms, implying that the disease is already defined. Because of this, choice C is inconsistent with the definition of medicalization, so it is not the best answer. Choice D is very similar to choice A in that it describes a biased view of medicalization. Medicalization serves more purposes than making more money for doctors so choice D is a biased interpretation that is too limited in scope. Choice B is the best answer.

16. **D is the best answer.** Values are standards of what is right or wrong in a given culture. If a child being hyperactive is considered "wrong," then values are contributing to the diagnosis of ADHD. Option I is a good answer and choice B can be ruled out. Norms are behaviors that are predictable and acceptable in a culture. If a child being hyperactive is considered "abnormal," then norms are contributing to the diagnosis of ADHD. Option II should be included in the best answer, so choice A can be ruled out. Beliefs are less clearly related to defining illness, but could still play a role. If hyperactivity was believed to be a sign of possession by a demon, as is true in some cultures, children may be seen by an exorcist rather than receiving a diagnosis of ADHD from a doctor. Since options I, II, and III are all strong answers, choice D is the best answer.

17. **C is the best answer.** A health disparity is a difference in health or disease between two groups whereas a healthcare disparity is a difference in accessibility of health services. Although these concepts are closely related, the question stem describes a healthcare disparity rather a health disparity because it refers to access to care rather than incidence of disease. A global inequality describes a disparity across nations or regions of the world in many things, including healthcare. The question stem relates to global inequality but not clearly to health disparities so choice A is probably not the best answer. Environmental injustice is the unequal treatment of people with regard to prevention and relief from environmental and health hazards. This does not match the scenario described in the question, so choice B can be eliminated. As mentioned previously, a healthcare disparity is a difference is availability of healthcare. Spatial inequality is any unequal access to resources so healthcare disparity is a type of spatial inequality. These are both directly related to inaccessibility of clinics so choice C is a strong answer. Globalization is increased interaction between people of different countries and regions of the world. This is not directly related to availability of clinics, so choice D can be eliminated. By process of elimination, choice C is the best answer.

18. **A is the best answer.** The sick role describes the behaviors of people with an illness and the exemptions they receive from certain responsibilities. When a child has strep throat, they may have the day off from school, their parent may stay home to play with him or her, and they may only be expected to watch TV, nap, and eat ice cream. The sick role can be desirable in some cases. However, some children and adults avoid the sick role to avoid having to take time off from work or receiving too much attention, among other reasons. The students in the study are self-medicating and are presumably avoiding the sick role by avoiding interaction with a doctor for an illness that is "too trivial" or "to save time." Choice A is a strong answer. Medicalization is the defining of behavior as illness. The students are not avoiding medicalization, but rather avoiding medical care. Choice B is not the best answer. Health inequity is a difference in health between groups of people. Medical students may be more or less healthy than another group of people, but Table 1 does not provide this type of information. Choice C is not a strong answer. The illness experience is the entire episode of being sick. It includes the interpretation of symptoms and the assumption of the sick role. The students are not avoiding being sick by self-medicating, but they are avoiding the expectations of others about how they should behave when sick. Choice A more specifically describes what the students are avoiding, so it is a stronger answer than choice D.

Stand-alones (Questions 19-23)

19. **D is the best answer.** Absolute poverty describes a lack of essential resources, such as food or shelter. It can often be a life-threatening situation. By contrast, relative poverty describes a social inequality in which individuals are poor relative to others in their society or social group. Since this individual is homeless and jobless, choice D is the best answer. Isolation and social exclusion describe the same concept: the idea that individuals in poverty lack opportunities and options. These are both possibilities in poverty, but the question stem does not specifically refer to these concepts. Additionally, it would be impossible to decide which of the two is the better answer. When two answer choices are synonyms, usually neither is the correct answer. Choices A and B can be eliminated..

20. **D is the best answer.** Symbolic culture is non-material culture that conveys meaning only in the mind. A fork is an example of material culture since it is an object that supports a specific action and conveys similar meaning in separate cultures. A handshake and a thumbs up do not suggest a specific meaning on their own but rather through symbolic expectations. For this reason, choices A and B can be eliminated. Language is also a form of symbolic culture, since the writing must be interpreted to convey meaning. A novel communicates with an individual through symbolism, so choice C is not as strong an answer as choice D.

21. **D is the best answer.** Notice the emphasis on ECONOMIC hardship in the question stem. This should lead you to the conclusion that the best answer is more likely related to poverty than prejudice, making choices C and D more likely than choices A or B. Social exclusion is the systematic exclusion of individuals or groups from certain rights, opportunities, or meaningful participation in certain aspects of society. This concept fits the given situation of excluding ex-prisoners from work and housing opportunities much more closely than socioeconomic status, spatial inequality, or social capital. Note that social capital should improve economic opportunities rather than contribute to economic hardship; this is another reason that choice C can be eliminated.

22. **B is the best answer.** The possible answers to this question each have two parts, a description of a position and a description of a social context. Both parts must be true for the answer to be the strongest choice. The first part, describing the position, is not very useful in narrowing down the answer choices because the office of President is a position of power and prestige and is also a white-collar position. The position is likely a move toward upward mobility (depending on where that person started) but it does not have to be, so choice C is called into question. The second part of the answer choices is more revealing. The United States is not a true meritocracy, so choice A can be eliminated. The U.S. is also not a social class, but rather contains many social classes, so choice C can be eliminated. Choice D is also eliminated because the U.S. is not a social movement, which requires common ideals and works toward a common goal. Instead, the U.S. contains many conflicting opinions as well as many opposing goals. As a country and as a government, the U.S. is a social institution. Therefore, choice B is the best answer.

23. **C is the best answer.** Culture shock refers to the discomfort people experience when encountering social norms that are different from what they are used to. The anxiety produced from being expected to eat an animal that is respected and loved in her own culture produces culture shock in the traveler. Material culture is tangentially related to the question, but is certainly less related than culture shock, so choice B is not the best answer. Choice C might seem tempting because of the involvement of global travel in the question stem, but globalization is a much broader concept than the travel of a single person. Like globalization, demographic transition is a widespread process that occurs over time, and is not applicable to the situation described here; choice D can also be eliminated.

EXPLANATIONS TO IN-CLASS EXAM FOR LECTURE 2

Passage I (Questions 24-27)

24. **C is the best answer.** The "previously neutral event" is a stimulus that originally has no significance but came to elicit a fearful response. This is best described as a conditioned stimulus. Choices A and B can be eliminated. The "associative fear after acquisition" is a response that follows conditioning, rather than a naturally existing behavior. It is a conditioned response, not an unconditioned response. Choice D can be eliminated, and choice C is the best answer.

25. **A is the best answer.** The question describes "learning from other mice," which is another way of saying observational learning. The only type of cell involved with observational learning that you are required to know for the MCAT® is the mirror neuron, which are believed to help us learn by example; choice A is the strongest answer. "Empathy cells" is a made-up term, though observational learning and mirror neurons are thought to be related to the development of empathy. However, this is beyond the scope of the MCAT®; choice B is wrong. Somatic motor neurons are part of the nervous system, but their deficits would contribute to loss of muscle control, not inhibited learning. Choice C can be eliminated. Erythrocytes, or red blood cells, are not relevant to the question stem, so choice D is also a weak answer.

26. **D is the best answer.** Figure 1 shows that participants' fear responses increased after worrisome thinking in response to both picture stimuli. Since only one of these pictures was conditioned to a fear-inducing stimulus, the worry must be causing participants to show a conditioned response to other stimuli that are similar to the conditioned picture. This is consistent with stimulus generalization, making choice D the best answer. In contrast, stimulus discrimination is the ability to distinguish and respond differently to similar stimuli, which is the opposite of what Figure 1 shows; choice C is a weak answer. If worry were driving fear extinction, you would expect to see DECREASES in fear response after worrying, so choice A can be eliminated. Choice B might seem like a tempting answer choice, but remember what Figure 1 is actually measuring: the change in fear response after acquisition has already taken place. It is possible that worry is causing greater fear acquisition, but the passage does not provide enough information to draw this conclusion. Choice D is the better answer.

27. **A is the best answer.** This question asks about operant conditioning, while the passage is focused on classical conditioning, so the answer will probably come from your background knowledge rather than from the passage. The question also states that the researchers want to encourage a specific behavior for as long as possible. In other words, they want to use a reward schedule that best delays extinction. Punishing participants every time they view the picture should lead to avoidance and fewer views, so choice C is a weak answer. Choice D would only be a strong answer if all of the other answer choices involved punishment, as there is no reason to believe that participants would choose to continue viewing the picture more in the absence of rewards than they would if rewarded. Since choices A and B contain rewards, D can be eliminated. Choice B is an example of a continuous reinforcement schedule, whereas choice A represents partial reinforcement. While continuous reinforcement is the best way to establish a response rapidly, behaviors that are partially reinforced are more resistant to extinction. Choice A is the better choice.

Passage II (Questions 28-32)

28. **B is the best answer.** Of the choices presented, ethical concerns pose the largest hindrance in replicating the events surrounding the murder of Kitty Genovese. A modern day ethics review board would never allow for the level of deception required for participants to view what they believe is a violent assault in order to study the participants' reactions. However, such realism is necessary in order to observe the bystander effect. This study attempts to circumvent these ethical considerations by placing subjects in a virtual reality environment that is sufficiently authentic to trigger realistic responses, but wherein subjects will be certain that they are not watching an act of violence against another human. Potential group effects can be controlled for by using confederates, eliminating choice D. There is no indication that the scenario was too complex to control for in an experiment—the fact that a general principle of psychology (the bystander effect) was discovered as a result of this incident implies that this was not an isolated finding, but rather a general tendency of human nature, which is something that can be measured in a properly designed experiment. This eliminates choice A. There is no reason this experiment cannot have a control group, eliminating choice C.

29. **C is the best answer**. The use of an IVE walks a fine line in this experiment. It must be sufficiently realistic to trigger realistic responses, but participants must also be aware that they are in a virtual scenario, lest they become distressed, raising ethical concerns. As the purpose of the study is to study the bystander effect, participants must feel as though they are witnessing a live emergency situation and also feel that it is possible to intervene. If participants feel as though the IVE is not realistic, they may not feel that either of these conditions are met, making choice C the best answer. Subjects are expected to feel some level of discomfort; this indicates that they find the simulation to be realistic, eliminating choice A. The whole point of the study is to measure differing levels of verbal intervention, so choice B is wrong. Group affiliation often lies along a continuum, with some members feeling stronger affiliation to a group than others. This fact alone is not sufficient to disqualify average effects, eliminating choice D.

30. **C is the best answer**. Eye contact between the victim and a member of the crowd should help to combat diffusion of responsibility, one of the purported underlying causes of the bystander effect. Rather than feeling like an anonymous member of a crowd, eye contact between victim and crowd member should empower the crowd member to intervene, so choice C is the best answer. Note that this finding was not demonstrated in this study, but the question asked what would be expected, not what actually happened. Choice B has the possibility to be a strong choice, but it is vague since it is unclear what conclusions are drawn about the bystander effect. Since *LookAt* was one of the study's independent variables, an effect would be expected; choice A is eliminated. In the absence of information stating otherwise, it is unreasonable to conclude that this independent variable acted as a confounding variable, so D is a weak answer.

31. **C is the best answer.** Deviant behavior is defined as behavior that violates social norms. Violence against another (outside of a context where this may be expected, such as within a boxing ring) qualifies as a violation of social expectations, making choice C the best answer. Institutional discrimination occurs when social institutions, not individuals, perform discriminatory actions; choice A can be eliminated. Social facilitation occurs when performance improves due to being watched. This effect is not involved in the attacker's actions, so choice B is a weak answer. Social loafing occurs when members of a group "slack off," letting other group members do a disproportionate amount of work; choice D is wrong.

32. **B is the best answer**. In group polarization, a group forms an opinion that is more extreme than the initial opinion of any individual group member. The best answer will refer to both initial opinions of individuals and the stronger final opinion of the group. Choice A does not specify a strengthened group opinion, and choice C does not reference individual and group opinions. Of the two remaining choices, B is most consistent with group polarization. The initial opinion of individuals (support of a verbal attack) changes to a more extreme view (support of a physical assault).

Passage III (Questions 33-37)

33. A is the best answer. Agents of socialization refer to the multiple and varied influences that provide information about social norms. In this study, Western media influences provided a context of acceptable behavior that informed Chinese university students about what constituted acceptable drinking behavior. Although Western-influenced Chinese university students may arguably be a subculture within the broader Chinese culture, this question specifically asks about the role of media, which is not a subculture, making choice B a weak answer. Assimilation refers to the process by which a person or group from a foreign culture becomes absorbed into a new culture. This does not accurately describe the situation depicted in this study, where Chinese students remain immersed in their home culture. In fact, cultural assimilant and socionormative influence are fabricated terms, making choices C and D weak answers. When you do not recognize the terms in answer choices, trust your instincts that they may be invented or at least beyond the scope of the MCAT®.

34. A is the best answer. Peer pressure occurs when people alter their behavior as a result of the influence of others. It is quite possible that respondents could change their answers to indicate either a higher or lower level of drinking to conform to the norms of the group, making option I a strong answer. Groupthink occurs when unpopular opinions are silenced in order to attain consensus in decision making. As this data collection does not involve making group decisions, groupthink is not possible, making option II a weak choice. Group polarization occurs when the opinions of the group become stronger than those of any one individual. Because this question implies the mere presence of others when administering the survey, but no group discussion or decision making, option III is a weak answer. This leaves choice A as the best answer.

35. B is the best answer. Impression management describes the process of modifying one's behavior in order to consciously change the perception that others have of oneself. Impression management does not involve self-image, eliminating choice A. Likewise, impression management implies a modification on the part of the actor, not the observer, making choice C a weak answer. Choice D is a distractor that does not involve the behavior modification that is required in impression management.

36. D is the best answer. Cultural relativists attempt to understand a culture on its own terms, recognizing that each culture has different values and standards. Cultural relativism specifically does not imply comparisons between cultures, which means that choice A can be eliminated, despite the misleading similarity of this answer choice. Cultural relativism only involves the understanding of different cultures, not necessarily acceptance of them, making choice B a weak answer. Cultural relativism does not forbid judging the practices or viewpoints of other cultures, eliminating choice C.

37. A is the best answer. Obeying the commands of an authority figure is defined as obedience. Conformity requires pressure from peers, rather than authority figures, making B a weak answer. There is no mention of reinforcement or punishment, so there is no indication that operant conditioning is being used; choice C can be eliminated. Self-fulfilling prophecy is completely unrelated to this situation, ruling out choice D.

Passage IV (Questions 38-41)

38. C is the best answer. This question is testing concepts related to the elements of social interaction. The scenario in the question stem describes an individual who is acting differently with regard to his or her diet when around coworkers relative to how he or she behaves at home. Choice A states that this individual is modifying his or her behavior when around fit coworkers to appear healthier. This is consistent with the idea that people will modify their behavior in order to change how they are perceived. This is known as self-presentation, and choice A can be eliminated. Choice B states that this individual is making behavior choices with the intent of shaping the impressions of others. This concept is known as impression management, and is consistent with this individual's behaviors, so choice B can be eliminated. The dramaturgical approach is one theory of impression management that states behavior is an ongoing performance of self that changes according to the situation. Choice C states that the person's behavior at work is not "true self." This is inconsistent with the dramaturgical approach, as the dramaturgical approach makes no such distinctions as "true self" and not "true self." Instead, this approach suggests that all behaviors are a portrayal of some aspect of the individual's self, and the portrayal of self only varies with respect to the audience at any given time. Choice C is untrue, so it is the best answer. Choice D states that the individual fears judgement for eating unhealthy food around their healthy peers. This could explain why this individual eats healthier foods at work, eliminating choice D.

39. **C is the best answer.** This question tests topics related to learning and behavior change. Obedience describes a behavioral change made in response to a command by an authority figure. Because the information in the passage and data in Table 1 do not suggest that any metric of health measured was due to the direct command of an authority figure, choice A can be eliminated. Peer pressure is the social influence exerted by one's peers to act in a way that is acceptable or similar to their own behaviors. Looking to Table 1, individuals working in larger workplaces said that health was important to their company more often than those in small and mid-sized workplaces. Choice B can be eliminated because it would not be expected that the effects of peer pressure in environments with relatively less emphasis on health would lead to the highest performance on a nutrition and fitness exam. Social norms describe a set of expectations that members of a given group are required to uphold. If the social norm for a work environment was to place high emphasis on health, the workers would be expected to have lower BMIs, eat less fast food, and report that their company values health. Table 1 indicates that white workers reported eating less fast food, working out more, having lower BMIs, and having a higher rating of company health than did African-Americans. Based on this data, the cohort in choice C would be expected to perform best on a nutrition and fitness assessment due to the social norms of their workplace.

40. **A is the best answer.** The question stem describes a group of people who share a preconceived set of beliefs about another group of individuals. Discrimination is the unfair treatment of others based on beliefs about them or the group to which they belong. While discrimination can be the result of a belief, it describes actions rather than the beliefs themselves. Choice A is not consistent with scenario presented in the question stem and is likely the best answer. Remember to consider all four choices before selecting the best answer. Stigma is a negative social label that classifies a person or group as abnormal or tainted in some respect. This concept is consistent with the question stem, and choice B can be eliminated. Prejudice describes strict generalizations or beliefs about groups of people that can often lead to antagonistic feelings. Because it describes thoughts and beliefs rather than actions, prejudice is more consistent with the question stem than discrimination, so choice C can be eliminated. A stereotype is a concept about a group or category of people that includes the belief that all members of that group share certain characteristics. Though stereotypes are not always negative, they can be. Choice D is consistent with the information presented in the question stem, so it can be eliminated. This leaves choice A as the best answer.

41. **C is the best answer.** Prejudice always has the potential for detrimental effects on those it touches. However, power, prestige, and class contribute most significantly to the effect that prejudice has on the lives and opportunities of individuals as well as the structure of social institutions. Individuals in a powerful social position can likely cause more damage with their prejudice than individuals in a less powerful position. Wealth is a primary consideration in social class, so choice C is the strongest answer. There is insufficient evidence to conclude that prejudice regarding weight would be more detrimental from men than women, from African-Americans than those of other racial groups, or from individuals who are single rather than married.

Stand-alones (Questions 42-46)

42. **C is the best answer.** This is a straightforward definition question. Know that a change in behavior that allows an individual to avoid an unpleasant stimulus is defined as avoidance conditioning. Choice C is the best answer. Escape conditioning involves learned behaviors that help someone to escape an unpleasant stimulus *after* he or she has encountered it, so choice D is not the best answer for this question. Shaping is a type of conditioning that allows behavior to be "shaped" in small, discrete steps. While it may be involved in the scenario described by the question stem, shaping does not answer the question and is not a better answer than avoidance conditioning. Choice A is a weak choice.

43. **C is the best answer.** Cultural relativism describes the practice of trying to understand a culture on its own terms and to judge a culture by its own standards. This is the opposite of ethnocentrism, which is the belief that one's group is of central importance. Choice A inaccurately characterizes cultural relativism and can be eliminated. Choice B uses the definition of cultural relativism to explain ethnocentrism, which is incorrect, and this choice can also be eliminated. Multiculturalism is the practice of valuing and respecting differences in culture. Trying to understand cultures and judge them on their own terms, as one would do under the auspices of cultural relativism, would promote multiculturalism. Assimilation is the process by which an individual or group becomes part of a new culture. The practice of cultural relativism does not directly address the idea of assimilation, so choice D is not a strong answer and can be eliminated, leaving choice C as the best answer.

44. **B is the best answer.** This question requires you to have a good grasp on some of the vocabulary used to describe operant conditioning. Recall that a reinforcement is anything that increases the likelihood of a desired behavior, while a punishment is anything that decreases the likelihood of an undesired behavior. Positive reinforcement or punishment means that something has been added to the system, whereas negative reinforcement or punishment means something has been taken away. The question asks for an example of negative punishment, so it is looking for the answer choice that involves something being taken from the system to discourage an undesired behavior. A mother spanking her son in response to a temper tantrum is an example of a positive punishment: the mother is adding something (the spanking) to discourage a bad behavior. Choice A is a weak answer. A father giving his son a toy in order to encourage him not to throw tantrums is an example of positive reinforcement, eliminating choice C. A mother who stops spanking a child to encourage them to continue not throwing a tantrum is using negative reinforcement by removing something (the spanking) from the system; choice D can be eliminated. Only choice B, which describes a father removing his son's favorite toy in order to discourage bad behavior, is an example of negative punishment.

45. **B is the best answer.** Altruism describes behavior that is disadvantageous to an individual, but advantageous to his for her social group. It can be thought of as selflessness, which best describes the situation presented in the question stem. Some people argue that inclusive fitness is one of the factors behind the evolution of altruism but choice A does not describe the situation presented as accurately as choice B. Foraging behavior is about searching for food, making choice C irrelevant. Game theory, is a mathematical modeling of behavior that could be used to model the situation but does not help describe the behavior presented.

46. **C is the best answer**. Multiculturalism involves valuing cultural differences and the belief that different cultures can and should coexist together. Banning immigration would be contrary to this goal so choice A can be eliminated. Choice B would also minimize the difference between cultures rather than preserving them, so it is also a weak answer. Choice D more accurately describes a viewpoint someone with a perspective of cultural relativism might take.

EXPLANATIONS TO IN-CLASS EXAM FOR LECTURE 3

Passage I (Questions 47-51)

47. **D is the best answer.** This question requires you to apply prior knowledge to a scenario that is related to the passage. You may immediately recognize that the question stem is describing the self-serving bias, making choice D the strongest answer. You could also answer the question by process of elimination. In either case, you should read through every answer choice. Locus of control is somewhat related to the self-serving bias, but is a more general process than the one described by the question stem. Unlike the self-serving bias, locus of control is not specific to successes and failures. Choice A can be eliminated. Role-taking describes the process of "trying on" an identity and is not related to the question stem, so choice B is wrong. Choice C, identity crisis, also does not address the finding described by the question stem and can be eliminated.

48. **C is the best answer.** The MCAT® expects you to be aware of the monoamine hypothesis, which suggests that depression is caused by insufficient levels of monoamine neurotransmitters. Look for the answer choice that would increase the levels and/or activity of monoamine NTs. Choice A is wrong because a monoamine antagonist would prevent these neurotransmitters from stimulating postsynaptic neurons, which would be more likely to increase depressive symptoms. Choice B would have a similar effect and can also be eliminated. To choose between choices C and D, recall that reuptake clears neurotransmitters from the synapse. Increased reuptake causes decreased NTs in the synapse, while decreased reuptake has the opposite effect. To increase the amount of monoamine NTs in the synapses, reuptake should be decreased (inhibited) rather than increased. This makes choice C the strongest answer. Notice that A, B, and D are very similar answer choices. This observation alone helps point you to choice C as the best answer, even if you did not recall the monoamine hypothesis and the typical mechanism of antidepressant drugs.

49. **C is the best answer.** The finding described in the question stem states that an aspect of temperament, which is closely associated with personality and thought to be strongly influenced by genetics, changes as a result of MDD treatment. The major theories of personality differ in terms of the extent to which they believe change in personality traits is possible. The question can be rephrased as, "Which perspective on personality places the most emphasis on stability of personality?" Social cognitive theory allows for change in personality and behavior as a result of environmental influences—for example, treatment for MDD. Choice A can be eliminated. The situational approach emphasizes the influence of changing environmental circumstances over stable personality traits, so choice B can be eliminated. Trait theory is centered on the stability of personality traits over time, making choice C the best answer. Out of all the theories of personality, humanistic theory is perhaps the most open to change and is definitely consistent with the finding presented in the question stem; choice D can be eliminated.

50. **A is the best answer.** The passage directly states that temperament has a "strong genetic component," so temperament must be influenced by genetic factors; choice C can be eliminated. However, the passage also says that one study showed changes in harm avoidance (a dimension of temperament) after antidepressant treatment (an environmental factor). Temperament is influenced by both genetic and environmental factors, so choices B and D can be eliminated, leaving choice A as the best answer. You can double-check your answer by considering the course of MDD as well. The passage starts by saying that MDD often responds to antidepressant treatment, so the course of MDD is affected by an environmental factor. However, the passage also states that siblings of depressed patients have a heightened risk of developing MDD, suggesting a genetic component. Again, choice A is the best answer.

51. **C is the best answer.** You should be familiar with the general features of the common tests described in the Research Skills Lecture of the CARS book: regression, correlation, chi-square, t-test, and ANOVA. The psychosocial section of the MCAT® is where you are most likely to see questions about these tests. The easiest way to answer this question is to examine Figure 1. A correlation can be used when all variables are continuous rather than categorical. Although the question stem states that TCI scores are continuous, you can tell from looking at the figure that the subjects are divided into groups according to cutoff scores rating scale, meaning that this variable is categorical. A correlation cannot be used for the data as it currently stands, so choice A can be eliminated. As stated in the question stem, the personality scores are already continuous, so choice B can be eliminated. Given the description of the depression rating scale in the passage, the change described in choice C would be a possible change to the methods of measurement that would allow the use of a correlation. Choice D can be eliminated, and choice C is the answer.

Passage II (Questions 52-55)

52. **C is the best answer.** Recall that identity is influenced by both internal and social factors. Looking at the answer explanations, "role-taking" and "imitation" stand out as key processes that facilitate identity formation. Option I accurately describes the process by which role-taking influences identity. However, notice that choice II refers to *out-group* members. Based on both passage information and your previous knowledge, it seems likely that imitation would involve in-group members, not out-group members. Option II is false, meaning that choices B and D can be eliminated. To select between choices A and C, consider option III. Cultural factors, including values, contribute to identity formation, so option III is true. This makes choice C the best answer.

53. **A is the best answer.** The relationship between in-group/out-group identity and ethnocentrism was discussed in Lecture 2, and is also consistent with the findings of the first study discussed in the passage. The creation of shared meanings in symbolic culture may be related to in-group/out-group identity, but any relationship between these processes is out of the scope of the MCAT®. Choice C can be eliminated because the characteristics described are personality traits, which are usually thought to be stable over the lifetime and would not be significantly altered by group membership. Finally, choice D is wrong because operant conditioning is determined by rewards and punishments and is not generally thought to be mediated by identity.

54. **D is the best answer.** Answering this question only requires basic familiarity with the named theorists, despite the reference to passage topics. The question could be rephrased as: "Which theorist was most interested in identity formation?" As discussed in the lecture, Erikson's work focused on identity formation over the lifetime. Although Freud and Vygotsky each addressed identity formation to some extent, it was not the defining feature of their work. Freud was more interested in subconscious processes of mental life, and Vygotsky focused on socially guided learning. Skinner was a major contributor to our understanding of operant conditioning, as described in Lecture 2, but did not study the issue of identity formation.

55. **C is the best answer.** When reading a passage, you should always try to understand the purpose of each study described, including dependent and independent variables. In the second study of this passage, the researchers wanted to see "how political beliefs mediate religious in-group favoritism." This sentence alone indicates that the dependent variable has something to do with "in-group favoritism." The study design indicates that participants were asked to donate money to various charities that were either religious or non-religious. Choice D describes the independent variable that was manipulated by the researchers, so it can be eliminated. Choice C describes the variable that was measured by the researchers—the dependent variable. This makes choice C the best answer.

Note that you could have eliminated choices A and B at the outset. The design of the second study is experimental, meaning that the dependent variable will be a characteristic or behavior of the participants that is expected to change based on the independent variable. It is not reasonable to think that participants' religious or political identities could change due to a feature of the experiment.

Passage III (Questions 56-60)

56. **A is the best answer.** This question is asking which of the Big Five traits is associated with emotional stability and anxiety. Individuals fall along a continuum for each of the five major traits, with neuroticism describing levels of emotional stability and anxiety. Low emotional instability and anxiety are associated with low neuroticism. The passage states that participants with low neuroticism had greater aerobic capacity, so choice A is the best answer.

57. **C is the best answer.** The trait theory of personality focuses on five main traits that vary between individuals but are constant over time. Choice A describes trait theory rather than biological theory, so it can be eliminated. The biological theory of personality focuses on genes and the heritability of personality. This theory proposes that many genes across a number of chromosomes interact to influence personality, and that the expression of these genes can be influence by environmental factors. There are not simply a few genes that "control" personality, so choice B is untrue. Since identical or monozygotic twins share all of their genetic material while dizygotic twins share only half, a greater similarity between the personalities of monozygotic twins is a strong indicator of biological influence. Choice C is consistent with the biological theory of personality and is the best answer. Choice D describes a scenario that could be biological in nature but could also be explained by the child learning from his or her parents. Choice D is not as strong an answer as choice C.

58. **D is the best answer.** The passage states that high neuroticism is associated with lower aerobic capacity, which is a predictor of poor health. The elevation in aerobic capacity five years later suggests that neuroticism is low at that time. Personality is thought to be constant over time in all major personality theories except the humanistic theory, so the humanistic theory is the only theory that can account for these findings. Choice D is the best answer.

59. **C is the best answer.** The MCAT® requires knowledge of the general prevalence of psychological disorders. Personality disorders have a prevalence of roughly 10%, so choice C is the best answer. Schizophrenia is less common, with a 1% prevalence. Anxiety disorders are more common, with a 20% prevalence.

60. **C is the best answer.** Neuroticism is one of the five traits in the trait theory of personality. High neuroticism is correlated with depression and suicide risk, so choice A can be eliminated. According to the passage, high neuroticism is associated with low aerobic capacity, so choice B can also be eliminated. The MCAT® does not require memorization of that specific information. The key to this question is that personality traits do not arise from specific genes. As with psychological disorders, the heritability of personality is complex, and no single gene determinant has been identified. Choice C is a false statement, making it the best answer. Low self-esteem and self-efficacy are also associated with high neuroticism, so choice D is not the best answer.

Passage IV (Questions 61-64)

61. **B is the best answer.** This question is testing the incidence of various psychological disorders. The MCAT® requires test takers to be familiar with the prevalence of mood disorders, anxiety disorders, personality disorders, and schizophrenia. The one-year prevalence of mood disorders in individuals 18 years and older is 9.5%. Choice B is the best answer, as it is closest to the true value. Schizophrenia is a less common condition with a prevalence of about 1%. Personality disorders occur at a prevalence of about 9%, similar to that of mood disorders. Anxiety disorders encompass a number of diagnoses with a wide range of severity and have a yearly prevalence of 20%.

62. **B is the best answer.** This question is testing the concept of the biomedical versus the biopsychosocial approaches. In the biomedical approach, emphasis is placed on biological mechanisms like genetics and neuronal functioning, while in the biopsychosocial model, psychological and social factors are weighed in addition to biological factors. On this basis alone, choices A and D can be eliminated because they inaccurately explain the biomedical and biopsychosocial models. The final paragraph of the passage states that the altered biological mechanism is the sole underpinning of apathy and cognitive dysfunction, suggesting that these researchers are attempting to explain their findings using a biomedical approach. Choice B is the best answer.

63. **B is the best answer.** This question is testing knowledge about the different types of psychological disorders. The four main categories include anxiety disorders, mood disorders, personality disorders, and schizophrenia. Each class has certain characteristics associated with it, so the best answer for this question would be an answer that inaccurately characterizes one of the classes. Somatoform disorders are characterized by bodily symptoms, such as pain, fatigue, and motor problems, along with associated psychological symptoms that cause significant problems for the individual. Based on the presentation of these types of disorders, a biopsychosocial approach would be best able to characterize the symptoms because there are symptoms with biological origins such as pain paired with psychological systems, so choice A can be eliminated. Choice B states that generalized anxiety and major depression comprise two ends of the spectrum of mood disorders. This statement is false because anxiety disorders are a distinct category from mood disorders. The two ends of the mood disorder spectrum are mania and depression. Schizophrenia is a very broad category of psychological disorder, but a common feature is a disconnect with reality, so choice C is not the best answer. Personality disorders have many subtypes, but one of the distinguishing features of this category of disorders is that they persist over the course of the lifetime, unlike many of the other psychological disorders. Therefore, choice D is true and can be eliminated, leaving choice B as the best answer.

64. **C is the best answer.** This question is testing both the biological basis of Parkinson's disease as well as the monoamine hypothesis of depression. Parkinson's disease is a neurodegenerative disease that involves death of dopaminergic neurons, which ultimately leads to a decrease in the neuronal transmission of the monoamine dopamine. The monoamine hypothesis proposes that the depletion of monoamines, including dopamine, norepinephrine, and serotonin, at the neuronal synapse leads to depressive symptoms. There is no direct evidence in the passage to suggest that depletion of dopaminergic neurons in the substantia nigra leads to overcompensation elsewhere in the brain, so choice A can be eliminated. This would not explain the depressive symptoms because overcompensation would mean that more monoamine was being released, not less, which is inconsistent with the monoamine hypothesis of depression. While difficulty performing daily activities could lead to depressive symptoms, this is not a biological mechanism, so choice B is not the best answer. The depletion of dopaminergic neurons that occurs in Parkinson's would directly lead to a decrease in monoamine transmission. According to the monoamine hypothesis of depression, this would lead to depressive symptoms, so choice C provides a biological mechanism that explains the reasoning for the proposed hypothesis. A dopamine precursor drug would provide PD patients with increased levels of dopamine precursor to be transformed into dopamine, yielding increased concentrations of this monoamine. Choice D would not explain the depressive symptoms in PD patients, leaving choice C as the best answer.

Stand-alones (Questions 65-69)

65. **B is the best answer.** The humanistic theory of personality reflects an individual's own influence on his or her personality by completing certain acts that make that individual feel fulfilled. Choice B is the best answer. Biological theory focuses on the biological contribution to personality, which is not related to this question stem, so choice A can be eliminated. The trait theory proposes that there are characteristics that exist over a spectrum, and since this question does not describe multiple traits, choice C is not the best answer. The behaviorist theory suggests that environmental situations shape an individual, and because this question involves an individual's internal motivation, choice D can be eliminated.

66. **C is the best answer.** Familiarity with the design and rationale of twin studies will serve you well on the psychosocial section. If monozygotic twins are more similar to each other than are dizygotic twins, a genetic influence is indicated. In other words, since environment is shared for both types of twins, the higher genetic relatedness (almost 100%) between monozygotic twins is assumed to explain the elevated similarity. Thus, the classical twin design allows separation of shared environment and genetic influences, as described in choice C. Choice A is wrong because monozygotic twins raised in the same household share both environment and genetics; any differences in the twins would be attributed to an unknown third variable. Choice B is wrong because dizygotic twins raised in different households do not share genetics or environment, so any differences in the twins could be due to either factor. As for choice D, twins that are raised together are assumed to have shared environment, so studying only twins that were raised together cannot shed light on non-shared environment.

67. **D is the best answer.** The MCAT® requires an understanding of cultural differences in the process of making attributions. As described in the lecture, studies have demonstrated that in certain contexts, Eastern subjects are more likely than Western subjects to favor situational attributions over dispositional attributions. Answer choices A and C, which indicate a higher likelihood of situational attributions among Western subjects, can be eliminated. In general, you should be suspicious of answer choices that include "always." A good MCAT® answer is usually less definitive. Eastern subjects favor situational attributions when situational factors are emphasized, as described in choice D. When situational factors are not emphasized, Eastern and Western subjects make similar attributions; choice B can be eliminated, and choice D is the best answer.

68. **D is the best answer.** Answering this question requires knowledge of the general features of different types of psychological disorders. The dissociative disorders include dissociative amnesia and dissociative identity disorder, as well as other types of disruption in psychological functioning, making choice D the best answer. The question stem does not reference the core features of the psychological disorders featured in the other answer choices: anxiety for choice A, mood for choice B, and physical symptoms for choice C.

69. **C is the best answer.** This question is an assessment of your understanding of biological features of schizophrenia. When you see schizophrenia, think high levels of dopamine. Choice D is directly contradictory to this major feature of schizophrenia, and choice C is the best answer. Like choice D, choice A is the opposite of what would be expected: schizophrenia is associated with SMALLER structures in the brain. Choice B describes a physiological process that is thought to be associated with depression. Although there is some evidence that the HPA axis is associated with schizophrenia as well, this is beyond the scope of the MCAT®; choice C is a better answer.

EXPLANATIONS TO IN-CLASS EXAM FOR LECTURE 4

Passage I (Questions 70-74)

70. **A is the best answer.** Epinephrine would raise subjects' heart rates, among other effects. This increased physiological arousal is one of the hallmarks of the emotional response, in addition to the cognitive and behavioral components of emotion. The James-Lange theory states that the cognitive component of emotion results from an appraisal of one's physiological arousal ("I feel my heart beating through my chest, so I must be stressed"). According to this theory, subjects who were administered epinephrine would ascribe their heightened arousal to an emotional state, consistent with the findings of the experiment; choice A is the best answer. The Cannon-Bard theory states that the physiological response and cognitive appraisal of emotion occur simultaneously, so this theory would not predict that increasing physiological response would increase reported emotional response; choice C can be eliminated. Cognitive dissonance and the fundamental attribution error are not directly related to emotional response, so choices B and D are wrong.

71. **B is the best answer.** One of the adaptive functions of emotions is that they are universal: the most basic emotions and their corresponding facial expressions do not differ between cultures. Of the options given, choice B most closely corresponds with this general principle; choice D can be eliminated. Choices A and C take the principle of universality a bit too far. We have no information suggesting that the role of the Māori medicine man is sufficiently similar to that of a Western physician to anticipate a similar trend among empathic abilities. Likewise, no information is presented explaining the age-dependent decline in empathic abilities, so we cannot say with confidence whether the same factors causing this decline also apply to the Māori population.

72. **B is the best answer.** The theory of multiple intelligences states that every person has a unique combination of strengths and weaknesses across a variety of domains; a person who is highly skilled in one domain may be less skilled in another domain, and performance on tasks can be improved by harnessing intelligences across a range of domains. You can rephrase the question as: "Which answer choice suggests the existence of a single level of intelligence that holds across different skills?" Choice A suggests that enhanced abilities in one domain may be assessed by different tests, choice C suggests that performance in one domain does not correspond to performance in another domain, and choice D suggests that performance can be improved by drawing upon multiple modalities. These are all consistent with the theory of multiple intelligences. Choice B points to the existence of g, a general intelligence factor, by suggesting that skill in one modality corresponds to skills in another modality. This makes choice B the best answer.

73. **C is the best answer.** This doctor is describing a quick decision rule or rule of thumb that she uses (when X happens, do Y). This is consistent with the definition of a heuristic; choice C is the best answer.

74. **B is the best answer.** The occipital lobe is responsible for high-level visual processing, so a lesion in this region would likely affect performance on this visually-based test. The prefrontal cortex is responsible for executive control. The hypothalamus controls some physiological responses to emotions, such as increased pulse or blood pressure. Although the prefrontal cortex and hypothalamus are likely somewhat involved in the 'eyes' task, these regions are not as directly related as the occipital lobe. Choices A and C can be eliminated. The ventral tegmental area is a portion of the midbrain involved in the release of dopamine; this information is out of the scope of the MCAT®. Choice D is a distractor.

Passage II (Questions 75-78)

75. **B is the best answer.** Sensation is the process of converting stimuli into electrical signals. Perception is the process of paying attention to and noticing the sensed stimuli. Cognition is the process of analyzing the stimuli for meaning. The passage states that hearing is intact in children with SLI. A hearing test assesses auditory perception because a child has to indicate that he or she heard the sound. If perception is intact, sensation must be intact since perception first requires sensation. Choices that include options I or II can be eliminated. It is possible that cognition is not impaired in SLI children, but the questions asks which feature of sensory processing *may* be impaired, so choice B is the best answer.

76. **A is the best answer.** The two primary parts of the brain used in language are Broca's area and Wernicke's area in the frontal and temporal lobes, respectively. Broca's area contributes to the production of speech and Wernicke's area contributes to the understanding of speech. When choosing between these two answer choices, the one most applicable to this study is Broca's area. The participants had trouble repeating words and using the past tense, which is a primarily a problem producing speech. Wernicke's area would be more applicable to an inability to follow directions, as it is involved in the interpretation of speech. A person with a problem in Wernicke's area can produce words but the sentences have no understandable meaning. This makes choice A a better answer than choice D. Choices B and C are less relevant to language than Broca's area and Wernicke's area. The occipital lobe is involved in visual processing, so choice B can be eliminated. The lenticular nucleus is not tested by the MCAT® but comprises two parts of the basal ganglia, which are mostly associated with movement. Using speech does involve moving the vocal cords and the mouth, but choice A is more directly related to the study than choice C.

77. **C is the best answer.** The question is asking which theory of language development is correctly defined. This is only true for choice C. As stated, the learning or behaviorist theory uses conditioning to explain language. The definitions of the nativist theory and interactionist theory are switched: the nativist theory focuses on biology and the interactionist theory incorporates biology and environment. Choices A and D can be eliminated. The empiricist theory is not tested by the MCAT® but actually opposes the nativist theory. It argues that there is no reason to believe biology controls language. Choice B inaccurately defines the interactionist theory and can be eliminated.

78. **B is the best answer.** This question is testing the theory of multiple intelligences. Participants in the SLI group struggle with language so any task involving language would be more difficult. Describing their weekend, taking a spelling test, and taking a college admissions test all involve language and would be challenging for the SLI group. Choices A, C, and D can be eliminated. Drawing a self-portrait would not require language and participants may excel at this task. Choice B is the best answer by process of elimination.

Passage III (Questions 79-82)

79. **A is the best answer.** Figure 1 shows the relationship between cognitive workload and gestational age. Gestational age is the age since conception so it is lowest in very preterm infants. Choice A describes defects in the temporal lobe. The temporal lobe is involved mostly with sensation, including olfaction and hearing. This is not closely related to cognition so choice A is inaccurate and likely the best answer. Choice B describes the relationship between cognition and the cerebral cortex. The cerebral cortex refers generally to the outer portion of the brain and is heavily involved in information processing and cognition. Choice B is true and therefore not a good answer to the question. Choice C describes only the relationship between cognition impairment and cognitive load. In general, cognitive impairment is worse for high cognitive workload since the solid line shows the greatest deviation from normal. Choice C is true and so it is not the best answer to the question. Choice D states that gestational age has an inverse correlation to cognitive impairment. Figure 1 shows that cognitive impairment increases with increasing prematurity or decreased gestational age. As gestational age increases, cognitive impairment decreases. This is consistent with an inverse correlation, so choice D is true and not the best answer. This leaves choice A as the best answer because it is the only answer choice not supported by Figure 1.

80. **C is the best answer.** Choice A is an accurate conclusion from Figure 1 but it is not relevant to the statements in the last paragraph so choice A is not the best answer to this question. Choice B may be a true statement but it is not supported by findings in the article or statements in the last paragraph, so it is likewise not a strong answer. The last paragraph states that the findings have implications for educational intervention. This is explained by choice C, where children with low IQs may need additional or specialized instruction in school. Choice C is a good answer choice. Like choice B, choice D may be true, but it is not supported by the passage. Choice D is not as strong as choice C, so it can be eliminated. Choice C is the best answer.

81. **C is the best answer.** Confounding variables are those that may interfere with the effect that the independent variable (gestational age) has on the dependent variable (cognition). Since choice A is the independent variable, it is not a confounding variable. The passage states that all children in the study were 8 years old. Since age was controlled for, it is not a confounding variable and choice B is not the best answer. Culture can affect cognitive development and may also affect gestational age. In fact, culture is a common confounding variable. Choice C is a strong answer. The passage states that all children were healthy, suggesting that genetic disorders are not present. Choice D is less likely than choice C, which makes choice C the best answer.

82. **C is the best answer.** The passage states that the children were 8 years old. This corresponds to Piaget's concrete operational stage which occurs from ages 7-11. Choice C is the best answer. This question can be answered from pure memorization, which is uncommon for the MCAT®. However, it is important to memorize such facts that are likely to be tested.

Passage IV (Questions 83-87)

83. **C is the best answer.** The passages describes the Stoop Color-Word Test as a task where subjects need to identify the color in which the name of a color is written as quickly and accurately as possible, which relies on attention. The two main types of attention tested on the MCAT® are selective attention and divided attention. Selective attention occurs when attention is focused on one stimulus while excluding other stimuli, while divided attention occurs when attention is split between several stimuli. A task like the one described requires subjects to focus on the color of the word and not be distracted by the written color name. The need to ignore the stimulus of the written color word rather than pay attention to multiple stimuli rules out choice A. Choice C is the best answer. Signal detection is the core concept in of signal detection theory, which focuses on differentiating meaningful from background or "noise" stimuli. Both stimuli are meaningful signals in this case, though, so signal detection does not answer the question as well as selective attention. Choice B can be eliminated. A difference threshold describes the smallest difference that is sufficient for a change in a stimulus to be noticed. This is not applicable to the Stroop test, so choice D can be ruled out.

84. **D is the best answer.** This question is assessing understanding of the physiological response to stress. Study 2 evaluates the reactivity of the autonomic nervous system (ANS) using salivary alpha-amylase (sAA) levels as a proxy for ANS activity. sAA levels are emerging biomarkers of ANS activity because ANS activation stimulates salivation, and during salivation sAA levels increase. The results state that male participants in the non-stressed group have increased sAA levels after an acute stressor, indicating that they have increased ANS activity. The catecholamines released due to increases in ANS activity have many physiological outcomes that are important to remember. These responses are part of the fight-or-flight response stimulated by stress and typically include responses that would help an organism flee a predator. Increased sweat helps regulate body temperature, which increases with expenditures of energy, eliminating choice A. Increased heart rate and contraction would increase blood flow to vital muscles for fleeing, eliminating choice B. Increased dilation of bronchioles also occurs to increase oxygenation of blood, ruling out choice C. While there is increased blood flow to the skeletal muscles, there is decreased blood flow to muscle groups not necessary for fight-or-flight, such as the smooth muscles of internal organs. Answers including the word "all" tend not to be the best answer on the MCAT® because they are too extreme. Choice D is the best answer.

85. **C is the best answer.** The behavioral effects of stress refer to changes in behavior that occur due to stress. This includes impaired performance on cognitive tasks like the color-word task, as well as effects such as impaired memory. In Study 1, the researchers investigate the discrepancy in performance between chronically stressed and non-stressed subjects on color-word task as an example of a behavioral outcome. Figure 1 shows that the accuracy of stressed males on the color-word task is decreased compared to their non-stressed counterparts. It is helpful to read the y-axis and note that while its label is accuracy, the unit is errors, so an increase in number actually indicates a decrease in performance. The comparison of stressed subjects' performance to non-stressed subjects' performance shows that stressed individuals are experiencing a decrease in performance relative to non-stressed individuals. Choice C is the best answer. Choice A indicates the opposite. Remember to read the units on graphs carefully to avoid traps like choice A. Stress can have physiologic effects as well, which is shown by the differences in ANS activation measured by sAA in this study. Changes in salivation are not behavioral though, so choices B and D can be eliminated.

86. **C is the best answer.** This question is testing an understanding of the effect of biological factors on cognition. Figure 1 shows that chronically stressed individuals have impaired performance on a cognitive task. The passage states that stress can affect neuronal activation, making choice A a reasonable hypothesis. While acute stress increases HPA axis activity, the passage says that in chronically stressed individuals, there is an abnormal response with decreased activity. Choice B could also be a possible explanation for the decreased cognitive performance of chronically stressed subjects. The results of Study 2 shows that non-stressed males have increased ANS activity, but this is not observed in chronically stressed males, nor in either group of females. Since non-stressed males actually performed better on the task than chronically stressed males did, this conclusion is not supported by Figure 1, making choice C the best answer. Choice D broadly encompasses specific examples described in choices A and C and can be ruled out.

87. **B is the best answer.** Stress can be described as the strain on an individual when his or her equilibrium is disrupted, requiring adaptation. The researchers show that stress affects the ANS in a gender-specific manner. Non-stressed males have increased ANS activity in response to an acute stressor, but the same is not true in non-stressed women. The increased ANS activity seen in non-stressed males in response to an acute stressor is not observed in chronically stressed males. The gender-specific ANS response can be described as blunted in chronically stressed males, so choice A is not as strong of an answer as choice B. This kind of gender difference in responses to stress is not observed in the color-word task, which shows attention deficits in chronically stressed men and women, eliminating choice C. The passage describes many health-related repercussions of stress, such as insomnia and hypertension. It does not specify a gender difference in these representation of these repercussions, so choice D can be ruled out.

Stand-alones (Questions 88-92)

88. **B is the best answer.** This question addresses the body's response to a physiological drive, thirst. Physiological drives are often regulated by negative feedback systems, which operate by decreasing a stimulus to correct a drive once homeostasis has been reestablished. Choice A describes the drive rather than the return to homeostasis, so it can be eliminated. The physiological drive of thirst results from the need of hydration, so a return to normal levels of hydration indicates a return to homeostasis. Once homeostasis has been achieved, thirst is no longer triggered. Choice B describes the negative feedback for thirst, so it is the best answer. Negative feedback will not begin as soon correction begins. If it did, homeostasis would not be achieved! Choice C can be eliminated. For the opposite reason, choice D can be ruled out as well. Negative feedback would begin before the body reached an overhydrated state.

89. **D is the best answer.** Wernicke's area is involved in speech comprehension, but not speech production; choice D is the strongest answer. Broca's area is required for speech production, but not comprehension; choice C is a weak answer. Wernicke's area is found in the temporal lobe, eliminating choices A and B.

90. **B is the best answer.** The nativist theory of language development posits that humans have an innate capacity to comprehend and produce language. The lack of feedback supports the argument that language development is an innate ability, rather than a learned one. The learning theory of development supposes exactly the opposite—that language is just like any other learned behavior. The fact that children with significantly less feedback were able to develop language skills without impairment hints that there is something deeper at play than the mechanisms that underlie other behavioral learning; choice A is a weak answer. The interactionist theory accepts the premises of both the learning and nativist theories. Because nothing in the question supports the learning theory, choice C can be eliminated. There is no such thing as the developmentalist theory of language development, ruling out choice D.

91. **D is the best answer.** While particularly low SES is associated with negative outcomes, there are no data to support the idea that particularly high SES impacts cognitive abilities. Of course, genetic information plays a significant role in determining one's cognitive abilities, eliminating choice A. Environmental conditions while in the womb also have a significant impact on cognitive development. Choices B and C constitute detrimental environmental conditions with the potential to negatively impact cognitive development. Choice D is the best answer.

92. **A is the best answer.** The limbic system, among many other functions, is involved in the storage and retrieval of memories, particularly those that are tied to emotion. The limbic system is not involved in visual processing, the regulation of temperament, or language comprehension.

EXPLANATIONS TO IN-CLASS EXAM FOR LECTURE 5

Passage I (Questions 93-97)

93. **B is the best answer.** Since caffeine is only involved in one of the experiments, it is easiest to start by looking at answer choices C and D. The difference between the caffeine and placebo group in Experiment 4 shows that caffeine has an effect on memory retrieval, so choice D can be eliminated. Although it is possible that caffeine increases long term potentiation, there is no way of coming to this conclusion using only the information in figure 1. Choice C is also wrong. To find the best answer, you must choose between choices A and B. The results of Experiment 1 show that sleep deprivation affects false memory rate, but since sleep deprivation occurs both immediately after memory encoding and immediately before memory retrieval, it is unclear which process is affected. Experiments 2 and 3 include modifications to the experimental setup that allow encoding and retrieval to be distinguished. Figure 1 shows that false memory rate is significantly higher when participants are sleep deprived immediately before retrieval of a memory (Experiment 2), but not when sleep deprivation occurs immediately after learning (Experiment 3). This means that retrieval, rather than encoding, is significantly affected by sleep deprivation. Choice A can be eliminated, therefore choice B is the best answer.

94. **D is the best answer.** You should know that sleep-related memory consolidation occurs during REM sleep. Choices A, B, and C are all forms of non-REM sleep, and can be eliminated. Notice that choice A encompasses both B and C. Anytime there are two answer choices that must both be strong choices if either is a strong choice (in this example, A and C or A and B), both choices must be eliminated.

95. **C is the best answer.** This question really only requires background knowledge of the terms, not an interpretation of the passage. The primacy effect describes the tendency to remember items that occur early on in a set, independent of semantic meaning; choice A can be eliminated. Weber's Law describes the change required to meet the difference threshold, and is unrelated to the question, ruling out choice B. Spreading activation is the process by which retrieval of memories leads to retrieval of semantically related memories. This could explain the relationship between real and false memories. Neural plasticity is important for memory processes and is likely involved in the formation of false memories, but it does not explain the link that the question is asking about. Therefore choice D is a weak answer, and choice C is the best choice.

96. **D is the best answer.** This is another question that calls for background knowledge of definitions. Interference is a process that prevents the proper retrieval of memories, ruling out choice A. Synaptic potentiation could lead to better recall, but it is a physiological phenomenon, not a technique. Remember that the best answer choice must be true AND answer the question; choice B can be eliminated. Hypnosis is a technique used to enter a state of deep relaxation, and usually requires the participation of another person. No passage or lecture information indicates that it helps with memory recall, so choice C is a weak answer. Chunking is a memory technique that involves breaking down large information sets into smaller "chunks" to improve memory. This technique would certainly help recall accurately and could have been selected by the participants within the experimental setup; choice D is the best answer.

97. **B is the best answer.** The question starts with "given the passage information," so the best answer likely involves a sleep disorder. Neither epilepsy nor schizophrenia are sleep disorders, so choices A and D can be eliminated. Narcolepsy involves sudden onset of REM sleep. Based on the passage information, this should not lead to high false memory rates, so choice C is eliminated. Insomnia, or the inability to achieve normal sleep, should have similar effects to those seen in the sleep-deprived groups in the passage. This makes choice B the best answer.

Passage II (Questions 98-101)

98. **C is the best answer.** Since the question stem refers to species-wide change over millions of years, you should immediately think of evolution. If new social pressures affected all phenotypes equally, natural selection would not favor any particular genotype, and behavior would not change, so choice A is eliminated. Choice B describes a change in transcription. While this might help explain a change in behavior in an individual, it is not adequate to explain an evolutionary change over millions of years; choice B can be discarded. The question stem does not indicate that artificial selection has taken place – remember that natural selection is the mechanism of evolution; choice D is also a weak answer. As described in the lecture, genotypes leading to behaviors with higher adaptive values lead to natural selection for those genotypes. This effect would account for the change described in the question, so choice C is the best answer.

99. **A is the best answer.** This question is asking about the relationship between a gene (*5-HTT*), an environmental stimulus, and a behavior (gun ownership), so you should look for an answer choice that involves all three. (Recall that one of the central ideas of Lecture 5 is that genes and the environment interact to produce behavior.) Choice D involves only genotype and behavior, so it cannot explain the effect of the fearful stimulus and can be eliminated. Choices B and C list changes in the gene pool as the only explanation, so both can be eliminated. There is also no reason to suspect that the gene pool would have substantially changed in the six months after the stimulus was received. Choice A describes a plausible relationship between genes, behavior, and the environment, and is the strongest answer.

100. **C is the best answer.** Choices A and B go beyond the scope of the passage by describing a causal relationship between genotype and popularity. The passage tells you only that researchers were looking at the correlation between popularity and certain social traits, not the actual causes of popularity. Remember that correlation does not necessarily mean causation. Furthermore, these answer choices describe a simplistic relationship between gene expression and a psychological trait. The study described in this passage examined the complex interaction between genetics, environment, and behavior, and on the MCAT® an answer choice that poses a simplistic causal relationship between genetics and behavior is usually not the strongest answer. The passage states that popularity is correlated with number of female friends. Figure 1 shows that the correlation is positive amongst all genotypes—that is, as number of female friends increases, so does popularity—but the slope of the correlation is increased among males with two $5HT^{2A}$ G alleles, indicating a stronger relationship. Choice D falsely claims that having two A alleles enhances the correlation between popularity and female friends, so it can be eliminated. Choice C is the best answer because it accurately describes the effect of two G alleles on the correlation being studied.

101. **B is the best answer.** Do not overthink this definition question. The question stem and passage state that an environmental factor is altering gene expression. You should know that regulatory genes are involved in environmental control of gene expression, making choice B the best answer. Absolute thresholds are important for sensation but are irrelevant to environmental gene regulation, so choice C can be eliminated. While it is possible that a tumor suppressor gene is also a regulatory gene, this answer choice goes way beyond anything in the passage or the knowledge of genetics required for the psychosocial question; choice D can be eliminated. Choice A is ruled out because allele frequencies refer to the entire gene pool and change during evolution. This question is only asking you to think about an individual.

Passage III (Questions 102-106)

102. **D is the best answer.** When you see a reference to difference thresholds, you should think of Weber's Law, which states that the amount of change in a stimulus that is required for detection of the change depends on the intensity of the originally presented stimulus. When an initial stimulus is more intense, small changes in intensity are harder to perceive, and the difference threshold will be higher. In the scenario described in the question stem, a faster initial speed of rotation corresponds to a more intense initial stimulus. According to Weber's law, both hearing and deaf participants should have HIGHER difference thresholds when there is a higher initial speed of rotation. Since the question asks for the lowest difference threshold, choices A and B can be eliminated. The passage states that deaf individuals have lower thresholds on average for the rotation discrimination task, so C is eliminated and D is the best answer.

103. **B is the best answer.** This is another question about Weber's Law. When you see a question about difference thresholds and the answer choices are numerical, the first thing you should think of is the Weber fraction, or the fraction of the original stimulus represented by the difference threshold. In this question, the difference threshold for an initial stimulus of 48 cm is 6 cm. This gives a Weber fraction of $\frac{6}{48}$, or $\frac{1}{8}$. To calculate the difference threshold given a new original stimulus, you simply multiply the stimulus by the Weber fraction. $12 \times \frac{1}{8} = \frac{3}{2}$, which is the new difference threshold. Notice that you could immediately eliminate choice A without doing any math; since the initial stimulus has changed, the difference threshold must change.

104. **C is the best answer.** This definition question describes neuronal pathways re-wiring following the loss of auditory sensation to accommodate more visual processing. This is a classic example of neural plasticity, making choice C the strongest answer. Gestalt principles are important for top-down organization of sensory information, but are not relevant to the question; choice A is a weak answer. Selective attention and divided attention are psychological processes that change how information from multiple stimuli or tasks is processed, but neither describe the physiological change described in the question stem. For this reason, choices B and D can be eliminated.

105. **C is the best answer.** Figure 1 shows a change from baseline sensory threshold when an arousing stimulus is experienced, demonstrating that sensory thresholds can change within an individual according to level of arousal. This means that arousal has a measurable effect on perception, and choice A can be eliminated. As described in the lecture, perception depends on more than just physical sensation. This is also demonstrated by the passage – if only the physical stimulus mattered, arousal would not be able to change the depth threshold. For this reason, choice D can be eliminated. Choices B and C are not mutually exclusive answers, so you should look at each individually. Arousal DECREASED the threshold for determining depth changes, which indicates an INCREASE in sensitivity. This rules out choice B. The changes caused by arousal level indicate that perception is dependent on psychological state as well as physical sensation, making choice C the best answer.

106. **A is the best answer.** Do not worry about the specific details of the experiment described by this question. What you need to understand is the basic aim: to figure out the intensity at which participants are first able to hear a stimulus. This is the definition of an absolute threshold, making choice A the strongest answer. Difference thresholds in this setup would involve the detection of changes at intensities that are already audible, so B can be eliminated. Weber fractions relate to difference thresholds and how big of an intensity change is needed at different discernible intensity levels; C can be eliminated. Note that if either B or C were a strong answer, the other would also likely be a strong answer. Always eliminate answer choices that overlap like these. Visual acuity is irrelevant to a question about an auditory test, so D can also be eliminated.

Passage IV (Questions 107-110)

107. D is the best answer. This question requires an understanding of the influence of light on the drive for sleep. Sleep and wakefulness are in constant opposition. Throughout the day, the drive for sleep builds, but it is opposed by signals from the suprachiasmatic nucleus (SCN) in the hypothalamus. The SCN sends inhibitory signals to the pineal gland which blocks melatonin production, suppressing the drive for sleep. An overactive SCN would promote wakefulness by strongly inhibiting the pineal gland, which is inconsistent with the information presented in the question stem. Choice A can be eliminated. When inputs from the SCN diminish as the day goes on, melatonin production is increased and sleepiness ensues. Light contributes significantly to the regulation of circadian rhythms by stimulating the SCN and increasing the inhibitory effect on melatonin production. Choice B, excess melatonin production, could lead to increased ratings of sleepiness but does not explicitly address the effect of light exposure, so choice B is not the best answer. Since there is not enough information in the question stem to suggest that this aneurysm causes a visual impairment, choice C can be eliminated. If the connection between the SCN and the pineal gland were severed, there would be no way for the SCN to inhibit the pineal gland. Light exposure is able to affect circadian rhythms by signaling through the SCN to the pineal gland, so without this connection, light would be unable to affect sleepiness. This is consistent with the information provided in the question stem, so choice D is the best answer.

108. A is the best answer. This question requires knowledge of how different sleep disorders manifest and when in the sleep cycle they typically occur. The passage states that Equatorial workers rarely enter REM sleep. Sleep terror disorder is characterized by vivid, nightmare-like imagery that occurs in non-REM sleep. This is a major concern because when a patient has a night terror, they have not achieved REM sleep and the body is not immobilized. This can result in people acting out their dreams. Unlike night terrors, nightmares occurs in REM sleep, much like other dreams. They can be disturbing, but patients are not free to move around during this phase of sleep. The passage stated that Equatorial workers rarely enters REM sleep, so choice B can be eliminated. Insomnia describes a sleep disorder in which falling asleep is difficult and the quality of sleep is disrupted. The passage does not state that Equatorial workers had trouble falling asleep, nor does it comment on their quality of sleep, so choice C is not the best answer. Narcolepsy describes a sleep disorder in which sleep begins without warning and patients enter directly into REM sleep. Equatorial workers rarely enter REM sleep according to their EEGs, so a condition with rapid ascent into REM sleep would not be of great concern. Choice D can be eliminated and choice A is the best answer.

109. C is the best answer. The phases of sleep serve different functions. While in the deepest stage of sleep, Stage 4, there is recovery from the fatigue of the day. REM sleep, a lighter sleep, is believed to be the time when the brain processes experiences and consolidates memories. Based on the functions assigned to deep sleep versus REM sleep, it would be reasonable to assume that individuals achieving better REM sleep would perform better on memory tests. Choices A and B can be eliminated because while Stage 4 sleep is important for other functions, it is not thought to be directly responsible for memory consolidation. The passage states that Equatorial workers rarely achieve REM sleep. Choice C states that Arctic workers would outperform Equatorial workers because they achieve better REM sleep, which is consistent with the passage and the function of REM sleep. Choice D states that Arctic workers would perform more poorly than Equatorial workers because they achieve better REM sleep. This finding is inconsistent because better REM sleep should correlate with better memory consolidation, eliminating choice D. Choice C is the best answer.

110. C is the best answer. The question tests the function of different stages of sleep. Individuals with inadequate amounts or poor quality of deep sleep would be expected to experience daytime fatigue and problems awakening. It is stated in the passage that Arctic workers experience more sleep problems, which include sleep quality problems, awakening problems, and sleepiness. This indicates that Arctic workers are not achieving adequate deep sleep. Deep sleep is characterized by a delta wave EEG pattern, which is consistent with the information presented in the question stem, although it is not necessary to know this in order to select the best answer. Stage 1 sleep is a light sleep characterized by the presence of alpha waves. This stage of sleep is associated with a form of wakefulness that is more relaxed than full alertness, so choice A can be eliminated because stage 1 sleep is not considered deep sleep. Stage 2 sleep is characterized by bursts of activity that indicate a full transition into sleep. Although this stage of sleep represents an important transition into what is considered fully sleeping, it is still not a stage of deep sleep, so choice B is not the best answer and can be eliminated. Deep sleep, stages 3 and 4, is typically associated with rejuvenation of fatigue and recovery from the day. Delta waves can be observed on the EEG in Stage 3 and 4 sleep, consistent with the question stem. A lack of stage 3 sleep would lead to feelings of tiredness and problems awakening. Choice C is the best answer. REM sleep is characterized by a period of high brain activity. REM sleep is considered important for memory consolidation but not necessarily for relieving the fatigue. Since a lack of REM sleep would not best explain feelings of tiredness and problems awakening, choice D can be eliminated.

Stand-alones (Questions 111-115)

111. **A is the best answer.** Serotonin is a key neurotransmitter in the brain. While the role of serotonin levels in depression is not fully understood, selective serotonin reuptake inhibitors have been used for many years to treat depression. A reuptake inhibitor means that the drug blocks the reuptake of serotonin, increasing the levels of serotonin in the synapse. This information is not completely necessary to answer the question. The main point is that altering the neurotransmitter levels changes behavior, as seen by the efficacy of selective serotonin reuptake inhibitors in treating depression. Choice A is the best answer. While it is true that increasing serotonin levels can treat depression, correlation is not causation. Choice B is not as strong as choice A. Choice C can be ruled out because if altered levels permanently changed mood, the potential mood effects of low levels of serotonin could not be changed by increasing serotonin levels. There is most likely a genetic role in depression, but the efficacy of selective serotonin reuptake inhibitors does not directly indicate that point. Changes in serotonin levels could be due to many factors. Choice D is not the best answer.

112. **B is the best answer.** Due to the primacy effect, recall is strongest for items mentioned at the beginning of any list, so choice A can be eliminated. Sarah is also likely to remember items at the end of the list because they were mentioned most recently. This is the recency effect. Choice C can be eliminated. Items in the middle of the list are forgotten most often, as they fall between those remembered due to the primacy and recency effects. There is no reason to assume Sarah would remember only random items, so choice D is not as strong as choice B.

113. **B is the best answer.** Long-term potentiation is the strengthening of neural synapses and is used to form long-term memories. Long-term potentiation occurs between the hippocampus and the cortex. The hippocampus stores short-term memories and then encodes them through long-term potentiation in different regions of the cortex. Choice B is the best answer. The thalamus is the "relay center" of the brain and has many connections to the cortex but is not as central to long-term potentiation. Choice A can be eliminated. Choices C and D reference the brainstem which does not play a primary role in memory formation. The brainstem controls rudimentary biological functions such breathing, blood pressure, thirst, sleep, and sex-drive. Memory is a more "evolved" trait so it relies on the cortex. Choices C and D can be eliminated.

114. **D is the best answer.** The part of the brain associated with drug addiction and gambling is the reward pathway, which is found in the limbic system. Choice C identifies the correct pathway, but places it in the wrong location in the brain. Mirror neurons are activated both when a person performs and observes a certain behavior. Mirror neurons are associated with empathy and can play a role in drug addiction, but are not as central as the reward pathway. Choices A and B can be eliminated.

115. **B is the best answer.** You should know the major neurological diseases discussed in the lecture. Hypothyroidism is not a neurological disorder, and as such does not answer the question regardless of its symptoms or causes; choice D can be eliminated. Parkinson's disease is caused by decay of the dopaminergic cells of the substantia nigra. There is no given reason to believe similar symptoms would be caused by a vitamin deficiency, so choice C is a weak answer. Alzheimer's disease and Korsakoff's syndrome are both characterized by memory loss, but only Korsakoff's is caused by a vitamin deficiency. Alzheimer's is caused by neurodegeneration. For this reason, choice B is a better answer than choice A.

Exam Explanations

ANSWERS & EXPLANATIONS

FOR

QUESTIONS IN THE LECTURES

ANSWERS TO THE LECTURE QUESTIONS

Lecture 1	Lecture 2	Lecture 3	Lecture 4	Lecture 5
1. C	25. C	49. B	73. C	97. B
2. C	26. A	50. D	74. A	98. A
3. C	27. B	51. D	75. C	99. C
4. B	28. C	52. B	76. D	100. B
5. D	29. B	53. A	77. A	101. B
6. A	30. D	54. C	78. C	102. C
7. A	31. D	55. B	79. B	103. C
8. D	32. B	56. D	80. D	104. C
9. C	33. C	57. B	81. A	105. A
10. B	34. C	58. D	82. C	106. D
11. A	35. A	59. B	83. A	107. B
12. D	36. B	60. A	84. B	108. B
13. C	37. D	61. C	85. C	109. D
14. A	38. D	62. C	86. B	110. A
15. C	39. A	63. D	87. A	111. D
16. B	40. D	64. A	88. B	112. A
17. B	41. D	65. B	89. C	113. C
18. C	42. A	66. C	90. D	114. B
19. C	43. C	67. A	91. A	115. D
20. D	44. C	68. D	92. B	116. C
21. B	45. B	69. A	93. C	117. B
22. D	46. C	70. D	94. D	118. B
23. B	47. A	71. C	95. A	119. C
24. A	48. B	72. B	96. A	120. D

EXPLANATIONS TO QUESTIONS IN LECTURE 1

1. **C is the best answer.** Although the biomedical model focuses on biological dysfunction as the major contributor to medical disorders, including psychological disorders, it does not imply that psychological disorders must always be associated with other medical disorders. Choice A can be eliminated. In contrast to choice A, choice C provides a more accurate picture of the biomedical model and describes a feature that differs from the biopsychosocial model. Choice B misrepresents the biomedical model. First, a practitioner who subscribes to the biomedical model would not deny that treatment is needed for psychological disorders. Second, a critical part of the biomedical model is the assumption that the symptoms of a psychological disorder *are* based in some type of physical pathology. For both of these reasons, choice B can be eliminated. Choice D describes the biopsychosocial model rather than the biomedical model and thus does not answer the question.

2. **C is the best answer.** Choice A distorts both the BPS model and the sociological perspective. Although it is true that a provider who adheres to the biopsychosocial model would likely examine both biological and social factors, the biological factors would not be assumed to have a causal influence on the social factors, and more than just these two factors would be considered. Sociology focuses on social phenomena, not mental life. Choice B similarly reduces the biopsychosocial model to the limited consideration of two possible contributors. In addition, sociology does not focus only on interpersonal influences; it also considers society as a whole. Choice C provides a more accurate description of the BPS model and does not restrict sociology to the sphere of interpersonal interaction, so it is the best answer. Finally, although the first part of choice D is accurate, the theoretical perspectives adopted by the two providers would differ, so choice D is not the best answer.

3. **C is the best answer.** Although there is a conflict taking place, conflict theory examines conflicts between social groups, not between individuals. Choice B can be eliminated. Similarly, the theoretical perspectives of functionalism and social constructionism are far more likely to be applied to large-scale social phenomena. Only symbolic interactionism describes small-scale interactions in which symbolic meaning is created and interpreted, as in the scenario described in the question stem. This makes choice C the best answer.

4. **B is the best answer.** The question stem refers to shared understandings of "truth," or meaning, which is the major focus of social constructionism. Choice B is the best answer. Although symbolic interactionism also has to do with shared meanings, it focuses primarily on small-scale interactions, which is not consistent with the question stem. Choice C is not the best answer. Because the relative stability or instability of society is not under consideration, functionalism and conflict theory are not directly relevant. Choices A and D can be eliminated.

5. **D is the best answer.** Since conflict theory is interested in how conflict between groups leads to social change, it is not likely to be the perspective taken by this researcher. Choice A can be eliminated. The question stem describes the major interest of functionalism, which, in contrast to conflict theory, focuses on the interactions between parts of society that contribute to the functioning of society as a whole. This makes choice D the best answer. Since social constructionism and symbolic interactionism describe the creation of shared meaning, they are somewhat related to the interests of the researcher, but functionalism is much more directly relevant. Choices B and C do not answer the question as well as choice D.

6. **A is the best answer.** Social constructionism and symbolic interactionism are related perspectives, but they are not indistinguishable. Choice D can be eliminated. One major difference between the two perspectives is that of scale. While social constructionism examines meanings shared by society as a whole, symbolic interactionism, as the name suggests, tends to focus more on the construction of meaning during interactions between individuals. Out of the answers given, choice A best reflects the distinction between social constructionism and symbolic interactionism. Choices B and C both incorrectly attribute elements of conflict theory to one or both theories. Although social constructionism and symbolic interactionism could be used to examine societal conflict, there is no reason to assume that they will in the scenario given in the question stem. In addition, choice C includes no reference to shared meaning, a critical part of both perspectives.

7. **A is the best answer.** This question requires the understanding that conflict theory and functionalism are each suited to the study of particular social phenomena. There is no reason to think that one is more globally useful than the other, so choices C and D can be eliminated. Each perspective is specialized to particular aspects of society, so choice B can also be eliminated. Choice A accurately indicates that the phenomenon of interest determines which theoretical perspective will be most useful.

8. **D is the best answer.** The question stem includes elements of all three perspectives. Since the creation of shared knowledge systems is involved, social constructionism is relevant, and option I should be included in the answer. Choice C can be eliminated. Functionalism is also relevant, since the question stem describes smooth functioning between institutions and how institutions contribute to the functioning of society as a whole by promoting health. Option III is also relevant, so choice D is the best answer. Although it was not necessary to evaluate option II, the reference to individuals in the context of shared meanings implies that symbolic interactionism is also relevant.

9. **C is the best answer.** As a physical artifact, the bowls are an example of ancient material culture. The replacement of old technologies with the new bowl-making technique illustrates how material culture can change over time, so choice A can be eliminated. Knowledge of how to use the new technology was likely passed from generation to generation and from region to region through verbal communication and demonstration. This spread of ideas is an example of how the exchange of non-material culture can affect the types of artifacts left behind, making choice B relevant and therefore a weak answer. Because physical artifacts can be preserved and recovered thousands of years later, while many forms of non-material culture, such as worldviews and oral traditions, are not well recorded for future generations, archaeology generally has a much greater focus on material culture. This has relevance to the finding described in the question stem, so choice D can be eliminated. Choice C is the best answer because there is no reason to assume that non-material culture is more location-specific than material culture. In the case described in the question stem, changes in non-material culture, which included ideas about technology, likely spread together with associated changes in material culture, such as the style of bowl-making.

10. **B is the best answer.** Students are not being confronted with a new culture and therefore are not experiencing culture shock, eliminating choice A. Instead they are doing something that is not generally accepted as normal behavior within their own culture. They are acting in violation of social norms, supporting choice B as the best answer. Choice C can be eliminated because there is no discussion of social interaction in the question stem. Since the students are practicing obedience to the professor's instructions, choice D could be an attractive choice. However, there is no reason to assume that obedience automatically results in the discomfort and embarrassment described in the question stem. In fact, obedience could be comforting, depending on the circumstances. Choice B remains the best answer.

11. **A is the best answer.** Sufficient intelligence is necessary for the shared meanings and learned behaviors that constitute culture, making choice A the best answer. Choices B and C directly contradict information presented in the lecture about elements of culture that have been observed in non-human species. Since only humans use verbal communication, at least as we understand it, choices B and C are too similar for either to be the best answer, and both can be eliminated. Choice D is not true because evidence indicates that human culture has experienced an explosion of changes BEGINNING around 40,000 years ago. There is no reason to assume that the start date for that explosion was the peak of cultural development, as cultural development continues even today.

12. **D is the best answer.** Symbolic culture consists of the meanings that things hold in people's minds. Language is only useful because people jointly agree to assign specific meanings to various symbols (sounds, words, etc.), making language a significant example of symbolic culture. Choice D is the best answer. Language is an example of non-material culture, so choice C is a weak answer. Cultural relativism has to do with evaluating each culture according to its own cultural values rather than measuring against some external yardstick. Language does not inherently involve the practice of cultural relativism, eliminating choice A. Language is certainly related to, helps shape, and is shaped by cultural values, but it is not specifically a system of cultural values. Instead, it is a way for values to be expressed, communicated, and propagated. Choice B is not as strong an answer as choice D.

13. **C is the best answer.** A society is a collection of people who share at least some elements of cultural identity, while a culture consists of the beliefs and practices that make up a shared way of life. Choices A and B are true statements and can be eliminated. Choice D can also be eliminated because a society can both share elements of culture and consist of multiple cultures together, as in the case of the United States. In other words, a society can be multicultural. Society and culture are related, but have separate definitions and uses, making choice C the best answer.

14. **A is the best answer.** Choices B, C, and D are all true and part of the definition of social institutions. Social institutions are hierarchical systems created to address specific needs within a society and help organize both the society and the interactions of its peoples. Choice A is untrue and the best answer because not all cultures may have the need for the same social institutions. Similar social institutions can also be implemented in different ways across cultures (e.g. education).

15. **C is the best answer.** Choice C is the best answer because the information collected in the census includes typical examples of demographic information, such as age and race, and the census is performed by the government, a social institution. Choice A is not the best answer because a census cannot be collected by a culture, which is a set of beliefs and behaviors. Choice B can be eliminated because the information collected in the census is not cultural, but rather demographic. Choice D can be eliminated because the information collected in the census is not directly related to non-material culture and because the question stem does not provide any evidence that the information is collected to illustrate demographic transition.

16. **B is the best answer.** If greater urbanization is correlated with increased population size, the best answer will be the one that maximizes population size. The combination of high fertility and low mortality will inevitably increase population size, making choice B the best answer. Low fertility with high mortality would decrease population size, eliminating choice C. Choices A and D could either increase or decrease population size depending on the relative lowness or highness of the fertility and mortality rates, but any resulting population growth would not be as extreme as under the conditions of choice B.

17. **B is the best answer.** If the study aims to examine spatial inequality WITHIN the city of Chicago, there is no need to sample from other cities, so choice A can be eliminated. The most critical part of the study design will be sampling from different areas of Chicago in order to investigate differential access to resources based on location within the city, making choice B the strongest answer. Choices C and D would be nice additions to the study to ensure that differences found between locations are not actually differences due to age, sex, or race rather than location. However, these elements are not very practically applicable, as different neighborhoods may very well differ according to these demographic factors and random assignment of participants to live in different neighborhoods is not practical or ethical.

18. **C is the best answer.** Global inequality describes the extent to which wealth is unevenly distributed on a global scale. Differences in wealth, which is composed of both income and acquired assets, are best represented by the data set described, making choice C the best answer. Choice A may be tempting, because it also deals with geographic distribution of resources, but it is not as specifically or directly related to the data gathered as choice C. Demographic composition deals more with factors such as age, sex, and race than issues of wealth and resource access. Choice B does not describe the data set as well as choice C. Choice D is an invented term that is not commonly used to describe specific phenomena within the social sciences and is not a topic tested by the MCAT®.

19. **C is the best answer.** Environmental justice is characterized by equal protection from environmental hazards and equal access to resources that promote a healthy lifestyle. Choice A creates unequal access to the ability to make healthy life choices based on gender. Choice B creates unequal risk of health hazards based on income level. Choice D creates unequal risk of accidents based on income level. Choice C may indicate unequal access to benefits or unequal exposure to risk based on neighborhood/race, but without knowing the attributes of the neighborhoods, the threat to environmental justice due to racial segregation of neighborhoods cannot be assessed, making choice C the best answer.

20. **D is the best answer.** Social class is dependent on socioeconomic status as well as power, privilege, and prestige. The best answer will not involve a change in any of these characteristics. Choice A can be eliminated because being an elected member of the state legislature would provide an individual with new power, as well as prestige and privileges. Inheriting a large amount of money would increase wealth, thereby affecting socioeconomic status, so choice B can be eliminated. Choice C can also be eliminated because level of education as well as the associated job opportunities are part of social class, so obtaining higher education affects class advancement. Choice D remains the best answer because volunteer work in a homeless shelter does not affect wealth and likely will not affect factors such as prestige within the community.

21. **B is the best answer.** All of these statements are true of the caste system, but the best answer will fail to name a significant factor that makes the caste system DIFFERENT from the class system. Choice B is the best answer because the social hierarchy of a class system, like that of a caste system, provides differential opportunities. By contrast, the statements made in choices A, C, and D would not be true of a class system. In a class system, there is greater flexibility – class can change from one generation to the next, upward mobility is possible, and marriage between members of different classes is not prohibited.

22. **D is the best answer.** Because the study will compare the mobility of immigrants to different countries, only knowledge about the countries of immigration, not the countries of origin, is strictly necessary. Choice A can be eliminated because SES before immigration must be known in order to determine whether mobility after immigration is upward or downward. Choice B can be ruled out because SES from multiple generations must be known in order to examine intergenerational mobility. Likewise, choice C is a weak choice because information about multiple times during an individual's lifetime is needed to determine intragenerational mobility.

23. **B is the best answer.** Cultural capital involves factors that affect social mobility, but are non-monetary in nature, including the cultural knowledge of how to act in various situations in order to promote social advancement. Choice B is the best answer because the worker is able to obtain upward social mobility through the cultural capital of knowing the proper patterns of speech to fit into his workplace. Choice A is not the best answer because cultural capital is non-financial. Choice C is a better example of social capital than cultural capital. Finally, choice D most closely aligns with the idea of a meritocracy.

24. **A is the best answer.** All of the possible answer choices COULD be important to understanding health disparities. The MCAT® will sometimes have questions where all of the answer choices seem possible, or, conversely, where none of the choices seem like the right one. In these cases, it is important to remember that the MCAT® asks for the BEST (or the "least bad") of the possible choices. Choices B, C, and D describe tangible disparities that directly and differentially affect the health of different populations. Choice A could affect health disparities, such as if Native Americans would be more likely to visit a doctor if there were more Native American doctors. However, the health disparity implications of this scenario are not as direct as those of the other three answer choices, making choice A the best answer.

EXPLANATIONS TO QUESTIONS IN LECTURE 2

25. **C is the best answer.** This experiment demonstrates operant conditioning, which utilizes the consequences of behavior to drive learning. Anything that increases the likelihood of the behavior is a reinforcer, while anything that decreases the likelihood of the behavior is a punishment. In the scenario described in the question stem, the feeding of fish led to an increased likelihood of the fin waving behavior. The fish acted as reinforcement, not punishment, eliminating choice B and making choice C the best answer. This experiment utilized operant rather than classical conditioning. In a classical conditioning experiment, an unconditioned stimulus and associated unconditioned response would be paired with a conditioned stimulus. Choice A can be eliminated. Observational learning occurs when one learns by observing and replicating the behavior of others, which did not occur in this experiment, so choice D is not the best answer.

26. **A is the best answer.** Classical conditioning involves associating a conditioned stimulus with another unconditioned stimulus that is tied to an unconditioned response. In this case, the startling noise is the unconditioned stimulus, the fear vocalization is the unconditioned response, and the green light is the conditioned stimulus. In operant conditioning, reinforcers and/or punishments follow a behavior. In this case, no behavior performed by the macaque is followed by a reinforcer or punishment, so choice B can be eliminated. Aversive conditioning is the association of noxious stimuli with an undesired behavior, so choice C is inconsistent with the experiment described. The macaque did not learn to produce the fear response by observing behaviors performed by others, so choice D can also be eliminated.

27. **B is the best answer.** In classical conditioning, a neutral stimulus is one that does not elicit a response. Prior to conditioning, the green light elicits no response, making choice B the best answer. An unconditioned stimulus is one that provokes a response prior to conditioning. Choice A can be eliminated. Though the green light later becomes a conditioned stimulus, the question asks what it is considered to be BEFORE the experimental intervention. Since the green light did not elicit a response prior to the experiment, it could not have been a conditioned stimulus, eliminating choice C. The green light did not act as any type of reinforcer for a behavior performed by the macaque, so choice D can be eliminated.

28. **C is the best answer.** Stimulus generalization occurs when a subject becomes responsive to stimuli that are similar to the conditioned stimulus. Production of the conditioned response (fear vocalization) upon presentation of a blue light, a stimulus similar to the conditioned stimulus, demonstrates this effect. Acquisition describes the stage of classical conditioning in which a conditioned response to a new stimulus is formed. The question stem suggests that the association to the conditioned stimulus occurred spontaneously, rather than being produced by a new process of conditioning. Choice A can be eliminated. Spontaneous recovery occurs when a conditioned response reappears after a time interval in which the response was lessened. Since the question stem describes the response to a new stimulus, not the previous one, choice B can be eliminated. Stimulus discrimination occurs when there is a LACK of response to a stimulus that is similar to the conditioned stimulus, so choice D is not the best answer.

29. **B is the best answer.** Avoidance conditioning occurs when a subject learns a behavioral pattern that can be used to prevent the occurrence of an aversive stimulus. In this case, the behavioral pattern of fleeing is used to prevent aggressive behavior towards the female. Escape conditioning is similar to avoidance conditioning, but it involves the subject terminating an aversive stimulus, rather than preventing its occurrence altogether, as is the case in this situation. Choice A can be eliminated. Aversive conditioning is a general term that can be used to describe both escape and avoidance conditioning. Since a more specific answer is available, choice C can be eliminated. This situation describes a variant of operant conditioning, not classical conditioning, so choice D is not the best answer.

30. **D is the best answer.** Variable-interval schedules have rewards provided after an unpredictable time interval has passed. As the daughter cannot predict whether the reward will be provided immediately or half an hour later, this is a variable-interval schedule, making choice D the best answer. A fixed-interval schedule has rewards provided after the same time interval for every response, eliminating choice C. Fixed- or variable-ratio schedules involve the provision of reinforcement after a fixed or variable number of responses. Since the child receives reinforcement every time that she uses the bathroom, rather than every three times or some other number, it is the time interval rather than the number of responses that is relevant. For this reason, choices A and B can be eliminated.

31. **D is the best answer.** Shaping involves rewarding successive approximations towards the desired behavior. Choice D best exemplifies this technique by describing how the dog is first rewarded for rolling onto its back, an intermediate step, and then for completing the entire action. Choices A and B can immediately be eliminated because they do not involve reinforcement, which is a key component of shaping. Choice C can be eliminated because it only describes the provision of a reward for the complete behavior, rather than including rewards for successive approximations toward that behavior.

32. **B is the best answer.** Mirror neurons fire when a person is completing an action and when the person observes another individual completing that same action. The only answer choice involving one person observing another is choice B. Choices A, C, and D are not as strong as choice B.

33. **C is the best answer.** Behavior involves responses to both internal and external stimuli, so choice A can be eliminated. Behavior is partially influenced by the biology of the organism, eliminating choice B. Genetics and neural connections can predispose organisms toward certain behavioral patterns, so choice D is true of behavior and can be eliminated. There is no requirement that behavior involve an emotional component, so choice C is the best answer.

34. **C is the best answer.** Nonverbal communication, mating behavior, and aggressive behavior all inherently involve interactions between individuals, the definition of social behavior. Choices A, B, and D are weak answers. Although learning may involve other people, this is not a *necessary* condition, making choice C the best answer.

35. **A is the best answer.** Altruism describes a behavior that is not advantageous to the person who carries out the behavior but is beneficial to other organisms in the acting individual's social group. This choice best describes the scenario given in the question stem, making choice A the best answer. Inclusive fitness is a particular type of altruism directed towards relatives. The drowning person is a stranger rather than a relative, so choice A is a better answer than choice B. Game theory involves decision-making in reaction to decisions made by others, such as in competitive situations, which is unrelated to the scenario described. Choice C can be eliminated. The question stem describes a situation that is contradictory to self-interest, eliminating choice D.

36. **B is the best answer.** Game theory involves the use of mathematical reasoning to guide decision making that is tied to decisions made by other people. Choices A, C, and D all represent situations where there are multiple actors and potentially limited information about the actors' motives and intentions. Choice B describes a situation where other actors are not involved, so game theory would not be well suited to it. Choice B is the best answer.

37. **D is the best answer.** Groupthink occurs when members of a group think alike for the sake of group harmony. Often, groupthink causes people to self-censor their ideas, which is likely what happened in this instance. Diffusion of responsibility is a phenomenon that occurs in a large crowd when individual people are less likely to feel accountable for the outcome of a situation. Since only a small group is involved in the question stem, choice A can be eliminated. Group polarization occurs when the attitudes of a group as a whole become stronger than the attitudes of any one group member. In this case, group polarization would have been occurring if the passengers as a group decided that they absolutely hated country music and would refuse to go on the trip if the driver continued playing it. Group dynamics is a general term for the behavior of individuals within a group, or the group as a whole. It is much less specific than groupthink and can be eliminated.

38. **D is the best answer.** Social facilitation occurs when performance in a task is better when others are watching, as described in the question stem. The dramaturgical approach is a theory of impression management that proposes that a person's behavior is an ongoing performance of self that changes according to the situation. This approach does not explain the scenario described in the question stem, so choice A can be eliminated. No influence of peers on each other is implied, so choice B is not the best answer. Deindividuation is the loss of the sense of individuality when part of a crowd, which is also not indicated by the question stem.

39. **A is the best answer.** Social loafing is the phenomenon where people intentionally work less when part of a group, assuming that other group members will make up for it. Only choice A involves a group member decreasing his or her contribution to the group, so choice A is the best answer and the other answer choices can be eliminated.

40. **D is the best answer.** The bystander effect occurs when a person is in trouble in a crowd and onlookers are less likely to help because they assume someone else will help. In this situation, telling the crowd as a whole to call 911 may result in nobody calling, as everyone thinks somebody else will. Choice D is the best answer. Group dynamics is a very general term, and given the presence of bystander effect as another choice, it is not the best answer available. Choice A can be eliminated. Group polarization and social facilitation do not fit the scenario described in the question stem, eliminating choices C and D.

41. **D is the best answer.** Agents of socialization are comprised of the groups and individuals who influence personal attitudes, beliefs, and behaviors. Choices A, B, and C are all stated to play a role in the life of the person in question. Choice D, on the other hand, may not be applicable to the person in question. If the individual does not have direct or indirect exposure to the works of this particular philosopher, they do not constitute an agent of socialization for that individual. Philosophers may serve as agents of socialization for some people, but do not necessarily do so for all people, making choice D the best answer.

42. **A is the best answer.** Conformity is the process of changing one's own thoughts and behaviors to line up with social norms, as in the scenario described in the question stem. By contrast, obedience describes changes in behavior resulting from explicit demands by someone who holds a position of authority. Because this behavior change does not occur at the request of an authority figure, choice B can be eliminated. Compliance is not explicitly covered on the MCAT®, but like obedience, compliance involves behavior change at the request of someone else. This was not the case in the question stem, making choice C a weak answer. Assimilation refers to the process of becoming absorbed into a new culture, rather than a smaller social group. Choice D is not as strong as choice A.

43. **C is the best answer.** Institutional discrimination occurs when social institutions, such as governments, schools, or the medical establishment, employ policies that differentiate between people based on social grouping. Only choice C demonstrates a situation where a discriminatory situation occurs on an institutional, rather than individual, level. In this case, the use of standardized tests biases college admissions in favor of certain cultures. Choices A, B, and D each involve the actions of an individual, so they can be eliminated.

44. **C is the best answer.** Prejudices are generalizations about people who are not part of one's in-group. The conclusion that Native Americans, an out-group of the European tourist, are irresponsible parents based solely on the observation that adolescents consume tobacco in tribal ceremonies constitutes prejudice, making option III true. Choice A can be eliminated. Ethnocentrism involves the usage of the cultural standards of one's own group to judge cultural practices of an out-group. This situation demonstrates ethnocentrism, as the indigenous culture is judged according to the tourist's cultural standards. This makes option I true. Choice B can be eliminated. Since cultural relativism is essentially the opposite of ethnocentrism, option III cannot also be true. Choice D can be eliminated, and choice C is the best answer.

45. **B is the best answer.** A subculture is a distinct culture shared by a smaller group of people who are also part of the larger culture. Of the answer choices presented, it is least likely that a fraternity constitutes a subculture, since the question stem does not indicate that a fraternity includes the marked differences from the dominant culture that are required for a group to be considered a subculture. It seems likely that members of a fraternity would feel a sense of shared identity with the group, particularly given the reference to expressions of pride. This is characteristic of an in-group, so choice A can be eliminated. Similarly, participation in the fraternity will likely influence an individual member's attitudes and behaviors, consistent with socialization. Choice C can be eliminated. Since members of a fraternity interact together as a group, the fraternity acts as a social group, and choice D can also be eliminated.

46. **C is the best answer.** Though the stereotype states that hazel-eyed people are not athletic, the question stem does not provide any indication that hazel-eyed people actually differ from other students in athletic ability, so choices A and B can be eliminated. People who are reminded of a negative stereotype about their group may experience decreased performance in the task that is the subject of the stereotype, a phenomenon known as stereotype threat. Choice C is the best answer. Choice D is the opposite of the expected outcome, so it can be eliminated.

47. **A is the best answer.** Bias occurs when one favors an in-group at the expense of an out-group. In this instance, the advertiser hires within her in-group of athletic types. The question stem does not provide any information about the person's attitudes towards non-athletic people, only indicating a preference for athletic in-group members. Since prejudice and stereotyping involve ideas about out-groups, choices B and C can be eliminated. Nepotism is not a required topic for the MCAT®. It is the practice of favoring relatives or friends, which is not indicated by the question stem. Choice D is not the best answer.

48. **B is the best answer.** Choice B most describes a situation where one's belief-driven actions cause the belief to become true. In this instance, the belief that the stock market is crashing drives an action that brings about the crashing of the stock market. Choices A and C do not include any reference to outcomes, so they do not describe self-fulfilling prophecies and can be eliminated. A son becoming angry at his mother for being angry at him does not constitute a self-fulfilling prophecy: the actions of the mother do not bring about a state that she originally believes to be true. Choice D can be eliminated.

EXPLANATIONS TO QUESTIONS IN LECTURE 3

49. **B is the best answer.** Choice A describes only one small piece of personality and does not include the essential point that personality influences behavior. In addition, some personality theories, like the behaviorist theory, do not consider internal mental life at all. Choice B is not an ideal definition of personality, but it is better than choice A. Choice C can be eliminated because personality is influenced by genetics. Choice D describes temperament rather than personality. Choice B is the best answer.

50. **D is the best answer.** In the field of psychology, the basic setup of a twin study is the comparison of monozygotic (identical) and dizygotic (fraternal) twins in order to separate the effects of the environment and genetics on some aspect of psychological functioning, particularly personality. A twin study compares the two types of twins, not twins and non-twins, so choice A is not the best answer. Choice B describes an experimental setup that could be used to separate genetic and environmental effects and draw conclusions of causality, but poses ethical and practical problems and cannot actually be carried out. Choice C is not the best answer for multiple reasons. For one thing, it suggests that only genetic OR environmental factors would cause (be "responsible for") a trait, but both types of factors influence the development of traits. Furthermore, a key point in twin studies and the study of personality in general is that traits are not "either/or" characteristics. Instead, people differ in the level to which they demonstrate a trait. Finally, choice D accurately describes the purpose of twin studies. By comparing twin pairs that have different levels of genetic relatedness but similar environments, a twin study allows the determination of how much heredity influences the expression of a trait.

51. **D is the best answer.** The behaviorist theory states that personality is made up of behaviors, which are shaped by learning experiences. Individual choice does not play a significant role in the behaviorist theory, so choice A can be eliminated. Choice A would be a better example of the social cognitive theory of personality. Choice B is an appealing answer choice, since the MCAT® usually rewards the understanding that multiple factors contribute to the development and psychological life of individuals. However, someone who adheres to the behaviorist theory of personality would express a more narrow view on personality development, so choice B is wrong. Similarly, choice C can be eliminated because the behaviorist theory pays little attention to mental life. Choice D indicates the importance of learning from the environment and focuses on behavior, so it is the best answer.

52. **B is the best answer.** According to the situational approach, the accuracy of predictions made using trait theory is limited by the effect that varying environments have on behavior. The situational approach asserts that behaviors are modified by circumstances, not personality traits. Choice A can be eliminated. Choice B accurately describes the major idea of the situational approach that some stability can be found in behavioral responses. Choice C goes a step too far; the situational approach says that behavior varies according to the situation, but does not indicate that behavior cannot be predicted. Choice D might be appealing due to the reference to varying situations, but does not use the term correctly, and points to a "stable personality," which is inconsistent with the situational approach.

53. **A is the best answer.** The key to answering this question is understanding that, according to the psychoanalytic approach, the psychological processes involved in personality are not consciously perceived. The best answer will allow the researcher to study psychological phenomena of which the participants are not aware. Choices B, C, and D all require subjects to report on their experience, requiring conscious awareness, so they can be eliminated. By using the experimental design described in choice A, the researcher can draw inferences about the unconscious personality processes that presumably lead participants to make decisions. Also note that the role-playing scenario involves a choice that would be of interest to a researcher who takes a psychoanalytic perspective: "impulse gratification" is governed by the id, while the decision to instead carry out "societally appropriate behaviors" is governed by the ego.

54. **C is the best answer.** This question requires a psychological and sociological understanding of social categories. Recall from Lecture 1 that demographic categories, which organize people into social groups, are used in sociological research. Choice C accurately points out that sexual orientation and gender, among other categories, have meaning to individuals and groups and are also used by social science researchers. Choice A is a weaker answer because it ignores the importance of these terms as types of identities. The use of "imposed," which has a negative connotation, also makes this answer choice suspect. Choice B mistakenly identifies sexual orientation and gender as "agents of socialization," when they are instead identities that could be arrived at due, in part, to socialization. Choice D can be eliminated because the development of identity is significantly influenced by social factors.

55. **B is the best answer.** Freud's theory of superego development involves the internalization of cultural values, imparted by the parents or other figures close to the child, quite similar to the process of socialization. Self-efficacy is a personal factor and cannot account for the development of the principles that make up the superego, so choice A is wrong. Peer pressure is not implicated in the development of the superego, since parents, rather than peers, are involved and "pressure" is not part of the process; choice C can be eliminated. The looking-glass self would probably not be directly tested on MCAT®, but it is a part of role-taking in social interactions. It could be included in the development of the superego, but is not a major part of the process and is not as closely related a concept as socialization.

56. **D is the best answer.** Although self-esteem and self-efficacy are closely related concepts, self-esteem refers to the overall evaluation of self-worth, while self-efficacy is tied to the ability to carry out tasks. Self-efficacy is a better fit with the scenario of failing to meet a goal, so choices A and B can be eliminated. According to the question stem, the experience of self-efficacy influenced the "overall perception of self." No value judgment is indicated, as would be the case for self-esteem, so choice D is a better answer than choice C.

57. **B is the best answer.** The three stages of Kohlberg's theory of moral development are the preconventional stage, the conventional stage, and the postconventional stage. The preconventional stage is characterized by moral judgments based on the anticipated consequences of behaviors. The conventional stage is characterized by consideration of the potential for disapproval by others and a desire to obey rules and laws. The postconventional stage takes into consideration universal principles and fully-developed ideas about right and wrong. The student described by the question is primarily concerned with following rules, so choice B is the best answer. The obedience level is not a stage of Kohlberg's theory, so choice D can be eliminated.

58. **D is the best answer.** Recall that Vygotsky's theory describes a gradual process of sociocultural learning, in contrast to the theories that describe stages that must be achieved in a set order. For this reason, choices B and C can be eliminated. Choice B also misuses the term "potential developmental level" by making it seem that Vygotsky described a particular set of levels. A potential developmental level is unique to a given child's current level of development. Although Vygotsky was interested in how children learn to fulfill social roles, and thus follow social norms, there is no indication that his theory points to the influence of in-groups. Instead, knowledgeable individuals guide the child's learning. Choice A can be eliminated. Choice D is the only answer that accurately describes Vygotsky's theory.

59. **B is the best answer.** Freud and Erikson both developed theories that included distinct stages rather than continuous development, so choice A can be eliminated. Choice C would be reasonable if not for the use of the word "only." It is true that Freud emphasized internal factors while Erikson's theory focused more on social factors, but neither of them completely discounted personal or social factors. Choice D flips the two theories: Freud proposed a theory of psychosexual development, which Erikson revised by focusing on psychosocial development. Choice B accurately points out that Freud's theory was mainly concerned with early life, while Erikson's theory extended across the entirety of an individual's lifetime.

60. **A is the best answer.** The child's focus on consequences shows that she is in the preconventional level, which is characterized by moral judgements based on the anticipated consequences of behaviors. Choice A is the best answer. The description of the child's reasoning is not consistent with the conventional level of moral reasoning, which takes into account social repercussions. Choice B can be eliminated. Since the child is concerned with personal consequences, she is not at the highest level of moral reasoning, the post-conventional level, which involves universal moral principles. Choice C can be eliminated. The "super-conventional" stage does not exist, so choice D can be eliminated.

61. **C is the best answer.** Answering this question does not require an exact knowledge of the stages of identity achievement and how they are related to Kohlberg's stages of moral reasoning. General familiarity with Kohlberg's stages and the types of identity status based on Erikson's work is sufficient to logically determine the best answer. The preconventional level is the lowest level of moral reasoning according to Kohlberg, based on simplistic ideas of reward and punishment. The person described in the question stem has advanced beyond this stage, so the best answer must be choice C or D. As indicated by their names, identity achievement and identity diffusion describe opposite ends of a spectrum of identity development. A person in identity diffusion has no strong identity; a person in identity achievement has a clear sense of identity and unique personal values. A person who has managed to reach the highest stage of moral reasoning is likely to also have had success in identity development. In fact, Kohlberg posited that achieving the postconventional level of moral reasoning required the type of self-exploration that is involved in reaching identity achievement. Choice D can be eliminated, and choice C is the best answer.

62. **C is the best answer.** Choice B mistakenly suggests that attribution theory is concerned with personal attributes (individual characteristics) rather than attributions of causality to the actions of others. Choice D can be eliminated because attribution theory examines beliefs about the behaviors of others, not the self. Choice A could be a reasonable answer in the absence of choice C, but choice C is a better answer because attribution theory considers both conscious and unconscious influences on the formation of attributions.

63. **D is the best answer.** Answering this question requires determining which answer choice describes a dispositional attribution – the belief that another person's actions were due to internal factors rather than situational ones. All of the answers except for choice D describe situational attributions, where success or failure is said to occur due to external factors. Choice D is consistent with the fundamental attribution error in that a student's poor performance is assumed to be due to her intelligence level, rather than possible environmental influences.

64. **A is the best answer.** An experimental protocol was used to divide participants into those who are and are not focusing on social identities (independent variable). Since social identity is an aspect of self, choice A is the best answer. The question stem does not indicate any manipulation of environmental factors, so choice B can be eliminated. It is possible that participants might engage in the self-serving bias while making attributions, but the question stem does not give enough information to determine if this is the case. Further, there is no indication that the researchers manipulated participants' perceptions of the self-serving bias itself. Choice C can be eliminated. Choice D might seem tempting because social identity is influenced by culture, but it is not as directly applicable to the question stem as is choice A. The fact that participants' perceptions of their social identities were manipulated does not necessarily mean that their perceptions of culture were affected as well.

65. **B is the best answer.** Anxiety disorders are generally oriented toward concerns about the future and hypothetical situations, rather than present circumstances. While it is possible to have an anxiety disorder triggered by one's present circumstances, it is the least likely of the answer choices. Unwanted fear, a physical manifestation of excessive sympathetic nervous system activation, and the frequent experience of excessive response to stress are all defining characteristics of anxiety disorders. Choices A, C, and D can be eliminated and choice B is the best answer.

66. **C is the best answer.** The prevalence of anxiety disorders is about 18%, the prevalence of mood disorders is roughly 10%, and the prevalence of personality disorders is about 9%. Schizophrenia affects roughly 1% of the population, so it is the least prevalent. Consider that choices A, B, and D represent classes of disorders encompassing a number of diagnoses, so they are more likely to be common than schizophrenia, which is a single disorder. Choice C is the best answer.

67. **A is the best answer.** Both physical and psychological symptoms are required for a diagnosis of a somatic symptom disorder; the psychological symptoms consist of the response to the physical ("somatic") symptoms. Choice A best describes the defining criteria of somatic symptom and related disorders. Choice B can be eliminated because a diagnosis of a somatic symptom disorder does not include the assumption that psychological factors "cause" the physical symptoms. Instead, physical and psychological symptoms are interrelated. While somatic symptom and related disorders are often initially treated by clinicians that do not specialize in psychiatric care, this does not constitute a definition of the disorder, ruling out choice C. Choice D is a nonsense answer and can be eliminated.

68. **D is the best answer.** Depression is considered to be a mood disorder, so choice A can be eliminated. Depression is associated with a number of physical symptoms, including insomnia and fatigue, so B can be eliminated. Because depression results in altered psychological functioning, it necessarily results in altered neural functioning as well, eliminating choice C. Depression, though heritable, is not a recessive phenotype. This would imply that there is one locus where the "depression gene" is located, but depression, like any psychological disorder, is much more complex, involving the contribution of multiple genes. Choice D is untrue, so it is the best answer.

69. **A is the best answer.** Although all psychological disorders seem to be influenced in part by genetics, evidence shows that genes contribute more significantly to the development of schizophrenia than other psychological disorders. Choice A is the best answer.

70. **D is the best answer.** Schizophrenia is a classic demonstration of a genotype-environment interaction: while having a particular genotype may predispose a person to exhibit schizophrenia, schizophrenia will not be exhibited unless environmental stressors are encountered, making option I a strong answer. Choices B and C can be eliminated. Option II presents the three primary symptoms of schizophrenia, at least one of which must be present for schizophrenia to be diagnosed. Since option II is accurate, choice A can be eliminated and D is the best answer. Option III is also true: schizophrenia is associated with excess dopamine activity.

71. **C is the best answer.** Negative symptoms involve the loss of normal behaviors or feelings, while positive symptoms generally involve new feelings or behaviors, beyond those that are typical. Choices A, B, and D all describe the loss of a typical ability or characteristic: the loss of motivation, social connectedness, and emotion, respectively. Hallucinations are sensory experiences beyond what is normal and constitute a positive symptom. Choice C is the best answer.

72. **B is the best answer.** The general term "psychological disorders" includes many that do not fit the characteristics described in the question stem, so choice A can be eliminated. The characteristics described are most consistent with the definition of personality disorders: disorders that persist across situations and over one's lifetime. Choice B is the best answer. Choices C and D do not necessarily endure temporally, so these choices can be eliminated.

EXPLANATIONS TO QUESTIONS IN LECTURE 4

73. **C is the best answer.** Engaging in conversation is a dynamic activity. It requires recognizing the contributions of the conversation partner via sensory inputs—auditory input if this is a verbal conversation, or visual input if this is a conversation via text messaging. This demonstrates the involvement of perception. It also requires processing of sensory inputs: figuring out what the conversation partner is saying, reacting to this information, formulating an opinion, determining what to say in response, etc. All of these examples of processing constitute cognition. Cognition and perception are both involved. Choice C is the best answer.

74. **A is the best answer.** The situation described first involves the processing of visual input as the student views the artwork. This function takes place in the occipital lobe, eliminating choices B and D. The next action described is formulation of an opinion. It is not necessary to recognize that forming an opinion is a type of information processing that takes place in the frontal lobe, but it can be inferred that an opinion is an example of the type of complex thought that generally takes place in the frontal lobe. The last action is delivering an oral presentation. Speech production is localized to the frontal lobe as well, making choice A the best answer. Choice C can be eliminated. For the MCAT®, it is necessary to know that Broca's area is required for speech production and is located in the frontal lobe. In addition, the occipital lobe is almost exclusively responsible for visual processing, so choice C can be eliminated.

75. **C is the best answer.** The situation described illustrates a failure to understand *conservation*, the notion that a quantity remains unchanged despite changes of its shape or container. Understanding of conservation is one of the hallmarks of the concrete operational phase of development, making choice C the best answer. There is no information to suggest that the child has not reached either the sensorimotor or preoperational stage, eliminating choices A and B. Piaget's stages do not include a logical operational stage, so choice D can also be eliminated.

76. **D is the best answer.** The learning theory emphasizes the role of external (social) influences on language development, believing that language is just like any other behavior, and that behaviors that are reinforced are learned. The nativist theory posits that language is an innate biologically-facilitated ability and downplays the necessity of external cues for the development of language. The interactionist theory includes aspects of both of these theories, recognizing that the brain develops to facilitate social influence. This most closely matches the information presented in the question, making choice D the best answer. Choices A and C are both more restrictive than the question stem. A proponent of the learning theory would not point to the involvement of the brain, and a proponent of the nativist theory would not indicate an effect of social reinforcement. Choices A and C can be eliminated. There is no cognitive theory of language development, or at least not one that must be known for the MCAT®, which eliminates choice B.

77. **A is the best answer.** Choice A is the only answer choice that does not contain any allusion to a process related to cognition. While it is likely that a language containing only gender-neutral pronouns might affect patterns of thought, such an effect is not implied in this choice. By contrast, all the other choices point to effects on cognition. Choice B describes how enhanced vocabulary within a particular domain of a language facilitates memory. There is an implied facilitation of cognition in this scenario: different shades of blue are better remembered because they are *thought of* as different colors to that language speaker. It is much easier to remember that one object is cerulean and another is azure rather than that one is a medium blue-gray and the other is a deep sky blue. Choice B is not the best answer. Choice C describes a scenario where language makes thought easier, demonstrating an effect of language on cognition. Choice C can be eliminated. The lack of relative directions in Guugu Yimithirr affects cognition by making it impossible to think in terms of relative directions and only allowing thought in terms of cardinal directions, eliminating choice D.

78. **C is the best answer.** Broca's area is necessary for language production, so it must be included in the best answer. Choices B and D can be eliminated. Wernicke's area is necessary for language comprehension. Since the stroke patient is also unable to understand speech, choice A can be eliminated and choice C is the best answer. The additional information that the patient can produce and process other auditory cues implies that the deficit is localized to speech, rather than affecting hearing more broadly.

79. **B is the best answer.** The serial information processing model of cognition posits that the brain first receives a stimulus, then processes the stimulus, and then selects an output function. This is best described in choice B, where the child hears the dinner bell (stimulus), recognizes its significance (processing), and then walks home (output). Choice A involves simultaneous stimulus input (hearing the dinner bell) and cognition (recognizing that it is dinner time). This scenario is consistent with parallel processing rather than serial processing, so choice A can be eliminated. Choice C lacks processing, so it is not the best answer. Choice D lacks a stimulus input, so it can also be eliminated.

80. **D is the best answer.** Though test-retest reliability is not defined explicitly in the lecture, this simply means that scores are consistent if the same person takes the same test at roughly the same point in time. This should make sense: an IQ test would not be a useful measure if it returned wildly different results every time the test was administered. Even without being familiar with the test-retest reliability of IQ test, choice D could be reached as the best answer by using process of elimination. IQ scores are not predictive of later career success, so choice A can be eliminated. A specific criticism of IQ testing is that it is biased against minorities, eliminating choice B. IQ tests specifically assess skills and abilities that are relevant in an academic context, ruling out choice C. Also notice that choices A and C are quite similar: "career success" could be seen as a type of "non-academic pursuit." This provides a clue that neither answer choice is the best answer.

81. **A is the best answer.** Although tests of multiple intelligences emphasize the variety of modalities they assess, this does not mean that traditional IQ tests only test one ability. This is evidenced by the fact that scores are often composed of a verbal and a performance metric, as well as the fact that IQ scores correlate with performance in a variety of domains, including math and verbal skills. The use of IQ tests to diagnose global learning disabilities (however flawed a practice this may be) is unique to IQ tests as compared to tests of multiple intelligences, eliminating choice B. Performance on traditional IQ tests does predict performance on a variety of intelligence tests. This implies the presence of a *g*, or a general intelligence, a notion that is antithetical to the theory of multiple intelligences; choice C can be eliminated. While it is true that traditional IQ tests correlate with academic performance, there is no indication that tests of multiple intelligences share this correlation, ruling out choice D.

82. **C is the best answer.** Algorithms use a step-by-step procedure that leads to a definite solution. Choice A describes analogic problem solving and is therefore a weak answer. Choice B does not accurately depict the use of a systematic list of steps that are used in algorithms to reach an answer, so it can be eliminated. Choice D describes intuition, making it a weak answer.

83. **A is the best answer.** In this situation, the contestant is presented with information that indicates that her initial guess is not the best guess: chance alone dictates that there would be a 33% chance that the prize would be found behind any one door. The revelation that there is only a 20% chance that the prize is behind her chosen door indicates that there is an 80% chance that the prize can be found behind either door B or C (and a 40% for each one), making it more logical to switch her guess to one of those two options. Her unwillingness to change her position after being presented with information to the contrary demonstrates belief perseverance. While belief perseverance is closely related to confirmation bias, confirmation bias requires both ignoring information to the contrary and valuing information that supports one's position. Because there is no information presented that supports the contestant's original position, choice B is a weak answer. Overconfidence specifically refers to an inflated belief in one's abilities. Because this is a game of chance, rather than a game of skill, it is unlikely that the contestant believes she has superior abilities in guessing. Overconfidence and belief perseverance often overlap, but this situation more clearly implies belief perseverance, eliminating choice C. Self-serving bias is the attribution of one's own actions to external circumstances; no information in the question stem indicates that this occurs in the given scenario, so choice D can be eliminated.

84. **B is the best answer.** The father's health during pregnancy is irrelevant to the child's cognitive development. His biological contribution ceases after he contributes his sperm, but the mother's health continues to be relevant, as her body serves as the fetus's environment during gestation. Choice B is a better answer than choice A. Both culture and language have demonstrable effects on cognitive development, making choices C and D weak answers.

85. **C is the best answer.** The fundamental attribution error occurs when one attributes others' actions to internal factors, rather than external circumstances. This often occurs in tandem with the self-serving bias, in which one attributes their own actions to external circumstances. In this question, both elements are present, as the referee attributes the other referee's actions to incompetence (an internal factor), while explaining away her own performance due to poor visibility (an external factor), making choice C the best answer. Causation bias refers to the tendency to assume a cause and effect relationship between correlated variables. This is not implied here; choices A and D can be eliminated.

86. **B is the best answer.** Emotion is a powerful force, tying together not only thought (choice A), but also autonomic nervous system activation or arousal (choice C) and a behavioral response (choice D). The cognitive, physiological, and behavioral responses are all facilitated by neural processes, but for the purposes of the MCAT®, emotion does not have a specific neural "component."

87. **A is the best answer.** The amygdala is associated with the emotional responses of fear and anger. Administration of random, unpredictable electric shocks is a laboratory technique commonly used to produce fear in rats. The prefrontal cortex is associated with regulation of emotional states, temperament, and decision making, none of which are implicated in this question, ruling out choice B. The hippocampus is associated with memory formation, which is not implicated in this question, ruling out choice C. The ventral tegmental area is involved in the reward circuitry of the brain, so it certainly is not activated in response to painful shocks. It is unlikely that it would be necessary to know the function of the ventral tegmental area for the MCAT®.

88. **B is the best answer.** Choice A describes the James-Lange theory, which says that a physiological response is interpreted as an emotional experience; choice A can be eliminated. The Cannon-Bard theory of emotion states that emotional and physiological responses to a situation are experienced simultaneously, as described in choice B. Choice C demonstrates the Schachter-Singer theory, which emphasizes the interpretation of a physiological response based on situational cues, so it is a weak answer. Choice D does not accurately represent any of the three theories of emotion described in the lecture, and lacks the simultaneous emotional and physiological response to a stimulus described by the Cannon-Bard theory, making it a weak answer as well.

89. **C is the best answer.** The parent's emphasis on "how good it feels to know…" demonstrates an intrinsic motivation (an internal feeling of satisfaction that will be experienced by the child). This is in contrast to an extrinsic motivation, which, in this case, would be some type of tangible award received by the child after eating her vegetables. The use of intrinsic motivation most closely aligns with a cognitive theory in the absence of any further information, making choice C the best answer. Drive reduction theories focus on limiting basic physiological drives, such as hunger and thirst. As the parent does not emphasize reducing the feeling of hunger, choice A can be eliminated. Incentive theories use external rewards to motivate behavior, such as in operant conditioning. Because the reward here is internal, rather than external, choice B can be eliminated. Need-based theories refer to motivation driven by the desire to fulfill unmet needs. Because there is no mention or implication that the child's good feeling of knowing that she will grow up to be strong and healthy satisfies an unmet need, choice D can be eliminated.

90. **D is the best answer.** Choices A, B, and C describe the Affective, Behavioral, and Cognitive components of attitudes, respectively. These three components can be remembered using the ABC mnemonic. The description in choice D does not match one of these three components of attitudes, making it the best answer.

91. **A is the best answer.** The foot-in-the-door phenomenon occurs when one has more success requesting a larger task after having the other party agree to a smaller one. This is the case here, where the IT specialist is more likely to fix the larger technical issue after helping with the seemingly less significant task of moving the equipment a small distance. Choice A is the best answer. The door-in-the-face technique is not covered on the MCAT®, but one can infer that it is the opposite of the foot-in-the-door technique: it involves first requesting a large task that the other party turns down in order to increase the likelihood that they will then agree to perform a smaller, more reasonable task. The scenario described in the question stem is the opposite of the door-in-the-face phenomenon, so choice B can be eliminated. Compliance might be a tempting choice, and could be the best answer if the foot-in-the-door phenomenon was not one of the choices, but it does not describe the question stem scenario as specifically as does the foot-in-the-door phenomenon. In fact, both choices A and B could be described as types of compliance, another reason to eliminate choice C. Finally, there is no evidence that the scenario described involves role-playing, so choice D is a weak answer.

92. **B is the best answer.** Social-cognitive theory states that behavior is driven by social learning, in addition to internal and external drives. It does not specifically apply to attitudes, so it is not as relevant as cognitive dissonance, ruling out choice A. Cognitive dissonance describes a situation where one's internal attitudes conflict with external behaviors. In order to resolve this conflict, one can either change an attitude or a behavior. As such, it is possible that either behavior drives a change in attitude or attitude drives a change in behavior. Central and peripheral route processing are both components of the elaboration likelihood model, which posits that there are two routes to attitude formation and change: one driven by logic and reason and one that is more automatic. Neither of these demonstrate how attitudes change behaviors, so choices C and D are weak answers.

93. **C is the best answer.** Social-cognitive theory involves behavior change that is not only influenced by internal and external drives, but also informed by observation of the actions of others. Choice C provides the most complete explanation of social-cognitive theory. Choice D is a weak answer because it indicates that internal and external drives are not involved. Choice A leaves out the important aspect of learning through observation. Finally, choice B inaccurately posits that attitudes are the main focus of social-cognitive theory. Note that social-cognitive theory also emphasizes the control of behavior in the absence of reward and punishment, though this is not reflected in any of the answer choices.

94. **D is the best answer.** Choices A, B, and C all describe characteristics of the target, or the person whose attitude is to be changed. A target with relevant knowledge and a willingness to engage will be more likely to use central route processing, ruling out choices A and C. Age is also an important factor: children respond more emotionally than rationally, making choice B a weak answer. The credibility of the speaker is a characteristic of the message, not the target, so choice D can be eliminated.

95. **A is the best answer.** Cognitive appraisal describes the modulation of a fear response as a result of thinking about the stressor. More specifically, a situation is evaluated for the presence of a potential threat. A secondary appraisal assesses one's personal ability to cope with the threat, with a greater stress response triggered if the threat cannot be dealt with. While the fight-or-flight response is likely involved in this situation, the sequence of events presented more closely aligns with a cognitive appraisal, ruling out choice B. More mention of a physiological stress response would have been necessary to favor choice B over choice A as a stronger answer. A cataclysmic event is a momentous, violent event and does not inherently refer to individuals' emotional responses, eliminating choice C. The elaboration likelihood model describes how people can be persuaded and is not relevant to the scenario described in the question stem; choice D can be eliminated.

96. **A is the best answer.** Chronic stress is most associated with elevated levels of cortisol, though there is significant overlap between the release of epinephrine and cortisol. Epinephrine and norepinephrine are released immediately after a stressful event, while the release of cortisol is more delayed and cortisol remains in the blood for a longer time span. The phrasing of the question does not address a sudden stressful event, one cannot be a strong answer without the other being a strong answer as well, another reason that choices B and C must both be weak answers. Though cortisol does result in increased circulating levels of glucose, glucose is not a hormone, eliminating choice D.

EXPLANATIONS TO QUESTIONS IN LECTURE 5

97. **B is the best answer.** The question stem states that schizophrenia is more prevalent in males than females. This indicates that the genetic component of the disease is likely sex-linked. On the MCAT®, a question about a phenotype that is more prevalent in males will likely turn out to be "X-linked." Y-linked diseases would not affect females at all, since they do not possess Y chromosomes. Since the question stem implies that women are susceptible to schizophrenia, choice A can be eliminated. One of the most important psychobiological concepts for the MCAT® is that the interaction between genes and the environment influences behavior. Purely genetic explanations are rarely adequate for complex behaviors such as those associated with schizophrenia. Since both choices C and D are restricted to genetic influences, they can both be eliminated. Choice B describes a relationship between an environmental factor and a genetic predisposition, and is the most likely explanation.

98. **A is the best answer.** Behavioral evolution occurs when certain combinations of alleles lead to behaviors that give the organism a selective advantage, increasing the prevalence of those alleles (and thus the behavior) in the gene pool over time. Choice D accurately describes the general idea of behavioral evolution and can be eliminated. Choice B gives an example of a behavior becoming more prevalent due to a selective advantage, making it a weak choice. Note that choice B specifically mentions that the change took place over many generations. For any question about evolution, be on the lookout for answers that involve a short period of time, as they are usually false. Choice C also describes a change in allele frequency due to some change in behavioral fitness, so it can be eliminated. Note that, as in choice C, behavioral evolution can involve a decrease in behavior rather than an increase. Choice A describes a genotype that has its lethal effect before any behavior can occur, making it an example of natural selection, but not behavioral evolution.

99. **C is the best answer.** It is important to know the definitions of sensation and perception for the MCAT®. Sensation is the process that converts physical stimuli into electrical signals that can be interpreted by the nervous system. The processing of these signals to create a working representation of the world is known as perception. Choice C is a strong answer, and choice B can be eliminated. Olfaction is another name for the sense of smell. Although olfaction involves the conversion of physical signals to electrical ones, it is not the name for that process; choice A can be eliminated. Sensitivity describes how well someone is able to pick out sensory information from "noise," but does not describe the actual process by which that information is received and turned into action potentials, so choice D can be eliminated.

100. **B is the best answer.** Absolute sensory thresholds are set by the physical limitations of the actual sensory receptor cells, and correspond with the minimum amount of a physical stimulus necessary to generate action potentials in those cells. Since neither the visual cortex nor the auditory cortex are part of sensory organs, choices C and D can be eliminated. Both hair cells in the cochlea and bipolar cells in the retina are found in sensory organs. However, bipolar cells are not the sensory cells of the retina (photoreceptor cells are), whereas the hair cells are the site of sensation in the inner ear. For this reason, choice A can be ruled out and choice B is the best answer.

101. **B is the best answer.** The mice had a Weber fraction of ¼, meaning that the stimulus had to change by at least one quarter of its original value for the change to be detected. If the starting frequency is eight times per second (8 Hz), the control mice should need a change of 25% × 8 Hz, or 2 Hz, in order for perception to occur. This makes choice B the best answer.

102. **C is the best answer.** This question requires knowledge of some basic definitions related to signal detection theory. The hit rate describes the frequency that an individual is able to distinguish a signal from noise when the signal is actually there. A false alarm occurs when the individual perceives a signal that is really just noise. Choice B is an inaccurate statement and can be eliminated. Sensitivity is the individual's overall ability to discern signal from noise. In simplified terms, sensitivity is the hit rate minus the false alarm rate. Someone with equivalent hit and false alarm rates would have very low sensitivity, eliminating choice A. Whether or not someone interprets a signal as such does not depend entirely on physical sensitivity levels. The individual has some level of conscious control over whether an input is interpreted as signal or noise, and this control is affected by biases. Bias is the reason that two individuals with the same physical abilities can differ in their detection of meaningful stimuli, making choice C a strong answer and choice D a weak answer.

103. **C is the best answer.** The first part of this question stem is extraneous, as the question only asks about the second half. The important information here is that viewing a recording with video and audio out of sync causes a severe decline in an individual's ability to remember details about *either* the auditory or visual information from the recording. If the question had described both auditory and visual memory decreasing for each participant, this would be a clear example of divided attention, which causes attention paid to each input to decline. Since the question states that either one or the other declines, the best explanation is that one input, either auditory or visual, is receiving all or most available attention at the expense of the other input. This is an example of selective attention. Choice C is a strong answer and choice D is a weak answer. Since absolute thresholds are largely (but not entirely) determined by the physical parameters of sense organs, it is unlikely that they are being altered in this experiment, ruling out choice B. Sensation is a relevant term but does not directly address the question, eliminating choice A.

104. **C is the best answer.** This question is testing knowledge of the distinction between absolute and difference thresholds. Whereas an absolute threshold describes the minimum amount of some stimulus needed to detect the presence of the stimulus, a difference threshold describes the amount of *change* in an already present stimulus necessary to detect the change. Option I is listed in every answer choice, so it is not necessary to spend time analyzing it; assume it is not an example of a difference threshold. (The minimum intensity necessary to detect the presence of a sound is in fact an absolute threshold, not a difference threshold.) Choice II describes an acceleration, which is a change in an already detectable stimulus (velocity). This is a difference threshold, eliminating choices B and D. Option III also describes a minimum input level necessary for detection, making it another example of an absolute threshold rather than a difference threshold. Choice A can be eliminated, and choice C is the best answer.

105. **A is the best answer.** This is a straightforward definition question. Choice A provides an accurate and complete description of perception. The process of translating physical stimuli into action potentials is sensation, ruling out choice B. It is important to be familiar with the difference between sensation and perception. Choice C describes an absolute threshold, while choice D describes selective attention.

106. **D is the best answer.** Selective attention involves brain regions "higher up" than the sensory organs exerting control over how information from stimuli arriving at those organs is used to construct a perception. This is an example of top-down processing, making choice D a strong answer and choice A a weak answer. Sensitivity, which describes an individual's ability to detect signals from sensory noise, is not directly relevant to the question stem; choice B can be eliminated. While sensation is required to generate the information used by attention, selective attention is a perceptual process, so choice C is also a weak answer.

107. **B is the best answer.** Gestalt principles are used to group objects through top-down processing. Two important Gestalt principles are the principles of similarity and nearness. The principle of similarity says that objects with common features will be perceived as a distinct group. The principle of nearness says the same about objects that are clustered spatially. Note that all of the answer choices contain two parts: one related to nearness and another related to similarity. Choices A, C, and D can be eliminated, since the question is asking for objects that will NOT be grouped. Only objects that are dispersed and unique would not be perceived as grouped. Note that although the answer choices reflect specific Gestalt principles, recalling the specific principles of similarity and nearness is not necessary to answer the question. The best answer could also be found simply by looking for the answer choice that describes the objects that are most dissimilar to each other.

108. **B is the best answer.** First of all, note that choices A and D are essentially the same answer. If performance is best at long distance, it should be worst at short distance. If either of these answers were a strong answer, the other would also have to be a strong answer. Choices A and D can both be eliminated on that basis. Judgments of depth are primarily based on the relative position of the object on each retina. At close distances, the difference between the images from each eye is substantial enough that determining depth is relatively easy. At longer distances, the image on each retina is nearly identical, meaning other visual cues must be used to judge depth. This makes it more difficult to make a distinction between the depths of two objects when both objects are far away, so choice B is the best answer. Even without remembering the details of depth perception, it would be possible to intuitively eliminate choice C– if the only thing that matters for a depth discrimination task is the absolute difference in depth, a six-inch gap between objects would be just as obvious at 500 feet from the viewer as it is at 5 feet!

109. D is the best answer. This question stem can be simplified to: "Which region of the visual pathway is responsible for identifying specific characteristics in the visual field?" Ablating the retina or optic chiasm would eliminate all visual processing rather than just the perception of specific shapes, so choices A and B can be eliminated. While ablating parts of the LGN could have a slightly more targeted effect (destroying shape and color information while preserving motion information, for example), feature detection occurs in the visual cortex. For this reason, researchers wanting to target the detection of a specific shape feature should focus on the cortex, making choice D a better answer than choice C.

110. A is the best answer. Parallel processing occurs when different types of ganglion cells in the retina respond simultaneously to different aspects of the visual scene. These cells send projections to two different pathways, one representing "form" and the other "motion." Since both of these pathways respond simultaneously to all visual information, this processing is designated "parallel." Once these projections reach the visual cortex, feature detection occurs in both pathways. Feature detection is referred to as "sequential" processing because increasingly complex features are analyzed in a serial (or sequential) fashion rather than parallel fashion. (For example, vertical and horizontal lines, shapes, and complex features like shadows might be detected in that order.) For this reason, choices B and D can be eliminated. Since feature detection occurs in both of the parallel pathways, choice C is also a weak answer.

111. D is the best answer. Consciousness can be described simply as the sum of all information that we are aware of, at the exclusion of all unconscious information. For example, a person reading a book might be conscious of the visual information conveying the words on each page, but not conscious of the sensory information coming from the left foot that has not been moved for an hour. The fact that not all information is available to consciousness at any given time makes choice B a weak answer, and necessitates some mechanism for controlling what information reaches the level of conscious perception. Attention is the "gatekeeper" that performs this function. For this reason, choice D is the best answer. Consciousness and attention are intimately related, meaning choice A can be eliminated. Although choice C describes a relationship between the consciousness and attention, the relationship is reversed so choice C is a weak answer.

112. A is the best answer. This is a basic feedback loop question. Questions like this are common in biology MCAT® passages, but can incorporate psychology phenomena as well, as in this case. Alertness is promoted by suppressing the activity of melatonin, so melatonin is a sleep-promoting agent. In a functioning feedback loop, sleep deprivation should lead to an increased sleep drive through increased levels of melatonin. This makes choice A a strong answer and choice B a weak answer. There is no indication in the question stem that the individual has taken stimulants or depressants, so choice A is a better answer than choices C or D.

113. C is the best answer. Choice B can immediately be eliminated because working memory is a type of declarative memory; if it were a strong answer, choice A would have to be a strong answer as well. There are types of declarative memory that are not working memory, so choice A cannot be eliminated based only on the overlap with choice B. However, the question stem does not describe factual knowledge or memory of particular events, so declarative memory is not involved, and choice A is eliminated. Practicing a physical task leads to the formation of new procedural memory, sometimes referred to as "muscle memory." Sensory coding is irrelevant to the question, ruling out choice D. Although the MCAT® is more likely to ask questions about types of declarative memory, it is important to have a basic understanding of procedural memory and the type of information it stores.

114. B is the best answer. This question requires an understanding of how working memory is encoded. Whereas sensory memory involves information from all sensory modalities, working memory is usually encoded through an auditory representation. Think, for example, of trying to remember a phone number in the time between hearing it and writing it down. For most people this task involves repeating the number sequence, either out loud or mentally, generating a phonetic representation. Choice B is the only answer that lists a brain region directly involved with auditory processing, so it is the best answer. The visual cortex is more likely to play a role in sensory or long term memory, so choice D can be eliminated. Although the hypothalamus is a brain region, it is associated with circadian rhythms and the endocrine system rather than memory encoding; choice C can be eliminated. Sympathetic ganglia, which are part of the peripheral autonomic nervous system, are not brain structures, so they cannot be a component of the strongest answer.

115. **D is the best answer.** Two major techniques that aid in memory encoding are chunking and rehearsal. A person repeating a piece of information many times to facilitate memory formation is utilizing rehearsal, whereas chunking involves reorganizing large pieces of information into smaller segments to bypass the limits of working memory. Since the question stem involves the use of repetition to facilitate encoding, choice D a strong answer and choice C is a weak answer. Feature recognition and hypnosis are unrelated to the question stem, and can both be eliminated.

116. **C is the best answer.** This question has two-part answer choices – a common MCAT® occurrence – so it can be helpful to look at each part individually. Two answer choices describe long term memory as being more durable than other forms of memory, while the other two claim that it is less durable. Since long term memory can last many times longer than memories held in sensory or working memory, and is less vulnerable to decay, choices A and B can be eliminated. The second component of the answer choices tests knowledge of when long term memory is available. If we could only maintain long term memories by consciously focusing on them, the amount of information potentially encoded by these memories would be severely limited by attention. In reality, there is no known limit on long term memory capacity, making choice C a strong answer and choice D a weak answer.

117. **B is the best answer.** This question can be rephrased as: "Which type of memory is least dependent on new synapse formation?" Long term memory is dependent on the formation and strengthening of new synaptic networks, so choice C can be eliminated. Sensory memory, on the other hand, is encoded in the immediate firing patterns of already established sensory neural networks. In the short term, sensory memory would not be affected by a loss of the ability to form new synapses. Working memory is encoded from sensory memory, but is also retrieved from long term memory. For this reason, it would be indirectly affected by gabapentin, so choice B is a better answer than choice A. Finally, although the MCAT® does not require knowledge of the mechanism of procedural memory formation, it is likely similar to that of long term memory, given that both types of memory are durable and can be retrieved from unconsciousness. This eliminates choice D, and choice B is the best answer.

118. **B is the best answer.** Long term potentiation (LTP) is the increase in likelihood that presynaptic input will trigger an action potential in the postsynaptic neuron, occurring after repeated communication between two neurons. Given that the question stem calls long term depression (LTD) the "opposing process" to LTP, LTD must involve a *decrease* in the likelihood that presynaptic activity will trigger an action potential at a given synapse. This makes choice B a false statement, and therefore the best answer. If LTP and LTD are opposing processes, they should be active in the same cells and regions of the brain, eliminating choices C and D incorrect. Since LTP is important for memory formation, it is likely that LTD, as an opposing process, is involved in memory loss; choice A can be eliminated.

119. **C is the best answer.** A student wanting to maximize her recall of material during a test should utilize retrieval cues – environmental stimuli that were present when she originally studied for the test. For these cues to be useful, it is essential that they are identical when studying and when taking the test. Choices B and D describe the opposite approach, and can be eliminated. While choice A might initially seem consistent with the use of retrieval cues, note that there is no mention of similarity between the study environment and the actual test environment. In other words, there is not enough information to determine whether the retrieval cues would actually be applicable to the test. Choice C, on the other hand, involves utilizing a stimulus that will be present during the test while preparing; for this reason choice C is a better answer than choice A.

120. **D is the best answer.** Retroactive interference occurs when newly learned material prevents successful retrieval of related older memories. Since this process involves highly similar memories, option I must be true, and choices A and C can be eliminated. Note that choices B and D both include option III, meaning that it must also be true. To save time, focus only on evaluating option II. (Proactive interference – option III – is the opposite of retroactive interference, in that previously learned material prevents learning of new material, but it also involves similar memories.) Spreading activation occurs when the retrieval of a memory triggers the retrieval of other highly similar memories, meaning that option II is true. Since options I, II, and III all involve highly similar memories, choice D is the best answer.

Photo Credits

Covers

Front cover, Brain wireframe model: © Jezperklauzen/ iStockphoto. com; People in Berlin: © lechatnoir/ iStockphoto.com

Lecture 1

Pg. 1, Open book: © Bienchen-s/iStockphoto.com

Pg. 14, Thumbs up: © jorgeantonio/iStockphoto.com

Pg. 15, Washing dog: © Cade Martin/CDC Public Health Image Library

Pg. 21, Aerial view of downtown Chicago's skyline: © Davel5957/ iStockphoto.com

Pg. 23 Search for smallpox in Sylet district of North-eastern Bangladesh: © Dr. Michael Schwartz/CDC Public Health Image Library

Pg. 24, Playground: © DenisTangneyJr/iStockphoto.com

Pg. 27, Blood pressure examination: © Amanda Mills/CDC Public Health Image Library

Lecture 2

Pg. 31, Against the crowd: © Track5/iStockphoto.com

Pg. 32, Pavlov and dog: © Science Source/Science Photo Library

Pg. 36, Gardening: © Dawn Arlotta/CDC Public Health Image Library

Pg. 39, Two ring-tailed lemurs relaxing on a rock: © sjallenphotography/iStockphoto.com

Pg. 44, Group of fans cheering: © AfricaImages/iStockphoto.com

Pg. 51, Closed society: © timsa/iStockphoto.com

Lecture 3

Pg. 55, Dynamic Mapping of Human Cortical Development during Childhood through Early Adulthood: © Nitin Gogtay MD, Jay N. Giedd MD, Leslie Lusk BA, Kiralee M. Hayashi BS, Deanna Greenstein PhD, A. Catherine Vaituzis, David H. Herman BS, Tom F. Nugent III AB, Liv Clasen PhD, Arthur W. Toga PhD, Judith L. Rapoport MD, and Paul M. Thompson PhD / NIMH and USC

Pg. 57, Factors Contributing to the Facial Aging of Identical Twins: © Dr. Bahman Guyuron / Department of Plastic Surgery, University Hospitals, Case Western Reserve University

Pg. 82, Schizophrenia: © Wellcome Dept. of Cognitive Neurology/ Science Photo Library

Lecture 4

Pg. 89, Woman consults with doctor: © Rhoda Baer/ National Cancer Institute

Pg. 95, White board discussion: © Clare McLean, Courtesy of University of Washington

Pg. 98, Dr. John E. Niederhuber, former Director, National Cancer Institute (NCI), (2006-2010): © National Cancer Institute (NCI)

Pg. 98, Label with amino acid phenylalanine: © Dana Kelley

Pg. 113, Meditation: © Amanda Mills/CDC Public Health Image Library

Lecture 5

Pg. 121, Brain MRI: © Dr. Leon Kaufman, University Of California, San Francisco/National Cancer Institute

Pg. 126, Child sleeping: © Juanmonino/ iStockphoto.com

Pg. 138, Healthy brain and severe AD brain: © National Institute on Aging/National Institutes of Health

Index

A

ABC model 107
absolute poverty 26, 144, 147, 184
absolute threshold 119-122, 177-176, 201, 222
accommodation 91
achieved status 40
acquisition 32, 37, 150, 187
action 110
acute stress disorder 81
adaptive 104
adaptive values 118, 200
adjustment 48, 81
adjustment disorder 81
affective component [of attitude] 107
age 18-19, 20, 23, 25-26, 62, 154, 158, 160, 166, 183, 209
age cohorts 18-19
agents of socialization 46, 66, 189, 212, 214
aggression 38, 175
aging and memory 137
aging and the life course 18
agonists 128
alertness 125-126, 128, 146, 202, 223
algorithm 99, 105, 218
alpha waves 126, 202
altruism 38-39, 45, 155, 191, 211
amygdala 102, 105, 219
amyloid plaques 138
analogies 99, 151
anal stage 68
analytical intelligence 97
anger 101-104, 135, 219
anomie 47
antagonists 128, 159
anxiety disorders 79-81, 85-86, 150, 155, 163, 193-194, 216
appraisal view of stress 111
arousal 98, 102-103, 106, 112, 176-177, 195, 201, 219
ascribed status 40
aspects of collective behavior 40
assimilation (into a culture) 48, 52, 144, 155, 184, 189, 190, 212
assimilation (Piaget's theory of cognitive development) 91
attachment 38
attention 119, 121-123, 125-126, 128, 130-132, 146, 161, 170, 177, 196-198, 201, 222-224
attitude 42, 46, 50-51, 107-110, 114, 212-213, 220
attraction 38
attribution theory 55, 73-75, 216

authority 14, 15, 31, 46-47, 54, 153, 159, 189-190, 212
autonomic nervous system 101-102, 111, 170, 198, 219, 223
autonomy vs. shame and doubt 69
avoidance conditioning 35, 37, 155, 190, 211

B

back stage self 41, 42
behavior 38-43, 45-48, 51
behavioral [component of emotion] 101, 105
behavioral [component of attitude] 107
behavior change 110, 114, 190, 212, 220
behaviorist theory (of personality) 58-59, 66, 162, 194, 214
behaviorist theory (of language) 93, 196
belief perseverance 100-101, 105, 219
beliefs 12-16
beta wave 125-126
bias 50-52, 54, 100-101, 105, 213, 219, 221
biological basis of depression 81
biological basis of schizophrenia 83
biological theory (of personality) 57, 160-161, 193
biomedical approach 3, 17, 78, 194
biopsychosocial approach 3, 6, 17, 162, 194
bipolar disorders 81-82
bodily-kinesthetic intelligence 97
body dysmorphic disorder 80
bottom-up processing 123, 125, 130
Broca's aphasia 95
Broca's area 95-96, 168, 171, 196, 199, 217, 218
bureaucracy 15, 40
bureaucratization 20
bystander effect 43, 151, 188, 212

C

Cannon-Bard theory of emotion 103-105, 166, 195, 219
capitalism 15, 26
caste system 25, 28, 209
cataclysmic events 111
causation bias 100-101, 105, 219
central route processing 109, 220
cerebral cortex 90, 95, 169, 197
characteristics of an ideal bureaucracy 40
characteristics of the target 110
charismatic authority 15
chunking 132, 224
church 16
circadian rhythm 125
civil unrest 21

class 24-28, 62, 142, 147, 183, 187, 190, 209
class consciousness 26
classical conditioning 32, 35-36, 187, 210, 211
classification of psychological disorders 77, 162
coalescence 20
cognition 90-91, 94, 96, 103, 106, 109-111, 167-170, 196-198, 218
cognitive (component of emotion) 101, 105
cognitive appraisals 111
cognitive changes 137
cognitive component of attitude 107
cognitive dissonance 108-110, 220
cognitive dissonance theory 108
cognitive processes 90, 93, 100-101, 137
cognitive theories 106
cohort study 19
comparative economic and political systems 15
concrete operational 92, 197, 217
conditioned reinforcers 34
conditioned response 32-33, 150, 187, 211
conditioned stimulus 32-33, 37, 187, 210, 211
confirmation bias 100, 105, 219
conflict theory 8-9, 11, 183, 207
conformity 31, 42, 46-47, 54
consciousness 125, 128-132, 135, 223
consciousness altering drugs 128-129
conservation 92, 217
constancy 124-125
contemplation 110
context-dependent 135
continuous theories 92
conventional level 71-72, 215
cortisol 82, 111, 113, 220
creative intelligence 97
crude death rate 19
cult 16
cultural capital 25-26, 28, 143-144, 183, 210
cultural relativism 22, 49, 155, 190-191, 208, 213
culture 12-14, 17, 19, 22, 27, 40, 46, 48-49, 62, 66, 73, 75, 93-94, 142, 145-147, 152-153, 155-156, 160, 183-187, 189-190, 192, 197, 208-209, 212-213, 216, 219
culture shock 12, 22, 48, 187, 208
current developmental level 70

D

decay 136, 203, 224
declarative memory 131, 133, 137, 139, 223
deductive reasoning 92
deindividuation 44-45
delta waves 126, 178
demographics 18-19, 21, 62, 142, 154
demographic transition 19, 22, 187, 209
depressants 128, 130, 223

depression 56, 77, 81-83, 86, 111, 139, 142, 158-159, 161-162, 178-179, 191-195, 203, 216, 224
depressive disorders 81-82
depth 124-125, 130, 176-177, 201, 222
developmental psychology 91-92
deviance 47-48, 151
Diagnostic and Statistical Manual of Mental Disorders, Fifth Edition (DSM-5) 77
difference threshold 119-120, 122, 170, 177, 197, 201, 222
different types of identities 62
diffusion 48
diffusion of responsibility 43, 188
discrimination 18, 23, 31, 33, 37, 50-54, 130, 144, 150 -151, 155, 159, 176, 187-188, 190, 201, 211-212, 222
disgust 104
dispositional attribution 73, 101, 216
dissociative disorders 84, 195
dissociative identity disorder 84, 195
divided attention 121-122, 170, 177, 197, 201, 222
division of labor 15
downward mobility 25
dramaturgical approach 41, 45, 155, 189, 212
dreaming 126
drive reduction theory 106-107
drives 106-107, 199, 219, 220
drug addiction 129, 179, 203
dyad 39

E

education 15, 17-18, 23-25, 28, 183-184, 208-209
educational segregation 15
education level 18
ego 6, 58, 61, 214
egocentric 92
elaboration likelihood model 109-110, 114, 220
electroencephalogram (EEG) 125, 178
emigration 20
emotion 101-106, 111, 135, 166-167, 195, 199, 217, 219
emotional intelligence 98
encoding 117, 131-134, 136, 139, 174-175, 199, 223-224
environmental influences 57, 73, 76, 83, 192, 216
environmental justice 23, 28, 209
enzyme inhibitors 128
epigenetics 118
epinephrine (adrenaline) 111
Erik Erikson 68
escape conditioning 35
ethnicity 16, 18, 50, 62
ethnocentrism 49, 64, 155, 160, 190, 192, 213
evolutionary psychology 57
exchange theory 9
excitatory postsynaptic potential 133
exercise 56, 84, 108, 112-113, 128, 136

expressive aphasia 95

extended family 16, 62

extinction 32, 35, 150, 187

extrinsic motivation 106, 219

F

factors contributing to globalization 21

fad 40

false consciousness 26

family 16-17, 24-25, 46, 62-63, 69, 101, 143, 171, 184

fashion 40, 223

fear 101-105, 111, 150, 219-220

feature detection 125, 223

feminist theory 8, 9

fertility 19, 22, 209

figure 123

Five Stages of Change 110

folkways 13

foot-in-the-door phenomenon 108, 114, 220

foraging behavior 38

formal operational 92

formal organization 40

forms of kinship 16

Freud's theory of developmental stages 68

frontal lobe 90, 95-96, 99, 179, 217

front stage self 41

functional fixedness 100

functionalism 8, 9, 11, 183, 207

fundamental attribution error 73-75, 101, 105, 162, 166, 195, 216, 219

G

game theory 39, 45, 212

gender 5, 15-16, 18, 23, 25-27, 40, 49, 62-63, 66, 68, 96, 154, 158, 198, 209, 214, 218

generalized anxiety disorder 80

general learning disability 97-98

generativity vs. stagnation 69

genital stage 68

Gestalt principles 123, 125, 130, 177, 201, 222

global inequalities 23

globalization 18, 21, 48, 146, 187

ground 123

group polarization 42-43, 152, 188, 212

groupthink 42, 46, 110, 189, 212

H

hallucinogens 128

happiness 104, 169

heredity 57, 81, 98, 118, 122, 214

heuristics 99, 100

hidden curriculum 15

hoarding disorder 80

honeymoon phase 48

how culture affects attributions 73

humanistic theory 59-60, 161, 192-194

hyper-globalist perspective 21

hypnosis 128, 224

hypothalamic-pituitary-adrenal (HPA) axis 82, 170

hypothalamus 82, 102, 125, 167, 178, 196, 202, 223

I

Id 6, 58, 61, 68, 214

identity 60-65, 67-75, 87, 191-192, 213-216

identity vs. role confusion 69

illness experience 17, 146, 186

imitation 36, 61, 63, 192

immigration 18, 28, 144, 156, 184, 191, 210

immigration status 18, 144

impression management 41, 153, 189, 212

incentive theory 106

inclusive fitness 39, 45, 191

income 15, 23-25, 28, 154, 184, 209

individual discrimination 51

inductive reasoning 92

industrialization and urban growth 21

industry vs. inferiority 69

influence of culture and socialization 62

influence of individuals 62

information processing models 125

in-group 31, 50, 52, 54, 63, 74, 110, 151, 159-160, 192-193, 213

initiative vs. guilt 69

innate behaviors 36

insomnia 127, 170, 198, 216

instinct 36, 106

institutional discrimination 51-52, 151

integrity vs. despair 69

intelligence 13, 22, 36, 89, 97-98, 105, 169, 196, 208, 216, 218

interactionist theory 93, 96, 168, 196, 199, 217

interference 136

intergenerational mobility 25, 143, 210

intermittent reinforcement 35

interpersonal intelligence 97

intimacy vs. isolation 69

intragenerational mobility 25, 28, 210

intrinsic motivation 107, 219

intuition 99, 135, 218

IQ (intelligence quotient) 97

iron law of oligarchy 40

J

James-Lange theory of emotion 103, 166
joy 104
just noticeable difference 119-120

K

kinship 16
Kohlberg's theory of moral development 71-72, 75, 215
Korsakoff's syndrome 138, 179, 203

L

language 14, 93-96, 98, 167-168, 171, 196, 199, 217-219
language acquisition device 93
latent period 68
learning 32-37, 133, 136, 146, 150, 155, 161, 168, 170, 174,
    187, 190, 192-193, 196, 199, 210-211, 214-215, 217-218,
    220, 224
learning theory 93, 96, 168, 199, 217
limbic system 102, 129, 171, 179, 199, 203
linguistic intelligence 97
locus of control 61, 65, 70, 73, 158, 191
logical-mathematical intelligence 97
long-term memory 90, 132-133, 134, 136
lower class 24-25

M

macrosociology 9
maintenance 110
Marx, Karl 26
Maslow, Abraham 107
mass media 40, 46, 48, 49
mastery 25, 48
material culture 13-14, 22, 142, 183, 186, 208-209
mating behavior 38, 211
McDonaldization 40
medicalization 17, 146, 185, 186
meditation 113, 128
melatonin 126, 130, 178, 202, 223
memory 84, 90, 112, 117, 126, 129, 131-139, 161, 163,
    167, 170, 174-175, 178-179, 198-200, 202-203, 218-219,
    222-224
memory consolidation 133, 174-175, 199, 202
memory construction 136
meritocracy 25, 144, 147, 184, 187, 210
microsociology 9
midbrain 138, 196
middle class 24
migration 20
mirror neurons 36, 187
mnemonics 135
model 6-7
modeling 6, 36, 191

modernization 15
monoamine hypothesis 81, 191, 194
monotheistic 16
mood disorders 85, 150, 194, 216
mores 13
mortality 19, 22, 26, 209
motion 124, 125, 223
motivation 106-107, 114, 185, 194, 217, 219
multiculturalism 48-49, 155, 190
multiple personality disorder 84
musical intelligence 97

N

narcolepsy 127
nationality 18
nativist theory 93, 96, 168, 196, 199, 217
nature versus nurture 91, 93, 98
need-based theories 106
needs 106-107
negative feedback system 106
negative punishment 34, 155, 191
negative reinforcement 34, 191
negotiation phase 48
networks 25, 40, 133, 135, 137, 139, 224
neural plasticity 133, 201
neurofibrillary tangles 138
neutral stimulus 32, 37, 210
non-material culture 13-14, 22, 186, 208-209
non-REM (NREM) sleep 126
norepinephrine (noradrenaline) 111
nuclear family 16

O

obedience 22, 31, 46-47, 54, 189, 208, 212, 215
object permanence 92
observational learning 36, 46, 59, 187
obsessive-compulsive disorder 80
occipital lobe 90, 96, 121, 167, 196, 217
operant conditioning 32, 34-36, 46, 93, 106, 150, 160, 187,
    189, 191-192, 210-211, 219
oral stage 68
organization 40
organization of social movements 20
out-group 31, 50, 54, 63, 74, 110, 151, 159-160, 192, 213
overconfidence 42, 100, 105

P

parallel processing 90, 125, 218
parietal lobe 90, 96
Parkinson's disease 138, 161, 168, 179, 194, 203
partial reinforcement 35, 187
patterns in fertility and mortality 19

patterns of immigration 18

peer pressure 45, 155, 190

perception 74-75, 90, 96, 119, 121-126, 128, 130-132, 136, 176-177, 196, 217, 221-223

perceptions of the environment 74

period study 19

peripheral route processing 109, 220

personal events 111

personality 55-62, 65-66, 68, 72, 74, 80-81, 84-85, 91, 101, 110, 118, 126, 158-159, 160, 162, 192-194, 214, 216-217

personality disorders 84-85, 194, 216-217

perspectives on bureaucracy 40

perspectives on deviance 47

perspectives on globalization 21

phallic stage 68

phobias 33

physiological markers of emotion 102

Piaget, Jean 70, 91

polyandry 16

polygamy 16

polygyny 16

polytheistic 16

popular culture 48-49

population pyramid 19

positive punishment 34, 191

positive reinforcement 34, 106, 108, 191

postconventional level 71-72, 75, 215

post-traumatic stress disorder (PTSD) 111

potential developmental level 70, 75, 215

poverty 25-26, 144, 147, 184, 186

power 8, 9, 11, 14-15, 20, 24-25, 33, 39-40, 47, 50-51, 90, 129, 142, 147, 187, 190, 209

practical intelligence 98

pre-contemplation 110

preconventional level 71-72, 75, 215

prefrontal cortex 102, 133, 137, 167, 196, 219

prejudices 50-51

preoperational 217

preparation 110

prestige 24, 34, 50-51, 142, 145, 147, 187, 190, 209

primacy effect 136, 200, 203

primary group 39

primary punisher 34

primary reinforcer 34, 37

priming 135

principle of closure 123

principle of common region 123

principle of continuity 123

principle of nearness 123, 222

principle of similarity 123, 222

privilege 24-25, 209

proactive interference 136

procedural memory 131, 223, 224

processes that contribute to prejudice 50

psychoanalytic theory 58, 126

psychological disorders 10, 55-56, 76-79, 81, 83-86, 94, 111, 118, 162-163, 193-195, 207, 216-217

psychotic disorders 82

punishment 9, 31, 34-35, 46-47, 54, 71, 74, 93, 106, 108, 110, 155, 187, 189, 191, 210, 215, 220

R

race 15-16, 18, 22-26, 28, 40, 43, 49-50, 62, 154, 209

race/ethnicity 62

racialization 18

rapid eye movement (REM) sleep 126

rational choice theory 9

rational-legal authority 15

recall 135-136

recency effect 136, 203

receptive aphasia 95

receptive fields 125

reciprocal causation 59, 110

recognition 26, 71, 103, 135-136, 139, 224

reference group 63-64, 74

regulatory genes 118, 201

reinforcement 31, 34-35, 37, 54, 93, 96, 106, 108, 187, 189, 191, 210-211, 217

reinforcement schedule 35, 37, 187

relative poverty 26, 144, 147, 184, 186

relearning 136

religion 15-16, 18, 33, 46, 52, 113

religion and social change 16

representativeness heuristic 100

residential segregation 24, 28, 144, 184

response expectancy 100

retrieval 117, 131, 133-137, 174-175, 199-200, 224

retrieval cues 135-136, 224

retroactive interference 136, 224

reuptake inhibitors 128-129, 179, 203

reverse culture shock 48

reward pathway 107, 129, 179, 203

riot 40

rituals 14

Rogers, Carl 59

role 40

role conflict 40

role exit 40

role of culture in cognitive development 93

role of emotion 135

role-playing 66, 108, 110, 114, 128, 214, 220

role strain 40

role-taking 63, 158, 192, 215

S

sadness 81, 104

sanctions 13

Schachter-Singer theory of emotion 103

schemas 50, 91

schizophrenia 76, 81-86, 94, 122, 163, 194-195, 200, 216-217, 221

secondary appraisal 111, 220

secondary group 39

secondary reinforcers 34

sect 16

secularization 16

selective attention 121-122, 130, 170, 177, 197, 222

self-actualization 59-60

self-concept 59, 61-62, 64-65, 67, 82, 108, 158

self-efficacy 61, 64-65, 67, 69, 161, 193, 215

self-esteem 2, 43, 61, 64-65, 67, 73, 82, 161, 193, 215

self-fulfilling prophecies 50, 213

self-presentation 41, 189

self-regulate 110

self-serving bias 73-75, 101, 105, 158, 191, 216, 219

semantic networks 135

sensation 117, 119, 121-123, 130-132, 168, 176-177, 196-197, 200-201, 221-222

sensitivity 27, 120-122, 130, 132, 176-177, 201, 221

sensorimotor 217

sensory memory 132, 136, 223-224

sex 16, 18-19, 26, 28, 68, 106, 160, 166, 203, 209, 221

sexual orientation 16, 18, 26, 62, 214

shape constancy 124

shaping 36-37

short-term memory 132, 136

sick role 17, 146, 186

signal detection theory 120, 122, 197, 221

situational approach to explaining behavior 60

situational attribution 73

size constancy 124

skeptical perspective 21

Skinner box 34

sleep 81, 101, 111, 117, 125-127, 130, 133, 136, 174-175, 178, 199-200, 202-203, 223

sleep cycles 126

sleep disorders 127, 200, 202

sleep terror disorder 127

social behavior 38-39, 45, 66, 114, 211

social capital 25, 143-144, 147, 183-184, 186, 210

social changes in globalization 21

social class 24-25, 28, 142, 147, 183, 187, 190, 209

social cognitive theory 59, 65, 161, 214

social-cognitive theory 60, 110, 167, 220

social constructionism 7-9, 207-208

social construction of gender 18

social construction of race 18

social facilitation 43, 45, 151, 212

social factors 1-3, 5, 12, 18, 25-26, 30, 64, 66, 72, 76, 78, 110, 117, 143, 162, 192, 194, 207, 214-215

social groups 9, 13, 27, 46, 62, 142, 183-184, 207, 214

social identity 47, 50, 62-63, 64, 216

social inequality 23

social institutions 1, 9, 14, 22, 30, 46, 50-51, 142, 183, 188, 190, 208, 212

socialism 15

socialization 46, 52, 61-62, 66, 70-71, 153, 189, 212-215

social loafing 43, 45, 151

social movement 20, 147, 187

social norms 13-15, 22, 40, 44, 46-48, 58, 75, 154-155, 184, 187-190, 208, 212, 215

social reproduction 25, 144, 184

social significance of aging 18

social support 38, 113

society 3-4, 14

socioeconomic gradient in health 26

socioeconomic status (SES) 24, 99, 143

somatic symptom and related disorders 216

somatic symptom disorder 216

source monitoring 137

spatial inequality 23, 28, 146-147, 186, 209

spatial intelligence 97

spirituality 113

spontaneous recovery 32

spreading activation 135

stages of cognitive development 70, 92

stages of sleep 126, 202

stage theory 92

Stanford-Binet scale 97

state-dependent 135

status 24-28, 40, 142-145, 147, 151, 183-186, 209

stem cell based therapy 138

stereotype 50-52, 74, 137, 155, 190, 213

stereotype threat 50, 213

Sternberg's triarchic theory 97

stigma 47, 94, 155

stimulants 128, 130, 146, 223

stimulus discrimination 33, 150, 187

stimulus generalization 33, 150, 187

strain theory 47

strategy 20

stress 111-113, 128-129, 144, 146, 150, 170, 198, 216, 220

stressor 81, 111-112, 170, 198, 220

subculture 48, 52, 153, 189, 213

subjective experience 101

substantia nigra 138, 162, 194, 203

suburbanization and urban decline 21

superego 6, 58, 61, 67-68, 215

suprachiasmatic nucleus (SCN) 125, 202

surprise 73, 104

symbolic culture 14, 22, 147, 160, 186, 192, 208
symbolic interactionism 7-9, 63, 183, 207, 208
symbols 8, 14, 63, 208

T

taboo 13
teacher expectancy 15
temperament 57, 102, 118, 158-159, 171, 192, 199, 214, 219
temperament and decision making 102
temporal lobe 90, 95, 102, 169, 197, 199
temporally 135
terrorism 21, 50
theories of attitude and behavior change 109
theory of multiple intelligences 97, 105, 167, 196, 218
top-down processing 123, 125, 130, 222
traits 56-57, 59-61, 66, 74, 158, 160, 192-194
trait theory 56, 160-161, 193, 194
transformationalist perspective 21
transmission 48
triad 39
trial and error 99
trichotillomania 80
trust vs. mistrust 69
twin studies 98, 195, 214
two-factor theory of emotion 103
types of memory storage 131
types of religious organizations 16
types of status 40

U

unconditioned response 32, 150, 187, 210
unconditioned stimulus 32, 37, 150, 210
upper class 24-25
upward mobility 25, 28, 147, 187, 209
urbanization 18, 21-22, 209
urban renewal 21

V

values 14
verbal communication 22, 38, 95, 208
vicarious emotions 36
visual processing 125, 171, 196, 199, 201, 217, 223
vitamin B1 138
Vygotsky, Lev 70, 92

W

wealth 24-26, 145, 184-185, 209
Weber fraction 120, 122, 201, 221
Weber's law 120, 201
Weber, Max 14, 40
Wechsler Adult Intelligence Scale 97

Wernicke's aphasia 95
Wernicke's area 95-96, 168, 171, 196, 199, 218
working memory 132, 134, 136-137, 139, 161, 223-224

Z

zone of proximal development 70

A Student Review of This Book

The following review of this book was written by Teri from New York.

"The Examkrackers MCAT® books are the best MCAT® prep materials I've seen-and I looked at many before deciding. The worst part about studying for the MCAT® is figuring out what you need to cover and getting the material organized. These books do all that for you so that you can spend your time learning. The books are well and carefully written, with great diagrams and really useful mnemonic tricks, so you don't waste time trying to figure out what the book is saying. They are concise enough that you can get through all of the subjects without cramming unnecessary details, and they really give you a strategy for the exam. The study questions in each section cover all the important concepts, and let you check your learning after each section. Alternating between reading and answering questions in MCAT® format really helps make the material stick, and means there are no surprises on the day of the exam-the exam format seems really familiar and this helps enormously with the anxiety. Basically, these books make it clear what you need to do to be completely prepared for the MCAT® and deliver it to you in a straightforward and easy-to-follow form. The mass of material you could study is overwhelming, so I decided to trust these books—I used nothing but the Examkrackers books in all subjects and scored in the 99th percentile in all sections. Thanks to Jonathan Orsay and Examkrackers, I was admitted to all of my top-choice schools (Columbia, Cornell, Stanford, and UCSF). I will always be grateful. I could not recommend the Examkrackers books more strongly. Please contact me if you have any questions."